Policy Making in Britain

Also by Peter Dorey:

British Politics Since 1945
The Conservative Party and the Trade Unions
The Major Premiership: Politics and Policies Under John Major, 1990–7 (ed.)
Wage Politics in Britain: The Rise and Fall of Incomes Policies Since 1945
The 1964–70 Labour Governments (ed.)
Developments in Public Policy in Britain Since 1945 (ed.) (available late 2005)

Policy Making in Britain
An Introduction

Peter Dorey

SAGE Publications

London ● Thousand Oaks ● New Delhi

SAGE Publications Ltd
1 Oliver's Yard
55 City Road
London EC1Y 1SP

SAGE Publications Inc.
2455 Teller Road
Thousand Oaks, California 91320

SAGE Publications India Pvt Ltd
B-42, Panchsheel Enclave
Post Box 4109
New Delhi 110 017

British Library Cataloguing in Publication data

A catalogue record for this book is available
from the British Library

ISBN 0-7619-4903-8
ISBN 0-7619-4904-6 (pbk)

Library of Congress Control Number available

Typeset by C&M Digitals (P) Ltd., Chennai, India
Printed in Great Britain by The Alden Press, Oxford

To Barry Jones – with sincerest thanks for all your support and encouragement,
and wishing you a long and happy retirement.

When I was a young man and first joined this Department … I thought [it] was Whitehall's equivalent of the signal box at Clapham Junction – we pulled the levers and guided activities or politics onto this track or that. I spent several happy years manipulating those levers. Only after a very long time did I realise there were no wires underneath them – they were connected to nothing at all.

(Former Treasury official quoted in Peter Hennessy, *Whitehall*, Pimlico, 2001: 398)

The history of post-war British Cabinets has been a continuous story of people trying to do too much, believing that they had power over events which in fact they lacked, treating national circumstances as entirely within their control and twirling the wheel on the bridge as though every move would provide an instant response in some well-oiled engine room below.

David Howell [former Minister], 'lead book review', *The Political Quarterly*, 58:1, 1987: 102)

We knew ourselves to be as corrupt as any other community of our size … but there was no tale-bearing then, or ringing up 999: transgressors were dealt with by local opinion, by silence, by lampoons, by nicknames … it is certain that most of us…would have been rounded up under present law … Instead, we emerged … unclassified in criminal record…we were less ensnared by bye-laws … It is not crime that has increased, but its definition.

(Laurie Lee, *Cider With Rosie*, The Book Club, 1959: 219–20)

Contents

Tables and figures

Acknowledgements

One of the joys of having a book published is the opportunity to thank publicly all of those people who have inspired it, provided support and encouragement, and thereby made it possible.

First, I would like to express my sincere thanks to Lucy Robinson and David Mainwaring at Sage, who originally approached me with the idea of writing a text on policy making in Britain. I would like to thank them, not only for commissioning the book and providing support and encouragement throughout, but also for their patience and understanding when – like an errant student – I kept asking for extensions to the submission deadline.

I would also like to thank the various anonymous referees who read drafts of the chapters and offered 'constructive criticisms' on how they could be improved. I have tried to incorporate the majority of these and believe that their suggestions have significantly improved this text. I am deeply grateful to them and hope that they are happy with the finished product. Any deficiencies which remain are mine alone.

Also deserving thanks are the hundreds of 'public policy' students I have taught over the years at Cardiff University, and who sustained my enjoyment of teaching (during a time when the obsession with research has taken over Higher Education). They also constantly reminded me about the lack of a suitable 'core text' on policy making in Britain, and so, in their own way, also provided the inspiration for this book. Some of them, I am delighted to hear, have subsequently embarked upon policy-related careers, working for: various British political parties; a range of government agencies; the Cabinet Office; MPs; the National Assembly for Wales; think tanks; the CBI; the civil service; and placements in the European Union.

My colleagues in the Politics Section in the School of European Studies at Cardiff University also deserve special mention. In particular, I would like to express my sincere thanks to David Broughton, Mark Donovan, Steve Marsh, Peter Sutch and Stephen Thornton. In the over-regulated, RAE-obsessed tyranny that is academia today, they have helped to support and sustain me with their encouragement, good humour, integrity and professionalism.

So too has Barry Jones, with whom I devised the Final Year Public Policy course back in the mid-1990s, and with whom I subsequently co-taught it. I am particularly indebted to Barry for his advice and wisdom over the years, not to mention his reservoir of anecdotes (many of them unrepeatable!) derived from 30 years of teaching in Higher Education. Now that Barry has retired, he will be greatly missed, and it is to him that I would like to dedicate this book.

Finally, I would like to thank my wife, Jane – her love, affection and unstinting support make all the difference between living, and merely existing.

Pete Dorey
Bath, Somerset
November 2004

Abbreviations and acronyms

ALF	Animal Liberation Front
ASBO	Anti-social Behaviour Order
BBC	British Broadcasting Corporation
BMA	British Medical Association
CAP	Common Agricultural Policy
CBI	Confederation of British Industry
CND	Campaign for Nuclear Disarmament
CPAG	Child Poverty Action Group
CPS	Centre for Policy Studies
CRE	Commission for Racial Equality
CSA	Child Support Agency
DEFRA	Department of the Environment, Food and Rural Affairs
DES	Department for Education and Science
DOE	Department of Education
DOH	Department of Health
DSS	Department of Social Security
DTI	Department of Trade and Industry
EDM	Early Day Motion
EEC	European Economic Community
EMU	Economic and Monetary Union
EOC	Equal Opportunities Commission
ERM	Exchange Rate Mechanism
EU	European Union
FCO	Foreign and Commonwealth Office
G7	Economic summits comprizing Britain, Canada, France, Germany, Italy, Japan and United States
G8	As above, but with additional membership of Russia (since 1998)
GLA	Greater London Authority
IGO	International Governmental Organization
IMF	International Monetary Fund
INGO	International Non-governmental Organization
IOD	Institute of Directors

IPPR	Institute for Public Policy Research
LEA	Local Education Authority
LSE	London School of Economics
MAFF	Ministry of Agriculture, Fisheries and Food
MOT	Ministry of Transport
MSC	Manpower Services Commission
MSP	Member of the Scottish Parliament
NATO	North Atlantic Treaty Organization
NEDC	National Economic Development Council
NFU	National Farmers Union
NHS	National Health Service
NI	National Insurance
NUS	National Union of Students
OFGAS	Office of Gas Supply
OFGEM	Office of Gas and Electricity Markets
OFSTED	Office for Standards in Education
OFTEL	Office of Telecommunications
OFWAT	Office of Water Services
PFI	Private Finance Initiative
PLP	Parliamentary Labour Party
PPP	Public–Private Partnership
PPS	Parliamentary Private Secretary
PRO	Public Record Office
PSBR	Public Sector Borrowing Requirement
QMV	Qualified Majority Voting
RAE	Research Assessment Exercise
SDP	Social Democratic Party
SMP	Scottish Member of Parliament
TEC	Training and Enterprise Council
TUC	Trades Union Congress

1 Introduction: The Study of Policy Making in Britain

The need for a new textbook on policy making in Britain

This book arose out of frustration with the dearth of up-to-date texts on policy making in Britain, which made it difficult to recommend a specific text to my third year and post-graduate 'public policy' students. In contrast to the super-abundance of textbooks on British politics and government in general, there has been a paucity of books on policy making in Britain. Of the few that do exist, some are now woefully out of date, such as Brian Hogwood's *From Crisis to Complacency: Shaping Public Policy in Britain*, and A.G. Jordan and J.J. Richardson's *British Politics and the Policy Process*, both of which were published originally in 1987, but sadly, neither has been updated since. In terms of both organization and content, both were excellent texts for students of policy making in Britain, lucidly written as they were by leading academic experts in this aspect of British politics.

The necessity of a much more contemporary text is due not merely to the obvious need for more recent examples to illustrate aspects of policy making in Britain, but also because since the 1980s, new trends have themselves led to the development of new issues, both conceptually and empirically. For example, as we will note in Chapter 2, the concept of agenda setting has been enriched by the notion of 'policy streams', while new sources of ideas for public policy have been provided by the marked expansion of think tanks, and the increasingly important phenomenon of 'policy transfer'.

Meanwhile, as Chapters 3 and 4 will illustrate, traditional discussions about the role of the Cabinet, ministers and civil servants in policy making have been superseded by the rise of 'core executive studies'. This draws attention to the increased role and importance of junior ministers, the growing significance of Special (Policy) Advisers, the changing role of senior civil servants (and thus their changing relationship with ministers), the role of departments themselves, and the increasing importance of supporting and coordinating institutions at the heart of the core executive, most notably the Cabinet Office and the Prime Minister's Office. There is also now, of course, a much greater need to consider how the 'core executive' has responded to, and is affected by, the phenomenon of 'Europeanization'.

The concept of the core executive also places strong emphasis on the interdependence of the individuals and institutions who comprise the core executive, and challenges older accounts which often depicted relationships in terms of 'Prime Ministers *versus* Cabinet or Ministers' or 'ministers *versus* senior civil servants'. Instead, we will explain how the various 'actors' in the core executive are bound together by 'resource dependency', and therefore need to interact in order to achieve policy goals. Instead of viewing individuals as having a specific degree of power, as if it was 'fixed' and predetermined, we will show how power in the core executive is relatively fluid and contingent, in the sense that its possession, and the exercise of it, is heavily dependent on circumstances, personalities, styles of leadership and the type of issues or policies involved.

A further development in the policy making literature since the 1980s is the approach to organized interests, which now tend to be discussed in terms of 'policy networks'. As we will show in Chapter 5, the concept of policy networks draws attention to the way in which the role of organized interests (or pressure groups as they are sometimes known) varies from one policy subsystem (agriculture, health, transport, etc.) to another. Some policy subsystems have traditionally been characterized by a very close and closed relationship between a government department and a specific organized interest, who have largely determined policies between them, on the basis of bargaining, shared objectives and a highly clientelistic relationship. These are known as 'policy communities', and have tended to exert a broadly conservative influence on public policy within their subsystem, often thwarting or slowing down attempts by ministers or new governments to implement significant changes. The prevalence of such policy communities in certain subsystems also contributed to the notion of a discernible 'British policy style', which we critically evaluate in Chapter 9. Meanwhile, in both Chapters 5 and 9, we will note how some policy communities have been weakened or restructured since the 1980s.

The extent to which public policy in Britain has tended to be 'made' within the core executive but with the involvement, in certain policy subsystems, of important or powerful organized interests, has served to marginalize the role of Parliament in the British policy process. As we discuss in Chapter 6, Parliament has played a relatively minor role in policy making, having long been a primarily reactive body, in which the *relative* unity and strength of the governing party and its parliamentary majority, coupled with the government's overall control of the House of Commons timetable – thereby enabling it to prioritize governmental business – has usually ensured that government-initiated public policies have been formally approved by Parliament (as opposed to actually being 'made' or initiated by Parliament).

However, whereas some commentators are inclined to dismiss Parliament almost entirely as a meaningful actor in the policy process, we acknowledge that Parliament may play a more indirect role, one which its critics overlook or underestimate. For example, that the overwhelming majority of governmental measures are formally approved by Parliament, and thus enacted, reflects the fact that ministers generally pursue measures which they are confident will be supported by the vast majority of their own MPs. If enough of the governing party's MPs are seriously and implacably opposed to a particular measure, then this opposition is likely to be made clear to the whips, possibly via meetings of various backbench committees, so that the contentious measure will either be abandoned, or significantly modified. Meanwhile, backbench MPs may effect policy change through successfully introducing Private Members' Bills.

Furthermore, since 1979, a range of Select Committees have scrutinized the policies of the government departments and ministries, regularly cross-examining ministers, senior civil servants, and other witnesses either involved in the formulation or implementation of a policy, or affected by it. The reports published by these Select Committees can themselves sometimes prompt policy change or modification. These Select Committees are now also increasingly involved in 'prelegislative scrutiny', whereby 'draft Bills' are examined by MPs *before* being formally introduced into Parliament as a whole. The increasing use of prelegislative scrutiny by Select Committees means that Parliament now has the opportunity to play a rather more active and potentially influential role in the legislative stage of policy making than it has hitherto.

Select Committees also play a valuable role in examining the *implementation* of public policy. Until relatively recently, implementation was considered a largely unproblematic or straightforward aspect of the policy process, representing the final part of a series of 'stages' through which public polices proceeded. However, as we explain in Chapter 7, implementation is often the 'stage' at which policies unravel or falter, as problems become apparent during the practical application and administration of them. A policy which was enthusiastically formulated in the core executive, and then formally approved by Parliament, may then encounter unforeseen difficulties when it is being applied in the real world, or it may have unintended consequences. What also has an impact on the success of a policy is the manner in which it is interpreted and applied by those ultimately responsible for implementation, namely 'street level bureaucrats'.

Consequently, whereas implementation was previously viewed as largely a 'top-down' process which followed the policy making 'stage', it is now widely recognized that implementation should also be seen as a 'bottom-up' process too, whereby street level bureaucrats – doctors, local authorities, police officers, social workers, teachers, etc. – both shape public policy through the manner in which they apply it 'on the ground', and themselves identify problems with the original policy, which can then be reported back, and eventually lead to policy modification. In other words, it is now recognized that the implementation 'stage' itself contributes to policy making, rather than merely following it: an integral part of a dynamic, ongoing 'process', not simply the end point.

A further significant development since the 1980s, which we examine in Chapter 8, is the transition from government to governance. This refers to a number of simultaneous, often interlinked, trends whereby policy making has become increasingly fragmented, and conducted at different levels – international, European, national and regional – while also involving a more diverse set of policy actors drawn from the public, private and voluntary sectors. The concept of governance emphasizes the extent to which 'the government' is now only one of many participants in the policy process, and which is increasingly concerned with 'steering' and coordinating public policy, rather than directly determining it from the centre. This, in turn, places a premium on both vertical and horizontal coordination, and greater interaction, cooperation, partnership and 'exchange relationships' between the plethora of actors now involved in the formulation and/or implementation of public policy.

All of the above changes will be synthesized and summarized in Chapter 9, when we conclude with an overview of the main trends and trajectories in policy making in Britain. We will highlight these changes by contrasting contemporary developments on policy making with the notion of a unique 'British policy style' advanced by Jordan and Richardson back in 1982. This concept was effectively buttressed by the work of Richard Rose during the early 1980s – and again in the early 1990s – when he suggested that in the short term political parties, when in government, made little substantive difference to public policy in Britain. These authors identified a variety of factors which contributed towards significant policy continuity in many policy areas in Britain, with short-term changes in public policy proving to be the exception rather than the norm. Jordan and Richardson (1982) emphasized the extent to which policy making was subject to a process of 'bureaucratic accommodation', whereby negotiation between the key policy actors invariably facilitated only relatively modest or incremental policy changes, while Rose (1984, 1990; see also Rose and Davies, 1994) drew attention to the extent to which policies and governmental programmes were 'inherited', or characterized by a form of inertia: governments generally needed at least two consecutive terms in power in order to effect significant or durable changes in public policy.

We will suggest that while the work of eminent authors such as Jordan and Richardson, and Rose, still offers valuable insights into aspects of policy making and the policy process in contemporary Britain, recent developments suggest that, in some respects, there is greater fluidity and less predictability in policy making and the policy process in Britain at the beginning of the 21st century. Some of these changes can be attributed to initiatives pursued by the Blair governments *per se*, but other trends can be traced back to the late 1980s and 1990s, even if their impact or implications have only become fully apparent in more recent years.

Before we commence our study properly, though, there is one particular aspect of policy making and the policy 'process' which we need briefly to consider, by way of providing context or background to some of the themes and issues which will variously be alluded to in the chapters which follow.

Policy making as a series of stages?

Many models of policy making have assumed or implied that there is a clear sequence of stages through which public policies proceed, and which therefore constitute the 'policy process'. As Figure 1.1 illustrates, this 'stagist' version of the policy process starts with agenda setting, and then portrays policy proceeding through a logical sequence of stages: recognition of problem; consideration of options; agreement on most suitable option; legislation or introduction of new policy; and implementation.

Although there have been variations on this model, they have all reflected and rein-forced the notion that policies proceed through a sequential series of stages, and that there is a 'policy process' with a clear beginning, middle and end (although to be fair, revised versions of this model have sometimes added an 'evaluation' stage after implementation, which then feeds back to agenda setting).

One famous version of this 'stagist' approach was provided by David Easton's wider notion of the political system, in which societal demands were processed inside the 'black box' of the political system, and then emerged as outputs in the form of allocation of resources, legislation and public programmes, as illustrated by Figure 1.2.

In reality, of course, matters are rather less clear-cut and straightforward. We noted above, for example, how policy is still 'made' while it is being implemented, and as such, may be transformed in ways that were not originally imagined or intended. Another criticism of the 'stagist' approach to policy making is its failure to distinguish between different

Figure 1.1   The 'stagist' model of the policy process

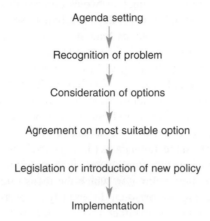

Agenda setting

Recognition of problem

Consideration of options

Agreement on most suitable option

Legislation or introduction of new policy

Implementation

Figure 1.2   Simplified version of Easton's model of the political system

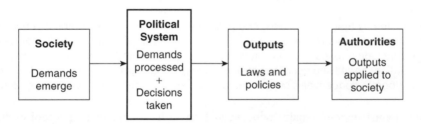

Source: Adapted from Easton, 1965.

policy areas or subsystems. It does not disaggregate or distinguish between discrete areas of public policy, or convey the extent to which different policies will involve different policy actors and modes of interaction or influence. For example, the poor have generally had rather less input in shaping welfare policy than farmers have had in shaping postwar agricultural policy in Britain.

Consequently, the 'stagist' version of the policy process has been criticized for providing an inaccurate account of how policies are 'made', because it depicts policy making as a linear process, with a clear beginning, middle and end. This sequential model, its critics argue, not only grossly oversimplifies the manner in which policies are apparently initiated, developed and implemented, but also fails, crucially, to explain *how* issues emerge, *why* some enter the political system (but not others), *how* they are 'processed' inside the 'black box' of the political system (and *who* is involved, and in *which* role or capacity), and *why* the policies (the outputs) subsequently encounter various difficulties, or enjoy varying degrees of success.

In short, the 'stagist' model can be criticized for failing to provide either a realistic or an explanatory account of policy making (for two examples of such criticism, see Jenkins-Smith and Sabatier, 1993: 3–4; John, 1998: 25–7). Sabatier especially emerged as a prominent critic of what he termed 'the stages heuristic' – or what Nakamura (1987) more prosaically called 'the textbook process' – claiming that while it 'served a useful purpose in the 1970s and early 1980s by dividing the very complex policy process into discrete stages', subsequent research and analysis of policy making has exposed serious weaknesses with the 'stages heuristic' model of the policy process.

Not least of these deficiencies, Sabatier (1999: 6–7) elaborates, are: its failure to provide *causal* accounts of policy development; the sequence of the stages is inaccurate or misleading, because the 'first' stage (agenda setting) is itself intimately and inextricably affected by other stages, such as the 'final' stage (evaluation); it reflects a rather legalistic or top-down approach to policy making, in which the focus often appears to be on legislation *per se*; it fails to distinguish between different types or aspects of public policy; it reflects an emphasis on government rather than the recent trend towards governance, involving different actors at different levels.

In similar vein, a former senior civil servant in the Department of Trade and Industry in the early 1990s, who also served in the Cabinet Office during the first Blair government, asks rhetorically: 'What [policy] process?, emphasizing that:

> The problem is that new policies, and policy decisions, can arise in, and are handled in, a multitude of different ways. But it is often possible to discern a number of separate stages, including research, consultation and gaining knowledge, exploring options, more consultation, and taking decisions through to Ministerial agreement. The individual stages do not operate sequentially, but overlap as policies become firmed up. (Stanley, 2000: 44)

Yet the 'stagist' model remains popular, and can still be defended, as a tool or starting point which can help us to understand some of the aspects of policy making. The fact that policy making is frequently complex or messy actually makes it even more useful to provide a simplified model which identifies some of the constituent elements of 'the policy process', precisely so that the complex or messy reality can begin to be understood.

Indeed, the 'stagist' model has often been defended precisely on these grounds, namely that it is best understood as a 'heuristic device', rather than an accurate depiction of policy making in the real world. A 'heuristic device' is an analytical tool or pedagogic model – particularly in the social and political sciences – designed and deployed to aid understanding (particularly for educational purposes) of an otherwise highly complex issue or process. In this context, characterizing the policy process as a series or sequence of stages 'facilitates the understanding of public policy making by breaking the complexity of the process into a limited number of stages', even though in the real world of day-to-day policy making 'there is often no linear progression as conceived by the [stagist or sequential] model' (Howlett and Ramesh, 1995: 12).

In other words, we would argue that the 'policy stages' or 'stages heuristic' approach is still useful in helping us begin to understand aspects of policy making in Britain, particularly if we take on board Sabatier's criticism about the sequence of the stages: we can identify how policy making in Britain enshrines various of the stages, even though they overlap, are inextricably interlinked, and do not always occur in the sequential order which the 'stages heuristic' suggests.

For example, this book treats agenda setting and the role of ideas in a separate (and prior) chapter to those which examine the roles and relationships of the formal policy makers in the 'core executive' and how they formulate public policy, but we readily acknowledge that those inside the 'black box' of central or formal governmental institutions themselves sometimes shape the policy agenda, and promote influential ideas, rather than merely responding to them (as the sequential model clearly implies).

Ultimately, therefore, while acknowledging the limitations of the 'stages heuristic' approach, as enunciated by critics such as Sabatier (1999), and John (1998), we still believe that it can provide useful insights into some of the ways in which public policy is made or shaped in Britain, and by who (or what). Without it, it would be difficult, if not impossible, to know where to start.

2 Defining Problems and Devising Policies

Identifying issues and problems

Our starting point is to note how and why certain issues or conditions become recognized as problems which warrant attention from policy makers. Given that policy makers will invariably be faced with any number of demands for action to tackle particular issues at any one time, we need to understand, right from the outset, how and why only a few of those are likely to be deemed as problematic, and thereby prompt the development of policies to solve or ameliorate them. Or as one political scientist has expressed it: 'Of the thousands and thousands of demands made upon government, only a small portion receive serious attention from public policy-makers' (Anderson, 1975: 59). As this chapter illustrates, the identification of problems, and the policies developed to address them, involves such concepts as social construction, policy agendas, issue-attention cycles, and 'policy streams'. Each of these conceptual approaches is concerned to offer an account of how and why problems become recognized as such, and therefore lead, in some cases, to policy change. We will also identify the role of ideas, individuals and think tanks in defining problems and developing policies in contemporary Britain, along with the increasing recourse to evidence-based policy making and policy transfer.

The social construction of problems

It needs to be emphasized right from the outset, that the concept of 'social construction' often plays a role in determining what is, or is not, viewed as a problem warranting a response from policy makers. To a considerable extent, some 'problems' are socially constructed, meaning that they reflect social or ideological values about what is good or bad, acceptable or unacceptable, desirable or undesirable. Issues which are ignored or not even recognized in one era can become defined as problems in a subsequent era. The crucial point here is that a 'problem' is not always evident or recognized as such.

A change in certain societal values can result in a previously accepted phenomenon, or one whose scale was not fully acknowledged, subsequently being identified or defined as a problem, and thus attracting the attention of policy makers. Arguably, child abuse, be it sexual or physical, is not in itself new or novel – some children, presumably, have always been subject to various abuse by certain adults – but only in recent years has it been identified, defined and recognized as a social problem, and consequently resulted in action by social workers to identify children 'at risk', and legislation via Parliament to impose harsher penalties on those found guilty of abusing children.

Similarly, married women in Britain were once deemed the property or chattel of their husbands, whereupon the latter were effectively entitled to behave as they wished towards their wives. British society, and in particular the law, either did not recognize as problematic, or turned a blind eye to, such atrocities as wife-beating and sexual abuse; marriage was assumed to confer certain conjugal rights on the husband, to the extent that a wife was always expected to accede to his sexual demands, so that the notion of rape within marriage was not recognized. It is only relatively recently that rape within marriage has been rendered a criminal offence (like any other form of rape or sexual assault), while recognition of the crime of 'domestic violence' has led both to an expansion in the number of women's refuges and hostels, and more serious or sympathetic attention by the police (who, apparently, traditionally declined to become involved in 'a domestic' when a wife reported her husband for assault, tending to treat such instances as a purely private matter) (Hulley and Clarke, 1991: 18).

For various reasons, therefore, British society no longer deems acceptable the abuse of children or women, and hence public policies and laws have changed accordingly. Changing societal values have ensured that such abuse is now defined as a problem, whereas previously, it was widely disregarded.

On the other hand, social changes may sometimes occur before, or ahead of, changes in dominant societal values, so that the change is, initially at least, deemed a 'problem'. For example, the 1970s and 1980s heard increasing political concern being expressed about the growing number of single (lone) parents in Britain. There were a number of reasons for this concern, including the implications for the social security budget, and the links which some commentators alleged existed between lone parenthood and juvenile delinquency, but one key factor was that single parents clearly did not correspond to British society's long-standing view of what constitutes a normal and morally acceptable family. In Britain, for much of the 20th century, a 'normal' family was widely defined as a (heterosexual) married couple with their dependent children, with the husband engaged in paid employment, and the wife assuming the primary responsibility for child-rearing (even if she herself also went out to work).

Consequently, when the number of single parents increased during the 1970s and 1980s, there was mounting concern in some quarters, for lone parent households came to be considered 'deviant' in relation to the socially accepted, morally approved, two-parent family form which had prevailed for most, if not all, of the 20th century. In other words, single parents are not inherently or automatically a social problem: they are defined as such through the process of social construction, because they 'deviate' from what is (or was, until recently) an ideologically defined and determined view about what counts as a 'normal' (and thus morally acceptable or legitimate) family (see, for example, Edholm, 1991).

Similar processes of social construction also result in same-sex couples sometimes being defined as 'deviant' or socially problematic (for a discussion of how sexuality is defined as 'natural' or 'deviant', see Vance 1989; Weeks, 1992: 228–33, 240–6). Hence the recent controversies over whether gay and lesbian couples should be allowed to 'get married' and/or adopt children. As we have just noted, what has been commonly defined as a 'natural family' in British society is a man and woman united through marriage, and their dependent children. Consequently, the 'familial ideology' or social values which legitimize this particular type of family unit socially constructs gay and lesbian couples as 'deviant' or problematic, particularly if they then wish to raise children.

Meanwhile, if we return to the example of the 'normal' family, we can see how 'working mothers' (i.e. mothers who also undertake paid employment outside the family home) have also been viewed – in some quarters – as 'deviant' or problematic. This is because the same mode of social construction which defines single parents as a social problem also assumes that the normal family is one in which women remain at home to raise the children, while husbands fulfil the role of breadwinner to provide financially for the family. The traditional nuclear family tacitly assumed that women are naturally – biologically and psychologically or emotionally – predisposed to raise children and act as home-makers, while men, being 'naturally' more competitive, gregarious and physically stronger, are equally destined to enter the 'public' sphere of work and economic activity. This sexual division of labour is socially constructed as being natural, innate and biologically predestined. Consequently, when increasing numbers of women became economically active during the 1970s and 1980s by undertaking paid employment, many traditionalists, and some Conservatives, considered this to be problematic, and wished to discourage it. Hence 'working women' sometimes found themselves – and still do today, on occasions – being accused of selfishness (for putting themselves before their families, particularly their children), or blamed for creating a generation of 'latchkey' children who were prone to juvenile delinquency and crime, because they were left unsupervised after school (or during school holidays) while mothers were at work. Hence the periodic political and media debate about whether, and if so, how, 'working mums' can be encouraged to remain at home.

To provide a final example of how dominant social values and norms serve to define what is deemed desirable or deviant, and thereby socially construct who or what is defined as a problem which warrants attention from policy makers, we can refer briefly to drug use in Britain. Here, as Hulley and Clarke (1991: 14) note, there has long been a clear distinction between legitimate and legal drug use, in the form of smoking cigarettes and drinking alcohol, and deviant, illegal drugs, such as cannabis, cocaine and heroin. Indeed, cigarettes have often been portrayed, via the media, as 'cool', glamorous or a sign of sophistication – the attractive hero or heroine in a film drawing on a cigarette between delivering their lines, or while mulling over a problem – while drinking alcohol has become so popular and extensive (not to say increasingly excessive) that it is those who are teetotal who are often viewed as 'deviant'. Certainly, in many working-class communities and among many professional footballers, heavy drinking has been viewed as evidence of being 'hard' or macho, and 'one of the lads'.

By contrast, those who consume other types of drugs have invariably been viewed as 'deviant', and quite possibly a menace to society. Those defined as 'drug-users' (a label not usually applied to smokers or drinkers) are commonly assumed to be 'drop-outs' from society, and usually envisaged to be unhealthy and unkempt in appearance, as well as probably economically inactive, socially irresponsible and morally degenerate.

Now, one of the key arguments which has been invariably invoked against 'drugs' (other than cigarettes and alcohol) concerns the socially undesirable consequences of using them. Cannabis is often said to lead on to harder drugs (a misconception, because the overwhelming majority of people who smoke cannabis do *not* proceed to take heroin), while many drugs are deemed addictive, and can also lead to crime (as users steal in order to obtain the money necessary to 'feed their habit'). Yet similar arguments can just as readily be used against cigarettes and alcohol: cigarettes are addictive, to the extent that many smokers are unable to give them up, however much they want to, while for some people, alcohol also proves to be addictive – yet drinkers are not warned: 'It might only be a couple of pints now, but you mark my words, in a couple of years, it'll be a bottle of scotch or vodka every day.' Meanwhile, alcohol itself fuels crime, as evidenced by the violence and vandalism readily displayed in any British town or city at closing time on a Friday or Saturday night (although in other societies, such as Scandinavian countries, heavy drinking at weekends does *not* result in violence or antisocial behaviour, as anyone who has visited Reykjavik will doubtless testify, although of course, if such places become popular with British stag or hen parties, this will immediately change).

The point here, though, is that what is defined as a drug, or deemed a 'bad' drug to be prohibited, is socially constructed, reflecting dominant or widely-held social and moral values. These values have hitherto accepted, and even promoted via positive images, alcohol and cigarettes as natural and desirable – although things do seem to be changing somewhat, as evinced by the debate over a possible ban on smoking in public places, and growing political concern over 'binge drinking' – while cannabis and cocaine have been defined as 'drugs', with all the negative connotations this invariably implies.

Social construction, in turn, has major implications for public policy, because what is defined as 'deviant' will be subject to various laws or other sanctions to prohibit or regulate it, and quite possibly punish the 'deviants' who transgress these laws or social norms. In other words, 'how problems are defined, and who defines them, affect what response will be made to the problem' (Hulley and Clarke, 1991: 19).

The role of power in defining or denying problems

Conversely, some 'issues' might *not* be defined as problems warranting a public policy response, because they somehow conflict with the values or attitudes which are dominant in British society at any given juncture. For example, poverty and inequality often have *not* been accepted by policy makers as a problem *per se*, partly because of what might be termed a 'dominant ideology' in Britain, whereby inequalities and disparities of wealth and income are widely accepted as either natural, inevitable or desirable (in order to provide rewards and incentives for risks and responsibilities). Admittedly, social attitude surveys have also revealed certain relatively widespread social democratic values among British people, which include a belief that governments ought to help the less well-off, and create a fairer society, but there has also been a longstanding distinction in many people's minds between the 'deserving' and 'undeserving' poor, with many of those apparently living in poverty placed in the latter category. Indeed, in this context, much poverty in Britain has been attributed not to the structural inequalities and extremes of wealth intrinsic to a capitalist society, but to the 'undeserving' poor themselves, who are variously deemed to be feckless, irresponsible, lazy or work-shy, and whose allegedly 'lax attitudes' or 'lifestyles' would only be compounded by more generous welfare benefits to tackle poverty. To the extent that the 'undeserving' poor have been deemed worthy of policy makers' attention, it has often been to invoke sanctions in order to foster greater self-reliance or oblige them to find gainful employment.

In many cases, therefore, what constitutes a problem warranting attention from policy makers is *not* necessarily self-evident. Certain problems are 'socially constructed', defined in accordance with dominant ideas and values prevalent in society at any particular juncture. As such, ideas not only provide potential solutions to societal problems, they also play an important, yet often subtle, part in defining which issues or particular state of affairs are defined as problems in the first place, and thus to be addressed by policy makers.

The point about 'dominant ideologies' and problem definition or denial itself reflects the notion that power operates at different levels in society, so that while a conflict over resources between individuals or groups is clearly a very visible power struggle, some writers have suggested that there are two other, much more discreet and subtle, levels at which power is exercised, and which play a part in determining whether certain issues are defined as problems, and whether policies are introduced to tackle them. Bachrach and Baratz, in particular, have become closely identified with the twin concepts of a 'hidden face of power' and 'non-decision-making', based on the premise that certain sections of society were so important or influential, that they could effectively ensure that certain 'problems' were not defined as such by policy makers, because this might result in policies being adopted which challenged their interests or socio-economic dominance. Their classic formula states that:

> power is also exercised when *A* devotes his energies to creating or reinforcing social and political values and institutional practices that limit the scope of the political process to public consideration of only those issues which are comparatively innocuous to *A*. To the extent that *A* succeeds in doing this, *B* is prevented, for all practical purposes, from bringing to the fore any issues that might in their resolution be seriously detrimental to *A*'s set of preferences.

> (Bachrach and Baratz, 1970: 7)

This perspective might explain why certain issues, such as poverty, inequality, excessive boardroom pay, have only sporadically been defined as problems, because in a capitalist society in which inequalities of wealth are widely deemed natural or necessary, defining these features as problems might then entail policies which would be damaging or detrimental to the material interests of corporations and the business community. Recognizing the likely response of these sections of society to 'punitive' measures against them – more tax evasion, investing overseas, relocating business abroad, etc. – policy makers have usually shied away from consideration of anything more than the mildest of redistributive policies, a point clearly exemplified by the Blair governments in Britain since 1997. Indeed, more radical policies – such as a freeze on company directors' pay to counter 'boardroom greed' – are not even formally considered, or placed on the 'agenda', so that no decision is actually taken *not* to pursue such policies, they are not seriously considered in the first place. They are automatically simply deemed 'out of bounds' or 'off-message' from the outset; they are 'non-decisions'.

In a similar context, Crenson investigated why the US city of Gary, Indiana, avoided, for many years, antipollution policies with regard to the city's industries. He discovered that US Steel was a major employer in the city, but might relocate and impose redundancies, if antipollution legislation was introduced which it deemed damaging to its commercial interests. This 'anticipated reaction' ensured that Gary's policy makers avoided, for many years, antipollution measures, while US Steel itself did not have to mobilize or enter the political arena (Crenson, 1971: 77–8).

This 'second' or 'hidden face' of power was also recognized by Schattschneider, when he declared that: 'All forms of political organisation have a bias in favor of the exploitation of some kinds of conflicts and the suppression of others, because *organisation is the mobilisation of bias*. Some issues are organised into politics while others are organized out' (1960: 71).

Lukes goes even further, identifying what he terms a 'third face' of power, whereby the most powerful group(s) in society can effectively impose a dominant set of values or beliefs on the rest of society. This helps to ensure that certain social phenomena are not even recognized as being problematic, but, instead, are simply assumed to be natural and taken for granted. It is not merely that certain issues or problems are kept off the agenda, they are not even recognized as being issues, yet alone problems, in the first place. Or as Lukes expresses it:

> is it not the supreme and most insidious use of power to prevent people, to whatever degree, from having grievances by shaping their perceptions, cognitions and preferences in such a way that they accept their role in the existing order of things, either because they can see or imagine no alternative to it, or because they see it as natural and unchangeable, or because they value it as divinely ordained and beneficial?

> (1974: 24)

Yet while Bachrach and Baratz, Crenson and Lukes, each made a valuable contribution to the study of power, problem definition and policy agendas, we need to consider other factors which can either inhibit change, and thereby contribute towards policy continuity, or which alternatively, in certain circumstances, can prompt policy change.

The role of ideas

The impact of ideas on public policy and agenda setting can be discerned on at least two discrete levels (Seldon, 1996: 264). There is a general or 'macro' level of ideas, which might be deemed ideological, in the sense that they constitute a dominant or *hegemonic* set of ideas and values concerning the purpose and objectives of government and public policy. In this respect, certain ideas become prevalent and pervasive during particular periods of history, and thereby shape and constrain the policies that are pursued.

For example, *laissez-faire* and individualism constituted the dominant framework of ideas during the Victorian era in late-19th-century Britain, with social phenomena such as poverty, and even ill-health, often attributed to individual failings, fecklessness and immorality. It was therefore deemed neither desirable nor appropriate for the state to intervene to ameliorate such conditions or circumstances, unless it was in a punitive manner to 'remoralize' the individuals concerned.

By contrast, the 1945–79 period was an era in which the dominant set of 'macro' ideas were those of social democracy (or at least a mild, British variant of it), entailing

Keynesian economic management and a Beveridgian welfare state. In stark contrast to the Victorian era, it was widely accepted that governments could – and therefore should – intervene in the economy to sustain or stimulate demand, and thereby underpin full employment and increased prosperity. Similarly, this period entailed a widespread acceptance that the state had a responsibility to ensure that there was an education system and health service available to everyone (free at the point of access or admission), irrespective of their background or material circumstances, as well as a system of public (council) housing for those who could not afford to buy their own homes. Furthermore, this social democratic era entailed a social security system whereby a range of benefits were available to people on the basis of their circumstances and needs 'from the cradle to the grave'.

So pervasive did this set of ideas become, particularly from the late 1940s to the 1960s, that many senior Conservatives sought to accommodate their party to it, deeming it to be in accordance with the 'one nation' strand of Toryism attributed to the 19th-century Conservative leader and Prime Minister, Benjamin Disraeli. Thus did the late 1940s, for example, hear a number of prominent Conservatives, such as Rab Butler, explicitly rejecting *laissez-faire* and the unfettered free market, and insisting that the Conservative Party had always acknowledged a more active role for the state in contributing towards the material welfare and prosperity of its citizens (Butler, 1971: 135, 146; see also Alport, 1946: 14; Hinchingbrooke, 1944: 21).

The Conservative Party's attempt at accommodating itself to the ideas of social democracy after 1945 was evident in the 1947 policy document, *The Industrial Charter*, in which the party publicly committed itself to the pursuit of 'high and stable levels of employment', government regulation of the economy where appropriate or necessary, and acceptance of the trade unions as important and valuable institutions who therefore deserved to be treated with respect.

Since the late 1970s, another set of 'macro' ideas has prevailed, thereby displacing those of social democracy, namely those of neo-liberalism and individualism, although whether these were actually a new set of ideas, or merely a revival of those which prevailed in the 19th century, is a matter of conjecture. Promoted and implemented by the New Right and Thatcherism during the 1980s and 1990s, this new *hegemony* lauded the primacy of the market economy, both on normative and practical grounds, and enthusiastically encouraged individualism (instead of collectivism). Whereas social democracy had viewed many socio-economic problems as a consequence of 'market failure', thereby justifying state intervention and trade union partnership as appropriate policy responses, the neo-liberalism of the New Right decreed that so-called 'market failures' were actually a consequence of excessive state intervention and trade union power. A different framework of ideas, therefore, provided the basis for a fundamentally different set of priorities and policies during the 1980s and 1990s.

So entrenched did these ideas become during this period, that (just as many Conservatives had accommodated themselves to social democracy from the late 1940s to the 1960s) Labour 'modernizers' sought to restructure and reposition the party in a manner which entailed it not merely accepting, but actually embracing 'the market', and thereby ditching its *dirigiste*, interventionist past (hence the rewriting of Clause IV and abandonment of nationalization as a principal policy objective) (Heffernan, 2000). This repositioning, which resulted in the emergence of New Labour, also entailed the party formally accepting the importance of the consumer over producer interests, and a much looser and cooler relationship with the trade unions. Indeed, since becoming Prime Minister in May 1997, Tony Blair – the personification of New Labour – has exuded the same admiration of businessmen as Margaret Thatcher did, much to the chagrin of many trade union leaders.

While the 'macro' level of ideas provides the dominant paradigm during different eras, there are also ideas at the 'meso' or 'micro' levels, which influence policies in particular areas and on specific issues. Of course, they will be significantly shaped and constrained by the dominant paradigm within the area articulated, but they will nonetheless often have an importance and impact in their own right, and certainly add to the multiplicity of influences shaping public policy overall.

When the social democratic paradigm was *hegemonic*, for example, the overall emphasis on equality of opportunity and reducing inequality facilitated specific ideas and policies promoting comprehensive schools and an expansion of Higher Education (to widen access), while the principle of government regulation of the economy (to mitigate the deficiencies and dysfunctions of the free market) yielded, among other things, acceptance of the need for some public ownership (nationalization) of key industries and services, and the adoption of incomes policies as a means of preventing 'excessive' or inflationary pay increases.

Once the social democratic paradigm was superseded by that of neo-liberalism and individualism, many 'micro-' or 'meso-' level ideas yielded corresponding changes in specific policies. The overarching importance of private enterprise and ownership facilitated the privatization of nationalized industries and the selling off of council houses, while the rejection of governmental responsibility for full employment, coupled with an alternative – 'money supply' – theory of the cause of inflation, led to the abandonment of incomes policies and partnership with the trade unions. Similarly, with the New Right disputing the previously held view (among many policy makers) that crime was largely attributable to socio-economic deprivation, there was much greater emphasis on catching and prosecuting criminals, through increasing both police numbers and powers, as well as encouraging the use of more custodial (prison) sentences by the courts.

Individuals as progenitors of ideas and policies

A few individuals can be said to have exerted a significant influence with regard to key ideas or the 'macro' level intellectual framework since 1945. First, John Maynard Keynes and William Beveridge are widely recognized as the intellectual architects of what became the postwar social democratic settlement in Britain, lasting from 1945 to the 1970s. Keynes' economic ideas provided a clear alternative to the hitherto dominance of unfettered market forces and *laissez-faire*, by explaining how governments could – and should – seek to regulate economic activity in order to sustain demand, and thereby both avoid oscillations between booms and slumps, and foster full employment. These ideas, considered quite radical when first enunciated (via Keynes' 1936 book, *The General Theory of*

Employment, Interest and Money) gained credence as a consequence of government intervention in, and regulation of, the British economy during World War II – when Keynes himself was appointed to work in the Treasury – to the extent that when the war ended in 1945, there was a widespread intellectual and political acceptance that the country should not seek to turn back the clock by reverting to pre-war economics. As previously noted, even the majority of senior Conservatives publicly accepted the need for state regulation of the economy from the mid-1940s onwards, and thereby acknowledged that there could be no return to Victorian economic liberalism. Indeed, by this time, the future Conservative Prime Minister, Harold Macmillan, had already urged the pursuit of a 'middle way' between state socialism and *laissez-faire* capitalism, whereby the state and industry, along with management and workers, would work together as partners to pursue common goals, rather than continuing to permit untrammelled market forces and rampant individualism, both of which were potentially, if not actually, destabilizing of the social and political order (Macmillan, 1927; Macmillan, 1937).

William Beveridge, meanwhile, was a former civil servant and sometime director of the London School of Economics (LSE), and is widely acknowledged to be the architect of the postwar welfare state, for it was his 1942 *Report on Social Insurance and Allied Services* which provided the intellectual and political framework for many of the social polices and institutions introduced by the 1945–51 Labour governments (and generally maintained by subsequent governments), although elements of the welfare state were already in existence before 1942. Certainly, one distinguished academic has characterized Beveridge as 'the emblematic Keynesian social democrat of the 1940s' (Marquand, 1996: 23).

The two intellectuals who have become most closely identified with the subsequent Conservative counter-revolution against the Keynesian–Beveridgian consensus are Friedrich Hayek and Milton Friedman, although their ideas were then popularized during the 1970s and 1980s by various British academics. Hayek provided a strong intellectual case against state intervention to regulate the economy or provide a comprehensive welfare state, arguing that this heralded a 'road to serfdom' (Hayek, 1944), and thus firmly believing that the State's role should be kept to the minimum necessary to maintain the framework of a market economy and law and order, beyond which individuals ought to be permitted maximum choice about how they lived their lives. Although Hayek insisted that he was a (classical) liberal rather than a Conservative (Hayek, 1960: 397–411), his ideas were enthusiastically adopted and cited by many of those Conservatives who came to constitute the New Right, and who increasingly coalesced around Margaret Thatcher, herself a self-confessed admirer of Hayek (Thatcher, 1993: 12–13, 1995: 50–1).

The monetarist economic theory popularized by Milton Friedman, meanwhile, was enthusiastically adopted or espoused by various Conservative politicians and adherents from the late 1970s onwards, and even though the first Thatcher government's 'monetarist experiment' was relatively short-lived (Ingham, 2000: 104–7; Keegan, 1984; Riddell, 1989: 18–22), Friedman's general views about the alleged inherent superiority of free markets and the immutable laws of supply and demand continued to inform the thinking of many senior Conservatives during the 1980s, as did his view that much unemployment was 'voluntary' (Friedman, 1962; Friedman and Friedman, 1980).

The main intellectual associated with New Labour and the Blair government, meanwhile, is Anthony Giddens, an academic sociologist and Director of the LSE (Fielding, 2003: 80; Kelly, 2003: 242). Prior to 1997, it had also been widely considered that Will Hutton – economic journalist for *The Observer* Sunday broad-sheet newspaper, for whom he was appointed editor in 1996 – was emerging as an intellectual influence on Tony Blair's Labour Party, particularly when the former promoted the 'stakeholder' economy as a third way between New Right neo-liberalism and Old Left *dirigisme*, but this apparent influence did not last (see, for example, Seldon, 2004: 241), and many of Hutton's weekly columns in *The Observer* have since been rather critical of the Blair governments' apparent lack of radicalism in many areas of policy, not least their approach to the economy, and their timidity towards European integration.

Individuals, often academic economists or sociologists, have also exercised an occasional influence on specific policies in postwar Britain. For example, Robert Hall, the Director of the Cabinet Office's Economic Section throughout the 1950s and into the beginning of the 1960s, seems to have played a major role in persuading Harold Macmillan and his senior Conservative ministers of the need to pursue an incomes policy after 1960, in order to maintain full employment and curb inflation (Hall, 1961: 1042). The subsequent Labour government of Harold Wilson entered Office in 1964, itself committed to 'a policy for incomes' (albeit shying away from the term incomes policy due to the trade unions' suspicion that this was invariably a euphemism for wage restraint), reflecting the strong influence on both Wilson and his first Chancellor, James Callaghan, of Thomas Balogh. Formerly an Oxbridge economist, Balogh subsequently became Wilson's personal economic adviser, and was a strong proponent of 'a policy for incomes' (Balogh, 1963: 14–15; PRO PREM 13/1875, Balogh to Wilson, 28 February 1967).

The 1964–70 Labour governments also seemed initially to be influenced by sociologists such as Brian Abel-Smith and Peter Townsend, who were instrumental in the 'rediscovery of poverty' during the first half of the 1960s, which therefore challenged the widely held view that full employment, rising incomes and the welfare state had, by this time, finally eradicated poverty. These sociologists provided analyses which refuted this complacent assumption (see, for example, Abel-Smith and Townsend, 1965; Titmuss, 1962), and thereby appeared to shape various of the Wilson governments' early social policies (Seldon, 1996: 268). Aspects of education policy especially bore the imprint of the sociologist Michael Young, who not only underpinned Tony Crosland's determination to expand comprehensive education, but was instrumental in convincing Harold Wilson himself to pursue the innovation of what was to become the Open University (Hollis, 1997: 303; Pimlott, 1993: 514).

During the same period, the Conservative Opposition was formulating a highly legalistic industrial relations policy, which would eventually become the 1971 Industrial Relations Act. Although this policy reflected the view of a number of senior Conservatives at the time, that 'appeasement' of the trade unions had been pursued too far and for too long, one particular individual, Stephen Abbott, seemed to have played a significant role in promoting the adoption of much more legalistic policy after 1965. As a company executive who began working for the Conservative Party in 1960, Abbott was convinced of the need to pursue greater legal regulation of industrial relations, a perspective which he was able to advocate through his subsequent membership of the Conservative Opposition's policy review group on 'trade union practice and law' (Abbott, 1966; Moran, 1977: 57–8).

The 1974–9 Labour governments, meanwhile, particularly its two leaders, Harold Wilson, until his resignation in the spring of 1976, and James Callaghan thereafter, were apparently strongly influenced on a range of policies by Bernard Donoughue, a former Reader in Politics at the LSE, who subsequently became a Special Policy Adviser to the two Labour Prime Ministers, and Head of the (10 Downing Street) Policy Unit. According to one leading political historian, his 'influence penetrated the heart of government' (Seldon, 1996: 271), and certainly, his influence – along with that of Wilson's Press Secretary, Joe Haines – was clearly discernible with regard to incomes policy in 1975–6, as well as aspects of social policy under Callaghan. However Donoughue and Haines were less successful in persuading the Cabinet to adopt a policy of selling council houses to their tenants (Donoughue, 1987: 63–4, 103–27), a policy which subsequently became indelibly associated with Margaret Thatcher and her Conservative governments in the 1980s.

During the early years of Margaret Thatcher's premiership, Ferdinand Mount – briefly head of the Policy Unit during 1982–3 – apparently 'contributed to her [Margaret Thatcher's] philosophical and moral approach', for he too was 'a firm advocate of the renewal of discipline and responsibility'. Consequently 'a number of policy proposals flowed from Mount's philosophy', including tax changes beneficial to married couples, education vouchers (not subsequently introduced), stronger policing and more generous discounts for those wishing to buy their council house (Blick, 2004: 200; Thatcher, 1993: 278–9).

During John Major's 1990–7 premiership, the Deputy Head of Policy Unit, Nick True, became closely associated with two particular policy initiatives, namely the 1991 Citizen's Charter, and the 1993 'back to basics' campaign (Hogg and Hill, 1995: 95–7; Seldon, 1996: 272). Meanwhile one of the most controversial policies of the Major governments was the Child Support Agency (CSA), whose intellectual antecedents could partly be attributed to the neo-conservative American sociologist Charles Murray (see below).

More recently, since 1997, Tony Blair seems to have been strongly influenced by individuals such as Peter Mandelson, widely recognized as a key architect of 'New Labour' and the party's modernization process, and by Philip Gould, Blair's personal poll adviser and overall organizer of the party's 'focus groups'. Mandelson and Blair have developed a very close friendship, with Mandelson regularly acting as a 'confidant' of Tony Blair, and thus enjoying regular meetings with the Prime Minister, even when he was not actually a minister (Mandelson and Liddle, 1996). It is partly because of the ultra-revisionist and 'modernizing' views to which he has long subscribed with regard to the Labour Party, and the apparent influence he has exercised over Tony Blair – coupled with the regularity and ease of access to him for bilateral meetings and advice-offering sessions – that Peter Mandelson became deeply unpopular among many Labour backbenchers. Even some senior ministers – including Gordon Brown and John Prescott – have reportedly been uneasy about Mandelson's apparent influence over Tony Blair's political thinking on occasions.

Meanwhile, Philip Gould has arguably played a central role in advising Blair on the aspirations and anxieties of 'Middle England', as ascertained through conducting regular private polling for the Labour Party, coupled with the organization of 'focus groups', which seek to elicit people's views and concerns on particular issues. This has enabled

New Labour to tailor – or present ('spin') – many of its policies accordingly, both publicly, but also privately, in the sense of persuading sceptical backbenchers that particular policy proposals which they want to see adopted would be unpopular with voters, and might therefore diminish the party's electoral support. In these respects, Gould can also be seen – like Mandelson – as a major influence on Tony Blair's political outlook, and thus on the establishment of New Labour (Gould, 1999).

Think tanks as progenitors of ideas and agenda setting

Since the late 1970s, there has been an increase in the number of 'think tanks' in Britain, and an apparent increase in their influence. We say apparent because 'influence' is often difficult to gauge in political science, due to the problem of identifying independent variables, or determining the degree to which a particular variable has shaped a political event or policy outcome. Consequently, while it is fairly straightforward to measure the rise of 'think tanks' quantitatively, it is rather less easy to gauge their actual contribution to public policy in Britain, especially as some such bodies might want to claim credit for certain policies in order to enhance their credibility – and attract new clients and funding – in an increasingly crowded think tank universe (for an overview on the rise and role of think tanks in Britain see Denham and Garnett, 1998, 1999, 2004; James, 1993; Stone, 1996).

One commentator has referred to think tanks as 'idea brokers', defining them as formally independent (from government) bodies 'engaged in multidisciplinary research intended to influence public policy'. In this context, the 'distinctive contribution of think tanks to British politics has been to broaden the repertoire of politicians by offering an extra, unorthodox alternative which makes it easier to question the premises of existing policy' (James, 1993: 492, 505). Although formally independent of government – a necessary precondition of being able to conduct independent research and promote original ideas – the ideological orientation of some think tanks means that two broad types can be identified.

First, there are those which are recognized as being politically neutral, or what Denham and Garnett term as 'traditional' (1996: 49) think tanks. These aim to provide objective information and evidence on issues, which they hope will influence the ideas of policy makers, irrespective of which political party is in government, or which overarching set of ideas is prevalent at any given time. The three most notable examples of such think tanks in Britain are indicated in Table 2.1.

The second category of think tanks are those that, while remaining formally independent of government, have a clear political or ideological orientation, to the extent that they often become identified with a particular ideology, a specific political party, or even a particular 'strand' within that party. In this respect, these have been labelled 'advocacy' think tanks (Denham and Garnett, 1998: 49), for they clearly seek to influence policy makers on the basis of a particular ideological orientation or political perspective. Similarly, in his essay on the Adam Smith Institute (a think tank cited below), Heffernan adopts the term 'policy advocate' clearly characterizing it as 'political', rather than an 'independent' think tank' (1996: 81). As such, these 'think tanks' are generally either on the political Right

Table 2.1 **'Traditional' think tanks in contemporary Britain**

Name of think tank	Date formed	Focus or orientation
Institute of Fiscal Studies	1969	'To provide top quality economic analysis' and provide 'a source of authoritative, impartial comment on fiscal matters', particularly with regard to taxation. The Institute sees itself as exercising 'substantial influence through publications, the media, close contacts with civil servants and regular meetings with Cabinet and Shadow Cabinet members' (www.ifs.org.uk).
National Institute of Economic and Social Research	1938	'To promote, through quantitative research, a deeper understanding of the interaction of economic and social forces that affect people's lives, so that they may be improved' (www.niesr.ac.uk).
Policy Studies Institute	1978	Aims to conduct 'rigorous and impartial' research and disseminate information – via publications (including a journal), workshops and conferences – which will 'promote economic well-being and improve quality of life' (www.psi.org.uk).

(and particularly what became known from the 1970s as the New Right), or towards the centre-Left (often associated with New Labour or the 'third way'), although some of the latter are sceptical about the continued relevance of terms such as Left and Right, and thus prefer to depict themselves as 'progressive' instead. Table 2.2 indicates the think tanks associated with the political Right in Britain, and particularly the New Right or Thatcherism.

These think tanks seek to influence public policy and policy makers in various ways, most notably through hosting conferences and seminars, submitting proposals to relevant civil servants and ministers, writing articles in newspapers and publishing books and pamphlets. Some of them, such as the Institute of Economic Affairs, even publish their own journal. Politeia, meanwhile, publishes about 10 pamphlets each year, and hosts numerous conferences and lectures, with many of the participants drawn from academia, journalism, other think tanks, 'the City', and the Conservative Party.

Most of these think tanks claim to have exerted an influence on public policy in Britain during the 1980s and 1990s, with the Adam Smith Institute claiming to have published 'over 300 *influential* policy reports' between 1977 and the end of 2002 (www.adamsmith. org.uk, emphasis added), while also claiming that the Thatcher governments implemented 200 of the 624 policy proposals recommended in the Adam Smith Institute's 1985 *Omega File*. The

Table 2.2   Think tanks associated with the political Right in Britain

Name of think tank	Date formed	Focus or orientation
Adam Smith Institute	1977	Leading advocate of ideas concerning private enterprise, the virtues of competition and the need to base economic activity and variables (such as prices, wages, and levels of employment) on the 'laws' of supply and demand. Sees itself providing suggestions and concrete proposals about how to put these principles into practice *vis-à-vis* particular policies.
Centre for Policy Studies	1974	Margaret Thatcher and Sir Keith Joseph founded the Centre for Policy Studies (CPS) in order to promote the case for a social market economy and greater freedom (from the state) for individuals. Strong emphasis on the importance of individual choice and responsibility, and the concepts of duty, family, respect for the law, national independence, individualism and liberty' (www.cps.org.uk/mission; see also, Harris, 1996).
Institute of Economic Affairs	1957	Has always advocated applying market principles (competition, contracting out, internal markets, private sector involvement or practices, etc) and consumer choice to the provision of public services and the welfare state, but only from the mid-1970s did the Institute find these ideas being taken seriously and sympathetically by an increasing number of Conservative politicians.
Politeia	1995	Founded by Sheila Lawlor, formerly a Deputy Director of the Centre for Policy Studies, Politeia is primarily concerned with such issues as: the proper role of government, appropriate or acceptable levels of taxation, and the balance to be struck between the state and the private sector in the provision of such services as health, education, pensions (www.politeia.co.uk).
Social Affairs Unit	1980	Initially established under the auspices of the Institute of Economic Affairs, the Social Affairs Unit eventually acquired complete institutional independence. Much of its work has provided a sociological 'parallel' to the IEA's economic critique of collectivism, concentrating on the apparently detrimental social effects of universal welfarism, and the alleged influence of 'self-serving' welfare professionals and Left-inclined sociologists on postwar social policy in Britain.

Institute, or individuals closely associated with it, also claim that it influenced various privatizations during the 1980s, along with the Poll Tax, the introduction of 'Freeports', and parts of the 1988 Education Act (which, among other things, enabled schools to opt out of Local Education Authority (LEA) control, and purported to increase 'parent power'). The Adam Smith Institute has also claimed at least some of the credit for John Major's introduction, in 1991, of a Citizen's Charter, formally intended to empower or enhance the rights of consumers of public services (Heffernan, 1996: 84–5).

The Social Affairs Unit similarly claims that many of the ideas it initially espoused have subsequently 'found their way into the policy mainstream', particularly in the sphere of education, such as local autonomy for schools and further education colleges, parental choice and accountability, standards and academic rigour in curricula, etc. (www.socialaffairsunit. org.uk).

Of course, as previously mentioned, discerning the actual influence of think tanks is methodologically difficult, primarily because we cannot know whether policy makers would have adopted the relevant policies anyway, irrespective of the arguments, or even the very existence, of certain think tanks. It is quite likely, for example, that Margaret Thatcher would have adopted the Poll Tax and pursued various privatizations regardless of the advocacy of both polices by the Adam Smith Institute.

However, think tanks might well serve either to embolden policy makers contemplating a particular policy, providing them with the intellectual confidence to proceed, or they might help to imbue a policy initiative with greater legitimacy, either among other political elites and opinion formers, or possibly among sections of the British public. Certainly, some commentators believe that the influence of think tanks is greater in helping to shape the overall intellectual framework, than in directly and explicitly influencing specific policies. Writing about the Institute of Economic Affairs, for example, Muller argues that the think tank 'engaged less in offering practical solutions and means of implementation to government, and rather sought to change the climate in which government thinking was taking place' (1996: 95), or, as Denham and Garnett elaborate, the Institute's main audience 'was (and continues to be) not so much people with day-to-day policy making responsibilities as those who help to frame the context in which policy making takes place' (1998: 93). More generally, Cockett's major study argues that New Right think tanks, and various individuals within them 'did as much intellectually to convert a generation of "opinion formers" and politicians to a new set of ideas as the Fabians had done with a former generation at the turn of the century' (Cockett, 1994: 5), while Seldon, although fully acknowledging the difficulties of accurately gauging their precise influence on particular policies, concurs that since the 1970s, think tanks 'have had an influential role in collating the thoughts of like-minded intellectuals and funnelling them into governing circles' (1996: 273).

One key point to note, though, is the extent to which the ideas propagated by think tanks – and, indeed, individuals – will only gain intellectual or political credence if they are perceived to correspond to actual circumstances, and offer a plausible explanation of the underlying causes of particular problems at a given historical juncture. For example, having been formed in 1957, the Institute of Economic Affairs spent its early years ploughing 'a lonely intellectual furrow' in espousing 'the then unfashionable case for the free market'

Table 2.3   Centre-Left or New Labour-orientated think tanks in Britain

Name of think tank	Date formed	Focus or orientation
Demos	1993	Describes itself as 'a greenhouse of new ideas' intended to underpin five main themes, namely democracy, learning, enterprise, global change and quality of life. Strong focus on cultural issues – environmental affairs, drugs, gender relations, political apathy, parenting, etc. Demos claims that its ideas 'regularly influence government policy' (www.demos.co.uk; see also, Bale, 1996).
Fabian Society	1884	Always espoused a gradualist yet progressive approach to social reform to establish a fairer society, but has experienced something of a renaissance, claiming to have made a significant contribution to the Labour Party's process of modernization since 1992, particularly the 1995 rewriting of Clause IV. Sees itself as the Blair government's 'critical friend' (see Callaghan, 1996, for an overview).
Institute for Public Policy Research	1988	Claims to be 'the leading independent think tank on the centre left', whose 'well-researched and clearly argued policy analysis' makes a significant contribution to 'maintaining the momentum of progressive thought'. Through its ideas and policy proposals, the Institute aims to create 'a fairer, more inclusive and more environmentally sustainable world', deriving from its values of 'social justice, equality, and democratic empowerment' (www.ippr.org.uk).

(James, 1993: 495). Not until the economic crises and apparent 'overload of government' of the 1970s did its ideas, and those of cognate think tanks formed around this time start to correspond to wider experiences and perceptions, whereupon they seemed to offer – at least to some commentators and policy makers – solutions to the mounting problems affecting Britain. As the social democratic, Keynesian, welfare consensus crumbled, so some of the ideas canvassed by the think tanks of the Right began to be taken more seriously by certain journalists, newspapers and politicians (most notably Sir Keith Joseph, who, in turn, strongly influenced Margaret Thatcher herself) (see Desai, 1994).

Irrespective of how much influence the Right's think tanks actually exercised from the mid-1970s onwards, some figures on the centre-Left evidently deemed them serious enough to warrant forming their own think tanks during the late 1980s and 1990s, or breathe new life into those which already had a long history. The main centre-Left – in fact, they are generally associated with New Labour – or self-proclaimed 'progressive' think tanks are outlined in Table 2.3.

Like their Conservative or New Right counterparts, most of the centre-Left or 'progressives' claim to have exercised at least some influence on the Labour Party since the early 1990s, even to the extent of partly fashioning 'New Labour', even before the term was actually invoked. For example, the Institute for Public Policy Research (IPPR) claims to have played a major role in the establishment (by the Labour Party) in 1992, of the (Borrie) Commission on Social Justice, which, in turn, provided the basis for such New Labour policies as the 'New Deal', tax-and-pension integration and pensions reform. The Institute also claims to have had various of its other policy ideas and initiatives embraced by the Blair governments, including environmental taxation, the Human Rights Act, and social housing. Since the Blair government's re-election in June 2001, the Institute has gained prominence for its endorsement of Public-Private Partnerships (PPP) (something which many Labour MPs view with profound suspicion). As we will note in the next two chapters, several of the Institute's staff have been appointed as Special Advisers to Cabinet Ministers and the Prime Minister himself since 1997. Certainly, the IPPR is deemed to have exercised so much influence on New Labour's policy development since the mid-1990s, that it has wryly been referred to as 'New Labour's civil service' (Rowan, 2003: 17; see also, Ruben, 1996).

A further indication of the apparent affinity between these think tanks and New Labour is indicated by the fact that following the party's 1997 election victory, the co-founder of Demos, Geoff Mulgan, was appointed by Blair to serve in the Cabinet Office, helping to oversee or coordinate the implementation of various policies, thereby assisting in the goal of creating 'joined-up government'.

Two other think tanks worth mentioning very briefly, but which are somewhat more difficult to locate clearly on a traditional Left-Right continuum, are the Social Market Foundation and Civitas. Founded in 1989, the Social Market Foundation claims to be non-ideological and independent of party politics, but has generally acquired a reputation for being closer to the centre-Right (for an overview, see Baston, 1996). Yet the political or ideological ambivalence of the Social Market Foundation is indicated by the ideologically eclectic range of figures who are either patrons or sit on its advisory board, including: Lord (David) Owen, a Labour Cabinet Minister in the 1970s and co-founder of the Social Democratic Party in 1981; the Conservative academic, Professor Lord (Robert) Skidelsky; Lord Sainsbury, the supermarket magnate and financial donor to New Labour; Daniel Finkelstein, who has worked in the Conservative Research Department since 1995; Professor Anthony Giddens, Director of the LSE and intellectual 'guru' of Tony Blair's 'third way'; Stephen Twigg, the Labour MP who defeated Michael Portillo in 1997 (and retained the Enfield and Southgate seat in the 2001 election); David Willetts, a former senior official in the Centre for Policy Studies and now a member of the Conservatives' Shadow Cabinet. It is this eclecticism which renders it so difficult to characterize the Social Market Foundation's political position.

Meanwhile, Civitas (the Institute for the Study of Civil Society), which was formed in 2000, claims to be 'politically non-partisan', its primary concern being 'to deepen public understanding of the legal, institutional and moral framework that makes a free and democratic society possible', and to promote 'a better division of responsibilities between government and civil society'. However, it believes that 'there are still areas where the realm of political decisions may have encroached too much onto the territory best left to the initiative of individuals freely co-operating in their own localities' (www.civitas.org.uk/hwu/mission). In the late summer of 2004, Civitas announced that it was opening a New Model School in London for children of primary school age, in which the emphasis would be on the '3 Rs' and developing good character'. The initiative derived from Civitas's concern that traditional British values and culture were being grievously undermined by excessive liberalism, multiculturalism and cultural relativism. In establishing the school – fees just under £3000 per annum – a senior official claimed that Civitas had changed from 'being a think-tank to a do-tank' (*The Guardian,* 31 August 2004).

Civitas is especially interested in four policy areas: education, family, health and welfare, and while declaring its political independence, its concern to ensure that hospitals and schools are more responsive to patients and parents, and that the social security system permits a greater role for individual responsibility and the voluntary sector, do suggest an orientation towards the centre-Right. In this respect, it is interesting to note that the founder of Civitas was previously the Director of the Institute of Economic Affairs' Health and Welfare Unit, while the Deputy Director of Civitas was formerly Assistant Director of this unit. Another senior official within Civitas was hitherto Deputy Director of the Social Market Foundation. Also 'ideologically' linked with Civitas (if not actually a member) is Melanie Phillips, a former *Guardian* journalist who now writes for *The Daily Mail*. Describing her political position as that of 'a liberal who has been mugged by reality', she apparently sees in Civitas 'the beginnings of a sympathetic network' (Beckett, 2003: 2).

One important way in which at least some of the ideas canvassed by the more political or partisan think tanks may have been transmitted to governments is through the appointment – often by the Prime Minister – of senior think tank personnel to key posts within the core executive (discussed in the next chapter).

Table 2.4 shows the most notable examples, since 1980, of think tank staff who were subsequently appointed to positions within the core executive, and therefore had regular and direct access to Cabinet Ministers, including the Prime Minister.

Yet however many ideas and individuals are vying for attention, and seeking to shape the policy agenda at any given moment, their intellectual merits or ideological strengths are not in themselves usually sufficient to ensure that they will be adopted by policy makers. Instead, ideas and proposed policy solutions to problems need to correspond to appropriate political circumstances.

Hayek wrote *The Road to Serfdom* in the mid-1940s, for example, but from 1945 to the early 1970s, his critique of government intervention and welfarism attracted little serious or sympathetic attention in Britain, largely because state management of the economy, and welfare provision from 'cradle to grave' were what most British people seemed to want and expect. Furthermore, for much of this period, these general policies were widely perceived to be relatively successful, certainly more so than what had preceded them. Consequently, Hayek's ideas were not 'picked-up' by many people, beyond a small number of right-wing academics and Conservatives, who were themselves generally viewed as mavericks or 'outsiders' at the time. Only in the political circumstances which developed in Britain during the 1970s did the ideas of individuals like Hayek, and like-minded think tanks, gain wider, more popular currency, and became treated much more seriously, to the extent of actually becoming influential, and arguably contributing towards policy change.

In other words, as Seldon notes 'ideas are not enough'; to be effective 'they need advocates, they need to square with the facts, and to be launched into positive circumstances' (1996: 289). This leads us to a key concept developed by John Kingdon, in his book

Table 2.4 Think tank staff subsequently appointed to posts in the core executive, since 1979

Name	Former think tank membership or post	Subsequent political post
Daniel Finkelstein	Director of Social Market Foundation (1992–5)	Conservative Research Department from 1995.
John Hoskyns	Centre for Policy Studies	Head of 10 Downing Street Policy Unit under Margaret Thatcher (1979–82).
David Miliband	Researcher for the Institute for Public Policy Research	1. Head of 10 Downing Street Policy Unit under Tony Blair. 2. From 2001, a Labour MP, and Minister of State for Education.
Ferdinand Mount	Director of Centre for Policy Studies	Head of 10 Downing Street Policy Unit under Margaret Thatcher (1982–3).
Geoff Mulgan	Co-founder and Director of Demos	1. Special Adviser to Tony Blair (with particular reference to tackling social exclusion). 2. Head of Cabinet Office's Strategy Unit.
John Redwood	Centre for Policy Studies	1. Head of 10 Downing Street Policy Unit under Margaret Thatcher (1983–5). 2. Cabinet Minister under John Major (1990–5). 3. Conservative leadership challenger (unsuccessful) in 1995. 4. Shadow Cabinet under William Hague 1997–2001, and Michael Howard since 2004.
Sir Alfred Sherman	Director of Studies at the Centre for Policy Studies	10 Downing Street Policy Unit under Margaret Thatcher (Special Adviser).
Norman Strauss	Centre for Policy Studies	10 Downing Street Policy Unit under Margaret Thatcher (Special Adviser).
Matthew Taylor	Institute for Public Policy Research	Head of (Tony Blair's) 10 Downing Street Policy Directorate since summer 2003.
Sir Alan Walters	Centre for Policy Studies	Special (Economic) Adviser to Margaret Thatcher.
David Willetts	Director of Centre for Policy Studies (1987–92). Board Member of Social Market Foundation after 1992.	1. 10 Downing Street Policy Unit under Margaret Thatcher. 2. Conservative MP (since 1992). 3. Various Cabinet and Shadow Cabinet posts.

Agendas, Alternatives and Public Policies, which was first published in 1984, with a second edition appearing in 1995, in which he examined the conditions normally required in order for policy change to occur.

Policy Streams

Kingdon (1995) illustrated that in order to get onto the policy agenda, and thus have an input into public policy, particularly policy change, ideas need to be conjoined with two other factors, namely the existence of identifiable problems for which those ideas purport to be solutions, and appropriate circumstances and situations enabling the ideas and solutions to be implemented. In this context, Kingdon delineates three 'streams', (Figure 2.1), which need to flow together if ideas are to move up, or even onto, the policy agenda, and be translated into public policy.

Figure 2.1 John Kingdon's model of policy streams

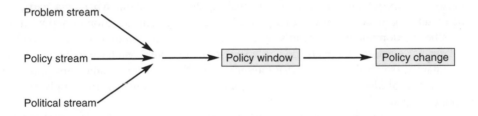

The problem stream

While many problems seem to be self-evident, especially when they produce a crisis compelling policy makers to act, other problems are not so often obvious, or even recognized as being problems, due to the manner in which they are socially constructed or ideologically defined. Consequently, it is not sufficient to assume that problems invariably or inevitably get onto the policy agenda, for not everyone involved in the policy process will recognize them as problems. On the other hand, some policy actors will actually look for a problem, because they have a particular theory or policy which they wish to pursue. As such, rather than assuming that problems generate a search for solutions, the policy process often comprises 'solutions' (via their advocates) searching for a problem to which they can be applied. Whether an issue is defined as a problem depends on a range of factors, which we might term the four 'I's:

- indicators
- interpretation
- ideology
- instances.

Indicators, usually of a quantitative or statistical kind, whereby statistics or other empirical evidence reveal that a particular phenomenon is increasing or decreasing in a manner which is deemed undesirable, unacceptable or unintended. For example, one of the reasons why Conservative governments decided, during the late 1980s and early 1990s, that single parents were a social problem, were figures which showed that their numbers had increased from 840,000 in 1979 to 1.5 million just over a decade later. Furthermore, while many of these were attributable to marital breakdown and divorce, it was also discovered that the number of unmarried mothers had increased from 160,000 in 1981 to 430,000 in 1991, with the total amount of welfare benefits paid annually to single parents having risen from £2.4 billion to £6 billion during the same period. For Conservatives subscribing to a particular view of the family – based on a married couple jointly bringing up their children – and also committed to curbing public expenditure (one-third of which was consumed by social security), these statistics were clearly a cause for concern, so that lone parents became a problem which policy makers needed to address. Hence the establishment of the CSA in 1993, and John Major's 'back to basics' campaign (Dorey, 1998, 2000).

Interpretation, whereby policy makers make judgements about whether a particular issue or set of indicators constitutes a problem warranting their attention or action. It has always been axiomatic in the social sciences that, contrary to 'common sense' convention or saloon-bar wisdom, 'the facts' do *not* 'speak for themselves', but have to be interpreted and explained (see Irvine et al. 1979). Interpretation of data or other indicators is itself an important part of identifying or defining a problem, and therefore of getting it placed onto the policy agenda.

Ideology, whereupon the dominant values, norms and beliefs of policy makers will play a significant role in defining an issue as a problem warranting attention or action. This, to a considerable extent, follows on from the previous point about interpretation, for a particular issue or phenomenon might be deemed a problem according to one ideological perspective, but not according to an alternative ideological stance. For example, a social democrat will acknowledge the existence of poverty, and deem it a problem requiring governmental action to ameliorate it, in accordance with the social democratic objective of establishing a fairer, more equal (less unequal) society. By contrast, the New Right would either deny the existence of poverty (either on the grounds that the existence of a welfare state means that no one need be hungry or homeless, for example, or by claiming that Britian does not have poverty, but merely inequality, which Conservatives deem both natural and necessary), or acknowledge that poverty does exist, but insist that those experiencing it are also responsible for their plight, due to the poor being 'lazy', 'workshy', 'feckless' or part of 'the dependency culture'. In this case, poverty is not deemed a problem necessitating action from policy makers, except insofar as eligibility for social security benefits might be tightened, and made more stringent, in order to compel the poor to find work and become more independent. Certainly, unlike social democrats, right-wing Conservatives who *are* prepared to acknowledge the existence of poverty, would not favour wealth redistribution via 'progressive taxation' (higher taxes on the better-off), more generous welfare benefits, or a minimum wage, to eradicate it. *Instances*, meaning that particular events, often receiving extensive or intensive media coverage, draw attention to an issue or social phenomenon, and prompt policy makers to respond accordingly.

The policy stream

This second component of Kingdon's 'policy streams' refers to the manner in which problems, once identified or defined as such, are accompanied by the advocacy of a particular policy, this policy deemed by its proponents to be the solution. Kingdon suggests that at any given juncture, there are a great many ideas and potential solutions being devised, developed or drafted by policy makers, and other 'policy advocates'. This plethora of potential or putative policies is deemed by Kingdon to resemble a 'primeval soup', in which ideas and possible policies are constantly floating around, sometimes reaching the surface, in which case, they may be extracted and applied to a particular problem, or be deemed inappropriate as a solution, and thus allowed to float back down onto the 'primeval soup', before resurfacing at a later stage. In this 'primeval soup', therefore, there are both policies which have not yet been successfully attached to a problem, and also policies which have previously been extracted, only to be thrown back in when they were no longer favoured.

This notion of a primeval soup is itself akin to March, Olsen and Cohen's concept of a 'garbage can' as a metaphor for the policy process, 'into which various problems and solutions are dumped by participants', but which are then retrieved at a later stage. The image is one of policy makers rummaging in the garbage can, either for a solution to solve a new (or recurring) problem, or for a previously discarded problem to which a favoured policy 'solution' can be applied (March and Olsen, 1976: 26; see also March et al., 1972).

While the policy stream therefore entails policy makers and policy advocates seeking to develop ideas and policies in response to the emergence and identification of particular problems, it also involves policy makers and policy advocates searching for problems to which they can attach or apply a favoured idea or policy. Or as Kingdon himself expresses it, as part of the process of agenda setting, policy advocates 'lie in wait in and around government with their solutions at hand, waiting for problems to float by to which they can attach a solution' (Kingdon, 1995: 165).

March et al. suggest that 'an organisation is a collection of choices looking for problems, issues … looking for decision structures in which they might be aired, solutions looking for issues to which they might be the answer, and decision-makers looking for work' (March et al., 1972: 2). This 'garbage can' model sought to illustrate the often chaotic or disjointed character of much policy making, and the manner in which both problems and solutions not only compete for attention from policy makers and agenda setters, but themselves rise and fall, before re-emerging, or being 'rediscovered' and revived by another policy maker (or policy entrepreneur) at a later date.

The political stream

It is not enough for a problem to be recognized, and a solution attached to it, for it to move sufficiently far up the policy agenda to be acted upon. What is also required are appropriate political circumstances, which will enable the policy to be implemented. In this context, Kingdon's model referred to such events or circumstances as 'swings of national mood, vagaries of public opinion, election results, changes of administration, shifts in partisan ideological distributions [in Parliament] and interest group pressure campaigns' (1995: 87). These phenomena will often occur independently of events in the problem and policy streams, according to Kingdon, although we would emphasise that wider recognition of a problem, and the successful advocacy of a popular solution, will themselves often contribute to the political stream, by facilitating a significant shift in public opinion, or even the election of a government with a rather different ideological orientation. A crisis will also provide an opportunity to put an idea and associated policy into practice, as may a significant change in public opinion or even the set of 'macro' ideas (these, of course, often yielding a change of government anyway).

Usually, only when political circumstances are right, or a particular crisis occurs, will a particular problem, and the apparent efficacy of a specific solution, be more widely recognized, even though some academics, analysts or 'policy entrepreneurs' might have been advocating a similar solution to the problem for many years, or even decades. Such advocacy will often be in vain unless political circumstances provide the opportunity to apply the ideas and associated policies. Or as Cortell expresses it: 'Every trigger – whether a crisis or non-crisis situation – creates the opportunity for structural change if it discredits existing institutions or raises concerns about the adequacy of current policy-making processes' (1997: 9; Cortell and Peterson, 1998).

For Kingdon, when these three 'streams' flow together, a 'policy window' opens, providing a unique opportunity for policy change to occur. On such occasions, the wider recognition of a particular problem, increased support for a proposed solution, and the 'right' political circumstances or the emergence of a crisis, combine to ensure that the issue moves to the top of the policy agenda, and is most likely to yield a change of policy: 'windows are either opened by the appearance of compelling problems or by happenings in the political stream … The separate streams of problems, policies and politics come together at certain critical times … Solutions become joined to problems, and both of them are joined to favourable political forces' (1995: 20). It is when all three occur simultaneously that a new policy is most likely to be introduced.

For example, some Conservatives, along with bodies such as the IEA, were viewing the trade unions as a problem back in the 1950s, and in so doing, they proposed various policies which they believed would solve the 'trade union problem'. However, these policies, of which secret ballots prior to strikes, and weakening the closed shop (i.e, compulsory trade union membership in some occupations) were the most frequently advocated, were at odds with the conciliatory approach of the 1951–64 Conservative governments, which were eager to avoid conflict or confrontation with the trade unions. Although Edward Heath's Conservative government then attempted to enact some of these measures in the 1971 Industrial Relations Act, he felt obliged to abandon the policy in the face of trade union opposition and 'industrial muscle', as well as anxiety among various of his ministerial colleagues. In retrospect, there was widespread agreement, both among many Conservatives and academic commentators, that Heath had attempted too much too soon, and that the time had not been quite right: the problem and policy streams had not met the political stream.

Not until 1979 did the political stream appear, and merge with the problem and policy streams to provide the necessary 'policy window' to attack the trade unions, and reduce their role and influence in economic affairs. By 1979, the trade unions were deemed a problem by many more people, while policies such as strike ballots, ballots to elect union leaders, curbing the closed shop, and curbing mass picketing during industrial disputes, were much more popular, both in the Conservative Party, and among the electorate. Crucially (but partly in response to increased public resentment of the trade unions and strikes during the 1970s), the Conservative Party which won the 1979 election contained many senior figures who were determined to tackle trade unionism, yet could ensure that in so doing, they did not repeat the mistakes of the Heath government a decade earlier.

This new Conservative government, increasingly dominated by ministers who rejected the paternalistic, conciliatory, 'one nation' Toryism of the 1940s and 1950s, and who were determined to 'put the trade unions back in their place', were emboldened by both the new political and intellectual climate (with New Right ideas and policies becoming increasingly influential), and a corresponding shift in public opinion against the trade unions, with the widespread disruption of the 1978–9 'winter of discontent' finally convincing many voters that 'something must be done' about trade union power and militancy: 'It needed further hard experience culminating in the Winter of Discontent in 1978 ... before the British people were ready to give continuous backing to a government for trade union reform' (Whitelaw, 1989: 75–6).

Thus did 1979 provide the 'policy window' which enabled trade union reform to move to the top of the policy agenda. Many of the problems were the same as those which had been identified by critics back in the 1950s, as were several of the policies pursued, yet not until the end of the 1970s did the political stream emerge, providing a change in government, ideological orientation and public opinion, sufficient to push trade union reform to the top of the policy agenda, thereby heralding a significantly and successful series of legislative reforms to weaken the trade unions.

In pursuing these reforms, Conservative ministers of the 1980s and 1990s were often extracting policies out of the 'policy primeval soup', ideas and proposals which had been swishing and swirling around since the 1950s, occasionally bubbling to the surface before sinking back down again. On other occasions, ministers who were impressed by a particular policy would search for a particular problem to which it would provide a solution, and which would therefore legitimize the favoured policy. Yet some new policy proposals, such as the prohibition of strikes in the public sector or 'essential services', were considered impracticable and unenforceable, and themselves discarded into the 'policy primeval soup', possibly to be extracted and implemented by a future government when another 'policy window' opens. Certainly, two figures very closely associated with New Labour and the Blair governments intimated, in 1996, that a future Labour government might consider 'restrictions on the freedom to undertake industrial action in the emergency services' (Mandelson and Liddle, 1996: 152).

However, because 'policy windows' are only usually open very briefly, before the three policy streams flow apart again, the opportunities for initiating new policies are often relatively rare or sporadic. If the 'policy window' closes before a policy initiative is enacted, the public and/or policy makers might well lose interest in the issue concerned, particularly if other issues have risen to prominence. Yet even if policy makers do successfully take advantage of a briefly open 'policy window', and introduce an apparently appropriate policy, public attention is likely to wane, not least because people blithely assume that the problem has been tackled. However, it is quite likely that the problem will re-emerge again at a later date, possibly in a different guise, because few economic, political or social problems are solved entirely or permanently.

Issues as diverse as animal welfare, child protection, environmental pollution, 'excessive' pay increases, food safety, inflation, juvenile crime and delinquency, trade union militancy, traffic congestion and welfare dependency, invariably move up and down the policy agenda over time. In so doing, they will become part of what policy analysts call an 'issue attention cycle'.

The 'issue attention cycle'

The notion of an 'issue attention cycle' was first developed by Anthony Downs (1972), who suggested that problems tend to progress through five discrete stages:

1. *Pre-problem stage*: Policy advocates might well be aware of an issue which they believe constitutes a problem warranting political attention, but at this stage, the nature or scope of the problem has not been recognized by either the public, the media, or policy makers themselves.
2. *Alarmed discovery and euphoric enthusiasm*: The issue is now recognized as a problem warranting attention from policy makers. Such recognition might be due to the success of policy advocates in persuading the media and/or policy makers of the seriousness or extent of a problem, or might be a consequence of a crisis which serves to bring the issue dramatically to public attention, thereby obliging policy makers to acknowledge the problem. This stage would correspond to the movement of an issue from the systemic agenda to the institutional agenda (see below).
3. *Realization of the costs which will be incurred by the solutions*: Having acknowledged the problem, and considered possible solutions, policy makers and/or the public become aware of the costs – which might be financial, environmental, loss of employment, curbs on individual liberty, etc. – and thus lose interest in the problem. At this stage, the problem might consequently be deemed less serious than the 'costs' likely to be incurred by applying solutions. Indeed, the problem might be 'redefined', in a manner which also serves to move it back down or off the policy agenda.

    For example, it might be decided that the costs of tackling the problem of traffic congestion or pollution caused by exhaust emissions, might be unacceptable in terms of restrictions on the use of private transport, or perhaps lead to a politically-sensitive loss of jobs in the car industry. Alternatively, proposals to limit the access of cars to city centres might meet opposition from retailers and shopkeepers fearing loss of trade, particularly if the result is that car-driving customers decide to travel to out-of-town shopping centres instead.

Or to provide another example, environmentalists' concerns about the health risks and other dangers apparently posed by nuclear power stations, and subsequent demands that nuclear power be phased out, might be countered by even greater concern, from residents in the vicinity of nuclear power stations, about the loss of jobs if much of the employment in their town is linked to the existence of such a power plant nearby. In this context, those residents who might be expected to be most concerned about the dangers of living near a nuclear power plant may well prove to be the most vocal opponents of proposals to close it down. In other words, once the 'costs' of tackling the problem (of nuclear power stations) in a particular locale become apparent, the proposed solution comes to be viewed as more unattractive than the problem it is supposed to solve.

4. *Decline in public interest in the issue*: Consequently, the public is likely to lose interest in the issue, or acquires an acceptance of it, possibly on the grounds that it represents the lesser of two (or three, or four, etc.) evils. Alternatively, the public's attention might be drawn to a new issue, reflecting the fact that many people have a limited attention span, particularly if they do not consider a problem to affect them or those directly around them. Of course, recognition of the fact that many people do have such a limited attention span may well encourage policy-makers to delay developing a policy, preferring to wait until public attention has waned, whereupon the issue can be 'buried'.

5. *Issue slips off, or back down, the policy agenda*: Following stage four, the issue effectively disappears, the 'policy window' having closed, and the problem – such as it was (and may still be to some policy advocates) – sinks back into the primeval soup. It might not entirely disappear, for subsequent events might result in its re-emergence – it may float back to the top of the primeval soup. Alternatively, policy advocates or entrepreneurs may seek to link the issue to other problems which subsequently emerge, or which they extract from the policy 'garbage can'.

While Downs' 'issue attention cycle' aims to explain why the placing of an issue on the policy agenda does not necessarily lead to policy change, we would argue that public interest in an issue also tends to dissipate – stage four – precisely when there is a change of policy, for once a problem appears to have been solved, or is thought likely to be solved imminently, due to action by policy-makers, then the issue is similarly likely to move back down or off the agenda, as the public loses interest, and new issues emerge to attract their attention.

Furthermore, although policies will invariably slip back down, or off, the policy agenda, as signified by stage five of Downs' model, we would emphasize that many, if not most, of them are likely to re-emerge at a later stage, either when the costs of *not* addressing the issue originally become apparent, or when it is realized that the policy originally introduced to tackle the problem has failed to achieve its professed objectives. In either case, many problems, sooner or later, will reappear at the top of the policy agenda, whereupon the cycle will repeat itself.

As such, Figure 2.2 offers a modified version of Downs' issue attention cycle.

The notions of 'policy streams' and 'issue attention cycles' are particularly useful to students of public policy because they provide valuable accounts of many of the factors determining policy change and continuity. Only when the three policy streams identified by Kingdon converge, is an issue likely to reach the top of the policy agenda, and thereupon

Figure 2.2   Modified version of Downs' issue attention cycle

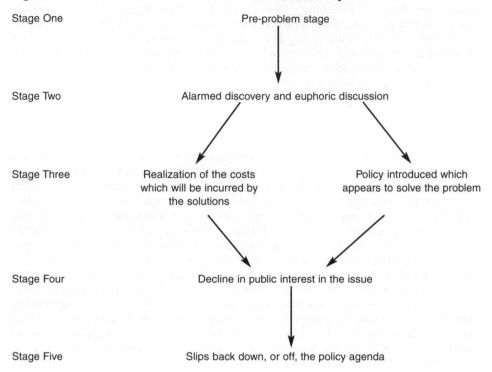

Stage One   Pre-problem stage

Stage Two   Alarmed discovery and euphoric discussion

Stage Three   Realization of the costs   Policy introduced which
                   which will be incurred by   appears to solve the problem
                        the solutions

Stage Four   Decline in public interest in the issue

Stage Five   Slips back down, or off, the policy agenda

generate a change of policy. If the three streams do not converge, then the 'policy window' will not open (or, at least, not sufficiently wide enough or long enough), and the policy will either fail to make it onto the policy agenda, or, if it has already nudged its way onto the agenda, it is likely to slip back down, or off the agenda entirely, both reflecting and reinforcing a loss of attention or interest in the issue.

Clearly, therefore, individual policy advocates and think tanks will be concerned to ensure that 'their' favoured policy is not merely pushed onto the policy agenda, but as near to the top of it as possible. They will seek to persuade policy makers that there is a serious problem which needs to be solved, that there is a particular policy which can effect such a solution, and that the issue is either sufficiently serious, or circumstances suitably appropriate, for the proposed policy to be introduced and implemented. Those advocating policies will be acutely aware that, because of the issue attention cycle, and the infrequency with which the 'policy window' normally opens, failure to persuade policy makers to act is likely to result in the issue slipping back down, or completely off, the policy agenda.

One other aspect which affects the likelihood of an issue reaching the policy agenda was identified by Solesbury (1976), who, like Downs, used the environment as a case study, but with the conclusions much more widely applicable. Solesbury suggested that a number of criteria affected whether or not a specific issue reached the policy agenda, and was considered worthy of attention and action from policy makers. Among the two most important of these criteria were *particularity* and *generality* (even though they seem, initially, to be mutually exclusive). What is meant by 'particularity' in this context is that a particular issue becomes recognized as a problem due to a dramatic or specific event, such as a disaster or other form of crisis. This makes an issue highly visible, and provides a clear example of the problem. For example, extreme weather (unusually severe or frequent tornadoes and hurricanes, prolonged droughts, or an unusually wet summer) can all serve as stark indicators of global warming, and thus of the need for policy makers to develop or encourage more environmentally-friendly forms of production and travel. Such particular instances or events will usually have a much greater impact in drawing attention to the issue of the environment than an occasional newspaper report about the depletion of the Amazon rainforests or melting of the polar ice caps, for specific events are clearly highly visible in their nature and visceral in their impact. Rail disasters, meanwhile – such as the Paddington or Hatfield crashes – will invariably serve to place the issue of rail safety on the policy agenda.

Alongside specificity, though, an issue will often need 'generality' in order to be placed on, or near the top, of the policy agenda. What Solesbury meant by this was that an issue or problem affects – or could affect – many people, so that public concern about it is increased or widened. The environment is once again a pertinent example, because everyone will be affected by aspects of environmental degradation, so that all citizens can be said to have an interest in supporting environmentally-friendly policies. Similarly, most citizens will, at various times in their lives, need health care – and at times when they do not, they will probably have friends or family members who do – which means that the NHS is consistently near the top of the policy agenda (for example, it has been one of the two 'most salient' issues in every general election since the 1980s).

Types of policy agenda

Although we have hitherto referred to the policy agenda, as if it were a single entity, some writers have suggested that there are actually different types of policy agenda, and have drawn a distinction between a systemic agenda and an institutional agenda (Cobb and Elder, 1972).

The systemic agenda

These are derived from issues which are 'out there' in the political system (hence systemic), and which sundry individuals, journalists, academics, think tanks, organized interests or other bodies are seeking to get accepted by policy makers as matters which are worthy of their attention and action. The actors involved in systemic agendas will either have identified problems which they believe policy makers and/or politicians should be tackling, or they will be promoting particular values and ideas which they believe political elites ought to be linking to problems, thereby providing a solution.

According to Cobb and Elder, the 'systemic agenda' 'consists of all issues that are commonly perceived by members of the political community as meriting public attention and as involving matters within the legitimate jurisdiction of existing governmental authority' (1972: 82), and as such, 'is essentially a discussion agenda' (Anderson, 1975: 59).

What those involved in the systemic agenda are ultimately seeking to influence is the institutional agenda.

The institutional agenda

These are the agendas deriving from policy makers' own objectives and priorities, based on the issues which they consider to be important at any particular juncture. The issues on an institutional agenda will have previously been recognized as problems deserving or demanding governmental action. The institutional agenda is therefore a more formal agenda, 'composed of those problems to which public officials give serious and active attention' (Cobb and Elder, 1972: 85), and is therefore 'an action agenda, and will be more specific and concrete than a systemic agenda' (Anderson, 1975: 59).

The institutional agenda, in turn, will comprise a combination of old, ongoing or regularly recurring problems, such as controlling public expenditure, raising educational standards or tackling social security fraud, and new problems – quite possibly emerging via the systemic agenda – such as relatively new forms of crime (mobile phone theft, crimes perpetrated via the internet, etc.), damage to the environment, or increasing obesity among sections of the British population derived from dietary and lifestyle changes. Of course, many of the 'new' problems will subsequently join the ongoing or recurring problems on the institutional agenda.

While this distinction between systemic and institutional agendas is undoubtedly useful, and reflects the processes of agenda setting and agenda management on many occasions, it does not adequately allow for the manner in which governments themselves will sometimes seek to develop support for an institutional agenda, based on ministers' own preferred policies for tackling issues defined by them as problems. Sometimes, ministers wishing to pursue a particular policy, particularly if it reflects particular partisan values or ideological objectives, will seek to secure wider support for their institutional agenda in order to imbue it with greater legitimacy and credibility.

Governments and the Policy Agenda

So far, we have considered how ideas and issues are defined and developed and thereby pushed onto, or further up the policy agenda. Yet as well as shaping the policy agenda, policy makers, and more particularly governments, will also seek to manage it. This will entail responding to certain issues in a number of ways, depending on whether ministers genuinely wish to tackle a problem or not.

Of course, if ministers accept the existence of a specific problem, are genuinely concerned to tackle it, and have an appropriate policy (either one which has emerged from the primeval soup, and/or one which the government itself is keen to apply) then it is highly likely that a policy will be introduced, leading to policy change. If this is the case, and the problem appears to have been solved, or looks as if it will be in the foreseeable future (once the policy has started to effect an impact), then the issue is likely to slip back down, or off, the policy agenda (stages four and five of Downs' 'issue attention cycle').

On other occasions, however, while ministers will be willing to acknowledge the emergence or existence of a particular problem, they might not have a policy readily available, or they might not really want to tackle it, in which case they are likely to insist on the need for further research into the issue, possibly involving some form of inquiry. Such an investigation might be undertaken by various bodies: a Cabinet committee; an official committee (comprising senior civil servants from the relevant department), a 'working party' (comprising ministers, senior civil servants policy advisers and/or outside experts); a Committee of Inquiry; a Royal Commission. A government resorting to such investigations into a particular issue will usually be guided by one of four motives:

1. It will genuinely be seeking a solution to the problem, recognizing the need to ascertain the underlying causes of a problem and/or the efficacy of possible policy solutions, on the basis of their respective costs and benefits.
2. Ministers will recognize the need to modify an existing policy, but will want any change legitimized by some form of independent and impartial inquiry, thereby imbuing the revised policy with greater justification or credibility in the eyes of the public, or even with the government's own backbenchers. For example, following repeated problems with aspects of its education reform programme in the early 1990s, and strong opposition from the teaching unions to various features of that programme, John Major's second (1992–7) Conservative government called upon Sir Ron Dearing to chair an inquiry into their education reforms, particularly aspects of the National Curriculum and associated tests for 7 and 14-year-olds. Of course, Major and his ministers might have taken action themselves to simplify the National Curriculum and its tests, but they may have been concerned that this might be viewed as a capitulation to – and thus a victory for – the teaching unions. By linking policy change or modification to the recommendations of an independent inquiry, chaired by a highly respected 'establishment figure' (a member of the 'great and good' as Peter Hennessy once nicely expressed it), John Major and his ministerial colleagues were able to modify the policy without appearing to have done so simply or directly in response to protests by the teaching unions. The government was therefore able to 'save face'.
3. The government will be expecting the inquiry to provide evidence or arguments which it can then cite as justification for *not* changing existing policy. The inquiry's report might highlight the financial, employment or social costs of a particular policy proposal, for example, or, perhaps, the manner in which implementation would be impracticable or unenforceable. This would then contribute to the third, fourth and fifth phases of Downs' 'issue attention cycle' (as outlined above), namely realization of the costs of a solution, the consequent loss of public interest and the issue's ensuing slippage back down the policy agenda.
4. It will be seeking to avoid a policy response – for economic, ideological or other political reasons – but recognizes that it must appear to be 'doing something'. In this scenario, ministers will doubtless be hoping that while the issue is being considered, the problem itself will somehow disappear, or even resolve itself. The ministers will also be envisaging that public interest will dissipate by the time any report and associated recommendations are produced by the inquiry, thereby further obviating the need to introduce a new policy. In this respect, Committees of Inquiry or Royal Commissions might be invoked as stalling mechanisms, enabling ministers to 'buy time'. For example, Tony Blair's establishment, in 1998, of a commission, chaired by the late Lord (Roy) Jenkins, to consider options for electoral reform, might be viewed as a means of avoiding having to introduce such a policy. Had Blair genuinely wanted to consider

which types of electoral system were available to a government committed to such reform, and what their respective strengths and weaknesses were, he could have read the Plant Report published in 1993, which was itself the result of an inquiry – commissioned by Labour's NEC – into different types of electoral systems, and how they might be applied to different types of elections and political institutions. Instead, Blair and Labour opponents of electoral reform could subsequently refer to potential problems identified in the Jenkins' Report as arguments for delaying – indefinitely – any change to the existing first-past-the-post electoral system for general elections (Dorey, 2003a).

Sometimes, however, a government might be faced with an apparent crisis or urgent problem, possibly reflecting a moral panic, which effectively obliges it to act (or to be seen to act) immediately, by rapidly developing a policy to address the new problem. While this might well satisfy the public or the media – and others involved in the systemic agenda – that the problem has been solved, the reality may prove otherwise, for not only might the policy encounter implementation problems (discussed in Chapter 7), it might also fall prey to the political maxim that 'rushed legislation is often bad legislation', because policies introduced with undue haste have obviously not benefited from proper consideration by policy makers, and adequate consultation with relevant organized interests or other 'affected parties'.

One notable example of this phenomenon concerns the 1991 Dangerous Dogs Act, which was introduced following a series of media reports about certain breeds of dogs – pit bull terriers, rottweilers, etc. – attacking babies and young children, and inflicting horrific injuries by virtue of their savagery and strength. The 'moral panic' and public anxiety prompted by intense media reportage of such attacks in the spring of 1991 led to swift action by John Major's Conservative government, in the form of the aforementioned Act, introduced by the then Home Secretary, Kenneth Baker. Indeed, so swift was the government's response that the Dangerous Dogs Bill 'was hurtled through the House of Commons' with all its parliamentary stages completed in one day (Hogg and Hill, 1995: 113), rather than over several weeks as would normally be the case.

The media and general public were therefore satisfied that the government had acted swiftly and decisively 'to rid the country of the menace of these … dogs' (as Kenneth Baker claimed), thereby enabling the issue to slip back off the agenda in accordance with the latter stages of the 'issue attention cycle'. Yet it was only after the enactment of the Bill that a range of practical problems and legal issues, deriving from its enforcement, became apparent, leading, eventually, to the Act being amended. Part of the problem arising from such hasty policy making was that those who might otherwise have been consulted, and thereupon offered advice pointing out problems of practicability, were neglected, resulting in flawed legislation (Mays, 2001).

One other way in which governments may seek to manage the institutional agenda, in order to keep off issues which they do not wish to act upon for whatever reason, is to place an alleged problem in comparative perspective in order to reduce its significance or seriousness. In this context, comparisons may be historical or international. Viewing an alleged problem historically will be intended to illustrate that the issue is less prevalent or potent than it was maybe 20, 50 or 100 years ago (or maybe even just last year), and does not, therefore, warrant special action by policy makers. This has often been the response of politicians when faced with calls to tackle poverty, for example, whereupon the position of the poor today is compared favourably with the plight of the poor in Victorian or inter-war Britain. In this context, the existence of poverty is either denied, or it is deemed to have been greatly diminished, so that new measures to combat poverty are deemed unnecessary.

Crime is another policy issue where governments are inclined to place statistics in historical-comparative context, in order to show either that levels of crime overall are falling, or, if this is not possible, that particular types of crime have diminished over the last *x* years. In so doing, they may also seek to show that the likelihood of being a victim of a particular type of crime is now 10,000: 1 compared with 5,000: 1 five or ten years ago, for example. Such statistics, of course, might not assuage public anxiety about crime, or the *perception* that crime is increasing, but they are nonetheless often cited by governments uncertain about what else they can do to combat crime, other than persevere with their existing law-and-order policy.

The other 'comparitor' sometimes invoked by policy makers seeking to avoid (further) action on a particular issue is to place the issue in an international context, and show that the alleged problem is less extensive or extreme in Britain than in various other countries. For example, if and when a government is faced by an increase in the number of people officially registered as unemployed, it will almost inevitably claim that the level of unemployment remains lower than that in France/Germany/Italy/Spain or wherever, or that it is increasing in Britain at a slower rate than in other such countries. Alternatively, it might cite figures to show that more jobs have been created in Britain during the last *x* months or years than in other comparable countries, so that Britain's jobless have a greater chance of finding employment than their foreign counterparts.

Through invoking such comparative 'evidence', governments will seek either to deny the existence of an alleged problem which is being canvassed on the systemic agenda, or deny that it is as serious or extensive as others are claiming, or insist that their policies are already successfully eradicating the problem.

Sometimes, though, if a government itself wants to tackle what it perceives to be a problem – possibly because it views an issue or trend as being incompatible with the government's own principles or objectives, or maybe because it wants to divert public attention away from other policy problems which it is struggling with – ministers might cite 'evidence' which purports to show that the problem is worse than it was *x* years ago, or is more prevalent than in comparable countries. In this context, ministers themselves may place an issue straight onto the institutional agenda, whereupon the media might highlight the issue, and ensure that it is discussed in the systemic agenda. The government might then earn plaudits for its prescience or courage in seizing the initiative to tackle the alleged problem. A relatively recent example might be that cited earlier, namely the Major governments' early 1990s offensive against single parents via the CSA, coupled with the 'back to basics' campaign, where ministers themselves cited the apparently dramatic increase in illegitimacy and unmarried mothers, and the consequent 'burden' on the welfare state and taxpayer, in order to legitimize certain policy initiatives.

In effect, we are back to our initial point, that problems are not always self-evident, but subject to interpretation, definition and contestation, as well as being, at least in part, historically contingent and socially constructed. Consequently, policy agendas are sites of conflict and struggle in some respects, as some policy actors (or would-be policy actors) seek to promote certain issues and push them onto the institutional agenda in particular, while other policy actors seek to keep – or push – certain issues off the institutional agenda, through the various responses delineated above.

Policy transfer

A relatively recent conceptual development in the study of public policy in Britain concerns the phenomenon of *policy transfer*, which refers to 'the occurrence of, and processes involved in, the development of programmes, policies and institutions, etc., within one political and/or social system which are based on the ideas, institutions, programmes and policies emanating from other political and/or social systems' (Dolowitz, 2000a: 3; see also Dolowitz and Marsh, 1996, 2000; Dolowitz et al., 1999; Deacon, 2000). Dolowitz believes that 'many of the changes in British public policy in the 1980s and 1990s can be traced directly to the process of policy transfer', most of it from the USA, which has been 'a source of ideas, inspirations, policies and institutions for various aspects of British public policy over the past twenty years' (Dolowitz, 2000a: 1, 2), although as is customary in political science, the emergence of a new concept soon prompts criticism from those who believe either that the definition is flawed, and/or that the concept is not as useful as its proponents claim in explaining a particular phenomenon (James and Lodge, 2003).

Admittedly, the actual phenomenon of looking abroad for policy ideas is not in itself new or novel, although the practice does seem to have become more extensive and explicit since the late 1980s. For example, in the early 1960s, when some senior Labour figures were beginning to consider how a Labour government would secure wage restraint by the trade unions, the party leader, Hugh Gaitskell, urged his Shadow Chancellor, James Callaghan, and the latter's advisers, to look at the type of incomes policies pursued in Sweden and the Netherlands (Morgan, 1997: 179). In the latter half of the 1960s, meanwhile, the Conservative Party, now itself in Opposition, looked partly to the USA in its formulation of a more legalistic industrial relations policy, with two of the leading architects of this new policy, Stephen Abbott (mentioned above) and Geoffrey Howe, having visited the USA, where they observed the role which the law played in American industrial relations (Moran, 1977: 57, 84).

Three specific policy initiatives will serve briefly to illustrate the manner in which ideas from the USA have been 'transferred' to Britain since the end of the 1980s, namely the establishment of the CSA, 'welfare-into-work' as a means of tackling unemployment and the so-called 'dependency culture', and 'zero tolerance' approaches to inner-city crime and juvenile delinquency.

The CSA was established in Britain in 1993, two years after the Child Support Act had received the Royal Assent. The CSA, and the legislation on which it was based (the 1991 Child Support Act), reflected concern among a number of senior Conservatives from the late 1980s onwards about Britain's growing number of 'lone parents' (from 570,000 in 1971 to 1,150,000 by 1989), particularly 'unmarried mothers'. While many Conservatives disapproved of 'lone parents' on moral grounds alone (believing that only a heterosexual, monogamous, marital relationship provided the proper basis for raising children), what reinforced a 'moral panic' about 'unmarried mothers' from the late 1980s was partly the costs in terms of welfare expenditure and social security entitlements (some Conservatives even claimed that Britain's 'generous' welfare state was encouraging young women to have illegitimate children, in order to qualify for Income Support, rather than undertake paid employment), and partly the alleged link between 'single parents', juvenile delinquency and urban decay. In short, 'unmarried mothers' were not only deemed to be a major consequence of the 'permissive society' and a key component of the 'dependency culture', they were also considered a significant element in the emerging 'underclass' which social commentators were turning their attention to during this period.

Charles Murray, a conservative US sociologist, became a prominent critic of the underclass, believing that the welfare state in Britain was providing a perverse incentive to young working-class women to have children outside of marriage, due both to their consequent eligibility for welfare support, and their apparent 'priority status' with regard to local authority housing. Furthermore, Murray argued, young working-class males had no incentive to be sexually responsible, for not only had the stigma or shame of 'illegitimacy' and 'pregnancy outside marriage' virtually disappeared from most parts of British society, these males knew that the welfare state would support 'their' children if they made a woman pregnant; they could, quite literally, leave her 'holding the baby' while they left to pursue their next short-term or casual relationship.

However, effectively deprived of the need to obtain and retain paid employment (because they were not held financially responsible for supporting 'their' children), some of these males existed on the margins of society, 'getting by' through claiming social security, but supplementing this meagre income via petty crime and drug-dealing (both of which also alleviated the boredom of having no job or family responsibilities). At the same time, though, the illegitimate children of the growing number of unmarried mothers were raised without the presence of a male role model. This meant that the boys of unmarried mothers lacked a father who could provide authority and discipline to complement the mother's love and nurturing, and so were likely to acquire values and behaviour patterns from their (often delinquent) peers and fellow 'gang members', who effectively became a surrogate family: they became 'feral children'. Consequently, the children of unmarried mothers were particularly prone to juvenile crime and delinquency, whereupon the inner city or urban housing estates where such lone parents tended to be located often became 'sink estates'. In turn, 'respectable' families moved away to escape the crime, vandalism, drug-dealing and general delinquency, and so the estate's downwards spiral and descent into a lawless virtual 'no-go' area (for the authorities and the police) continued (Murray, 1989, 1994a, 1994b).

For social commentators such as Murray, and many Conservatives, Britain was thus facing a socio-demographic crisis by the 1990s, and it was in this context that Conservative ministers began looking at ways of tackling this issue (it had now moved onto the institutional agenda). Given that Murray was himself American, and claimed that the socio-demographic trends he discerned in Britain were closely following those which had already manifested themselves in the USA a decade or two earlier, it was, perhaps, only natural that British policy makers wondered how their US counterparts had addressed the problem.

Consequently, the then Minister of State for State for Social Security, Tony Newton, visited Wisconsin, to see how the Americans had established what was believed to be the first child support system in the world, and one which was also deemed to be highly efficient. Enthused by what it observed, 'the Thatcher government transferred the design and structure of the Child Support Agency from the United States', although many of the Agency's ensuing problems reflected a failure by Conservative ministers to investigate the operation of child support more widely in the USA: 'the British government … concentrated on the Wisconsin system', elements of which subsequently proved inappropriate or inapplicable to Britain (Dolowitz, 2000b). The case of the CSA therefore provides both an example of policy transfer, and a lesson in the need either to investigate the wider operation or impact of a particular policy in another country, or to recognize the problems which are likely to arise from attempts at wholesale policy transfer which fail to take account of politico-administrative, legal or cultural differences between Britain and other countries.

The second contemporary example of 'policy transfer' concerns the 'welfare-into-work' programme, initiated in Britain in the mid-1990s by the same (Conservative) government which launched the CSA, but developed further – and perhaps more widely associated with – the New Labour/Blair governments since 1997. In certain respects, of course, welfare-into-work derives from many of the same socio-political concerns which underpinned the child support initiatives delineated above, most notably anxiety among some intellectuals and policy makers that Britain was experiencing the emergence of an underclass, who were not only unemployed and part of a growing 'dependency culture', but who were also, in many cases, virtually 'unemployable', either because they lacked the requisite qualifications or training, or because they were simply not imbued with the 'work ethic'.

For New Labour, therefore, 'welfare-into-work' was linked inextricably with its professed determination to tackle social exclusion, and reintegrate those who were economically inactive and socially marginalized. It was also linked explicitly to New Labour's proudly proclaimed principle (although it was one with which many, if not most, Conservatives, could readily agree) that citizens' rights had to be matched by responsibilities; in this particular case, welfare rights had to be matched by corresponding social responsibilities (see, for example, Department of Social Security, 1998: 23). There was also an assumption that by tackling the 'social exclusion' of this nascent underclass, crime would also be reduced. In this respect, the manner in which 'welfare-into-work' apparently dovetailed into other New Labour social objectives was lauded as an indication of the professed desire to pursue 'joined-up government'.

Yet while 'welfare-into-work' seemed to correspond neatly to many other New Labour objectives, the origins of the policy largely emanate from the USA (Annesley, 2003: 157–9; Deacon, 2000; Driver and Martell, 1997; King and Wickham-Jones, 1999). In noting the similarities between Britain and the USA with particular regard to 'welfare-into-work', Deacon notes the extent to which 'the British approach follows the American in its redefinition of welfare as a period of temporary assistance during which claimants would be equipped with the skills and capacities to re-enter the labour force, and then required to do so'. In making this observation, and noting the extent to which New Labour's welfare policy is no longer primarily concerned with raising the level of social security benefits *per se*, in order to tackle poverty, Deacon suggests that 'welfare-into-work' appears as 'yet another candidate for the new holy grail of transatlantic politics' (2000: 130).

Regardless of whether Blair and his Cabinet colleagues have actually sat down and read the academic work of such writers as Etzioni (1993) – whose concept of 'communitarianism' is widely deemed to be a major influence on New Labour's approaches to social policy – the general ideas seem to have permeated much of New Labour's thinking with regard to social policy, especially with regard to tackling unemployment. Furthermore, in this case, policy transfer has not necessarily required that New Labour politicians and policy makers actually visit the USA to learn and adopt similar social policies, for Etzioni, and the American conservative commentator, James Q. Wilson, are both reported to have been visitors to 10 Downing Street since Tony Blair became Prime Minister in May 1997 (Lewis, 2001: 493).

Third, and finally, 'policy transfer' seems to be evident in some of the Blair governments' law-and-order policies, particularly the second Blair government's espousal of a 'zero tolerance' policy *vis-à-vis* inner-city crime and juvenile delinquency. Once again, ministers appear to have looked across the Atlantic for inspiration, impressed, it seems, by the apparent success of Rudolph Giuliani, the former Mayor of New York during most of the 1990s. Giuliani became synonymous with the 'zero tolerance' form of policing, whereby even minor misdemeanours were pursued by the police, the reasoning being that if individuals went unpunished for committing petty crimes, many of them would proceed, unchecked, to more serious crimes, and thereby become serial offenders. The 'zero tolerance' policy was therefore intended to 'nip in the bud' a drift into serious crime. More generally, by making the streets safer, and restoring public confidence in the police and criminal justice system, it was envisaged that a process of urban regeneration would be instigated, as formerly run-down, even 'no go' districts began to attract new businesses and residents. Such a 'zero tolerance' policy is widely believed to have made New York a much safer city, to the extent that the once dangerous, crime-ridden, district known as Alphabet City, at the eastern end of the (lower) East Village, has now become a trendy, bohemian district, and undergone major regeneration and gentrification. Some critics, however, allege that 'zero tolerance' policing tends to involve certain minorities being systematically 'harassed' or singled out, and that urban regeneration and renewal derives more from economic growth and rising incomes than 'heavy' policing in inner city districts.

In spite of these criticisms, the perceived success of 'zero tolerance' policing has greatly impressed many in New Labour, and can be seen in the raft of initiatives announced since 1997 to tackle relatively minor forms of crime and public disorder, such as public drunkenness, noise nuisance, graffiti, vandalism and 'aggressive' begging. Meanwhile, local authorities have been empowered to apply for 'after-dark' curfews to be imposed on children under the age of 15, while both the police and local authorities are permitted to apply for the imposition of Anti-social Behaviour Orders (ASBOs) on troublesome individuals, the breach of which can result in a custodial sentence.

Ironically, though, while the Blair governments were looking to the USA for policy inspiration on certain issues, the otherwise Euro-sceptic Conservative Party and sympathetic think tanks were looking at health-care systems in France, Germany and Sweden for ideas about how to tackle the problems facing Britain's NHS (*The Guardian,* 7 December 2001).

However, British policy makers do not always or necessarily need to travel abroad in order to elicit ideas from overseas. The Cabinet Office's Strategy Unit usually includes a number of officials on secondment from governments around the world. For example, during the Blair government's second term of Office, the Strategy Unit included officials from governments in Australia, Canada, France, Germany and the USA (Cabinet Office, 2003a: 5).

The increasing willingness of policy makers to look abroad for ideas and examine the extent to which solutions to problems have been effective in other countries, can itself be placed in the context of a more general development in the British policy process, namely the greater use of 'evidence-based policy making'.

Evidence-based policy making

The use of evidence-based policy making is another relatively recent development in the policy process in Britain, and one which represents something of a shift away from incrementalism (involving piecemeal and reactive adjustments to existing policy, with an emphasis on minimal change and maximum continuity) towards greater rationality by policy makers (although a policy formulated on the basis of evidence and rationality might still be *implemented* on an incremental basis), whereby policy makers consider more carefully and explicitly their policy goals, and various ways in which these might best be achieved (for the seminal account of 'rational decision-taking', see Simon (1957). For the classic exposition of incrementalism, see Lindblom, 1959, 1979). One of the criticisms of incrementalism is the extent to which it not only uses the status quo or existing policy as the basis of further policy development or modification, but tacitly assumes that the extant policy is broadly correct or desirable, and thus only requires piecemeal adjustments. As such, incrementalism tends to neglect rather more fundamental questions, such as 'what are our policy goals?' and 'what are the alternatives to our current policy approach?'.

Certainly, the Blair governments since 1997 have explicitly stated their intention of making much greater use of evidence-based policies, as part of the emphasis on an apparently non-ideological – or post-ideological – 'what works' empiricism. Consequently, one commentator has asserted that evidence-based policy making has 'emerged as central to policy making and governance in Britain' (David, 2002: 1).

Since the 1980s, and particularly since 1997, policy makers have increasingly operated on the premise that existing policy is not working. Indeed, existing policies have sometimes been defined as a key part of the problem, so that incrementally amending the existing policy merely compounded or perpetuated the underlying problem(s). This partly reflects the 'paradigm shift' away from the social democratic consensus of the 1945–79 period (academic attacks on its existence notwithstanding), so that previous assumptions underpinning many policies have subsequently been challenged and rejected. For example, there has been a growing recognition from the 1980s to the present day that eradicating poverty will not be achieved simply by increasing the value of (up-rating) social security benefits each year. Instead, under both Conservative and New Labour governments, policy makers and ministerial advisers have – as noted above – looked overseas to discover alternative ways of tackling poverty or welfare dependency, and/or looked much more systematically at the ways in which the existing welfare state in Britain *fails* to tackle poverty and social exclusion (and maybe perpetuates them); whereupon new initiatives have been 'piloted' to test their effectiveness.

The greater recourse to evidence-based policy making in Britain today is reflected not only in the greater use now made of academic or professional experts appointed as Special Advisers (see Chapters 3 and 4) or to sundry task forces and 'working parties' (see Chapter 8), but also in the restructuring of the core executive (see Chapter 4). For example, one of the first institutional innovations of the first Blair government was the establishment of the Social Exclusion Unit in the Cabinet Office, which has been cited as 'an example of a partially rational approach to policy making' (Bochel and Bochel, 2004: 33).

It is important to emphasize, however, that evidence-based policy making does not necessarily mean 'objective' polices which are devoid of principles, priorities or preferences. Indeed, when discussing the notion of evidence-based policy making, three caveats need to be borne in mind. First, although evidence-based policy making might imply a cool, calm and careful analysis of 'the facts' (empirical evidence) in order to make an informed decision about what is most likely to work, it is vital to remember that the institutional agenda will still play a significant role in determining which issues are deemed worthy of policy makers' attention, via research and consideration of policy options. Policy makers' own perceptions of what constitutes a problem will play a significant role in determining whether they seek to acquire evidence with a view to devising a new policy.

Second, but following on directly from the above, even when undertaking (or commissioning) research into a problem, policy makers might either frame the terms of reference in a particular way, so as to narrow the field of inquiry, and preclude consideration of particular options, and/or they might treat certain forms of 'evidence' as being more reliable or relevant than others. This might also serve to restrict the range of organizations or individuals who are invited to submit evidence or information, so that only those who are judged 'responsible' or 'on message' are permitted to participate. This is likely further to 'skew' the findings, and thereby limit the range of policy options which are subsequently considered once the inquiry has been completed. For example, an inquiry into minimizing cruelty in scientific or medical experiments on animals would still be unlikely to invite representations from the Animal Liberation Front.

Alternatively, a government-sponsored inquiry into ways of tackling the widening gap between rich and poor in Britain would still, almost certainly, *not* include the options of increasing income tax for high earners or placing a limit on top salaries (i.e. specifying that the highest salary anyone can earn should be no more than 10 or 20 times the average salary or minimum wage, for example). In other words, even when resorting to evidence-based policy making, ministers can still limit the range of options to be considered, so that the 'objective' research is subtly steered in certain directions, and towards particular findings, which will then endorse or legitimize particular policy options instead of others.

Third, but following on from the above point two points, the evidence obtained – the 'facts' – will still be subject to interpretation prior to the adoption of the 'correct' policy. It is one of the so-called common-sense assumptions of everyday British life that 'the facts speak for themselves', yet very often, what passes for common sense is merely the absence of serious thought or careful consideration. The 'facts' are invariably taken-for-granted and assumed to be self-evident.

Yet once research and inquiries have been completed, the 'facts' have to be interpreted, but the way that they are interpreted will reflect, to varying degrees, the values and preferences of the policy makers themselves. For example, surveys of crime might reveal that its incidence is falling, whereupon ministers are likely to boast that their law and order policies are working: 'the facts speak for themselves'. Yet it might well be that lower levels of crime at any given time might reflect wider economic factors, such as greater employment opportunities or increased prosperity and rising living standards. Alternatively, statistics revealing lower levels of crime – based, for example, on the number of incidents reported to the police, or the number of convictions or court cases – might actually be due to fewer people bothering to report criminal acts, due to lack of confidence in the police's likelihood of catching the perpetrator(s) and/or a belief that the courts are likely to show leniency by imposing a 'soft' sentence if a conviction is secured. Either way, if fewer people report crime to the police, and fewer criminals are convicted, then official statistics are likely to 'prove' that crime in Britain is falling, and policy makers are likely to cite them as proof of their successful law and order measures, even though the actual incidence of crime is increasing.

Conversely, 'facts' which 'show' that crime *is* increasing might not necessarily mean that Britain is becoming a more criminal or lawless society. If people became more confident that criminals would actually be apprehended and convicted, then more citizens would probably report criminal offences to the police, whereupon official statistics would indicate an increase in crime. On the other hand, more arrests and convictions might reflect the 'criminalization' of previously legal activities. For example, in many towns and cities, drinking alcohol in 'non-designated' places (i.e. not sat at a table outside a pub or wine bar) has been outlawed in order to clamp down on public (dis)order. Yet this means that someone who, a few years ago, could lawfully have drunk a can of beer or bottle of cider sat on a park bench or in a shopping mall might now be liable to prosecution, and thus become a 'criminal statistic' subsequently cited as evidence that crime is increasing.

The point here is that 'facts' do not 'speak for themselves', but are subject to interpretation and contestation depending on social values and political perspectives. Even when the 'facts' are widely accepted, they might be cited in support of markedly different policy responses. For example, statistically, the rate of teenage and schoolgirl pregnancies in Britain is among the highest in western Europe, yet whereas social democrats and liberals cite this as evidence of the urgent need for more or 'better' sex education in schools, and the provision of more information about safe sex and contraception (and even the provision of contraception itself to under-16s in certain cases), conservatives generally believe that Britain's high incidence of teenage pregnancies derives from either too much sex education ('it encourages teenagers to experiment') or the wrong kind, meaning that there is insufficient emphasis on abstinence and the importance of marriage as the only moral framework for legitimate sexual relations. In other words, the same set of statistics can result in two – or more – very different conclusions and policy responses.

As such, it should not be assumed that greater reliance on evidence-based policy will actually take the politics out of policy making. The decisions about *which* issues or problems should be investigated, *how* the inquiry should be conducted and *what* questions should be asked, and *how* the evidence should then be interpreted or incorporated into a public policy, will all reflect, to varying degrees, the perspectives, priorities and preferences of the policy makers themselves.

Such observations, though, do not mean that evidence-based policy making should be dispensed with, or that policies based on the acquisition of evidence might not be a considerable improvement on what existed before, to the extent of enjoying greater success in tackling a problem. We merely seek to emphasize that evidence-based policy making will still, on many occasions, entail judgements and choices which are at least partly shaped by institutional interests, personal preferences or political perspectives.

Conclusion

In the sphere of policy making, problems are not necessarily self-evident or obvious, but are often subject to definition and identification, which, in turn, may be determined by political perspectives and social values. Only a proportion of issues become defined or officially recognized as problems at any given juncture, and thus deemed worthy of attention by policy makers. By focusing on the institutional agenda, policy makers seek to limit the number of problems to be addressed to a (more) manageable level, otherwise they would inevitably face a situation of 'overload'. For those in wider society who wish to influence public policy, and persuade policy makers that there is a problem which needs to be addressed, the aim must be to get 'their' issue from the systemic agenda to the institutional agenda, although even if they are successful, the issue attention cycle might then operate against them, as their issue slips back down or off the agenda without a policy actually being enacted.

We have also seen that it is not normally sufficient to show how a particular policy would solve a particular problem, it is also necessary for the right political circumstances to exist, in terms of a sympathetic minister (or Prime Minister) or favourable ideological climate, for example. If the right political circumstances do occur, however, then opportunities may well arise for certain individuals or think tanks to exercise considerable influence on policy makers. On such occasions, moreover, rather than simply create policies to tackle problems as and when they arise, in a reactive manner, policy makers (or those seeking to influence them) may search for problems to which they can apply a favoured pre-existing policy proposal, and which they may have been wanting to implement for some time.

As such, we have already noted how 'messy' the reality of policy making can be in Britain, and how public policy is developed through the combined impact and interaction of ideas and ideological perspectives, definitions or interpretations of problems, various policy actors and varying political circumstances. Having considered the role of ideas, ideologies and the importance of circumstances in this chapter, the next few chapters will examine the key actors involved in policy making in Britain, although various themes identified in this chapter will also recur at regular intervals.

Recommended texts and further reading

1 Peter Bachrach and Morton Baratz (1970) *Power and Poverty: Theory and Practice*, New York: Oxford University Press.

In spite of being published back in 1970, this remains a classic study of the 'hidden face of power' and the manner in which the political or policy agenda is confined to 'safe' issues, and entails 'non-decisions', thereby militating against radical change.

2 Andrew Denham and Mark Garnett (1998) *British Think Tanks and the Climate of Opinion*, UCL Press.

The first major survey of the rise of think tanks in Britain, paying particular attention to those which became prominent in the 1980s and 1990s, and examining the ways in which they sought to shape public policy, as well as evaluating their success in so doing. An update examining think tanks *vis-à-vis* New Labour would be warmly welcomed, though.

3 David Dolowitz (2000a), with Rob Hulme, Mike Nellis and Fiona O'Neill (2000), *Policy Transfer and British Social Policy*, Buckingham: Open University Press.

Fine overview of the phenomenon of policy transfer, detailing what it entails, why it has occurred apace since the 1980s, and providing empirical case studies of particular policies by way of examples and illustration.

4 John Kingdon (1995) *Agendas, Alternatives and Public Policies* 2nd edition. New York: Harper Collins.

The classic text on the concept of policy streams, examining how and why policy change occurs, through the interaction and confluence of problems, policies and favourable political circumstances.

5 Anthony Seldon (1996) 'Ideas are not Enough' in David Marquand and Anthony Seldon (eds) *The Ideas That Shaped Post-War Britain*, London: Fontana.

Explains how policies and policy change in Britain are shaped not just by ideas, but also by individuals, organized interests and circumstances.

3 The Core Executive, Part One: Key Individuals

The concept of the core executive was developed from the late 1980s onwards, primarily by political scientists dissatisfied with the limitations of the 'Prime Minister versus Cabinet' debate, which had been rehearsed and rehashed for at least the previous two decades. This debate implied that the possession and exercise of political power could be understood in 'either/or' terms, as a zero-sum phenomenon, whereby more power for the Prime Minister automatically meant less power for the Cabinet and its ministers, and vice versa. Furthermore, this model of power at the heart of British government often failed to acknowledge the increasingly important role of other individuals and institutions in central government, surrounding and supporting the Prime Minister and the Cabinet.

What the emergence of 'core executive studies' sought to illustrate, therefore, was not only the range of individuals and institutions involved in policy making in British government, but also their respective sources of power, which ensured that many policy decisions entailed bargaining and negotiation between individuals or institutions, each of whom possessed particular resources, and who adopted various tactics and strategies in deploying them to achieve their goals. Consequently, core executive studies emphatically reject any notion of policies being routinely imposed unilaterally, or top-down, from one central institution or individual; political reality and policy making are usually rather more complex, subtle and variable, and thus for those studying it, infinitely more interesting.

The classic definition of the core executive was provided by Rhodes, when he identified it as:

> *all those organisations and procedures which co-ordinate central government policies, and act as final arbiters of conflict between different parts of the government machine …* the 'core executive' is the heart of the machine, covering the complex web of institutions, networks and practices surrounding the prime minister, cabinet, cabinet committees and their official counterparts, less formalised ministerial 'clubs' or meetings, bilateral negotiations and interdepartmental committees. It also includes co-ordinating departments, chiefly the Cabinet Office, the Treasury [and] the Foreign Office.
>
> (1995a: 12, original emphasis)

To this list, Smith adds government departments in general, not only on the grounds that these are 'the core policy making units within central government', but also that they are headed by ministers, who themselves are 'key actors within the institutions of the core executive' (Smith, 1999: 5).

Figure 3.1   The core executive in Britain

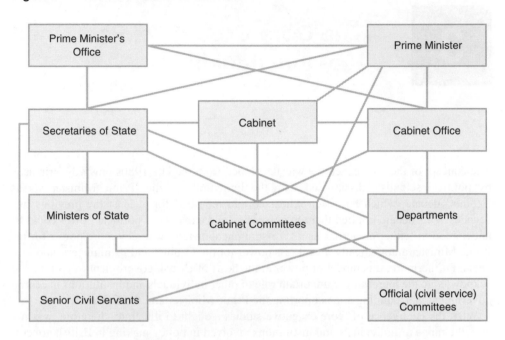

Figure 3.1 provides an illustration of the key actors who comprise the core executive, and the myriad linkages between them.

The central importance of the core executive to the policy process in Britain is clearly confirmed by the opening words of Smith's book on the topic, namely that: 'The core executive is at the heart of British government. It contains the key institutions and actors concerned with developing policy, co-ordinating government activity and providing the necessary resources for delivering public goods' (Smith, 1999: 1).

In similar vein, Holliday notes that: 'The heart of the UK state, and the key driving force in UK politics, is the core executive' (Holliday, 2000: 8).

Indeed, the importance of the core executive to policy making in Britain is such that it warrants two chapters in this text. The remainder of this chapter, therefore, will explore the roles and resources of the individuals who collectively comprise the core executive, and how these impact upon policy making in Britain. The next chapter will analyse the institutions of the core executive within which these individuals operate, and which provide many of the resources which those individuals draw upon in pursuing policy objectives. It will also consider some of the sources of tension within the core executive, and their implications for public policy in Britain.

Both chapters, though, will draw attention to the power relations which operate in the core executive, and the interactions between the individual and institutional policy actors. What will become apparent is the extent to which the core executive entails a dialectic of both centralization and fragmentation, as well as a tension between the need for central coordination against the tendency towards departmentalism and sectorization. As such, the chapters will emphasize the extent to which these policy actors are dependent on each other, due to the need to share or exchange the resources necessary for the formulation and implementation of public policy in Britain. It will be shown not only that each of the policy actors in the core executive possesses resources needed by others, but that these resources are themselves partly affected by exogenous circumstances and events. This, in turn, will indicate that within the core executive, power relations between the policy actors are *not* of a zero-sum character, nor are they fixed or static. Power within the core executive is relatively fluid and variable, varying according to the individuals and issues involved, and the differing contexts in which they are operating. A policy actor prevailing on one particular issue might not do so on a range of other issues, or if the original issue arises again, but in a different set of circumstances. The variability of power and influence is clearly illustrated by examining, first, the role of the Prime Minister in the policy process.

The Prime Minister

Since the 1960s, discussions about the role of the Prime Minister in British politics have almost invariably focused on his/her apparently increased powers, to the extent that a number of commentators have variously asserted that parliamentary government and Cabinet government have been supplanted by the establishment of 'prime ministerial government' (Benn, 1981: 67–22; Crossman, 1963: 51; Mackintosh, 1977: 629). According to this perspective, the increased role of government in 20th-century Britain, the corresponding expansion of the core executive, and the emergence of the 'career politician' dependent on prime ministerial patronage to further their political careers, all served to imbue the Prime Minister with ever greater powers. Indeed, Tony Blair's premiership heard this line of argument taken further, to the extent that some now speak of a new 'Presidentialism' (Foley, 2000; see also Foley, 1992; Pryce, 1997), with Blair accused of adopting a 'Napoleonic' style of leadership and control (although curiously, many of those most critical of Blair's allegedly autocratic or arrogant leadership are the very same critics who have complained that he relies too much on 'focus groups' or slavishly follows public opinion and opinion polls instead of providing clear leadership).

In response to the allegations about the rise of 'prime ministerial government' or 'British presidentialism', there have been three alternative – but not necessarily mutually exclusive – counter-perspectives, emphasizing the constraints facing contemporary British Prime Ministers. G.W. Jones was one of the first to rebut the 'prime ministerial government' thesis, arguing that the power of the postwar British premier has been exaggerated, for ultimately, a Prime Minister is dependent upon the support of Cabinet colleagues (and ultimately, one might add, backbench MPs too); Prime Ministers are only as powerful as their senior ministers allow them to be, Jones (1985) has insisted. Or as another commentator expressed it in the mid-1990s, 'Prime Ministers are, in effect, captains of their teams, but they owe their position (and its very real powers) … to the team itself' (Hodder-Williams, 1995: 232). For such commentators, what has been most notable about prime ministerial 'power' in Britain is precisely its contingent character, and the practical limitations which British premiers invariably encountered, irrespective of their formal or constitutional powers. The very complexity of contemporary British society, which has arguably served to downgrade the role of Parliament in policy making (as discussed in Chapter 6) and yielded a corresponding centralization of power in the core executive, can be cited as evidence of the (potential or actual) constraints facing any modern prime minister in Britain. No British Prime Minister can seriously expect to grasp the intricacies of more than a few policies at any particular time.

Indeed, beyond the realms of economic affairs and international relations, prime ministerial involvement in domestic policy initiatives has generally been sporadic and *ad hoc*, varying from one premier to another (Barber, 1991: Chapters 9 and 10). For example, during her first two years as Prime Minister, Margaret Thatcher took a particularly keen interest in trade union reform, much to the chagrin of her first Employment Secretary, James Prior (Prior, 1986: 165). Tony Blair, meanwhile, has sought to involve himself closely in the pursuit of peace in Northern Ireland, as did his Conservative predecessor, John Major. In general, though, lack of time and expertise, and a concern with the broader picture, means that Prime Ministers are obliged to leave many, if not most, domestic policies to their ministerial colleagues, thereby indicating that in many respects, a Prime Minister is as dependent upon his/her senior ministers for policy success as they are on him/her. Indeed, Kavanagh and Seldon suggest that (with the exception of Margaret Thatcher, and possibly Clement Attlee): 'Few post-war Prime Ministers … have left much of an intended and enduring legacy on public policy' (2000: 317). This is because many policies either originate, or are developed, elsewhere – particularly in government departments and policy networks, but also in both supranational or subnational institutions.

A second rebuttal of the 'prime ministerial government' thesis, therefore, is the fact that the Prime Minister is but one of several individuals and institutions at the centre of the British political system. In this respect, as noted at the beginning of this chapter, 'core executive studies' emphasizes the extensive interdependency of policy actors in the higher echelons of the British political system. This interdependency derives from the differing resources that each policy actor possesses or has ready access to. Consequently, against those who talk of increasing prime ministerial power, and who imply that power entails a 'zero-sum' relationship between political or policy actors, 'core executive studies' emphasizes the extent to which the policy actors in the core executive are dependent on each other much of the time, and therefore need to cooperate in order to achieve their policy goals.

The third critique of the 'prime ministerial government' thesis has been advanced by Richard Rose, who locates the contemporary British Prime Minister 'in a shrinking world' (Rose, 2001). Analysing the British premiership in the context of Europeanization and globalization (both of which are discussed in Chapter 8), Rose argues that while Prime Ministers now enjoy a higher profile than before, due to modern mass media, and the frequency of international summits, the power which this often implies is largely illusory, for in the world beyond Westminster – where the important policy decisions tend to originate – the Prime Minister is increasingly constrained by external or global factors; omnipresence does not mean omnipotence.

On the contrary, the extent to which contemporary British Prime Ministers seem to be involved in an almost constant series of high-profile meetings, summits and international conferences with their overseas counterparts, can actually be interpreted as a two-fold limitation on their power. First, because the increasing amount of time and energy expended in intergovernmental and supranational forums is time and energy not being expended at home on domestic affairs (although, of course, many international summits and their subsequent decisions will have an impact on domestic policies). Prime Ministers thus increasingly have to delegate matters to their ministerial colleagues, senior officials and advisers (discussed below).

Second, the increasing number of international meetings which Prime Ministers are obliged to attend, is itself an indication of the extent to which public policy is being 'Europeanized' and 'globalized', and thus subject to international agreement and coordination. Or as Rose expresses it: 'National policies are no longer national' (2001: 45, and Chapters 3 and 10). This is a key issue which will be alluded to at various points in subsequent chapters.

Meanwhile, to return to what still remains of domestic British politics, two other factors must be noted when considering the policy role of the Prime Minister in the core executive, both of which further indicate the contingent character of their power and authority. First, irrespective of their formal or constitutional powers, the actual power and authority of a Prime Minister cannot be isolated from the economic and political circumstances of their premiership (Elgie, 1995: 40–50). As Table 3.1 indicates, for example, the size of the government's parliamentary majority can have some impact on a Prime Minister's power, for a premier whose party has been (re)elected with a large majority in the House of Commons generally has more scope for exercising somewhat greater power than one who presides over a narrow, possibly dwindling, majority (for a discussion of Prime Ministers' relationships with the House of Commons since 1945, see Borthwick, 1995; for a discussion of their relations with their parliamentary parties, see Shell, 1995).

In this respect, Margaret Thatcher, presiding over majorities of 144 and 101 in 1983 and 1987 respectively, and Tony Blair, with majorities of 179 in 1997 and 166 in 2001, were generally able to exercise rather more power than John Major, whose Conservative government was re-elected in 1992 with a parliamentary majority of 21, which was then

Table 3.1   The variability of prime ministerial power: supports and constraints

Enhancing the PM's power	Constraining the PM's power
Large parliamentary majority	Small parliamentary majority
Unified Cabinet	Divided Cabinet
Cohesion on backbenches	Division among backbenchers
Recent general election victory	'Mid-term' blues
High opinion poll ratings	Low opinion poll ratings
Competence and integrity of ministerial colleagues	Incompetence or scandals involving ministerial colleagues
Clear objectives and strategy	Limited grasp of policy detail
Supportive media	Media hostility
Strong, stable economic situation	Recession/economic crisis
International crisis, well-handled	International crisis, poorly-handled
Weak, ineffective Opposition	Strong, credible Opposition

whittled away during the next five years, due to by-election defeats and defections. With such a narrow majority, John Major's room for manoeuvre was much more limited than Thatcher's and Blair's, hence the widespread perception that he was a weak Prime Minister (his former Chancellor, Norman Lamont, once caustically remarking that Major gave the impression of 'being in Office, but not in power'). This was quite apart from the fact that by temperament and inclination, Major was a more collegial Prime Minister than Thatcher and Blair, in the sense that he was inclined to encourage greater discussion of policy issues in Cabinet, rather than attempting to lead from the front (Baker, 1993: 427; Seldon, 1997: 739), although this merely led to Tony Blair's jibe, in the House of Commons, that 'I lead my party; he follows his'.

Yet even apparently strong Prime Ministers are not consistently strong throughout their premierships. As Table 3.1 also indicates, economic circumstances, events or crises can impact upon a Prime Minister's authority and influence, sometimes enhancing it, sometimes undermining it. Margaret Thatcher was rather constrained during the first three years of her premiership, presiding over a major recession, a significant loss of manufacturing jobs which increased unemployment to approximately 3 million, inner city riots in the summer of 1981, and a Cabinet divided between 'wets' and 'dries'. The 1982 Falklands War then transformed her position, as military success boosted her public popularity and restored a sense of national pride, and rallied more of the Conservative Party behind her. This strengthening of her leadership was both reflected and reinforced by the landslide election victory in 1983, further assisted by the ineffectiveness of a divided Opposition.

Thatcher was weakened again in the immediate aftermath of the 'Westland affair' in January 1986, to the extent that she found herself 'thinking hard about my own position. ... [I knew] there were those in my own Party and Government who would like to take the opportunity of getting rid of me' (Thatcher, 1993: 435). She was then bolstered by another convincing election victory in 1987, but by 1989, Thatcher was once again being undermined by events and individuals around her, to the extent that, with hindsight, these can be seen to have heralded the beginning of the end of her premiership. For example, in the summer of 1989, she was effectively compelled by Nigel Lawson, her Chancellor, and Sir Geoffrey Howe, the Foreign Secretary, to declare Britain's eventual intention to join the European Communities' (it had not yet become the European Union (EU)) Exchange Rate Mechanism (ERM), something to which she was strongly opposed. Lawson and Howe intimated that if Thatcher did not formally announce this intention, at a meeting of the European Council in Madrid, in June 1989, then they would resign, calculating, no doubt, that a joint resignation by her Chancellor and Foreign Secretary would do immense damage to her own credibility and legitimacy as Prime Minister. Not surprisingly, Thatcher believed that she had effectively been 'ambushed' by her two senior ministerial colleagues, although she did refuse to specify a date for Britain's entry. The important point here, though, is that the Prime Minister concluded that, on this issue at least, and at this particular juncture, she had to accede to their general demand on an issue of major economic and diplomatic importance, even though it was against her own views and policy preferences (Howe, 1995: 581–84; Lawson, 1992: 929–34; Thatcher, 1993: 709–12).

It could be claimed, though, that Thatcher exacted revenge very soon afterwards, for just four weeks later, she pursued a Cabinet reshuffle, in which Sir Geoffrey was moved from the Foreign Office to become Leader of the House (of Commons). On the other hand, this very public and humiliating demotion merely fuelled Sir Geoffrey's resentment at Thatcher's treatment of him, culminating in his devastating resignation speech – he had resigned as Leader of the House – to the House of Commons in November 1990. By this time, Thatcher had already faced a 'stalking horse' leadership challenge, in December 1989, from Sir Anthony Meyer, who attracted the votes of 33 Conservative MPs, while 27 Conservatives abstained. Although this was presented as a comfortable victory for Thatcher (a majority of 281) by her supporters, the fact that 60 Conservatives had not supported her was interpreted by her critics as a clear indication that a sizeable body of opinion in the party did not support her continued leadership. These critics were also quick to ask the key question of how many votes would be attained by a serious, 'heavy-weight', leadership challenger, if a virtually unknown backbencher had managed to deprive Thatcher of 60 votes?

One other indication of the variability of the Prime Minister's power was also provided by Nigel Lawson, just a few months after the Madrid summit 'ambush', when, in October 1989, Lawson resigned as Chancellor, due to Thatcher's refusal to dismiss her Special (Economic) Adviser, Sir Alan Walters. Lawson believed that Walters' advice to Thatcher, and various of his comments, both in 'the City' and in written journal articles, were undermining him and aspects of his economic strategy, particularly *vis-à-vis* Europe and the ERM. Walters himself felt obliged to resign immediately afterwards, meaning that Thatcher had embarrassingly lost both her Chancellor and her personal Economic Adviser virtually simultaneously.

Consequently, the damage inflicted on her credibility in this situation, and the concomitant questions about her political judgement, was such that her power was further constrained, for Thatcher needed to avoid antagonizing more of her Cabinet colleagues and Conservative backbenchers. This bears out Smith's point that 'Prime Ministerial authority is largely relational, and is dependent on the standing of the Prime Minister' (Smith, 2003: 65). At various times, and in relation to particular ministers and policy issues, Margaret Thatcher's 'standing' was rather lower than it had been in the immediate aftermath of the 1982 Falklands War, or the 1983 and 1987 general election victories.

This variability of prime ministerial power has recently been confirmed by Sir Richard Wilson, a former Cabinet Secretary, who explained to the House of Commons Select Committee on public administration that:

> His or her power varies from time to time according to the extent their Cabinet colleagues permit them to have that power, depending on whether the Cabinet is split, depending also on the strength of the Government majority in the House of Commons and also popular opinion in the electorate and attitudes in the Party.

> (Public Administration Committee, 2002)

One other factor to be considered is that of prime ministerial personality and style of leadership. Again, quite apart from the impact of wider economic and political circumstances, Prime Ministers will adopt different approaches to political leadership, deriving from their own particular personal style and personality (see, for example, Barber, 1991; James,

Table 3.2   Prime ministerial styles of leadership

Innovator	Reformer	Balancer	Egotist
Edward Heath (1970–4)	Clement Attlee (1945–51)	Harold Macmillan (1957–63)	Harold Wilson (1964–70)
Margaret Thatcher (1979–90) *Tony Blair* (1997–present)		Alec Douglas-Home (1963–4) *Harold Wilson* (1974–6) James Callaghan (1976–9) *John Major* (1990–7)	

Source: Adapted from Norton, 1987: 328–9. Names in italics have been added by this author

1999: 98–100; Hennessy, 2001a; Hodder-Williams, 1995). As such, the formal constitutional powers granted to all British Prime Ministers will actually be exercised in different ways, a key consideration which should further encourage scepticism when confronted by complaints about the rise of prime ministerial government or a new 'presidentialism'. Norton once devised a four-fold typology of prime ministerial styles, as indicated by Table 3.2, although he was quick to emphasize that these 'are not mutually exclusive', because premiers can, and often do, 'exhibit the characteristics of more than one type'. Norton's categorization thus sought to identify 'the preponderant characteristics of a particular type' (1987: 329).

What Norton meant by these four typologies is now explained in slightly more detail. *Innovator*: This refers to a Prime Minister who is determined to make an impact, and leave a lasting legacy, in terms of policy initiatives, but who has to lead a somewhat sceptical or hesitant parliamentary party. The Prime Minister will have certain policy objectives and goals which they personally wish to see pursued, but which some of their ministerial and backbench colleagues might have reservations about. Margaret Thatcher was clearly an example of such a Prime Minister, for as another of Norton's studies indicates, only about 19 per cent of Conservative MPs and ministers – even by 1989, when she had been Prime Minister for 10 years – could be categorized as 'Thatcherites'. The rest were either 'One Nation' critics of much of Thatcherism, or were 'agnostics' whose support for Thatcher was pragmatic, rather than ideological (Norton, 1990a). The crucial point here, though, in terms of prime ministerial leadership style and policy impact, was that Thatcher often felt obliged to take the lead, and seize the initiative, and then expect her parliamentary and ministerial colleagues to follow her.

More recently, Tony Blair – who has, on various occasions, spoken of his admiration of Margaret Thatcher – has assumed a similar style of leadership following New Labour's 1997 and 2001 general election victories. In so doing, Blair has pursued various policies, most notably 'Public-Private Partnerships' (PPP), the establishment of 'foundation' hospitals, the imminent introduction of university top-up fees and the pursuit (with the USA) of the March-April 2003 war 'to liberate' Iraq, all of which have been deeply unpopular with many Labour MPs. Faced with such scepticism, Blair (like Thatcher) has relied on a blend of exhortation, defiance and an insistence that 'there is no alternative', or that 'no change is not an option'.

Such a leadership style is invariably controversial, for while supporters and admirers of Thatcher or Blair invariably depict them as heroic, visionary leaders courageously battling against the 'forces of conservatism' resistant to new ideas and policy initiatives, their critics denounce them as arrogant or autocratic. It is precisely this type of Prime Minister who is deemed, by some, to be developing a 'prime ministerial' or even presidential system of government in Britain, in place of Cabinet or parliamentary government.

Reformer: This is a Prime Minister who also wants to achieve specific policy objectives, but in this case, the goals are broadly shared by their party. This type of Prime Minister is effectively aiming to implement agreed party policies, so that they themselves do not necessarily become personally associated with the policies. Labour's first postwar leader, Clement Attlee, was a 'reformer', for the pursuit of full employment, and establishment of a welfare state 'from cradle to grave', were policy goals strongly supported throughout the Labour Party; no one refers to 'Attleeism'!

Balancer: This typology refers to a prime minister whose primary concern is to maintain party unity, particularly when faced with ideological tensions and disagreements over policies, or possibly very difficult economic or political circumstances which render party unity more important than ever. It might also mean that they see their role as being to maintain (or restore) national unity and social stability after a period of political uncertainty or upheaval. Such Prime Ministers will, therefore, either adopt a predominantly managerialist stance, or pursue policies which are explicitly intended to ameliorate signs or sources of conflict, be they within government itself, or the country at large. If one were to deploy a maritime or nautical analogy, this style of leadership would reflect a 'steady-as-she goes' philosophy, whereby the primary objective is to keep the 'ship of state' afloat, and safely navigate – or, preferably avoid altogether – choppy waters, rather than sail towards any predetermined destination.

Norton placed the 1976–79 Labour prime minister, James Callaghan, in this category, but we would also add Callaghan's 1974–6 predecessor, Harold Wilson (his final premiership somewhat different to that of the 1960s), and John Major, 1990–7. Wilson was preoccupied for much of the 1974–6 period with keeping Labour's Left-Right ideological infighting under control – the 1975 referendum on Britain's continued membership of the European Communities primarily deployed by Wilson to overcome or bypass the deep Left-Right divisions in the Parliamentary Labour Party over Europe at that time – rather than pursuing clear policy objectives.

More recently, in the 1990s, John Major found himself expending considerable time and energy trying to maintain a semblance of unity to an increasingly fractious Conservative Party. Not only did this style reflect his own personality and character, he also deemed it necessary to act as a 'balancer' in order to heal the divisions wrought by Thatcher's 11 years as Prime Minister.

Egotist: Probably the most contentious of Norton's prime ministerial types, this refers to a premier who seeks to obtain and exercise power for its own sake, rather than having any particular policy objectives. Norton places Harold Wilson's 1964–70 premiership in this category, based, it seems, largely on some rather unflattering observations about Wilson's leadership in Richard Crossman's subsequent *Diaries of a Cabinet Minister* (for example, Crossman, 1976: 160, diary entry for 11 December 1966; Crossman, 1977: 459, diary entry for 27 April 1969).

A slightly different typology is proffered by Burch, who suggests that Prime Ministers tend to adopt one of three approaches towards ministerial colleagues and their departments, namely delegators, intervenors or overseers (1995: 111–13). Delegators (such as Clement Attlee and John Major) tend to trust or allow their ministers to proceed with their departmental and policy responsibilities, thereby granting considerable discretion and autonomy. By contrast, intervenors (of which Thatcher and Blair provide good examples) are inclined to involve themselves in the work of departments, perhaps feeling the need to push or cajole ministerial colleagues into the pursuit of a particular policy. This intervention does not necessarily have to be direct or in person; staff in the 10 Downing Street Policy Directorate (formerly Unit) or the Cabinet Office (both of which are discussed in the next chapter) can readily act on the Prime Minister's behalf to 'push' or 'chase-up' a minister or department to pursue a specific policy. Indeed, during Tony Blair's premiership, an unnamed Cabinet Minister claimed that 'Tony wants ...' had become 'the two most powerful words in Whitehall' (quoted in Hennessy, 2001b: 747). Overseers, by contrast (such as Callaghan), confine themselves to a more general purview of how ministerial colleagues and departments are developing policies.

Of course, the approach adopted will reflect, to a considerable degree, the personality or style of the Prime Minister (as delineated in Norton's above typology), and there will also be occasions or circumstances when a Prime Minister adopts one of the other approaches. For example, either the delegator approach or that of the overseer will be transformed into that of an intervenor if serious problems become apparent, or a crisis erupts.

Senior ministers (other than the Prime Minister)

Apart from the Prime Minister, most of the senior ministers in Britain's core executive (senior here referring primarily to those of cabinet rank) tend to have the official title of Secretary of State (although a few will have alternative appellations, such as Chancellor of the Exchequer), and most of these will be political heads of a key government department or ministry. In addition, two or three senior ministers will be appointed as 'Ministers without Portfolio' – usually free of any departmental responsibilities – with quaint, usually archaic, titles such as Lord President of the Council, Lord Privy Seal and Chancellor of the Duchy of Lancaster. It is these secretaries of state and 'Ministers without Portfolio', who, along with the Prime Minister, and the government's Chief Whip, collectively constitute the cabinet.

The precise role which any Secretary of State plays in policy making will vary from minister to minister, and depend upon a range of variables, most notably:

- The extent to which the minister has a clear policy objective which they are determined to pursue.
- The extent to which there is a strongly entrenched departmental philosophy, by which the minister becomes persuaded. Gerald Kaufman, a Labour minister in the 1970s, warns of the danger of contracting the disease of 'departmentalitis', whereby a minister views issues primarily from their department's perspective and interests, and pursues policy objectives accordingly (the notion of 'departmental philosophies' is discussed in the next chapter).

- The degree of support (or otherwise) which a minister receives from the Prime Minister. If a Cabinet Minister enjoys the full support of the Prime Minister, then they are much more likely successfully to pursue a policy initiative. Conversely, when a minister is seeking to introduce a policy which is not fully endorsed by the Prime Minister, then their chances of success are correspondingly diminished, especially if their ministerial colleagues and departmental officials are aware of the Prime Minister's displeasure. On a few occasions, a Cabinet Minister may even face a prime ministerial demand that they pursue a particular policy.
- The nature of the issues or problems with which a Cabinet Minister is faced during his/her tenure at a particular department. A crisis, for example, is both an opportunity and a threat: if successfully overcome, then the minister's political stature and authority are likely to increase accordingly, whereas failure to tackle the problem satisfactorily – even if it is unfair or unrealistic to expect them to have done so, given the nature or extent of the problem – is likely to have a detrimental impact on their political stature.
- The Cabinet Minister's own style and personality: just as Prime Ministers vary in their approach to leadership (as noted above), so do Cabinet Ministers adopt a range of roles with regard to policy making at their department, although as well as their own personality, the factors noted above – political circumstances, the departmental ethos, the degree of prime ministerial 'direction' – will also shape their approach to heading the department.

With regard to the last of these factors, Norton, having previously devised a taxonomy of prime ministerial styles, has devised a similar typology of ministerial styles. He identifies five main types of minister in Britain (2000: 109–10):

1. *Commanders*, who pursue policy goals based on personal experience or motivation of what they believe ought to be done.
2. *Ideologues*, who are concerned primarily to pursue policies based on a clear political philosophy or doctrine.
3. *Managers*, these being ministers who are essentially pragmatic decision takers, and who are generally more concerned with the efficient administration of their department.
4. *Agents*, namely ministers who effectively act on behalf of others, such as the Prime Minister or departmental civil servants.
5. *Team players*, being those ministers who believe in collective decision taking, and seek to secure the agreement of as many Cabinet colleagues as possible.

Marsh et al., meanwhile, develop Headey's original classification of ministers as either policy initiators, policy selectors or policy legitimators (Headey, 1974: 71), by subdividing the policy initiator role between those who do focus on initiating specific policies, and those ministers who seek to adopt an agenda-setting role, whereupon they seek to effect a more general reorientation of policy. This is certainly a role which the authors attribute to a number of Conservative Cabinet Ministers during the 1980s and 1990s, and which achieved, to varying degrees, changes in the 'departmental philosophies' (discussed in the next chapter) and institutional agendas (Marsh et al., 2001: 133–41).

Of course, as with prime ministerial styles, such a typology does not preclude occasional overlaps, and Norton himself is quick to emphasize that these are 'ideal types' (or what social scientists call 'heuristic devices'), thereby acknowledging that while ministers tend to exhibit *mostly* the characteristics of a particular style or role, aspects of another style might still be discernible. Hence their categorization depends upon which character-istics predominate overall. For example, we would suggest that a 'commander' minister's perception of what policy *ought* to be pursued may well reflect a particular ideological orientation, while an individual minister may adopt a different style or role if circum-stances warrant such a change. Nonetheless, Norton suggests that the two most common types of ministerial role are commander or manager. Indeed, for reasons which will become apparent subsequently, we would go even further by suggesting that an increasing number of senior ministers are adopting a commander role.

Whichever role is adopted by a Secretary of State, though, as departmental head, they are constitutionally responsible for the policies emanating from their department, reflect-ing the assumption that they are politically in charge, and that their junior ministers and senior civil servants act in accordance with instructions issued by them. This is the doctrine of 'individual ministerial responsibility', which, strictly interpreted, implies that in the case of a major policy failure or error, the Secretary of State should accept the blame (rather than blaming his/her subordinates), and resign accordingly. In practice, this does not happen very often, and when it does, it often owes much to the minister having lost the confidence or support of parliamentary or ministerial colleagues, rather than to genuine contrition over a significant policy error or failure (for an analysis of ministerial resigna-tions from 1964 to 1990, see Pyper, 1991).

The 'Ministers without Portfolio', meanwhile, will often be allocated specific tasks by the Prime Minister, these either not corresponding to particular departmental responsibil-ities, or being concerned with coordinating the work of various Government departments, and helping the Prime Minister – and the Cabinet Office – achieve 'joined-up government' and supervise policy 'delivery' (for a fuller discussion of the roles generally ascribed to 'ministers without portfolio', see Lee et al., 1998: Chapter 11).

In pursuing their departmental responsibilities, numerous Secretaries of State have encountered two particular problems, both of which militated against their ability to effect policy change or successfully introduce new policies. First, as mentioned above, there is what the former Labour minister, Gerald Kaufman has termed the disease of 'departmen-talitis', which many ministers apparently become afflicted with (1997: 14–15). This refers to a tendency for some Secretaries of State to 'go native' by adopting the views and values of their particular department (see next chapter), and consequently pursuing the perceived interests of their department, even if and when these might not be entirely compatible with the aims and objectives of the government itself. The memoirs and diaries of various for-mer Secretaries of State testify to the extent to which they – or other Cabinet Ministers – became preoccupied with their departmental interests and issues, and therefore paid little attention to policy proposals put forward by their ministerial colleagues (see, for example: Barnett, 1982: 81–2; Castle, 1993: 341; Crossman, 1975: 201, diary entry for 18 April 1965; Dell, 1980: 25; Healey, 1990: 326–7; Joseph, 1987: 27; Marsh, 1978: 87).

This tendency was well noted by Sir Douglas Wass, a former head of the Civil Service, when he observed that 'for each Minister, the test of success in office lies in his ability to deliver his departmental goals … No Minister I know of has won political distinction by his performance in the Cabinet or by his contribution to collective decision-taking'

(Wass, 1983: 25). Much more recently, within months of New Labour's May 1997 election victory, Tony Blair was bemoaning the already evident trend towards departmentalism among his ministerial colleagues: 'One of the things we have lost from Opposition is that shared sense of purpose and strategy. Ministers have become preoccupied by their departmental brief and we need to draw them back more' (*The Observer*, 23 November 1997). This tendency or trend clearly places a premium on other (non-departmental) individuals – particularly 'Ministers without Portfolio' and the Prime Minister – and institutions (most notably the Cabinet Office, discussed in the next chapter) within the core executive with regard to policy coordination.

The second problem which Secretaries of State often encounter in pursuing their departmental responsibilities, and which also has implications for the achievement of policy change, is the pressure of short-term decisions and events, which often, unavoidably, distract the minister from adopting a broader or more strategic perspective, or from devising a new policy. A newly appointed Secretary of State does not arrive at their department with a clear desk, an empty 'in' tray or a blank sheet of paper onto which they can immediately draft a new strategy or policy for immediate implementation. Instead, they will invariably find themselves immediately inundated with a range of ongoing issues, problems and cases requiring a decision, quite apart from the new issues and problems which occur during their tenure at the department. Many of these might be rather technical or administrative, or politically 'low-level', in which case, they might well be delegated to the department's civil servants, but a variety of issues and problems will still require ministerial consideration and authorization, and demand the minister's day-to-day attention. This corresponds to the notion of 'policy inheritance' developed by Richard Rose (1990; Rose and Davies, 1994) which is discussed briefly in Chapter 9.

This almost inevitably means that a new policy initiative will either have to be pursued alongside these other issues and cases, therefore limiting the time which the Secretary of State can devote to it, or that the minister will defer pursuit of a new policy until his/her desk 'clears' – which it is unlikely to do. Besides, a Secretary of State will only spend a limited amount of time each week actually in their department, because their other departmental and political responsibilities oblige them to be elsewhere, such as attending Cabinet committees, or holding meetings with one or two other ministers (bilaterals or trilaterals), as well as their various appearances in the House of Commons, such as Question Time, the Readings of a Bill they are 'sponsoring', and giving evidence to select committee inquiries. Secretaries of State will also need to attend meetings of the EU Council of Ministers (for their policy domain), as well as other occasional international summits or conferences. In addition, the vast majority of Secretaries of State are still MPs, and therefore retain constituency responsibilities as well.

These various responsibilities, and either ongoing issues (which they have 'inherited') or new ones which arise, have often left many Secretaries of State with little time or energy to pursue a new policy or strategy, at least in the short term, and this reinforced a trend towards policy continuity, or at the most, only incremental policy change. For example, when appointed Home Secretary in 1985 (a post in which he remained for the next four years), Douglas Hurd saw his role ... 'much more as managing the Department and keeping an eye open for any potential crisis looming on the horizon, rather than introducing my own social agenda on law and order ... I was most concerned to consult widely and heed the views of my senior officials' (quoted in Marsh et al., 2001: 140).

Furthermore, even if a Secretary of State does resolve to pursue a new policy, he/she would invariably need to engage in consultations with organized interests or 'affected parties' (or, more likely, delegate such consultations to their civil servants), thereby yielding further, usually unavoidable, delay in introducing the new policy. As Lord Croham, another former Head of the Civil Service, once explained, 'in general, the Minister is so captivated ... by the day-to-day affairs of being a Minister ... that he finds the long-term issue is something he'll do tomorrow – and tomorrow never comes' (quoted in Hennessy, 2001b: 492).

In view of the workload of most Secretaries of State, and the extent to which they have traditionally been heavily reliant upon the advice and cooperation of senior civil servants in their departments, there has been a long-running debate, both among political scientists and politicians themselves, about the (power) relationship between ministers and civil servants. It has sometimes been claimed that the longevity of senior civil servants' tenure, compared with the temporary, transient nature of Cabinet Ministers – many of whom are reshuffled every couple of years, on average – coupled with the civil servants' consequent acquisition of specialist knowledge and expertise, places ministers in a weak position, to the extent that senior civil servants are effectively the rulers of Britain, rather than elected politicians and ministers accountable to Parliament. There is also an implication, sometimes, that senior civil servants prefer a weak minister, on the grounds that he/she will be much more readily persuaded to accept their officials' advice.

However, civil servants themselves robustly reject this critique, and while it might be tempting to retort, 'well, they would, wouldn't they!', many former Cabinet Ministers have also dismissed the 'civil service dominance' perspective. The most important reason why a 'civil servants versus Cabinet Ministers' dichotomy should be rejected is the same as why the 'Prime Minister versus Cabinet' model should be rejected, namely that of 'resource dependency', whereby Cabinet Minister and civil servants are actually interdependent. This vital consideration will be returned to below.

In the meantime, there is a second reason for rejecting the notion that senior civil servants tend to prefer a weak or pliable minister, namely that such a minister would also probably be weak *vis-à-vis* his/her Cabinet colleagues or the Treasury, in terms of promoting or protecting the interests of the department. Senior civil servants will recognize that if *they* can easily dominate their Secretary of State, then other policy actors are likely to be able to do so as well, to the detriment of the department as a whole. As Roy Jenkins – who served both as Chancellor of the Exchequer and Home Secretary during his political career – once noted: 'If a Minister is putty in their hands, they have a nasty suspicion that he will be putty in the hands of everybody else too, and that policy will not so much be made by the civil servants as never properly made at all' (1971: 218). A similar point, but conveyed slightly differently, was made by Norman Tebbit, recalling his time as Secretary of State for Employment during the latter half of Margaret Thatcher's first term of office. He notes that while senior civil servants liked his predecessor at the Department of Employment, the emollient James Prior, they were nonetheless 'conscious that he [Prior] lacked the Prime Minister's support, and was unlikely to win Cabinet battles. Like all organizations, departments like to be on the winning side, and they saw me as a winner in the Whitehall civil wars' (Tebbit, 1988: 183).

The changing role of Cabinet Ministers

A further reason for rejecting the dichotomy of 'weak ministers – dominant civil servants' is that recent in-depth studies of the 'core executive' have drawn attention to changes in the role of Cabinet Ministers. In particular, a trend has been identified whereby a growing number of Secretaries of State are adopting a more proactive – commander – policy role in their departments. While there have always been some Cabinet Ministers adopting such a role in their departments – such as Roy Jenkins' socially liberal or 'permissive' reforms at the Home Office in the mid-1960s – their numbers have increased since the 1980s (Campbell and Wilson, 1995; Foster and Plowden, 1996; Marsh et al., 2001: Chapter 6; Richards, 1997). Initially, this was largely attributable to the ideological objectives of the Thatcher governments, and their determination to break with the postwar consensus in British politics. To achieve this, various Cabinet Ministers in the 1980s deemed it vital to challenge the long-established departmental philosophies and policy communities which militated against policy change and innovation. Hence the proactive, innovative or agenda-setting policy role adopted by senior ministers such as Nigel Lawson at the Department of Energy in the early 1980s, Lord (David) Young at the Department of Trade and Industry in the late 1980s, Michael Howard at the Home Office in the 1990s, and Peter Lilley at the Department of Social Security during the same decade (Marsh et al., 2001: Chapter 6).

This trend towards more proactive agenda-setting Cabinet Ministers has continued to the present day, as evinced by Gordon Brown's tenure at the Treasury, Blunkett's time at the Home Office and Clarke's tenure at the Department For Education and Skills. The latter two, in particular, became strongly identified with controversial policies – albeit polices which Tony Blair is known strongly to support – such as tough law-and-order measures and planned ID cards in Blunkett's case, and the imminent introduction of university top-up fees in the case of Charles Clarke.

The increasing trend towards more proactive or agenda-setting Cabinet Ministers has been both reflected and reinforced by such factors as: the increased use of Special (Policy) Advisers as a source of original – or more partisan – ideas (see below); the changed role of senior civil servants, who are now expected to focus more on policy 'delivery' and management; the weakening or restructuring of particular policy communities (discussed in Chapter 5); and the general increase in policy transfer and evidence-based policy making.

Of course, the extent to which an individual Cabinet Minister will adopt a proactive or agenda-setting role will depend on various factors, including the minister's own personality and style, the nature of the issue they are seeking to address, the wider economic, social or political context and circumstances, the degree of prime ministerial support, and the degree of cooperation (or acquiescence) emanating from the relevant policy network. Yet it remains the case that more Cabinet Ministers are adopting a more proactive or agenda-setting role in their departments. The image of senior ministers being content to act as reactive managers, responding to events and issues as and when they occurred, and looking primarily to their senior civil servants for policy initiatives, appears increasingly outdated and inaccurate.

Junior Ministers

Once largely unsung and almost unseen, junior ministers have increased both in number and importance since the 1970s. While the precise role ascribed to junior ministers varies from department to department, and is also heavily dependent on who their 'boss' (Secretary of State) happens to be, there is no doubt that junior ministers generally play a much more extensive policy role in the core executive than they did in the 1950s and 1960s. The increased importance of junior ministers is partly reflected in their growth in numbers during the last century, having more than quadrupled, from 15 junior ministers in 1914 to 66 in 1998 (Theakston, 1999a: 230–1). There remained 66 junior ministers by 2004.

There are actually two categories of junior minister, the higher-ranking of these being the Minister of State, with the second category comprising Parliamentary Under Secretaries. That junior ministers have increased in both number and importance is itself indicative of the greatly expanded role and responsibilities of British government during the last century, as well as the greater complexity of governing.

Junior ministers are normally selected by the Prime Minister, rather than by the Secretary of State under whom they serve, and to whom they are constitutionally account-able, although the Prime Minister may choose to consult the Secretary of State over pro-posed appointments. On other occasions, though, the Prime Minister's choice of junior minister might cause some dismay to the Secretary of State. Certainly, during her 11 years as Prime Minister, Margaret Thatcher was not averse to allocating a particular junior minister – who was closer to her political views – to a Cabinet Minister whom she con-sidered somewhat 'wet' or 'not one of us'. In such instances, the junior minister would be expected to 'keep an eye' on the Secretary of State, and possibly keep the Prime Minister informed about what was happening in the department. For example, James Prior, upon being appointed Secretary of State for Employment in May 1979, found himself obliged to accept the appointment of a Minister of State favoured by Margaret Thatcher herself, the latter adamant that she wanted '*someone* with backbone' in the department (Prior, 1986: 114), an allusion by Thatcher to Prior's congenial manner and consensual approach to trade union reform, which she did not share.

More recently, following the election of the first Blair government, an acrimonious personal relationship rapidly emerged – 'it was hate at first sight' – between the Secretary of State for Social Security, Harriet Harman, and Frank Field, the Minister of State (for Welfare Reform) in the department. Field apparently considered himself intellectually superior to Harman, and believed that he ought to have been appointed Secretary of State (indeed, a conversation he had had with Tony Blair the previous autumn had led him to believe that he would indeed be appointed Secretary of State following the election of a New Labour government). Field was therefore apparently dismayed at subsequently being appointed Harman's 'junior' at the DSS. His resentment was greatly fuelled by Harman allegedly attempting to prevent his 'personal advisers' from having access to the department, followed by her subsequent efforts at block-ing Field's appointment of Kate Hoey as his Parliamentary Private Secretary (PPS). An acri-monious meeting ensued, at which Harman intimated that it was the party whips who were obstructing Hoey's appointment. When Field claimed that he did not believe this, Harman retorted that: 'I can't work with someone who thinks I'm a liar', to which Field's furious retort was: 'And I can't work with someone who *is* a … liar' (Rawnsley, 2001: 106–9).

Meanwhile, John Prescott, during his late 1990s guise as Secretary of State for Transport, the Environment and the Regions (as well as Deputy Prime Minister) was apparently not enamoured with his first three Ministers of State for Transport, and made his dissatisfaction crystal clear to Tony Blair (Rawnsley, 2001: 296; Foster, 2001: 278). However, Prescott's apparent disdain towards these junior ministers probably owed much to the fact that they were appointed at Tony Blair's behest, 'to keep an eye on Prescott', for the Prime Minister was 'worried [that] Prescott was becoming an "unguided missile" in his huge department' (Seldon, 2004: 416).

Most of the key government departments now have two or three Ministers of State, each of whom is usually given responsibility for a particular area of policy within their department. The precise role and remit of each Minister of State will usually be determined by the Secretary of State heading the department, although, again, this might be subject to prime ministerial intervention on occasions. In many cases, the Minister of State's full title will indicate their primary policy responsibility in the department – such as Minister of State for Higher Education, Minister of State for the Armed Forces, etc. – yet as Theakston noted in his seminal study, their role and authority are 'essentially informal and indeterminate, depending upon personal and political, not statutory, factors'. Consequently, the precise policy role of junior ministers will partly depend upon their relationship with the Secretary of State heading their department; where there is a good professional relationship or personal rapport between a junior minister and his/her Secretary of State, it is likely that the former will be permitted – and trusted – to play a more extensive policy role in the department. Where the relationship is less cordial, however, the junior minister is likely to be given a very limited role in policy development, to the extent that they may be confined to administrative tasks, or replying to correspondence sent to the department by MPs, outside bodies or members of the public (Theakston, 1987: 93–4; Theakston, 1999a: 235–6).

A further variable which influences the precise role of Junior Ministers will be the size and jurisdiction of their department. The larger the government department or ministry, and the broader its range of responsibilities, the more likely it is that a junior minister will be granted a more significant policy role, for the Secretary of State would otherwise be overwhelmed (Theakston, 1987: 95).

Meanwhile, there is a certain ambiguity concerning the relationship between junior ministers and senior civil servants, for while 'the Permanent Secretary [the topmost civil servant in a department] is not subject to the direction of junior Ministers ... junior Ministers are not subject to the directions of the Permanent Secretary' (Cabinet Office, 1997). Instead, 'Civil Servants observe the balance of forces and operate accordingly. They gauge whether the junior Minister has his boss's confidence' (James, 1999: 20–1).

The other category of junior minister in the core executive is that of Under-Secretary of State (sometimes with the prefix Parliamentary). These are the most junior in the ministerial hierarchy, and are often allocated very specific tasks, often technically specialized or concerned with administrative minutiae (but still vitally important nonetheless). Again, their precise title usually reflects the nature of their precise remit, such as (Parliamentary) Under-Secretary of State for Skills and Vocational Education, for example.

Figures 3.2 and 3.3 illustrate the allocation of responsibilities between Secretaries of State (or their equivalent), Ministers of State and Under-Secretaries in two particular government departments in late 2004. Although ministerial reshuffles will mean that the

Figure 3.2 Division of responsibilities between ministers in the Treasury, 2004

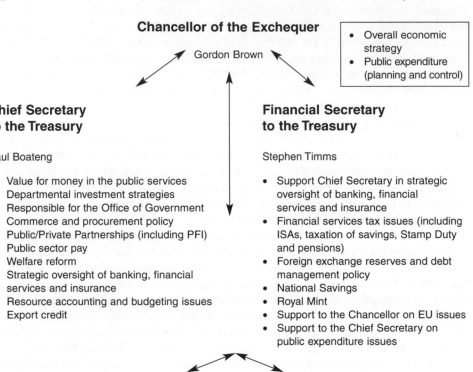

Chancellor of the Exchequer

Gordon Brown

- Overall economic strategy
- Public expenditure (planning and control)

Chief Secretary to the Treasury

Paul Boateng

- Value for money in the public services
- Departmental investment strategies
- Responsible for the Office of Government Commerce and procurement policy
- Public/Private Partnerships (including PFI)
- Public sector pay
- Welfare reform
- Strategic oversight of banking, financial services and insurance
- Resource accounting and budgeting issues
- Export credit

Financial Secretary to the Treasury

Stephen Timms

- Support Chief Secretary in strategic oversight of banking, financial services and insurance
- Financial services tax issues (including ISAs, taxation of savings, Stamp Duty and pensions)
- Foreign exchange reserves and debt management policy
- National Savings
- Royal Mint
- Support to the Chancellor on EU issues
- Support to the Chief Secretary on public expenditure issues

Economic Secretary to the Treasury

John Healey

- Departmental Minister for Customs and Excise
- VAT; alcohol and tobacco duties
- Betting and gaming taxation
- Environmental taxes (climate change levy, landfill tax)
- Transport taxes (road fuel, taxation of company cars, vehicle excise duty, air passenger duty)
- Urban regeneration
- Productivity and enterprise (working with Paymaster General on tax issues)
- Competition and deregulation policy
- Science, research and development
- Welfare to Work and social exclusion issues
- Charities and charity taxation
- Support to the Chancellor on international issues
- Support to the Chief Secretary on public spending issues and selected Cabinet committees
- Support to the Paymaster General on the Finance Bill

Paymaster General

Dawn Primarolo

- Strategic oversight of taxation
- Minister for Inland Revenue
- Income tax, NI contributions and personal tax credits
- Business tax and corporation tax
- Capital Gains tax
- Inheritance tax
- Welfare reform (combatting fraud)

Figure 3.3 Division of responsibilities between ministers in the Department For Education and Skills, 2004

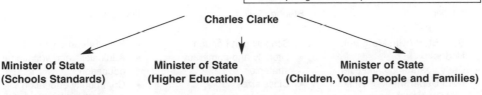

Secretary of State

- Overall responsibility for education policies and strategy, including finance and public expenditure on education
- Responsible for appointments to public bodies and 'quangos' in the sphere of education.

Charles Clarke

Minister of State (Schools Standards)	**Minister of State (Higher Education)**	**Minister of State (Children, Young People and Families)**
David Miliband	Kim Howells	Margaret Hodge

Raising school standards
- Key Stage 3 strategy
- OFSTED
- Excellence in cities
- Education action zones

Higher Education
- Standards in post-19 education
- Widening participation in HE
- Review of student support
- Quality assurance in HE
- Relations with DTI
- HE Funding Council (England)

Children and Young People
- Children's social services
- Child protection
- Children in care
- Youth Service
- Careers Service
- Young people at risk

Reform of Secondary Education
- Diversity in schools
- Specialist schools
- Beacon schools
- City academies

Lifelong learning
- Overview of lifelong learning
- Learning and Skills Council
- Pay in Higher Education
- Student support post-16
- Inspections post-16

Families
- Family and parenting law
- Families and parental responsibility for supporting schools (including family learning)

Remodelling the school workforce
- Support staff in schools
- Teachers' workload
- Teachers' pay, performance, supply and retention
- Teacher training/Teacher Training Agency
- General Teaching Council
- Teachers' pensions
- Teacher misconduct

Reform of 14–19 education/training
- Overview of 14–19 organization and curriculum
- Overview of qualifications policy
- Qualifications and Curriculum Authority

Local organization of schools
- Overview of 5–16 admissions policy
- Local Education Authorities (LEAs)

(Continued)

Figure 3.3   (Continued)

Parliamentary Under-Secretary of State (for Extended and Inclusive Schools and Sure Start (with Department of Work and Pensions))	Parliamentary Under-Secretary of State (for Schools)	Parliamentary Under-Secretary of State (for Skills and Vocational Education)
Lord Filkin	Stephen Twigg	Ivan Lewis
• Sure Start (with Margaret Hodge) • Early years and child care (with Department of Work and Pensions) • Special educational needs • Educational issues in the House of Lords	• Schooling in London • Literacy and numeracy strategies • Class sizes • National curriculum • Citizenship education • Sex education in schools • Equality issues • Rural schools	• Post-14 curriculum • Adult skills and vocational education • Community education • Apprenticeships • Prison education • Lifelong learning • Links between education and business

precise individuals will be moved periodically, the titles and division of departmental responsibilities will remain broadly similar in most cases.

Junior Ministers do not usually attend meetings of the full Cabinet, although they may appear on an *ad hoc* basis, if and when there is an item on the agenda relevant to their particular policy responsibilities. However, once their topic has been dealt with, they leave the Cabinet meeting prior to the next item on the agenda.

Interdependency between the Prime Minister and Cabinet Ministers

As suggested earlier, the power of British Prime Ministers is often exaggerated or misunderstood, so that its variability and contingent character have too often been overlooked. Whereas the 'prime ministerial versus Cabinet government' debate implies a zero-sum conception of political power – whereby greater power for one actor or institution automatically means correspondingly less for the other – the emergence of 'core executive studies' has focused attention on the variability of power relations, with different political actors possessing particular resources, which might themselves vary according to circumstances; power is contingent, as illustrated in Figure 3.4.

It is evident that while the Prime Minister's primary source of power is that of political authority, along with the dispensation of patronage (i.e., ministerial appointment, promotion, demotion and dismissal), individual ministers – along with their departmental civil servants and policy advisers (discussed below) – will generally possess greater time (in which to address a policy or a problem, unless it arises out of a crisis), and expertise,

Figure 3.4   Contextual influences on, and resource interdependency between, Prime Minister and ministerial colleagues

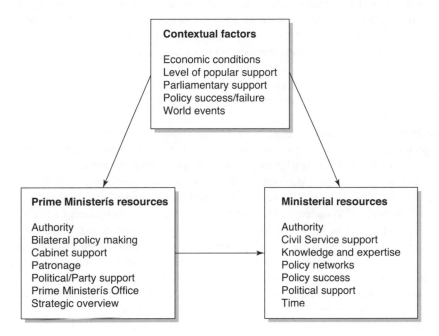

Source: Adapted from Smith, 1999: 75, 2003: 63

derived both from the accumulated wisdom and experience of their department and its senior civil servants, and from the specialist advice proffered by the department's 'client' groups. Also, some ministers will command greater authority by virtue of their – or their department's – status within the core executive; clearly, some ministries will be more prestigious or powerful than others, and this too is likely to enhance their power and bargaining position on particular issues. One only has to consider the brooding presence of Gordon Brown at the Treasury during Tony Blair's premiership to appreciate how a Prime Minister might be constrained on various policy issues by a particularly strong or popular (either in the country, or in the parliamentary party) ministerial colleague.

Furthermore, while a Prime Minister's power can be enhanced on particular policy issues by a high level of Cabinet support, on other issues or on other occasions, this support might not be forthcoming, thereby constraining the Prime Minister's power somewhat. For example, a ministerial reshuffle had been widely expected in July 2004, in which Peter Mandelson would return to the Cabinet, but with Ian McCartney being removed as Chair of the Labour Party. Meanwhile, Geoff Hoon, the Secretary of State for Defence, was being tipped for appointment as Britain's new EU Commissioner. However, a number of senior ministers – particularly John Prescott – apparently objected strongly to these proposed appointments and dismissals, to the extent that the reshuffle was postponed. At the same time, though, Peter Mandelson was despatched to Brussels as Britain's new EU Commissioner, after several senior ministers, including Prescott again, Gordon Brown – whose response, when Blair informed him that he intended reappointing Mandelson to the Cabinet, was 'more concise than it was polite' – and Charles Clarke, made clear to Tony Blair their strong objection to seeing Mandelson returned to the Cabinet for a third time (having been obliged to resign on two previous occasions) (McSmith, 2004; *The Independent on Sunday*, 25 July 2004). Again, therefore, we would emphasize that power in the core executive is neither zero-sum nor constant; it is relational and variable.

The Prime Minister and their ministerial colleagues are therefore heavily dependent upon each other, in various ways, and in varying degrees (depending on particular policies, personalities and circumstances) to ensure the successful development of public policy, and while the Prime Minister may have considerable authority over their Cabinet colleagues much of the time, he/she will still need their support and cooperation, as well as their departmental knowledge, in order to ensure that policy objectives are effectively pursued. In other words, the Prime Minister's authority with regard to Cabinet colleagues must not be characterized as a zero-sum power relationship. Smith is rightly emphatic that: 'Notions of Prime Ministerial government, Cabinet Government, or "Presidentialism" are irrelevant. Power within the core executive is based on dependency, not command', so that even 'resource-rich actors, such as the Prime Minister, are dependent on other actors to achieve their goals' (Smith, 2003: 62). Or as Barberis observes:

> It is certainly simplistic to assume a continuous contest, the Prime Minister set at odds with the rest of the Cabinet. More likely there will be a matrix of (shifting) alliances, the Prime Minister having certain allies (although not always the same ones), pitching alongside one, two or more ... identifiable 'opinion sets'. Besides, a strong Prime Minister may well mean not a weak Cabinet but a strong one and an effective government.
>
> (2000: 27)

Therefore, while some conflicts and disagreements between the Prime Minister and other senior ministers are inevitable from time to time, they must seek, as a far as possible, to work together. An apparently powerful Prime Minister still needs the advice, assistance and acquiescence of their ministerial colleagues, who themselves require the support of the Prime Minister in developing their policies. Furthermore, as already intimated, Prime Minister and Cabinet Ministers alike will sometimes be constrained, and sometimes aided, by exogenous circumstances.

Senior civil servants

Although the British civil service overall comprises more than 500,000 people, those who constitute the senior civil service represent less than 1 per cent of this tally. It is these senior civil servants who have long played a major role in the formulation and administration of public policy. Indeed, the senior civil service has been sporadically subject to the allegation that it is too powerful, having allegedly sought to impose its own views on Cabinet Ministers, or obstructed and undermined them when they declined to accept the civil service 'line' (Benn, 1989: 135, 136; Sedgemore, 1980: 11). Another criticism routinely levelled against senior civil servants concerns their socio-educational background, with the majority of most senior officials traditionally having attended Oxford or Cambridge universities as undergraduates. To their critics – usually towards the Left of the Labour Party – this exclusive or privileged background is either said to render senior civil servants highly conservative in their outlook (and thus instinctively sceptical of Labour governments and egalitarian policies), or 'out of touch' with the ordinary people they are supposed – along with governments – to serve. Indeed, the two criticisms have sometimes been combined, thereby depicting the senior civil service as 'Britain's ruling class' (Kellner and Crowther-Hunt, 1980; see also Benn, 1989: 135; Ponting, 1986: Chapter 3; Williams, 1972: 353). Certainly, it has sometimes been claimed that the socio-educational background of senior civil servants, and the generally conservative or 'establishment' views this allegedly fosters, provides a partial explanation for the alleged failure of 'Old Labour' governments to pursue more radical or 'socialist' policies: such governments and policies were apparently thwarted by senior civil servants who watered-down or otherwise undermined radical policies in order to defend the status quo and 'the establishment' of which they were themselves members.

Even the formal constitutional role ascribed to senior civil servants – also referred to as departmental officials, as well as mandarins – has courted criticism and controversy. The convention is that 'advisers advise, ministers decide' (advisers in this context meaning senior civil servants – 'Special Advisers' will be treated separately, below), and while, as with most aphorisms, there is some truth in this, it ultimately oversimplifies the relationship: the reality is rather more varied and nuanced.

Undoubtedly, a significant role of senior civil servants has been the provision of advice to ministers, this advice being proffered in a variety of guises, such as statistical evidence, the viewpoints elicited from consultations with organized interests, the 'pros and cons' of particular policy options, etc. In so doing, senior civil servants might present their advice in such a way as to 'steer' the minister towards a particular policy decision, one that the departmental officials themselves prefer, rather than one which the minister was known to favour. This is another of the criticisms which has variously been levelled against senior civil servants, namely that as 'gatekeepers' controlling the flow of information reaching their minister, they can exercise discretion, or be selective, in what they allow him/her to see, and thereby subtly influence the minister's policy decision. In describing the presentation of policy options by senior civil servants to ministers, former Labour minister, Gerald Kaufman, recalls that:

> Most submissions consist of three or four pages containing a concise summary of a problem with possible courses of action completing the document. Some officials will just suggest one course of action, for you to take or leave. Others, more cunning, will attempt to confuse you with a choice, while carefully steering you in the direction they want you to go'. (1997: 30)

Figure 3.5 Resource exchange and interdependency between ministers and civil servants

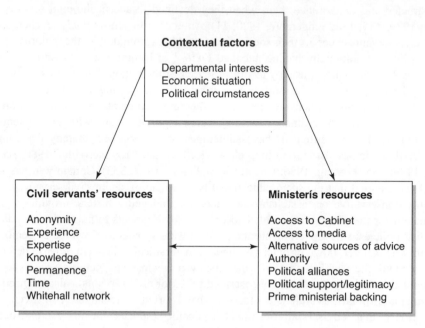

Source: Adapted from Marsh et al., 2001: 168; Smith, 1999: 118, 2003: 63

Yet for some ministers, a heavy reliance on departmental officials has been virtually unavoidable on many issues, not least because of the amount of time which a Cabinet Minister will normally spend outside of their department (as noted above). As a result, most Cabinet Ministers are only able to spend a limited amount of time actually in their departments, which means that a considerable degree of delegation to – and thus discretion by – senior civil servants has often been virtually unavoidable.

However to imply that the normal relationship between ministers and senior civil servants is one of distrust or duplicity is to overlook the extent to which they too depend upon each other to achieve their goals. Just as Prime Ministers and ministers depend upon each other to a large extent to achieve policy objectives, so are ministers and civil servants heavily interdependent, for as Figure 3.5 illustrates, each has resources required by the other, quite apart from the wider contextual political or economic circumstances and constraints within which they operate. For example, the longevity of many senior civil servants in a government department has tended to imbue them with a level of expertise and knowledge within a particular policy subsystem which a minister could rarely expect to match, yet the civil servants themselves will require the political authority and approval of their minister in order to secure the acceptance or adoption of a new policy. Similarly, while civil servants can seek to mobilize colleagues elsewhere in the 'Whitehall network', so too will a Cabinet Minister, when adjudged appropriate, develop alliances with his/her colleagues, and/or obtain the backing of the Prime Minister to overcome apparent civil service resistance.

Consequently, it is misleading to depict the normal relationship between ministers and senior civil servants as one of antagonism and the imposition of policy preferences. Instead, just as the Prime Minister and ministerial colleagues ultimately need the consent and cooperation of each other to achieve policy goals, so ministers and senior civil servants similarly need to work together as far as possible, even though occasional disputes and disagreements will be inevitable, as in all human relationships.

However, one notable trend has developed since the 1980s, and that is a partial downgrading of the senior civil servants' traditional policy advising role. This is partly because the civil service reforms of the Thatcher-Major governments sought to steer the civil service more towards policy delivery and management (Richards, 1997; Theakston, 1999b) – a trend continued apace under Tony Blair's premiership – and partly because ministers have increasingly sought other sources of policy ideas and advice, either as a partial alternative to or in addition to, that proffered by senior civil servants, thereby providing them either with more policy options to select from, or greater originality in terms of possible policy initiatives. This, of course, is linked to our earlier observation about the trend towards more proactive or agenda-setting Cabinet Ministers.

Again, however, we need to be wary of overgeneralizations. While there has been an overall trend towards more proactive or agenda-setting Cabinet Ministers, and a shift in the role of many senior civil servants towards policy management (rather than policy advice and formulation), it is very much a question of degree. Certainly, not all Cabinet Ministers since the 1980s have adopted a proactive or agenda-setting role, and as such, there will remain instances where some senior civil servants continue to play a traditional role in advising their Secretary of State, and presenting a range of policy options, accompanied by recommendations as to the most appropriate or practicable one to choose. As with other relationships in the core executive, much will depend on the context, in terms of specific issues, circumstances, resources, and the minister's own style or personality. According to one senior civil servant interviewed towards the end of the 1990s:

> Your experience around Whitehall depends very much on who your Minister is, and what his/her attitude is. Some Ministers think they are there to run the Department, and others think that the Permanent Secretary is there to do that and they are only there to give broad instructions. I think that will continue to vary depending on the personality and predilection of Ministers.
>
> (quoted in Marsh et al., 2001: 167)

In other words, although there has (as noted previously) been a trend towards more proactive or agenda-setting Cabinet Ministers since the 1980s, and a parallel reorientation of senior civil servants towards policy management and delivery, there remains a close professional and departmental relationship between many senior civil servants and Secretaries of State, along with continued resource dependency and interaction between ministers and mandarins. Nonetheless, many Cabinet Ministers are somewhat less dependent than they used to be on senior civil servants for policy ideas and advice, because of the increased employment, since the 1980s, of Special Advisers.

Special Advisers

As intimated earlier, when we looked at the Prime Minister's role in the policy process, there has been a significant increase in the employment of Special Advisers – sometimes referred to as Policy Advisers – in the core executive, an increase by no means confined to the Prime Minister's Office and Policy Directorate. Most Cabinet Ministers in recent years have appointed their own Special Advisers, therefore contributing greatly to the significant increase since the 1990s, for whereas there were 38 Special Advisers serving the 1990–7 Major governments, this figure has virtually doubled under Tony Blair's premiership. Table 3.3 illustrates the allocation of departmental Special Advisers since 2001 and their respective backgrounds.

The Ministerial Code (which, in 1997, replaced *Questions of Procedure for Ministers*) specifies that each Cabinet Minister is entitled to appoint up to two Special Advisers, subject to approval by the Prime Minister, although in departments with a wider policy remit, such as the Treasury, this limit is usually exceeded, but, again, only with the formal approval of the Prime Minister. In such cases, it is usually expected that the additional advisers will be unpaid.

Some Special Advisers develop such a good working relationship with a particular minister that they accompany them to another department when there is a Cabinet reshuffle. Furthermore, some of the Special Advisers serving ministers in the Blair governments had previously advised them as Shadow Ministers in Opposition prior to May 1997.

The precise role of Special Advisers will vary somewhat, in accordance with which function(s) their particular minister wishes them to fulfil, but most will be primarily involved either in dealing with the media in the presentation of policies (the so-called 'spin doctors'), liasing with the minister's political party, or in providing their minister with new or innovative policy ideas and proposals, whereupon they can – in contrast to senior civil servants, perhaps – 'bring a more adventurous cast of mind … able to suggest things that officials might dismiss as outlandish'. Ultimately, a Special Policy Adviser 'acts as counsellor, confidant and political ally to a Minister surrounded by officials who are – quite correctly – non-political' (James, 1999: 223, 224). According to Pat McFadden, who was formerly a member of Tony Blair's Policy Unit (now Directorate):

> the term 'Special Adviser' covers several different kinds of job. Sometimes it is policy expertise … general speech writing … contact with the media. It is quite difficult in government and in politics to put people into separate boxes and say that the person who deals with the media does not have policy expertise, because they might have both.
>
> (quoted in Blick, 2004: 260)

Many of the Special Advisers serving ministers in the Blair governments are close, not merely in political terms, but socially and personally too (Castle, 1997: 19; Ahmed, 2002: 14). Several of the Special Advisers identified in Table 3.3 were educated at Oxford or Cambridge, for example. Also, many of the Special Advisers embarked upon a 'political' career very soon after graduating. Meanwhile, there are a number of close friendships and

Table 3.3   Departmental Special Advisers since 2001

Department/Ministry	Special Adviser	Background/Previous post
Culture, Media and Sport	Bill Bush	Head of Political Research at the BBC, and former aide to Ken Livingstone at the GLC
	Ruth MacKenzie	Arts Council then General Director of Scottish Opera
Defence	Michael Dugher	Head of Policy for AEEU
	Andrew Hood	Journal Editor, and former Adviser at the Foreign Office
	Richard Taylor	Confederation of British Industry
Education and Skills	Chris Boffey	News Editor of *The Sunday Telegraph*
	William Cavendish	University Lecturer (Economics)
	Robert Hill	Audit Commission
	Lisa Tremble	N/K (not known)
Environment, Food and Rural Affairs	Nicci Collins	Westminster Labour Councillor
	Sheila Watson	Worked for Margaret Beckett since 1990; former Researcher for the Institute of Fiscal Studies
Foreign and Commonwealth Office	Ed Owen	Journalist for the *Stockport Messenger*; Research and Press Officer for Jack Straw in Opposition
	Michael Williams	Amnesty International; BBC World Service; Senior Consultant for United Nations
Health	Darren Murphy	Newcastle Labour Councillor; Economic Development Consultant
	Paul Corrigan	N/K
Home Office	Huw Evans	Home Office civil servant
	Sophie Lindon	Worked for Blunkett in Opposition to 1997, then Special Adviser to Blunkett at the Department of Education
	Nick Pearce	Institute for Public Policy Research
	Katherine Redmond	Former Director of Social Market Foundation
International Development	David Mepham	Labour Party Officer
Northern Ireland	Richard Olszewski	Royal College of Nursing, then lobbyist for Citigate
	Owen Smith	N/K
Scotland	Rhoda Macdonald	N/K
	George McGregor	N/K
Trade and Industry	Jim Godfrey	PR for Institute for Public Policy Research, then worked in Millbank (Labour Party HQ) Press Office

(Continued)

Table 3.3 **(Continued)**

Department/Ministry	Special Adviser	Background/Previous post
	Deborah Lincoln	N/K
	Roger Sharp	Lobbyist for GJW Government Relations
	Kitty Usher	Chief Economist for Britain in Europe Group
Transport	Dan Corry	Economist in Department of Employment, and Treasury, then a Labour Party official. Also worked for Institute for Public Policy Research
	Andrew Maugham	Bank of England; Labour Party official since 1991
	Tom Restrick	N/K
Treasury	Ed Balls	Leader-writer for *The Financial Times*
	Michael Jacobs	Former General Secretary of the Fabian Society
	Ed Miliband	Television researcher
	Sue Nye	Various posts in the Labour Party
Wales	Adrian McMenaman	Various posts in the Labour Party, including Millbank Press Office
	Andrew Bold	N/K
Work and Pensions	Tom Clark	N/K
	Chris Norton	N/K
	Kieran Simpson	Various posts in the Labour Party

Source: Blick, 2004: Chapter 9 and pp. 320–3; Dillon, 2001: 12–13;
www.politicallinks.co.uk/politics2/BIOG/MP; www.red-star-research.org.uk/spec4.html

romantic relationships among some of them, as well as the occasional family ties. For example, Ed Miliband, one of Gordon Brown's Special Advisers at the Treasury, is the brother of David Miliband, who (as we noted above), was one of Tony Blair's Special Advisers in the Downing Street Policy Unit/Directorate before becoming an MP in the 2001 election, and Minister of State for Education thereafter. Ed Miliband's partner, Liz Lloyd, meanwhile, also works in the Policy Directorate, as one of Blair's Special Advisers on Foreign Affairs. Another of Gordon Brown's Economic Advisers, Ed Balls, is married to the Labour MP (since 1997) Yvette Cooper, who subsequently became a Minister of State in the Office of the Deputy Prime Minister. Elsewhere, Professor Paul Corrigan, a Special Adviser in the Department of Health, is married to Labour's Chief Whip, Hilary Armstrong.

Some Policy Advisers also become MPs – and even ministers – themselves, in due course. For example, David Young, who was a Special Adviser to Sir Keith Joseph at the Department of Trade and Industry in the early 1980s, was subsequently appointed Secretary of State at the department following the 1987 election (having been awarded a peerage and a seat in the House of Lords three years earlier) (Blick, 2004: 193–4). More recently, Jack Straw, Foreign Secretary during the second Blair government, and Tony

Banks, Minister of Sport, were both Policy Advisers to ministers in the 1974–9 Labour government. More recently, Hilary Benn (son of veteran Labour Left-winger, Tony Benn) worked as Special Adviser to David Blunkett at the Department of Education for two years (having previously been a councillor in west London for many years), before successfully contesting a 1999 by-election in the Leeds Central constituency. Following the 2001 election, Benn was appointed a Minister of State in the Department for International Development. Even more recently, Ed Balls, just mentioned as one of Gordon Brown's Special Advisers, was adopted as Labour's parliamentary candidate – for the 2005 election – for the safe Labour seat in Normanton, Yorkshire – neighbouring his wife's (Yvette Cooper) Pontefract and Castleford constituency (*The Observer*, 28 December 2003).

One other characteristic of the burgeoning cadre of Special Advisers is the number who have previously worked for one of the plethora of think tanks (as indicated by Table 3.3) which, as we noted in Chapter 2, have also proliferated in Britain since the 1970s, and apparently become a significant source of policy advice and innovation. For example, Dan Corry, a Special Adviser in the Department of Transport after 1997, formerly worked for the Institute for Public Policy Research, as did Nick Pearce, a Special Adviser at the Home Office, and Jim Godfrey, a Special Adviser at the Department of Trade and Industry. Elsewhere, Michael Jacobs, appointed as a Special Adviser to Gordon Brown at the Treasury, in 2004, was formerly general-secretary of the Fabian Society, while Katherine Redmond, a Special Adviser at the Home Office, was once director of the Social Market Foundation.

Although it is difficult to attribute particular policies to specific individuals – not least because policies (as we note in Chapter 2) usually emanate from a variety of sources, and are invariably 'processed' by various individuals and institutions prior to being enacted – some policies since the 1980s do seem to have been closely associated with, or strongly influenced by, particular Special Advisers. For example, it has been suggested that David Young, during his aforementioned time as a Special Adviser to Sir Keith Joseph, played a key role in promoting and preparing the privatization of British Telecom, while in the early 1990s, Christopher Foster, a Special Adviser to John MacGregor, Secretary of State for Transport, played 'an important role in the privatization of British Rail' (Blick, 2004: 193, 231). Meanwhile, Michael Portillo, while a Special Adviser at the Department of Energy in the early 1980s, played an important role – in tandem with the Prime Minister's Policy Unit (see next chapter) – in supervising the stock-piling of coal reserves, which subsequently helped the Thatcher government to crush the 1984–5 miners' strike (Blick, 2004: 208).

More recently, Ed Balls has been deemed 'the brains behind' much of Gordon Brown's economic strategy and the decision to grant independence to the Bank of England immediately following the 1997 election (Ashley, 2002: 15), while Michael Jacobs was apparently instrumental in persuading the second Blair government to increase NI contributions by 1 per cent and spend the extra revenue solely on the NHS (Grice, 2004: 2).

The increasing use of Special Advisers both reflects and reinforces the downgrading of the traditional role of senior civil servants in proffering advice and developing policy – although this role is still important: it is a question of degree, and will depend, to some extent, on both the issues concerned, and the minister involved. However, with civil servants increasingly expected to focus on policy management and 'delivery', Special Advisers have acquired increased scope for initiating or developing policies with ministers. In so doing, they have also contributed to a discernible change in the British policy process to which we will return in the final chapter, namely a shift towards more anticipatory or proactive policy making, in place of the traditional British emphasis on 'reactive policy making'.

Conclusion

In identifying the individuals who collectively comprise the core executive, we have drawn particular attention to the variability of roles which they each play, as shaped by a combination of personal style, the extent to which each has clearly defined policy objectives, and the particular circumstances which prevail at any given juncture. Yet we have also noted some general trends which have occurred since the 1980s, most notably greater ministerial 'activism' in agenda setting and policy initiation, a greater emphasis on policy management and delivery by senior civil servants, and the increasing use, by Cabinet Ministers, of Special Advisers and junior ministers in policy making.

Second, we have emphasized a key theme of 'core executive studies', namely the extent to which the individuals who comprise the core executive are mutually dependent on each other to achieve policy goals (in spite of the changes and trends just summarized). This is intended to move the analysis away from debates about who ultimately possesses power, and therefore shapes public policy, within the core executive, towards a recognition that power is shared between the various actors, and that much policy making is an increasingly interactive process.

Consequently, the individuals within the core executive are dependent on each other to pursue policy objectives, and need regularly to share or exchange resources in order to do so. Crucially, power is not of a zero-sum character, but is both shared between individuals, and also partly contingent upon circumstances and policy issues. Certain individuals within the core executive will be able to exercise greater power on certain issues and in certain circumstances than others. Furthermore, what also enhances and constrains the power of these individual actors, and therefore affects their ability to achieve particular policy goals, are the institutions which are also integral to the core executive, and which often provide forums in which these individuals are obliged to work together. It is the institutional components of the core executive to which we will turn our attention in the next chapter.

Recommended texts and further reading

1. Andrew Blick (2004) *People Who Live in the Dark*, London: Politico's.

    Provides a good, up-to-date overview of the role of Special Advisers in British politics, and the manner in which they have increased, both in number and apparent influence, since the 1960s.

2. David Marsh, David Richards and Martin J. Smith (2001) *Changing Patterns of Governance in the United Kingdom: Reinventing Whitehall?*, Basingstoke; Palgrave, Chapters 6 and 7.

    Chapter 6 summarizes the changing role of Cabinet Ministers in Britain since the 1980s, noting the extent to which they have acquired a more active role in policy making, to the extent of increasingly challenging traditional departmental 'philosophies'. Chapter 7 notes how this, in turn, has had an impact on Cabinet Ministers' relationships with senior civil servants, as the latter have increasingly been steered towards a policy management role. However, there remains a significant degree of reciprocity and mutual dependence.

3. Donald Shell and Richard Hodder-Williams (eds) (1995) *Churchill to Major: The British Prime Ministership Since 1945*, Hurst.

    Useful series of essays focusing on particular aspects of the prime ministership in Britain, including separate chapters on the Prime Minister's relationship with the Cabinet, and Whitehall.

4. Kevin Theakston (1987) *Junior Ministers in British Government*, Oxford: Basil Blackwell.

    The definitive text on this previously under-researched topic. Examines how and why junior ministers have increased in both number and importance, to the extent that many of them have acquired a significant role in policy making within departments.

5. Kevin Theakston (2000) 'Permanent Secretaries: Comparative Biography and Leadership in Whitehall' in R.A.W. Rhodes (ed.) *Transforming British Government, Volume Two: Changing Roles and Relationships*, Basingstoke: Palgrave.

    Contemporary account of the changing roles and responsibilities of senior civil servants in Britain, drawing particular attention to the increased emphasis on policy management and delivery, rather than policy advice and policy making directly.

6. Martin J. Smith (2000) 'Prime Ministers, Ministers and Civil Servants in the Core Executive' in R.A.W. Rhodes (ed.) *Transforming British Government, Volume One: Changing Institutions*, Basingstoke: Palgrave.

    Examines the interaction between Prime Ministers, Cabinet Ministers and senior civil servants with particular reference to notions of mutual dependence and exchange relationships. Thus rejects a zero-sum conception of political power and emphasizes instead the manner and extent to which power is shared between the actors, albeit varying according to personalities, leadership styles, external circumstances and specific policy issues.

7. Gerald Kaufman (1997) *How to be a Minister*, Faber.

    Wry, but highly informative, account of life as a minister, based on the author's own experiences, and full of useful, often amusing, anecdotes. Offers advice on such issues as how a minister should: operate in Cabinet committees; work with organized interests; deal with 10 Downing Street; and 'how to make policy'.

4 The Core Executive, Part Two: Key Institutions

The individuals whose policy roles and responsibilities were discussed in the previous chapter are themselves part of a network of institutions which also constitute the core executive. Those individuals both shape, and are themselves shaped by, these institutions, although much will depend on who the individuals and institutions are, as well as on factors such as external support or circumstances.

What can safely be asserted here is that just as the individuals who form part of the core executive are mutually dependent, by virtue of each possessing resources which various of their colleagues require in order successfully to pursue policy objectives, so are the institutions of the core executive also resource-rich in particular ways, ensuring that they too are characterized by considerable interdependence leading to various exchange relationships. Furthermore, of course, these institutions provide many, if not most, of the resources which the individual policy actors are reliant upon in successfully pursuing policy goals.

The Prime Minister's Office

In order to fulfil his/her myriad functions and responsibilities, while simultaneously supervising the implementation of the government's policies and overall strategy, the Prime Minister is aided by a Prime Minister's Office, which actually comprises four discrete units (Figure 4.1).

The Private Office

This deals with correspondence to and from the Prime Minister, and in so doing, keeps him/her abreast of developments, issues and meetings, as well as keeping the Prime Minister in regular touch with the rest of the core executive and Parliament. In so doing, the Private Office, led by the Prime Minister's Principal Private Secretary, manages the premier's diary, arranges meetings and keeps a record of them. The Private Office is therefore a vital conduit between 10 Downing Street and government departments, or as Smith observes, 'the centre of the Prime Minister's Whitehall network, ensuring he is in touch with all the key actors and institutions within the core executive' (Smith, 1999: 174).

The Political Office

This is the body which keeps the Prime Minister in touch with his/her party, both at parliamentary and extra-parliamentary levels. Due to the constitutional obligation on civil

Figure 4.1 The Prime Minister's Office

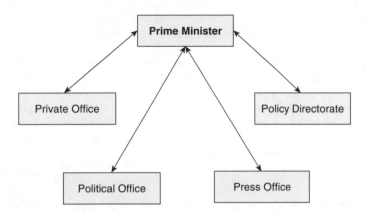

servants to remain politically neutral, the Political Office is actually staffed by political appointees, rather than senior civil servants. It is also partly financed by the governing party's own funds (Burch and Holliday, 1999: 34).

The Press Office

The Press Office both processes the questions submitted to the Prime Minister from the media, and arranges media interviews or press conferences involving the Prime Minister. The Press Office also provides regular – often twice each day – press briefings, via the leader of the Press Office, who also serves as the Prime Minister's official spokesperson or Press Secretary. Tony Blair originally appointed Alistair Campbell as his Press Secretary, although he was certainly not the first high profile or controversial (sometimes becoming the news item or talking point himself) Prime Ministerial Press Officer: an earlier Labour Prime Minister, Harold Wilson, appointed Joe Haines to the post, while Margaret Thatcher's press spokesperson was the pugnacious Bernard Ingham.

The Prime Minister's Press Office also liaises with the press offices located in each of the main government departments, thereby coordinating the release of government information or announcements to the media.

However, for the purpose of this particular study, the most important part of the Prime Minister's Office is the Policy Directorate.

The Policy Directorate

Originally established as the Policy Unit by Harold Wilson in 1974, what is now known as the Policy Directorate has become a major source of policy advice for Prime Ministers. Indeed, the Policy Directorate plays a dual role, for it both keeps the Prime Minister informed of policy proposals and progress in government departments (thereby aiding coordination from the centre of the core executive), while also assisting the Prime Minister in developing policy ideas and initiatives. In this respect, as Smith points out, the Policy

Directorate 'is both reactive and proactive' (1999: 174), while Burch and Holliday similarly note that the Policy Directorate is 'sometimes engaging in forward thinking and policy initiative, sometimes in evaluation of initiatives taken by government departments' (1999: 35). This is confirmed by to two former 'insiders', who explain that:

> The Policy Unit's [Directorate's] job is to keep the Prime Minister in touch with outside thinking, to work on his own ideas and to act as a sounding board for Ministers, advising on the flow of proposals and counter-proposals that pour in continually from all around Whitehall. The Prime Minister can use his Unit as storm troops, invading the complacent hinterland of Whitehall, or as peacemakers, building bridges between warring departments and Ministers. In practice, the Unit tried to do a bit of both: to be both grit and oil in the government machine.
>
> (Hogg and Hill, 1995: 24)

Under Margaret Thatcher's premiership in the 1980s, for example: the Policy Unit participated in her 'famous "judge and jury" sessions, in which Ministers would be called to No. 10 and interrogated on their policies and performance, and by the mid-1980s had become a feared and hated part of their lives' (Hennessy, 2001b: 424). Under Tony Blair's premiership, meanwhile, the Policy Unit/Directorate became 'central to Blair's style of leadership ... was systematically involved in the development of departmental proposals from a very early stage, representing the Prime Minister's preferences in central areas' (Blick, 2004: 276). Or as an eminent contemporary political historian observes: 'The Policy Directorate made Number 10 into more of a policy-making powerhouse for the Prime Minister' (Seldon, 2004: 631).

The Prime Minister's Special Advisers in the Policy Directorate

What has undoubtedly enhanced the 'powerhouse' role of the Policy Directorate is the extent to which it has increasingly been staffed by Special Advisers since the 1970s. Most of these Special Policy Advisers are recruited from outside the civil service, particularly if the Prime Minister wishes to elicit ideas independent of the civil service itself. Margaret Thatcher was renowned for her distrust of much of the senior civil service, and consequently appointed Sir Alan Walters – an academic economist – as her personal Economic Adviser. She did, however, appoint a senior civil servant, Sir Charles Powell (pronounced *pole*) as her special Foreign Policy Adviser.

Tony Blair has evinced a particular penchant for appointing Special Advisers, to the extent that by 2000 (three years after becoming Prime Minister), he had 27 of them working for him (out of a total of 149 staff in the Prime Minister's Office). By the end of 2004, however, the number of Special Advisers in the Policy Directorate had fallen to 19, of whom four were classified as Foreign Policy Advisers. One of the most notable appointments during Tony Blair's premiership was Jonathon Porritt, formerly Director of Friends of the Earth from 1984–90 (and an adviser on environmental matters to Prince Charles), who was appointed as Blair's Special Adviser on the Environment, and Director of the

Government's Sustainable Development Commission in July 2000. Then, following the 2001 general election victory, Blair appointed Andrew Adonis, previously a senior journalist for *The Observer* newspaper, as Head of the 10 Downing Street Policy Directorate, but with a special remit also for advising the Prime Minister on education policy. Another policy adviser appointed by Blair, early in his second term of office, was John Birt, the former Director-General of the BBC, who was allocated the role of advising the Prime Minister on transport issues. More recently, in the summer of 2003, Matthew Taylor, hitherto Director of the Institute for Public Policy Research – and son of the sociologist, journalist and broadcaster, Professor Laurie Taylor – was appointed as the head of the Policy Directorate (Rowan, 2003: 17). Taylor had previously been a keen advocate of Public-Private Partnerships (PPPs), the policy initiative much favoured by Tony Blair, but bitterly opposed by many Labour MPs as 'creeping privatization' of the public sector. Table 4.1 shows some of Special Advisers who have served Tony Blair in the Policy Unit/Directorate since 2000.

It is perhaps worth noting that during the last 20 years or so, several former advisers in the Prime Minister's Policy Unit/Directorate have proceeded to parliamentary or even ministerial careers, with Damian Green, Oliver Letwin, Michael Portillo, John Redwood and David Willetts being notable Conservative examples, and David Miliband, as already intimated, providing a more recent New Labour example of this particular career path.

Of course, the Prime Minister's appointment of such Policy Advisers can be a source of tension with ministerial colleagues, particularly if those Special Advisers are apparently persuading the Prime Minister of the alleged merits of a policy with which the departmental minister disagrees. Just how conflictual the relationships can be was dramatically illustrated by Nigel Lawson's resignation as Chancellor of the Exchequer in 1989, following Margaret Thatcher's refusal to dispense with her Economic Adviser, Sir Alan Walters (see below, in section on prime ministers versus chancellors).

Much more recently, October 2002 saw the resignation of Estelle Morris, Secretary of State for Education in the second Blair government. Although a variety of factors were cited by Morris to explain her decision to quit, it soon became apparent that one of the issues which had driven her to despair was the conflict between her own views on certain education issues, and those of Andrew Adonis, Blair's Head of the 10 Downing Street Policy Unit/Directorate and Special Adviser on education at the time. In particular, it was variously reported that Adonis was making known his support for the right of universities to charge 'top-up fees' as a means of increasing their income (Ahmed et al., 2002: 18; McSmith, 2002: 6; Wintour, 2002: 10). Morris, however, was strongly opposed to 'top-up fees', not least on the grounds that they would deter young people from working-class backgrounds from pursuing a university education (and in so doing, undermine the government's professed objective of widening access to higher education).

Meanwhile, during the first Blair government, John Prescott found himself increasingly at odds with Tony Blair's then transport adviser, Geoffrey Norris, to the extent that the latter, at Prescott's insistence, was given another policy brief (Rawnsley, 2001: 296). More recently, there has apparently been tension between Andrew Adonis and Estelle Morris's successor at the Department For Education and Skills, Charles Clarke, over the issue of

Table 4.1   Examples of Tony Blair's Special Advisers in the Policy Unit/Directorate since 2000

Policy area/issue	Policy adviser	Background/previous post
Head of Policy Unit/Directorate	David Miliband	Institute of Public Policy Research
	Andrew Adonis	Journalist with *The Financial Times*, then *The Observer*
	Matthew Taylor	Director of Institute of Public Policy Research
Devolution	Alasdair McGowan	Special Adviser in Ministry of Defence until 2000
Economy	Derek Scott	Economist with Shell, then Barclays Zoete Wedd Bank; Economic Adviser to the SDP
	Simon Virley	Civil servant in Department of Transport, then the Treasury
Foreign Affairs	Roger Liddle	Councillor in Oxford, then (for SDP) in Lambeth; consultancy
	Anna Wechberg	Official in the Department for International Development, and official with the International Monetary Fund
Health and Social Services	Robert Hill	Audit Commission
	Simon Stevens	Senior NHS Manager; Policy Adviser in Department of Health
	Julian Le Grand	Professor of Social Policy at the London School of Economics (LSE)
Home Affairs	David North	Civil Servant
	Justin Russell	Labour Party Official
Inequality and Social Exclusion	Geoff Mulgan	Director of DEMOS (think tank)
Trade and Industry and Employment	Geoffrey Norris	Labour Party researcher; Adviser to Blair on transport before being given trade and industry brief
Transport	Geoffrey Norris	Labour Party researcher
	John Birt	Director-General of the BBC
	Matthew Elson	Management consultant
Welfare (including children, the elderly and women)	Carey Oppenheim	Child Poverty Action Group; Senior Lecturer in Social Policy, South Bank University; Research Director, Institute for Public Policy Research

Source: Blick, 2004: 321–2; Kavanagh and Seldon, 2000: 266–7, 352; www.dodonline.co.uk; www.politicallinks.co.uk/politics2/BIOG; www.red-star-research.org.uk

sixth forms. Adonis was reported to be proposing the abolition of school sixth forms, so that all A-levels would be studied in sixth form colleges instead, a proposal to which Clarke was strongly opposed (*The Sunday Times*, 22 June 2003). Yet in spite of such conflicts, one in-depth study has suggested that: 'For a Department, they [Special Advisers] can be an irritant, not a major threat', not least because, on many issues, 'their grasp can only be superficial compared with the knowledge and expertise of civil servants in Ministers' Departments' (Lee et al., 1998: 117).

We noted in the previous chapter the difficulties of attributing specific policies directly to individual Special Advisers, although some were identifiable as advocates of, or strongly associated with, particular policy initiatives. With the same caveat in mind, we can cite a few policies, since the 1980s, which have been advocated by, or closely associated with, Special Advisers in the Prime Minister's Policy Unit/Directorate. At a general level, Ferdinand Mount – briefly head of the Policy Unit during 1982–3 – is credited with having 'contributed to her [Margaret Thatcher's] philosophical and moral approach', for he too was 'a firm advocate of the renewal of discipline and responsibility'. Consequently 'a number of policy proposals flowed form Mount's philosophy', including tax changes beneficial to married couples, education vouchers, stronger policing and more generous discounts for those wishing to buy their council house (Blick, 2004: 200; Thatcher, 1993: 278–9). Mount's successor as head of the Policy Unit, Brian Griffiths, also provided Thatcher with 'a moral basis for her ideological convictions' (Brown, 1990).

Meanwhile, in the early 1980s, during the first of his two periods as Margaret Thatcher's Special (Economic) Adviser, Alan Walters is credited with having played a significant role in influencing or emboldening her stance on aspects of economic policy, particularly curbing public expenditure and reducing the Public Sector Borrowing Requirement (PSBR), even to the extent that Thatcher's stance caused some concern to various of her Cabinet colleagues, including, on occasions, her then Chancellor Geoffrey Howe (Blick, 2004: 215; Hennessy, 2001a: 410–11; Hoskyns, 2000: 273; Thatcher, 1993: 133–6).

More specifically, following his recruitment to the Policy Unit after the Conservatives' 1983 election victory, John Redwood played a significant role in 'setting up a government mechanism for implementing the privatization agenda, which he'd been trying to persuade Thatcher to pursue since the early years of her leadership in the mid-1970s' (Blick, 2004: 201). Meanwhile, John Hoskyns, who was appointed Thatcher's first head of the Policy Unit in 1979 – but with the title 'Senior Policy Adviser to the Prime Minister' – seems to have played a significant role in shaping the Conservative governments' programme of trade union reform (Blick, 2004: 205–6).

During John Major's subsequent 1990–97 Conservative governments, Nick True, one of the Prime Minister's early appointments as a Special Adviser in the Policy Unit, played a notable role in developing the 'Citizen's Charter', an initiative which it was hoped would make public sector employees provide a more efficient and courteous service to their public sector 'clients' or 'consumers' (Hogg and Hill, 1995: 95–6; Blick, 2004: 240).

During Tony Blair's first term of Office, David Miliband – at one stage, head of the Policy Unit – 'helped develop Blair's ideological approach … [as] an advocate of what came to be labelled as the "Third Way"' (Blick, 2004: 273). Miliband also, along with Geoff Mulgan (another of Blair's Special Advisers in the Policy Unit during the first term of office), played a significant role in the development of New Labour's policies for tackling social exclusion and poverty (Riddell, 2001: 33). Meanwhile, as we noted above, Andrew Adonis was widely believed to have played a significant role in persuading Blair to proceed with the proposals for university top-up fees.

Contextualizing the Prime Minister's institutional support

The degree of institutional support provided by the Prime Minister's Office – especially the Policy Directorate – might seem to provide (further) evidence of prime ministerial power at the centre or apex of government, and dominance *vis-à-vis* their ministerial colleagues. However, it can just as readily be interpreted as an indication of relative weakness, for Prime Ministers are effectively seeking to match the support and resources which Cabinet colleagues derive from their departmental officials, Special Advisers and 'client' groups. After all, as Kavanagh and Seldon note:

> Compared with most Departmental Ministers, a Prime Minister has a tiny budget, a small staff, and few formal powers. He has to work through Secretaries of State, in whom statutory powers are vested. Viewed from Number Ten, Whitehall Departments can look at times like a series of baronial fiefdoms, to which it can only react. Departmental ministers have large staffs, budgets, policy networks, information and expertise ... The strength of most Departments is such that it requires enormous willpower, obstinacy, political authority, and excellent briefing for the Prime Minister to prevail.
>
> (2000: 318)

This perspective was effectively endorsed by Tony Blair's personal opinion poll and campaign adviser, and 'focus group' organizer, Philip Gould, when he asserted that:

> The centre actually has far less power than is typically ascribed to it. Anyone who spends time at Number 10 quickly realises that it is a tiny corner of a huge government machine, staffed with talented people, but lacking the resources necessary to be a commanding and dominating nerve centre. The idea that officials at Number 10 headquarters are smoothly pulling strings and levers, and effortlessly controlling events, is ridiculous.
>
> (1999: xxiii)

Furthermore, Prime Ministers also encounter the paradox that the more staff and resources they employ in order to underpin or bolster their authority, the greater can be the problem of coordination of such staff and resources, the possibility of conflict – either between these staff themselves or with others in the core executive – and the potential for 'information overload'. According to one academic expert on the core executive, 'whilst institutional resources have increased, the power of the Prime Minister to achieve his or her goals has not' (Smith, 2003: 62). With regard to the last point, for example, Richard Rose refers to Tony Blair's reported appointment of over 300 task forces during his first term of office, a tally which sounds highly impressive, Rose observes, before enquiring (rather rhetorically): 'How much time does he have to give to their reports?' (2001: 154). With particular reference to Tony Blair's enhanced and expanded Policy Directorate, for example, one writer has highlighted the risk of 'overburdening an already fully stretched Number 10'. (Seldon, 2004: 631).

Certainly, it is apparent that the more time or energy which any Prime Minister devotes to one particular policy, the less time and energy this leaves to pursue other policies. Hence: 'Management by exception is the only way to find time to deal with high priority matters' (Rose, 2001: 155). Even 'activist' or 'innovator' Prime Ministers – as personified by Margaret Thatcher and Tony Blair – cannot involve themselves in more than a small number of policy issues at any one time; they lack 'the time, resources and the inclination to occupy, on a significant and continuous basis, policy space outside that of high policy', high policy referring to economic and foreign affairs (Norton, 2000: 105–6). If Prime Ministers do attempt to intervene and involve themselves more widely, they are likely to deal only superficially with each individual policy issue or problem, while also potentially antagonizing more ministerial colleagues, each of whom may well resent what they consider to be ill-judged or half-hearted 'interference' in their departmental policy domain (Donoughue, 1987: 6; Pym, 1984: 16).

While most Prime Ministers have indeed sought to concern themselves with a few specific policies – Heath and Britain's entry into the (then) European Community in the early 1970s, Thatcher and the Poll Tax or Blair and peace in Northern Ireland – it has been suggested that: 'Few post-war Prime Ministers … have left much of an intended and enduring legacy on public policy', (with Thatcher as the obvious exception), reflecting the fact that while the precise origins of any individual policy are often difficult to pin-point accurately, 'most derive not from Number Ten, but from the parties' work in Opposition or friendly think tanks, or from within the Departments, which then go on to shape them and in so doing can change them beyond all recognition' (Kavanagh and Seldon, 2000: 316–7; Smith et al., 2000: 161–2).

Cabinet Office

The Cabinet Office plays a crucial role in the coordination of public policy in Britain. Located primarily at 70 Whitehall – but with a connecting corridor to 10 Downing Street – and a few offices in nearby streets, it has been described as 'something of a corporate headquarters overseeing government strategy' (Kavanagh and Seldon, 2000: 70). In pursuing this objective, the Cabinet Office has two organizational 'branches', as illustrated by Figure 4.2.

The Cabinet Secretariat

The primary role of the Cabinet Secretariat is to assist the Prime Minister and ministers in their role as chairs of Cabinet committees, and to ensure that such business is conducted as effectively and efficiently as possible, both before and after such committee meetings. It claims that:

Figure 4.2   The structure of the Cabinet Secretariat

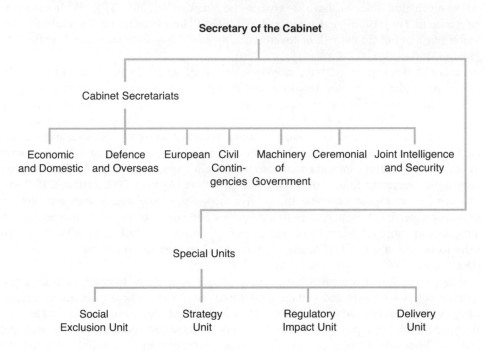

The sole objective of the Cabinet Office Secretariat is to provide an effective, efficient and impartial service to the Cabinet and its committees, and co-ordinating departmental contributions to the Government's work … The Office ensures that decisions are consistent with overall government policy and where appropriate, co-ordinates effective follow-up policy decisions.

(Cabinet Office, 1997: 5, 15).

This entails the Cabinet Secretariat:

- preparing Cabinet committee meetings, setting their agendas (as requested by the chairperson), and circulating the relevant papers to the relevant ministers in advance of the meetings;
- recording the minutes, conclusions and policy decisions, and distributing these to the relevant ministers;
- monitoring the subsequent progress of inter-departmental policy issues;
- facilitating coordination between departments when they are affected by, or involved in, a particular policy initiative.

The Cabinet Secretariat is actually comprised of seven discrete secretariats, namely:

1   *Economic and Domestic*, which deals with domestic and economic policy issues, working with the relevant Cabinet committees in these policy spheres, and also coordinating the

government's legislative programme. It also seeks to secure agreement between departments when disputes arise over policy issues.

2 *Defence and Overseas*, focusing on foreign affairs, and diplomatic or military responses to overseas crises or threats to national security. It seeks to ensure that all departments' existing or proposed policies are compatible with Britain's diplomatic, defence and national security interests. The head of the Defence and Overseas Secretariat also serves as the Prime Minister's Special Adviser on Foreign Policy in the Policy Directorate.

3 *European*, which coordinates European Union (EU) policies *vis-à-vis* the work of government departments, and ensures that departmental policies are compatible with EU directives and regulations, and with Britain's EU obligations.

4 *Civil Contingencies*, established immediately after the 2001 election (and partly prompted by the foot-and-mouth epidemic which itself had delayed the general election), dealing with events or emergencies likely to cause serious domestic disruption. The Civil Contingencies Secretariat not only seeks to ensure that policy makers can deal swiftly and effectively when faced with a national crisis or disaster, entailing the facilitating of interdepartmental coordination, it also engages in forward or predictive planning in order to identify, and thereby pre-empt or prevent, such crises from occurring. It also fosters policy learning by extrapolating the lessons which can be gleaned from previous crises, thereby considering how a similar crisis or disaster could be better tackled if it reoccurred.

5 *Machinery of Government* (Central Secretariat until 2001), is concerned with the operation and organization of the core executive and issues concerning ministerial responsibility and accountability as well as with standards and ethical issues arising from the relationships between ministers, civil servants and Special Advisers.

6 *Ceremonial*, whose primary responsibility concerns the award of honours, as in the New Year or Queen's Birthday Honours List.

7 *Joint Intelligence and Security*, is concerned with identifying, monitoring and resisting threats to national security, and combating terrorism.

Special units

Alongside the various secretariats, the Cabinet Office also enshrines several 'special units' which are either intended to facilitate better coordination of cross-departmental policy issues and initiatives, or to ensure that policies are being implemented effectively, and in accordance with specified government objectives.

The *Social Exclusion Unit* was established in December 1997 to tackle socio-economic deprivation and incorporate the 'underclass' back into British society, although in May 2002, the Social Exclusion Unit was relocated to the newly-established Office of the Deputy Prime Minister. The creation of the Social Exclusion Unit derived from recognition of the multidimensional and inter-connected character of 'social exclusion' – reflected and reinforced by such phenomena as crime and juvenile delinquency, deprived neighbourhoods, homelessness or substandard housing, teenage pregnancies, truancy, etc. – which therefore necessitated the active involvement of several government departments. The inauguration of the Social Exclusion Unit was thus intended to foster the interaction and coordination required to implement policies which would eradicate social exclusion. In this respect, it could be seen as a good example of Tony Blair's professed desire to pursue 'joined-up government'.

The *Strategy Unit* was established in July 2002, as a result of a merger of the Performance and Innovation Unit, the Prime Minister's Forward Strategy Unit, and the

Policy Studies Directorate of the Centre for Management and Policy Studies. Headed by Geoff Mulgan – previously director of both the Performance and Innovation Unit, and the Forward Strategy Unit, as well as a former head of DEMOS, one of the think tanks closely associated with New Labour – the role of the Strategy Unit is to facilitate 'joined-up' thinking and government. This will entail the Strategy Unit engaging in such exercises as long-term strategic reviews of major policies, as well as consideration of cross-cutting policy issues, and the need for interdepartmental coordination. It will also engage in 'strategic audits', to gauge progress towards specific targets or objectives.

In pursuit of this role, the Strategy Unit has a staff whose number fluctuates between 80–100, and which is recruited from a plethora of institutions, both within and beyond the core executive, including senior civil servants from government departments, businesses (such as Ford and Glaxo), voluntary sector organizations, universities (including the LSE, and Harvard), and think tanks such as the Institute of Economic Affairs (IEA) and the Institute for Public Policy Research (IPPR) (Cabinet Office, 2003a: 5).

Although part of the Cabinet Office, the Strategy Unit has very close links with 10 Downing Street, reporting to the Prime Minister via the Cabinet Secretary. Indeed, the closeness of the links are such that a 2003 Briefing Note on its role and responsibilities, published by the Cabinet Office, was entitled *The Prime Minister's Strategy Unit*. This illustrates how the formal boundaries between certain parts of the core executive can sometimes become blurred, or almost overlap, so close are the relationships, exchanges of information and coordination of policies in the pursuit of 'joined-up government'.

The Strategy Unit was established with the avowed objective of providing 'a strong focus on evidence-based policy and analytic rigour', yet with a 'strong emphasis on creativity and challenging conventional wisdom' (www.strategy.gov.uk/about). It simultaneously examines the progress and efficacy of existing policies, considers the implications of proposed policies which have yet to be finalized or implemented, and identifies areas or issues where new policies might be warranted. For example, in the late summer of 2003, the Strategy Unit published an interim report – in lieu of a full report in 2004 – into 'binge drinking' among young people. This report reflected growing ministerial concern about alcohol abuse (excessive drinking) by young people in Britain, particularly among women (*The Observer*, 21 December 2003). Although this was ostensibly a health issue, it also had serious implications for the Home Office, due to the public disorder – crime, violence and vandalism – deriving from drunkenness in Britain's towns and cities at weekends. Hence the need to formulate a coordinated, interdepartmental approach, under the auspices of the Cabinet Office's Strategy Unit.

The *Regulatory Impact Unit*, as its appellation implies, is concerned to gauge the impact of various regulations in the implementation of public policy. In particular, it seeks to evaluate the impact of regulations on business, although the impact of regulations on the public and voluntary sectors are also considered. In so doing, the Regulatory Impact Unit seeks to determine whether various regulations are absolutely necessary, so that if they cannot be dispensed with, removed, they are at least fair and effective in their application, and not too detrimental to enterprise, economic growth and innovation. In performing this function, the Regulatory Impact Unit is also concerned with the effects of regulations emanating from the EU, and their impact on business and public policy in Britain.

The *Delivery Unit* was established by Tony Blair, but under the auspices of the Cabinet Office, to facilitate the effective implementation of the government's professed policy priorities, most notably the modernization of public services, and the tackling of social exclusion. In so doing, the Delivery Unit keeps the Prime Minister informed of the progress which relevant government departments are making in meeting their particular policy objectives and performance targets. This, in turn, enables potential or actual problems and obstacles to be identified, and appropriate remedial action to be taken. The Delivery Unit is headed by one of Tony Blair's Special Advisers, Professor Michael Barber.

Through these various secretariats and units, therefore, the Cabinet Office seeks to counter the innate trend towards departmentalism (discussed below), and ensure that there is coherence and coordination between ministers and their departments at all 'stages' of the policy process. In this respect, the Cabinet Office has become even more important in the context of Tony Blair's avowed commitment to 'joined-up government', although critics are inclined to view this enhanced role, in conjunction with that of the Downing Street Policy Directorate (formerly Unit), as a further manifestation of Blair's alleged 'control freakery'.

Government departments

There has long been a widespread recognition among political scientists that government departments are the primary loci of most contemporary decision taking and policy making within the core executive (Burch and Holliday, 1996: 71; Headey, 1974: 60; Hogwood and Mackie, 1985: 47, 58; James, 1999: 12, 172; Madgwick, 1991: 169; Richardson and Jordan, 1979: 25–34; Smith, 1999: 109; 2003: 79; Smith et al., 1993: 567–94, 1995). Even following in-depth, interview-based research on the various changes and reforms in the core executive since the 1980s, Marsh et al. remain convinced that:

> departments are both the *key actors and institutions at the centre of the policy making process*. They continue to provide the foci in which policy is made. Thus, although we acknowledge that changes brought about by governance have altered both the actors and the distribution of resources in the policy making arena, most resources remain concentrated within Whitehall Departments. So, it is important to recognise that Departments continue to provide the key terrain in which power can be located within the British political system.
>
> (2001: 249, original emphasis)

Certainly, even when broad policy objectives and strategy have been determined via the Cabinet and/or the Prime Minister, the detailed formulation of most policies occurs inside individual departments, involving interaction and between ministers, junior ministers, special advisers and civil servants, for 'departments … are where concentrations of political and bureaucratic resources are located and, as such, they both influence the development of policy, and structure the behaviour of other actors within the core executive' (Smith et al., 2000: 163). However, a number of government departments will also be in regular discussions with their 'client' organized interests when developing policy, thereby constituting *policy communities* (whose importance is such that they will be discussed separately in the next chapter).

Although many government departments are concerned with one particular policy area or subsystem (health, transport, etc.) these are invariably highly detailed or specialized, and so the departments invariably comprise several policy directorates or units. These reflect the different aspects of policy within a particular subsystem, and the extent to which such fragmentation and specialization means that the technical details of many policies are determined deep within government departments. For example, the main subdivisions – directorates – within the Department of Health, each covering specific aspects of health care and medical provision, are:

- Children, Older People and Social Care Services Directorate
- Public Health and Clinical Quality Directorate
- Specialist Health Services Directorate
- Nursing, Health and Social Care Directorate
- NHS Human Resources Directorate
- Research Analysis and Information Directorate
- Policy Directorate.

The Home Office is similarly internally structured and subdivided, reflecting the range of highly specific or specialist areas of policy for which it is responsible. Among the directorates and 'groups' nested within the Home Office are the:

- Immigration and Nationality Directorate
- Community Policy Directorate
- Policing and Crime Reduction Group
- Criminal Policy Group
- Organized Crime, Drugs and International Directorate.

Many of these individual directorates and groups within the Home Office are themselves subdivided into a range of units, so that the Criminal Policy Group, for example, enshrines the:

- Criminal Justice Reform Unit
- Justice and Victims Unit
- Juvenile Offenders Unit
- Mental Health Unit
- Sentencing and Offences Unit
- Correctional Policy Unit.

Such degrees of specialization and subdivision mean that much detailed policy work is conducted deep within government departments, with senior ministers often seeking to provide strategic leadership and direction, based on their and/or the Cabinet's overall objectives, and only occasionally immersing themselves in the administrative minutiae of specific policies. The degree of specialization within government departments is such that junior ministers, rather than the Secretary of State, are more likely to become involved in issues concerning specific directorates and units, for as we noted in the previous chapter, junior ministers are usually ascribed responsibility for a particular aspect of a department's policy functions.

For example, in the Department of Health, an issue arising from the Children, Older People and Social Care Services Directorate, which requires political consideration or approval, is likely, in the first instance, to be brought to the attention of the Minister of State for Health, who has particular responsibility for community health issues, including those relating to children and the elderly.

The degree of specialization – often highly technical or administrative – which characterizes the policy work of many government departments, is a major reason why senior ministers have often found it difficult to make a significant impact, at least in the short term. Traditionally, much of the detailed or specialist work within the subdivisions of government departments has been undertaken by senior, or even middle-ranking, civil servants, with a relatively high degree of autonomy and discretion. Ministers generally lacked the time, expertise or inclination to immerse themselves in technical policy detail or day-to-day issues, and had they attempted so to involve themselves, they would have very quickly become overwhelmed. Only since the 1980s, as we noted in the previous chapter, have more ministers sought to adopt a more proactive policy role, aided by junior ministers – who have themselves acquired more extensive policy responsibilities in recent years – and Special Advisers.

Previously, many senior ministers adopted a primarily managerial or strategic oversight role with regard to their department. This, in turn, contributed towards the development or maintenance of discrete departmental philosophies. As we also noted in the previous chapter, even when certain ministers did seek to introduce changes of policy or departmental strategy, they were often 'defeated' by the strength or prevalence of a particular ethos within their department.

Departmental cultures

One of the most significant features of many of these government departments is the extent to which they have embodied a particular prevalent 'philosophy', or what Marsh et al. (2001: Chapter 4) characterize as 'departmental cultures'. These departmental philosophies or cultures have significantly shaped many departments' overall policy perspectives and approaches to problems, including how problems are defined – or denied – in the first place, thereby serving to shape the institutional agenda. The dominant ethos of various departments is summarized in Table 4.2. It can be seen, for example, that the Department of Trade and Industry has evinced a form of political schizophrenia, for the Trade side, according to one of its former permanent secretaries, has enshrined 'a strong Cobdenite[1] free trading ethos' (quoted in Smith, 1999: 132), while the Industry side tended to be rather more interventionist (Sewill, 1975: 44), although both 'sides' would claim that their particular perspectives, international free trade and domestic economic intervention, were intended to promote or protect British manufacturing industry and jobs, at least until the late 1980s, by which time a series of Thatcherite Secretaries of State had begun to effect a reorientation away from the department's hitherto *dirigisme* (Marsh et al., 2001: 82–4).

---

[1]Richard Cobden was a prominent mid-19th-century advocate of free trade and economic liberalism, and was thus an active supporter of the Anti-Corn Law League, formed in 1839.

Table 4.2   Dominant ethos in various government departments

Department or ministry	Prevailing policy ethos
Agriculture, Fisheries and Food (abolished in 2001)	Protecting British farmers through the defence of farm subsidies.
Defence	Until 1990, maintain Britain's military capability (in partnership with the USA) to deter or repel Soviet invasion of Western Europe.
Education	Until relatively recently, widely perceived to be in favour of extending comprehensive education.
Foreign and Commonwealth Office	1 Promoting/protecting British interests through diplomacy. 2 Pro-Europe.
Home Office	1 Social liberalism (from 1960s to 1980s) on law and order. 2 Increasingly tough on immigration and asylum-seeking. 3 Resistant to 'open government' and freedom of information.
Department of Social Security	Until mid-1980s, committed to 'universalist' principles of welfare entitlement delineated by 1942 Beveridge Report, but has since shifted towards greater emphasis on targeting, selectivity and tackling social security fraud.
Trade and Industry	1 Trade 'division' in favour of international free trade. 2 Industry 'division' interventionist in domestic industry, until late 1980s at least.
Transport	Promoting car ownership, road haulage and other forms of private transport, rather than expanding public transport.
Treasury	1 Maintaining strict control over public expenditure. 2 Maintaining 'the City's' role as a major international centre for currency transactions/investments and invisible earnings. Often accused of a bias against manufacturing industry, and thus of neglecting Britain's domestic manufacturing sector.

Source: Adapted from Smith et al., 2001: Chapter 4.

The Home Office, meanwhile, from the 1960s until at least the 1980s, was widely viewed as a source of social liberalism, due largely to the fact that the latter half of the 1960s witnessed the abolition of the death penalty, the end of theatre censorship, the liberalization of abortion and divorce, and the legalization of homosexuality, while both the 1960s and 1970s heralded various laws to outlaw racial and sexual discrimination. Even during the Thatcher years, some writers have claimed, successive Conservative Home Secretaries had little notable effect in bringing about significant or permanent change in the 'social liberalism' of the Home Office with regard to criminal justice and penal matters (Marsh et al., 2001: 72–7). Certainly, the Home Office's conservative critics have viewed it as too concerned with the rehabilitation of criminals and offenders, rather than retribution through harsher punishment and longer prison sentences. Yet during the same period, the Home Office has also presided over increasingly stringent controls on immigration, with various Acts of Parliament since the 1960s concerned to limit the right to enter Britain on a long-term or permanent basis.

In these respects, many Conservatives (and various pro-Conservative newspapers) hold the Home Office at least partly responsible for the alleged decline of morality and breakdown of social order in Britain since the late 1960s, as evinced by increased divorce, illegitimacy and single parents, along with increases in sexually transmitted diseases, crime and other forms of antisocial behaviour, as well as 'excessive' immigration (in spite of the increasingly stringent conditions and restrictions it has sought to impose on the latter).

Meanwhile, what was, until relatively recently, the Department for Education and Science, had been accused (by its Conservative critics) of being preoccupied with promoting comprehensive schools (and of therefore being hostile to private schooling and parental choice), and diluting academic standards in order to enable more pupils to obtain qualifications, as part of an apparent concern with pursuing egalitarianism and equality of opportunity. Certainly, a former Conservative Secretary of State for Education, Kenneth Baker, once claimed that: 'Of all the Whitehall Departments, the DES [Department for Education and Science] was among those with the strongest in-house ideology. There was a clear 1960s ethos and a very clear agenda which permeated virtually all civil servants … It was devoutly anti-excellence, anti-selection, and anti-market' (1993: 168).

The establishment of a 'departmental philosophy' can be explained by reference to three inter-related factors. First, there is the notion of 'custom and practice', whereby a certain way of approaching issues or problems becomes the operational norm within a department – 'how things are done'.

Second, this operational norm is internalized by the senior civil servants within a department, so that they adopt a particular set of principles and practices – praxis – when dealing with policies. Those in the highest echelons of the civil service are likely to have spent their whole careers – 30 years or more – in Whitehall, and thus internalized a specific set of norms and values which strongly influences how they approach decision making in their department. Younger civil servants, meanwhile, will be socialized, through their career development, into adopting these values also, thereby contributing to the continuity of the departmental philosophy irrespective, to a considerable degree, of the political complexion of the governing party at any particular juncture.

Crucially, the departmental philosophy can sometimes become so pronounced or ingrained that a new minister, intent on pursuing a significant change of policy, will find him/herself being 'persuaded' by their officials that the proposed policy is unrealistic, requires more consideration, needs to be moderated, or ought be deferred until circumstances are more propitious. As we will note below, many would-be radical or reform-minded ministers have 'gone native' by themselves adopting their department's perspective, so that relative continuity of policy, rather than radical change, has often prevailed.

Third, many government departments will have close links with particular organized interests, thereby facilitating the establishment of policy communities. As will be discussed more fully in the next chapter, such close linkages themselves serve to underpin a departmental philosophy, as senior civil servants and the leaders of the relevant organized interests adopt a broadly similar approach to issues. Indeed, with senior departmental officials and leaders of a department's 'client' group engaged in an ongoing process of consultation, bargaining and negotiation, the scope for radical departures from existing policies is further reduced, thus ensuring that the extant stance remains the 'norm'.

Needless to say, the existence of 'departmental philosophies' has often meant that much policy making in Britain has been predominantly incremental, with continuity more common than change, and such changes that have been effected often tending to be piecemeal. Rapid or dramatic policy change has been the exception rather than the norm.

Certainly, a department's 'in-house ideology' means that when faced with a problem, only a relatively narrow range of options or solutions have usually been considered, with senior officials insisting on the importance of effectiveness, practicability and what is deemed 'realistic'. This usually militates against (at least in the short term) the wholesale abandonment or repeal of existing policies, or radical new initiatives which depart significantly from the status quo.

Only occasionally, therefore, have individual ministers significantly changed a department's prevalent philosophy, and thereby successfully effected a change in policy orientation. Such occasions, of course, will also depend on propitious circumstances in the wider economic or political environment, in accordance with the third of Kingdon's three policy streams, that of the 'political stream'. Such change will also entail that, in accordance with the 'policy streams' model of agenda setting identified by Kingdon, a reform-minded minister will already have identified, or been persuaded of, a particular policy solution to an acknowledged problem.

Yet it is also the case that while individual ministers can occasionally instigate change in their department's prevailing philosophy or policy perspective – what Smith et al. term 'a paradigm shift' (2000: 151) – it is usually necessary for a subsequent minister to maintain the momentum in order for the initial change to become more permanent. Otherwise, when a Cabinet reshuffle moves the original reforming minister to another department (or he/she returns to the backbenches), the momentum of his/her reform is likely to dissipate, and the department is likely to revert back to its traditional policy perspective.

For example, Smith et al. (2000: 150–2; Smith, 1999: 133–6) suggest that it was David Young, during the late 1980s, rather than Sir Keith Joseph, at the beginning of the decade (and a subsequent succession of neo-liberal ministers during the mid-1980s), who enjoyed greater success in steering the Industry 'half' of the Department of Trade and Industry away from its interventionist ethos, towards a rather more neo-liberal stance (rebranding it as 'the Department for Enterprise'), while it was Peter Lilley, during the early 1990s, rather than Norman Fowler, in the mid-1980s, who 'successfully altered the policy bias' (Smith et al., 2000: 152) of the Department of Social Security. Similarly, at the Home Office, it was Michael Howard in the early 1990s, rather than David Waddington in the late 1980s, who achieved greater success in changing the department's perspective on issues pertaining to penal policy. In each case, the latter minister, aided by favourable economic or political circumstances, and enjoying prime ministerial backing, was able to build on the work initiated by their predecessors, and which therefore enabled the subsequent ministers more successfully to 'push through' reforms which the department might previously have resisted.

As we will note in Chapter 9, Richard Rose (1984) has suggested that a governing political party is unlikely to make a lasting impact if it only enjoys one term of office, for at least two terms are generally required in order to effect a lasting change of policy orientation. We would suggest that a similar principle applies to departmental change, in that a single minister in post for an average of 18 months is unlikely to effect significant or lasting change in the policy perspective of a department, for such change usually requires at least two ministers, in close succession, pursuing a similar 'agenda for change', and aided by propitious economic and political circumstances (including the clear support or encouragement of the Prime Minister).

The Cabinet

Comprising approximately 21 ministers, the Cabinet was, for much of the 20th century, regarded as the most important arena of decision taking and policy making, a notion lent added credence by the doctrine of collective ministerial responsibility. However, it is now widely accepted that the policy making role of the Cabinet has diminished, especially since the 1970s, partly through the transfer of certain powers to the EU, but also because an increasing volume of government business has effectively been delegated down to other policy arenas and modes of interaction, most notably Cabinet committees, official (civil service) committees, 'bilaterals', 'trilaterals', and written correspondence. Each of these will be discussed below, after we have considered the residual role of the Cabinet.

Apart from the Prime Minister, the vast majority of ministers belonging to the Cabinet are heads of key government departments, their official title usually being Secretary of State (for Defence, Education, Northern Ireland, etc.). In addition to these, two or three non-departmental ministers/ministers without portfolio (as discussed in the previous chapter) are usually appointed to the Cabinet. While most Cabinet Ministers are recruited from the government's MPs in the House of Commons, a couple or so will be selected from peers in the House of Lords. Also in regular attendance at meetings of the Cabinet is the government's Chief Whip, who acts as an important conduit of communication between ministers and their backbench colleagues.

It is now widely acknowledged, though, that the traditional textbook or constitutional model of Cabinet as a forum for systematic collective decision taking and policy making is no longer accurate, and has probably not been for quite some time (Burch, 1988a: 30–2; James, 1999: 81–7). As the complexities of governing Britain have increased since 1945, with a corresponding increase in governmental responsibilities and legislation, the Cabinet has ceased to be the arena in which detailed discussion takes place on most issues, leading to a considered collective decision being taken. As Smith et al. observe, 'Ministers are too overloaded and cabinet meetings are too short and ill-informed for the cabinet to be a significant decision-making body' (1995: 55).

The diminishing role of the Cabinet in policy making is reflected in, and reinforced by, the decline in both the number and duration of its meetings. Until the 1960s, the Cabinet often met twice each week, on Tuesday and Thursday mornings, with the standard length of these meetings being three hours (particularly for the Thursday meetings). By the 1980s and early 1990s, however, the Tuesday meetings of the Cabinet had largely been dispensed with, leaving just the Thursday meeting, starting at 10.00 am, but still usually lasting for about three hours. Under Tony Blair's premiership, though, the Thursday morning Cabinet meeting has become shorter in duration, often lasting 1½ hours at most (Hennessy, 2001a; Holliday, 2000: 89; Riddell, 2001: 32). This partly reflects prime ministerial style, for Blair – like Thatcher – recognizes the limitations of the Cabinet as an effective policy making forum, and therefore generally views lengthy meetings as a waste of his, and his ministerial colleagues', time. Indeed, Blair himself once referred contemptuously to 'the old days of Labour governments where meetings occasionally went on for two days and you had a show of hands at the end' (quoted in Rawnsley, 2001: 52). However, Blair's downgrading of the Cabinet prompted Lord (Robin) Butler, the former Cabinet Secretary, to refer – somewhat disparagingly and disapprovingly – to the 'sofa style' of decision taking (*The Times*, 8 September 2004).

Consequently, the Cabinet itself is widely deemed to have four main functions (Burch, 1988a, 1988b: 3–4; Burch and Holliday, 1996: 42), namely: ratification, coordination, arbitration, and information.

Ratification

The primary policy role of the contemporary Cabinet is the formal acceptance and approval of decisions and proposals presented to it, but which have normally been determined elsewhere in the core executive. In this respect, it is hardly an exaggeration to claim that with the majority of policy proposals, the Cabinet acts as a 'rubber stamp', endorsing measures already agreed upon by individual ministers, small groups of ministers or Cabinet committees. As such, it is extremely rare for the Cabinet to reject policy proposals if they have already been agreed elsewhere in the core executive.

It is relatively rare for Cabinet Ministers to oppose each other's policy proposals when they are presented to the full Cabinet for ratification. Quite apart from wishing to avoid antagonizing or alienating their ministerial colleagues, ministers will normally have little professional interest in the policies of their colleagues around the Cabinet table. This reflects the prevalence of departmentalism at senior ministerial level, with most ministers usually so immersed in the affairs of their own departments, that the activities of other departments and ministers will not generally concern them, unless a particular policy proposal impinges upon their department's jurisdiction or objectives. Yet if this were the case, then any potential conflicts would normally have been resolved via bilaterals, or in Cabinet committee. In most cases, therefore, potential or actual disputes over policy will not normally reach the full Cabinet, thereby ensuring that most policy proposals are 'nodded through' by this stage. Or as a former Chancellor of the Exchequer explains: 'Most Cabinet Ministers, particularly after a longish period in government, tend to be preoccupied with fighting their own battles, and pursuing the issues in their own bailiwick, and lose interest in the wider picture' (Lawson, 1992: 129).

Furthermore, by virtue of not being professionally or politically affected by a particular policy, most Cabinet Ministers will not have served on the relevant Cabinet committee which has discussed a policy in detail, prior to endorsing it. Consequently, most of the ministers around the Cabinet table will not possess a sufficient grasp of the technicalities or details of a finalized policy, and, as a result, will not usually be intellectually equipped or sufficiently well informed to mount a serious and informed objection when a colleague presents a policy for Cabinet approval. Ratification by the Cabinet of predetermined policies is, therefore, usually a formality.

Just occasionally, however, a policy proposal does attract criticism from around the Cabinet table, possibly to the extent that the relevant minister modifies it. This is an issue to which we will return below, when considering sources of tension within the core executive.

Coordination

Given the prevalence of departmentalism, and the concomitant risk that the policies of one department might detrimentally impact upon those of another, or even prove incompatible with the government's own objectives, the full Cabinet also plays a crucial role – increasingly assisted by the Cabinet Office – in ensuring that individual ministers are aware of the policy goals and measures being pursued by their ministerial colleagues. The inclusion in the Cabinet of a couple of Ministers without Portfolio can also prove valuable in facilitating coordination, for lacking departmental responsibilities more readily enables them to take a broader or strategic view of policy issues, thereby providing a corrective to the narrower departmental perspective adopted by some of the other ministers around the Cabinet table.

Arbitration

Very occasionally, the full Cabinet might be appealed to by a minister feeling aggrieved with a Cabinet committee decision, or dissatisfied with the outcome of a 'bilateral', quite possibly involving Treasury Minister. On such occasions, the minister concerned will hope to persuade his/her Cabinet colleagues to 'adjudicate' in their favour, effectively overriding or reversing the previous policy decision. However, if a minister wishes to take a Cabinet committee decision to the full Cabinet, with a view to having it reviewed or reversed, he/she needs the permission of the minister who chaired the committee, and this, perhaps understandably, is unlikely to be granted. Furthermore, the *The Ministerial Code* makes it clear that such appeals to the Cabinet should be 'infrequent', otherwise one of the key purposes of establishing Cabinet committees in the first place will be undermined, namely the alleviation of the Cabinet's workload, and the minimization of ministerial time which needs to be taken up attending meetings of the full Cabinet.

Even if such permission is granted, though, recourse to such action might make the minister concerned – or their preferred policy option – appear somewhat weak, for they will effectively be admitting to the full Cabinet that they had 'lost the argument' when and where it really mattered, in the committee or bilateral. Furthermore, the other Cabinet Ministers may not want to risk alienating the ministerial colleagues who served on the Cabinet committee by siding with the aggrieved minister, or incurring the displeasure of another senior minister if the aggrieved minister has 'lost' in a bilateral, particularly if it involved the Chancellor or the Prime Minister. Besides, if the policy does not directly affect their own department and its policy responsibilities, then they are not likely to be particularly interested in the issue, and therefore disinclined to get involved in it for the sake of pacifying one disgruntled ministerial colleague. For these reasons, aggrieved ministers rarely appeal to the full Cabinet in an attempt at having a Cabinet committee policy decision overturned or reversed.

Information

The Cabinet is undoubtedly a vitally important forum through which senior ministers are kept informed of the government's programme, including forthcoming legislation and parliamentary business for the next week. Cabinet meetings also include reports on international affairs by the Foreign Secretary, particularly those which have diplomatic, military or security implications for Britain.

We would, however, propose the addition of a fifth function for the full Cabinet, namely that of general policy determination.

General policy determination

While this particular dimension might partly be addressed via the function of coordination and information, it can also be a role in its own right, such as when the Cabinet collectively discusses or determines its overall objectives, or when there is a more general discussion concerning a particular (but relatively broad) area of policy.

In this context, the Cabinet may conduct an 'open discussion' over how the government ought to respond either to an ongoing and unresolved problem, or to an issue which has just risen to the top of the policy agenda. According to a former Chancellor of the Exchequer, Nigel Lawson: 'The Cabinet's customary role was to rubber stamp decisions that had already been taken, to keep all colleagues reasonably informed about what was going on, and to provide a forum for general political discussion if time permitted' (1992: 125).

However, only occasionally does time – and the Prime Minister – permit the Cabinet 'to provide a forum for general political discussion', particularly in view of the reduced frequency and length of Cabinet meetings, as noted above.

Cabinet committees

For much of the 20th century, and particularly after 1945, an increasing amount of decision taking and policy making was delegated to Cabinet committees, although their precise number or extent was often shrouded in considerable secrecy. However, a combination of factors have subsequently served to reveal more about the growth and use of Cabinet committees, thereby enabling political scientists and policy analysts to appreciate their immense importance in the policy process. These are:

- The availability of Cabinet papers and ministerial correspondence at the Public Records Office in Kew – subject to the 30-year rule – has provided political researchers with abundant evidence of the extent to which Prime Ministers and/or Cabinets have increasingly discharged detailed policy making to Cabinet committees.

- The excellent work of former *Times* Whitehall correspondent-turned-academic, Peter Hennessy (1986) who did much in the 1980s especially to reveal the use and extent of Cabinet committees as arenas of policy making in the core executive.
- The publication, particularly since the 1970s, of a plethora of ministerial memoirs and diaries, which gave many insights into the ways in which decisions are taken and policies determined. In so doing, these ministerial records and recollections also revealed much about the role played by Cabinet committees.
- Recent Prime Ministers, most notably Margaret Thatcher, John Major and Tony Blair, have revealed a little more about the existence and framework of Cabinet committees under their respective premierships.
- Political websites, in conjunction with some moves towards more open government and the release of previously confidential material, have enabled a clearer picture to be obtained of the plethora of Cabinet committees established, along with their remits and membership.

The increased delegation of detailed policy making to Cabinet committees reflects not only the increasing responsibilities of British governments in industrial, economic and social affairs during the last 100 years, but also the growing political and administrative complexities of governing contemporary Britain, and the corresponding need for greater specialization. In this respect, it is widely recognized that a Cabinet committee comprising a small number of ministers will usually be a more effective forum for detailed discussion and decision taking than the full Cabinet, where most other ministers will probably have limited understanding of, or interest in, the issue concerned.

Although the members of a Cabinet committee are normally selected by the Prime Minister, membership is usually functional, meaning that the ministers appointed will normally be those whose departments are most involved in, or affected by, a particular issue or policy, and thus have a direct interest; in such cases, membership is virtually automatic or self-selecting (Catterall and Brady, 1998: 74; Dorey, 1991; James, 1999: 67). However, one or two other ministers will sometimes be included too, possibly Ministers without Portfolio, or other senior ministers particularly trusted by the Prime Minister, who will normally provide a somewhat broader perspective by virtue of not being departmentally involved in the policy under discussion.

For example, the Cabinet committee on Northern Ireland comprises the following ministers:

- Prime Minister (chair)
- Deputy Prime Minister
- Chancellor of the Exchequer
- Foreign Secretary
- Home Secretary
- Northern Ireland Secretary
- Defence Secretary.

The Prime Minister's chairmanship of this particular Cabinet committee reflects not only the major importance of Northern Ireland as an issue in its own right, but also Tony Blair's personal interest in seeking a solution to 'the troubles'. Many of the other ministers serving on this committee can be seen to have a 'departmental interest', such as the Defence Secretary, for Northern Ireland is clearly a military issue, in the sense that British troops have been deployed in the province since August 1969. Similarly, the law and order and internal security dimensions of the Northern Ireland issue render it natural that the Home Secretary should also serve on this particular Cabinet committee.

Meanwhile, the membership of the Cabinet committee on Drugs Policy is comprised of:

- Home Secretary (chair)
- Secretary of State for Health
- Secretary of State for Education and Skills
- Chief Secretary to the Treasury
- Minister of State, Office of the Deputy Prime Minister
- Parliamentary Under Secretary of State, Foreign and Commonwealth Office
- Parliamentary Under Secretary of State, Home Office.

Again, the membership largely reflects the extent to which drugs policy impinges upon the work of particular departments, most notably the Home Office (responsible for law and order, criminal justice and policing issues), the Department of Health (in this context concerned with the health impact of drug abuse and treatment), the Department For Education and Skills (concerned here with educational campaigns warning of the dangers of illegal drugs), and the Foreign and Commonwealth Office (drug trafficking and smuggling clearly requiring a coordinated response at international level).

The size of Cabinet committees varies considerably, depending on the nature of the policy or issue being addressed, and the range of departments affected. As such, while many Cabinet committees – like the two above – comprise six to eight ministers, a few are even smaller, such as the Millennium Dome committee, which consists of just four ministers, and the Wembley Stadium committee, which had a ministerial membership of five. Many other Cabinet committees, however, are rather larger, such as the Ministerial Committee on the Environment, which comprises 20 ministers (almost all of the Cabinet, in effect), while the Ministerial Committee on Social Exclusion has a membership of 14 ministers.

Cabinet committees often include junior ministers in their membership, most notably when the issue under consideration is related to a Minister of State's or Parliamentary Under Secretary's particular policy remit or responsibilities.

Most Cabinet committees – especially those not being chaired by the Chancellor – will also include a Treasury Minister (if not the Chancellor in person, then either the Chief Secretary to the Treasury, or the Treasury's Financial Secretary), to ensure that the policy being considered does not entail unauthorized increases in public expenditure.

Cabinet committees are invariably chaired by a senior minister, with the Prime Minister chairing several of the most important ones, although as Table 4.3, below, illustrates, the Deputy Prime Minister and the Home Secretary chair the most Cabinet committees overall.

Cabinet committees normally enjoy full policy making authority, to the extent that their decisions, subsequently reported to the full Cabinet, are usually ratified as a formality. This is hardly surprising, given the earlier observation about the lack of detailed discussion which occurs in the Cabinet. As such, once a Cabinet committee comprising the most

Table 4.3   Chairs of Cabinet Committees during the second Blair government

Ministerial position	Cabinet committees chaired
Prime Minister	Defence and Overseas Policy Intelligence Services International Terrorism Northern Ireland Thames Gateway Welfare Reform
Deputy Prime Minister	Domestic Affairs Energy Policy Environment Equality Local Government Nations and Regions Social Exclusion Sustainable Development
Chancellor of the Exchequer	Children and Young People's Services Economic Affairs, Productivity and Competitiveness Employment Public Services and Public Expenditure
Foreign Secretary	European Issues
Home Secretary	Active Communities and Family Issues Animal Rights Activists Civil Contingencies Consequence Management and Resilience Crime Reduction Criminal Justice System Drugs Policy Protective and Preventive Security Social and Economic Aspects of Migration
Secretary of State for Education and Skills	Adult Basic Skills
Secretary of State for Environment, Food and Rural Affairs	Rural Revival
Secretary of State for Trade and Industry	European Aerospace and Defence Industry Science Policy
Secretary of State for Work and Pensions	Older People Universal Banking Service
Chief Secretary to the Treasury	Electronic Service Delivery Fraud

(Continued)

Table 4.3 (Continued)

Ministerial position	Cabinet committees chaired
President of the Council/Leader of the House of Commons	Legislative Programme Biotechnology E-Democracy
Chancellor of the Duchy of Lancaster/Minister for the Cabinet Office	Regulatory Accountability
Minister of State, Office of the Deputy Prime Minister	Local Public Service Agreements
Lord Chancellor	Constitutional Reform Reform of the House of Lords Freedom of Information Incorporation of European Convention on Human Rights

relevant or affected ministers has agreed on a policy, it is highly unlikely that other ministers will raise objections in the full Cabinet, particularly if the committee was chaired by the Prime Minister or another trusted senior ministerial colleague.

We can see, therefore, how Cabinet committees, rather than the full Cabinet, are one of the most important arenas of policy making in British government, with policies usually determined by a small number of ministers, most of whom serve on a committee due to their department's involvement or interest in a particular policy. They therefore constitute key 'institutional mechanisms for melding Departmental autonomy with collective government' (Smith, 1999: 168).

Official (Civil Service) Committees

The plethora of Cabinet committees in Britain's core executive is paralleled by a corresponding framework of 'official committees', comprising senior civil servants from the departments involved in a particular policy issue or initiative. In effect, these official committees 'shadow' the relevant Cabinet committee, playing an important role in both coordinating the information disseminated and deployed by ministers in the Cabinet committees, and in facilitating interdepartmental cooperation in the implementation of subsequent ministerial policy decisions (and thereby supplementing the coordinating and 'enforcement' roles of the Cabinet Office itself). As Seldon has observed: 'Interdepartmental co-ordination is institutionalised in Whitehall, and ranges from telephone calls and letters between officials, through interdepartmental committees, to the Cabinet Office' (1990: 116).

Furthermore, because of the extent to which these official committees are usually involved in the highly detailed administrative or technical aspects of policies, there are often rather more of them (Catterall and Brady, 1998: 72), although – unlike Cabinet committees themselves – their precise number cannot be ascertained, as they remain shrouded in rather more secrecy. To give just one example, though, of the way in which one Cabinet committee can be serviced by more than one official committee, the Cabinet committee on competitiveness is shadowed by both an official committee on public sector pay, and one on development of science policy (James, 1999: 51).

Whereas critics of the civil service and/or conspiracy theorists have inclined to the view that the plethora of official committees is a manifestation of mandarin power over, or domination of, Cabinet Ministers, James (1999) suggests that the committee system in the core executive reflects a clearer and more useful division of responsibilities, with official (civil service) committees focusing on the administrative aspects of a policy issue, and Cabinet committees thus left free to consider the political dimensions. Viewed from this perspective, the relationship between official committees and Cabinet committees is generally complementary, rather than competitive, and again reaffirms the view that institutions within the core executive – like those between individuals – are 'resource dependent', and are characterized by exchange relationships.

Other forms of ministerial interaction

Outside of the Cabinet and its sundry committees, there are three other modes of ministerial interaction, namely bilaterals, trilaterals and written correspondence.

Bilaterals

While Cabinet committees have clearly increased, both in number and significance, particularly since 1945, a more recent parallel development concerning policy making within the core executive has been the growing importance of bilaterals, whereby policy decisions are determined through discussions between just two ministers. These bilaterals can be divided into three general types:

1   Policies determined jointly between two departmental ministers, when a particular policy clearly requires the involvement and cooperation of their respective departments.
2   Decisions concerning departmental budgets and expenditure, thereby involving bargaining between the department's Cabinet Minister and a Treasury Minister. In such bilaterals, the latter is usually the Chief Secretary to the Treasury, rather than the Chancellor *per se*, for the Chief Secretary has particular responsibility for public expenditure, albeit within the context of the Chancellor's macro-economic strategy. These bilaterals have invariably entailed the Chief Secretary seeking to persuade the relevant minister to reduce their bid for increased departmental funding, or even to accept a reduction in their department's budget in times of economic retrenchment.
3   Meetings between the Prime Minister and a departmental minister, these having been particularly favoured by both Margaret Thatcher and Tony Blair. These bilaterals may simply be a means whereby the Prime Minister ensures that he/she is kept informed of a department's policy initiatives and progress (and *inter alia* how successfully the minister is fulfilling his/her departmental responsibilities), or they may be a means by which the Prime Minister seeks to impose their will on a minister, either by insisting on the adoption of a new policy which the premier is particularly keen on, or by exhorting the minister to pursue an existing policy with more urgency or vigour if it is felt that progress has been too tardy to date.

While the last of the above scenarios might be viewed as indicative of increased prime ministerial power, the greater use of bilaterals since the 1980s is better understood as a further manifestation of the constraints imposed on collective Cabinet policy making by both lack of time and greater complexity. Furthermore, even if the Prime Minister wishes to impose a policy initiative on a minister, it is unlikely to prove successful unless the minister and their department can be infused with the Prime Minister's enthusiasm, and even this might not be sufficient if inadequate resources or inappropriate circumstances undermine the efficacy of the policy (a consideration to which we return in Chapter 7, when implementation problems are discussed).

Consequently, rather than interpreting the increased penchant for bilaterals as further evidence of growing prime ministerial power, they might better be viewed as another indication of the 'resource dependency' which characterizes political relationships within the core executive, which thus renders the Prime Minister at least partially dependent upon the support and cooperation of individual ministers (and their departments) in pursuing particular policies.

Trilaterals

A further development evinced during Tony Blair's premiership is that of 'trilaterals', usually entailing the Prime Minister *and* the Chancellor meeting with another minister to discuss policy initiatives or progress. This development reflects the degree to which Gordon Brown has displayed an interest in policy issues and areas wider than the Treasury's usual concern with controlling public expenditure and macro-economic strategy (Riddell, 2001: 36–8). Obviously, many, if not most, policies have public expenditure implications and this partly explains the Chancellor's involvement, but Brown's interest has expanded beyond this particular concern, for he has appeared genuinely interested in such New Labour initiatives as 'welfare-into-work' and pensions reform.

Meanwhile, during the middle of May 2003, a series of trilaterals were initiated, involving the Prime Minister, the Chancellor and individual Cabinet Ministers, in order to discuss Britain's possible membership of the single European currency (the euro), although it was being emphasized that the final decision would *not* be based on a Cabinet vote or 'weighing-up' of ministerial views, but would be taken, ultimately, by Tony Blair and Gordon Brown (Ahmed, 2003: 19).

Written correspondence

Given the ever-increasing volume of government business, and the consequent increase in ministerial workloads and time constraints, it is hardly surprising that routine issues are often dealt with through correspondence between ministers, particularly in the era of the email. The Cabinet Office itself advises ministers that many issues 'can be settled through an exchange of letters', provided that copies are forwarded to the Prime Minister, ministers serving on the relevant Cabinet committee, and the Cabinet Secretary. Correspondence concerning policy issues with EU implications is also copied to the UK's Permanent Representative to the EU.

Sources of tension within the core executive

In view of the plethora of individuals and institutions collectively comprising the core executive, it is hardly surprising that disagreements and tensions occasionally arise, either between particular individuals, or between institutions. Such differences are generally derived either from differing ideological perspectives (in the case of ministers, and within the Cabinet generally), or policy disagreements (between either individual ministers, or between departments, or sometimes between a minister and his/her senior civil servants). Another source of tension which has become more widely acknowledged since the 1980s – although it certainly occurred in earlier decades too – is that between the Prime Minister and the Chancellor of the Exchequer.

Ideological: factions and tendencies

As there are invariably a variety of attitudes, opinions and outlooks within a political party, and a Prime Minister will normally feel obliged to ensure that these are formally represented at ministerial level (in order to keep different sections of the parliamentary party reasonably satisfied), it has often been the case in British politics that Cabinets have enshrined ideological tensions. These have manifested themselves both over general policy direction or strategy, and over specific policies, sometimes creating considerable conflict between ministers.

Until the advent of New Labour and the subsequent marginalization of the Left, ideological tensions were most commonly associated with the Labour Party, so that pre-1979 Labour Cabinets were particularly prone to Left versus Right disagreements. These had derived from tensions between those on the Left, who favoured more public ownership (nationalization) of industry, sometimes in tandem with demands for 'workers' control', and more vigorous efforts at redistributing wealth from rich to poor, while those on the (revisionist) Right or social democratic 'wing' of the Labour party had been rather more cautious or conservative in their approach to achieving 'socialism', and inclined more to the view capitalism should be reformed, rather than replaced. These ideological divisions, of course, then underpinned many disagreements which ensued over particular policies.

During the 1980s and 1990s, though, it was Conservative Cabinets which evinced ideological tensions and disagreements over the general orientation of policy, as Thatcherite ministers battled for supremacy against representatives of the party's paternalistic 'one nation' tradition. These tensions were most particularly prominent with regard to economic strategy during the early 1980s, when Thatcherite monetarists and neo-liberals insisted that the recession and rising unemployment rendered it essential that stricter control was exercised over the money supply, primarily through curbing public expenditure and cutting welfare provision. By contrast, 'one nation' Conservatives believed that the recession was not only being exacerbated by their government's economic strategy, but this was precisely the time to relax monetary policy and public expenditure in order to reflate the economy, in order to get the country out of recession. The 'one nation' Conservatives in the Cabinet of the early 1980s similarly reasoned that a period of high unemployment was exactly the time when the welfare state was most needed, in order to assist those who, due to economic circumstances beyond their control, were without jobs. To curb welfare entitlement at such a time was deemed both politically insensitive and potentially socially destabilizing.

This ideological demarcation was also replicated with regard to issues such as industrial relations reform, for while the Thatcherites were keen to emasculate the trade unions permanently, albeit on a step-by-step basis over a period of time, some 'one nation' ministers believed that beyond a few modest reforms to 'clip their wings', the Conservative governments ought to resume the pursuit of partnership and dialogue with organized labour which had been pursued by pre-Thatcher Conservative administrations (the 1970–1 Heath government notwithstanding) (Dorey, 1993b; Dorey, 2003b).

In the 1990s, meanwhile, the Left-Right divisions within the Conservative Cabinets of John Major manifested themselves most starkly with regard to the EU, to the extent that they came to symbolize publicly the tensions and conflicts within the Conservative Party. Thatcherite ministers (enthusiastically encouraged by numerous backbench Conservative MPs) adopted a highly sceptical, if not openly hostile, stance towards much of the EU, particularly *vis-à-vis* trends towards greater integration, and the corresponding Economic and Monetary Union (EMU). In sharp contrast, prominent ministers on the Left of the Conservative Party made no attempt to conceal their pro-European credentials, including their firm belief that Britain should join 'the euro'. For them, European integration was seen, not so much as a threat to Britain, particularly to British sovereignty, but as the source of new opportunities, and a 'pooling' (sharing) of sovereignty, whereupon policy goals could far more readily or realistically be attained through partnership with other member states than by isolation and self-imposed exclusion.

The general marginalization of the Left in New Labour has ensured that open ideological divisions have been relatively rare in Tony Blair's Cabinets since May 1997, with 'Old Labour' figures such as John Prescott proving reliable allies on most policy issues. To the extent that the Labour Cabinets of Tony Blair do contain disagreements over policies, they are less readily comprehensible in terms of ideology and Left versus Right, as we will note below (although some of the disagreements which have emerged between Tony Blair and Gordon Brown are partly explicable in terms of Brown being a little nearer to the remnants of 'Old Labour' than Blair). When disagreements have arisen in the Blair Cabinets, these have often been over policy priorities and strategy, rather than objectives; over means rather than ends.

For example, on various occasions, Blair's Cabinet has disagreed over the allocation of increased public expenditure, with some ministers, most notably, Gordon Brown, as Chancellor, favouring raising social security benefits and extending tax credits for the low paid, in order to tackle poverty, while others in the Cabinet – including Tony Blair himself – have preferred to target any public expenditure increases on services, most notably health and education, reasoning that increasing welfare benefits might be seen as merely providing 'hand outs' and increasing dependency amongst the poor, whereas 'investing' in public services will be viewed by more voters – particularly Middle England – as a worthwhile and justified way of spending their tax contributions, especially as they themselves will benefit from an improved NHS and 'better' schools. Besides, Blair was inclined to point out, poorer people would also be beneficiaries of better schools and hospitals (*The Observer*, 19 September 1999; *The Guardian*, 19 November 2001).

Policy conflicts

Ideology and Left-Right factionalism are by no means the only basis of disagreements and tensions within the core executive: differences of opinion can sometimes arise over particular policies which transcend ideological positions (although, as just noted, sometimes they can clearly be underpinned by, and reflect, those ideological divisions). As previously discussed, departmentalism is a widely recognized characteristic of the core executive in Britain, and this can result in ministers resisting a policy proposal which they consider to be detrimental to the interests or objectives of their department. Referring to the findings of a report into the mid-1990s BSE crisis which affected British farming and the meat industry, a Special Adviser to a senior Cabinet Minister declared that:

> The BSE report confirms everything we have been saying about Whitehall as a whole. Whenever there is a potential conflict between different departments, or an awkward problem, they do not search for the right answers. Their priority is to defend their own departmental position. They do not share knowledge, but keep information to themselves. They judge the quality of their work purely on the basis of how well they defend their own department.
>
> (quoted in Richards, 2000: 13; see also, Greer, 1999)

For example, the Blair government's 2000 Freedom of Information Act was widely criticized for its timidity, particularly when compared with the expectations which had been raised in Opposition by 'New Labour' about the need to tackle Britain's culture of official secrecy. Yet a significant reason for the timidity of the ensuing legislation was that a number of Cabinet Ministers on the relevant cabinet committee opposed radical freedom of information legislation, because of the implications for their departments. Indeed, the then Home Secretary himself, Jack Straw, was unenthusiastic about freedom of information, reflecting a long-standing Home Office view that 'too much' freedom of information would be inimical to good government and effective policy making, due to policy actors' apparent need to know that they could express views and make proposals which would remain confidential. Meanwhile, the Secretary of State for Social Security was anxious about the implications for the department, fearing that it would be unable to cope if tens of thousands of welfare claimants were granted a statutory right to demand certain types of information, while Geoffrey Robinson, the then Paymaster General was determined to ensure that commercial information possessed by the government was exempt from any statutory right of disclosure. The Minister of State for Defence also conveyed his ministry's opposition, insisting on the need for defence issues to remain secret for reasons of national security (Hencke, 1999: 12).

Similarly, ministers can occasionally clash because they believe that a policy proposal emanating from one of their Cabinet colleagues ought to be the responsibility of their own department; minister A is encroaching on the territory of minister B, and needs to be 'fought off'. For example, during the second Blair government, there were reported to be tensions between David Blunkett and the Home Office on the one hand, and the Lord Chancellor on the other, with the latter politically responsible for the British judicial system. In view of the Home Office's responsibility for law-and-order matters, and the Lord Chancellor's

Department, presiding over a judicial system involved (among other things) in the actual sentencing of convicted criminals, it is perhaps not surprising that the two departments, or their respective ministers, occasionally come into conflict. One such conflict, in the spring of 2003, concerned the role of coroners' courts, and whether they ought ultimately to remain under the formal jurisdiction of the Home Office, or whether this function should be transferred to the Lord Chancellor's Department (*The Independent on Sunday*, 11 May 2003).

Occasionally, though, two ministers or departments might actually seek to shift the responsibility for a policy initiative to the other, quite possibly because of the potential problems identified. This was certainly the case in the early 1990s, when the Child Support Agency (CSA) was being devised. The then Permanent Secretary in the DSS, Sir Michael Partridge, was apprehensive about aspects of the imminent CSA, and suggested that it should be operated via the Inland Revenue (and thus under the auspices of the Treasury), so that child support payments could be deducted from salaries at source, just as income tax was. In response, the then chair of the Board of the Inland Revenue, Sir Anthony Battishill, argued that child support payments were not a form of taxation, and should therefore be administered via the DSS. Sir Anthony was backed by one of the Treasury Ministers, Peter Lilley, who pointed out that if child support was portrayed or perceived to be a form of taxation, it would be viewed negatively from the outset (Channel 4, 1999; see also Maclean and Eekelaar, 1993: 224).

Yet while the Treasury did not want to assume responsibility for administering the CSA, it did insist – to the chagrin of the DSS – that all monies obtained from 'absent fathers' and paid to 'lone mothers' in receipt of social security should be deducted, pound for pound, from their Income Support. The Social Security Secretary, though, had envisaged 'lone mothers' being permitted to retain up to 50 per cent of child support payments before their Income Support was reduced, an approach which would simultaneously help to tackle poverty in 'lone parent' households, and enhance the credibility of the CSA. Not surprisingly, perhaps, it was the Treasury's approach which prevailed, but in so doing, ensured that the CSA proved highly unpopular right from the outset, not least amongst the very 'lone parents' in whose interests it was supposed to have been established.

Another form of policy conflict which emerged during the first Blair government, reflecting different perspectives between senior ministers, concerned that of transport. John Prescott was well known for his desire to improve public transport, and develop an 'integrated transport system' in Britain, and as Secretary of State for Transport, might have been expected to develop transport policies in this direction. Certainly, Prescott wanted to improve Britain's railways, partly as a good thing in itself, but also in the hope that if more people travelled by train, then traffic congestion and pollution would be ameliorated. Yet Blair, primarily concerned with the government's electoral and political popularity, apparently claimed that the railways 'are not a top priority', and also harboured fears that tangible measures to boost public transport would be portrayed by Labour's critics as 'anti-car', thereby alienating 'Middle England' (in spite of the fact that millions of 'Middle England' commuters would presumably have welcomed any improvement in the parlous state of Britain's railways). Hence, ideas such as congestion charges and taxes on out-of-town shopping were vetoed by 10 Downing Street – leading an exasperated Prescott to complain: 'They keep throwing the … focus groups at me. They're attacking me for what we were elected to do' (quoted in Rawnsley, 2001: 297).

As well as policy clashes between individual ministers, there are occasionally more general disagreements within the Cabinet over a specific policy proposal, as was the case during the spring of 2002, when it became known that Tony Blair favoured reducing or temporarily 'freezing' social security payments to the parents of persistent young offenders and juvenile delinquents. Blair was concerned that too many parents were effectively turning a blind eye to the delinquent, criminal or antisocial behaviour of their offspring, and, in some cases, actively colluding with their children in breaking the law, such as taking them shopping when they should be at school (thereby aiding and abetting truancy). Blair's approach was broadly supported by the then Education Secretary, Estelle Morris, and was in accordance with proposals previously developed by Frank Field, one of Blair's former Ministers of State for Welfare Reform.

Other Cabinet Ministers, however, including the Chancellor, Gordon Brown and the Secretary of State for Social Security, Alistair Darling, were dismissive of this punitive proposal, pointing out not only the practical, administrative difficulties of implementing such sanctions, but also the potentially counter-productive consequences, in terms of exacerbating poverty, and also making such families even more dysfunctional (*The Guardian*, 29 April 2002).

Then, during 2003, it emerged that there were deep differences of opinion within the Cabinet over the possible introduction of an identity card (ID) for all adults in Britain. An ID card was suggested to the Cabinet by the Home Secretary, David Blunkett – backed by Tony Blair – as a possible means of tackling fraud (particularly with regard to social security), for such a card would confirm its holder's legitimate entitlement to a range of public and welfare services. It was also envisaged that an ID card would help to combat illegal immigration and 'bogus' asylum seekers. Yet Blunkett himself acknowledged that: 'Members of the Cabinet have different views on this', and as such, he emphasized that he was merely exploring options for the medium to long term, and aiming to develop a debate, not merely between his Cabinet colleagues, but also among the British public, where opinion polls reported similar differences of opinion (*The Guardian*, 16 January 2003). The issue rumbled on throughout the rest of 2003, with John Reid (Health Secretary), Geoff Hoon (Defence Secretary) and Charles Clarke (Education Secretary) reported to be in favour, and John Prescott (Deputy Prime Minister), Alistair Darling (Transport Secretary) and Patricia Hewitt (Trade and Industry Secretary) apparently opposed to the scheme (*The Sunday Times*, 12 October 2003).

Although some of the ministerial opposition to ID cards derived from principles concerning civil liberties, or doubts about the practicability of such a scheme, some of the opposition also derived from departmentalism, with the Foreign Office expressing concern about the discrepancy whereby British citizens would have to pay for their ID card, while asylum seekers would be issued with one free of charge. Jack Straw, the Foreign Secretary, also expressed concern about the likely loss of Foreign Office revenue – amounting, perhaps, to more that £30 million – as people increasingly used their ID cards instead of purchasing a passport when visiting EU countries. Treasury Ministers, meanwhile, warned that if people had to pay for a compulsory ID card, the government would be vulnerable to accusations of imposing another 'stealth tax' (*The Sunday Times*, 12 October 2003).

However, by 2004 the proposals for an ID card became more concrete, although to assuage opponents of the initiative, the Home Office emphasized that the scheme would be phased in over several years, and on a voluntary basis during this period. Here, then, is an example of a policy being modified – even before being formally introduced – in order to overcome opposition from other Cabinet Ministers.

Another policy which caused considerable consternation in the Cabinet, in the autumn of 2004, was a legislative proposal to liberalize Britain's gambling laws, with a view to permitting the opening of 250 'super casinos', along with the installation of up to 100,000 slot-machines offering instant cash prizes of up to £1 million. Following publication of the relevant Gambling Bill in mid-October 2004, the Secretary of State for Culture, Media and Sport, Tessa Jowell, found her proposals being savaged by senior Cabinet colleagues, most notably Gordon Brown and John Prescott (the latter threatening to use planning laws to reject applications for the building of various casinos). Many Labour MPs were also aghast at the implications of the proposals, particularly as the summer had heard a succession of reports and news items about record levels of personal and household debt in Britain. It was also reckoned that about 350,0000 people in Britain were already addicted to gambling. Opposition to the proposals was compounded when it became apparent that Las Vegas-based gambling companies had spent £100 million on lobbying MPs in an attempt to secure political support for the initiative. As a result of the breadth and depth of Cabinet (and back-bench) opposition, Jowell was obliged to revise her proposals, to the extent that only about 20 'super casinos' were likely to be permitted (*The Observer*, 24 October 2004).

On a rather more controversial issue – the decision to support US military attacks on Saddam Hussein's Iraq in 2003 – there was a 'near mutiny' in the Cabinet, according to one minister present (but who resigned shortly afterwards due to his opposition to the war). Robin Cook – himself a Foreign Secretary earlier in the Blair premiership – claims that there was widespread opposition among most Cabinet Ministers, with David Blunkett, the Home Secretary, and Patricia Hewitt, Secretary of State for Trade and Industry, proving particularly prominent critics of Tony Blair's support for military attacks on Iraq (as part of an Anglo-American 'war against terror' in the aftermath of 9/11) (Cook, 2003: 115–6).

On this particular issue, of course, Tony Blair's view prevailed, in spite of Cabinet opposition, thereby providing a ready example to the advocates of the prime ministerial or presidential government thesis. On the other hand, though, subsequent events and inquiry reports concerning Iraq, could be said to have proven politically damaging to Tony Blair, and served to weaken his authority and credibility somewhat.

Prime Ministers versus Chancellors

One other source of tension which sometimes arises within the core executive concerns the working relationship and policy preferences between the Prime Minister and his/her Chancellor of the Exchequer. As the two most senior figures in the Cabinet, relations between the Prime Minister and the Chancellor can have a significant impact on the rest of the Cabinet, and serious repercussions for the overall performance of the government itself. A close and harmonious relationship can render a Prime Minister and Chancellor an extremely powerful force within the Cabinet, whereas divisions and disagreements between them might facilitate damaging factionalism, as each seeks to mobilize allies, or build coalitions, among other ministers (and also, perhaps, among the government's backbenchers).

One of the most notable examples in postwar British politics of a Prime Minister and their Chancellor 'falling-out' was in February 1958, when Peter Thorneycroft – along with his two Treasury Ministers – resigned because of (Prime Minister) Harold Macmillan's refusal to accept Thorneycroft's repeated advocacy of a deflationary budget – entailing cuts in public expenditure and a deliberate increase in unemployment – in order both to curb inflation, and weaken the trade unions (PRO CAB 129/88 195, 7 September 1957; PRO CAB 128(58) third conclusions, 5 January 1958). Macmillan blithely referred to the loss of his Treasury team as 'a little local difficulty'.

Just over 30 years later, in 1989, Nigel Lawson resigned as Margaret Thatcher's Chancellor, following her refusal to dismiss her Special Adviser on economic affairs, Sir Alan Walters. According to Lawson:

> I had gone to Margaret not to tell her I wished to resign, but to ask her to wave goodbye to Walters – making clear to her, however, what the consequences would be were she not to do so … She had made it clear that she would not do so. There was really nothing for me to reflect on … I wrote out … my draft resignation letter.

> (1992: 962)

In this resignation letter, Lawson emphasized that:

> The successful conduct of economic policy is possible only if there is, *and is seen to be*, full agreement between the Prime Minister and the Chancellor of the Exchequer. Recent events have confirmed that this essential requirement cannot be satisfied so long as Alan Walters remains your personal economic adviser. I have therefore regretfully concluded that it is in the best interest of the Government for me to resign my office without further ado.

> (1992: 964; see also Kavanagh and Seldon, 2000: 194–5;
> Thatcher, 1993: 715–7).

Walters actually resigned almost immediately afterwards, meaning that Margaret Thatcher had lost both her Chancellor, and her Special (Economic) Adviser, in the space of a few hours. The episode also meant that she lost some of her political authority, to the extent that just over a year later, she was replaced (by John Major) as Conservative leader and Prime Minister.

Much more recently, since New Labour's 1997 election victory, Tony Blair's relationship with his Chancellor, Gordon Brown, appears to have been subject to varying degrees of tension, and repeated rumours of rifts. The reported disagreements and disputes appear to be both policy orientated, and also to reflect a power struggle between the two men, which has apparently seriously – possibly irreparably – damaged their former friendship. We have already noted, above, the way in which Blair and Brown have disagreed over both government strategy or priorities, in terms of whether additional Treasury revenues should be apportioned to higher welfare benefits or increased expenditure on schools and hospitals, and over specific policies, such as curbing benefits paid to parents of persistent young offenders and delinquents, but their disagreements have been apparent with regard to various other policies.

For example, when, at the beginning of 2003, the government was preparing to announce details of the future funding of higher education, Gordon Brown made known his preference for a Graduate Tax as the most effective and socially just way of providing extra revenues for cash-strapped universities. Not only did Brown believe that the mooted alternative of 'top-up' fees would deter prospective students from poorer or disadvantaged socioeconomic backgrounds from going to university, he also believed that the result would be a two-tier – or more two-tier than it already is – university system, in which 'elite' universities would charge higher fees, and thereby attract pupils from richer families, thereby leaving other students attending 'cheaper' universities. Tony Blair, however, made equally clear his preference for universities to be permitted to charge 'top-up' fees in order to raise more money, insisting that limits would be placed on how much extra they would be able to charge, but also arguing that 'top-up' fees would enable students to 'shop around', thereby obliging universities to become more competitive, and raise their standards, in order to attract students willing to pay the fees being charged (*The Independent*, 18 January 2003). Eventually, a compromise ensued, whereby the limits on the level of 'top-up' fees which universities would be permitted to charge would also be linked to their record in admitting students from poorer backgrounds, as monitored by a proposed Access Regulator.

Another issue which was widely reported to be a source of ongoing tension between Tony Blair and Gordon Brown, in their respective roles as Prime Minister and Chancellor, was when Britain should – subject to a referendum – join the euro. Although both men were apparently agreed that Britain ought to acquire membership of the single European currency, they disagreed over the appropriate circumstances and timing, with Brown insisting that a referendum should only be held once the Treasury had confirmed that the five economic 'tests' or conditions had been met. Blair, though, was believed to be generally keener to conduct the referendum anyway, suspecting that Brown's 'five economic tests' were more of a delaying device than a genuinely objective assessment of the compatibility of the British economy *vis-à-vis* euro membership (Elliott et al., 2002: 10–11; Naughtie, 2001; Rawnsley, 2001, 2002: 29; Richards, 2003: 26). Certainly, few were surprised when Gordon Brown eventually announced, in June 2003, that only one of the five economic tests had been passed, although to pacify more pro-euro elements in the Labour Party, he also hinted that a referendum could still be held during the lifetime of the second Blair government, subject to the economic tests being passed in 2004 or 2005. Most commentators interpreted this, however, as a clear indication that there would, in fact, be no referendum on British membership of the euro until *after* the next general election (*The Guardian*, 19 June 2003).

Some of the tensions between Blair and Brown have manifested themselves through the guise of other ministers, known to be in either the Prime Minister's or the Chancellor's 'camp', or via Special Advisers. For example, when the then Health Secretary, Alan Milburn, recognized as a loyal Blairite, announced his intention of establishing 'foundation hospitals', which would still be part of the NHS, but permitted to raise capital from the private sector, Gordon Brown moved to veto the proposal, claiming that a hospital which subsequently defaulted on its loans would have to be 'bailed out' by the Treasury, something which he was not willing to countenance. However, this stance was widely interpreted as a warning by the Chancellor, to Blair himself, that there was a limit to how far the private sector and 'market solutions' could – and should – be involved in, and applied to, Britain's public services. Whereas Blair was favourable to the use of private sector finance and expertise in improving public services, provided that these services remained free to consumers at the point of access or usage, Brown was concerned not only about the extent to which the Treasury might subsequently be asked to 'bail out' public services which could not afford to repay money invested or lent by the private sector, but also about what he viewed as 'creeping privatization', a view shared by numerous Labour MPs and trade unions. Shortly afterwards, Brown's Economic Adviser, Ed Balls, claimed that 'there is a limit to how far you can apply market principles … In an area like health or education, if you go down that marketising route, you run grave risks with [the] ethic of public service' (*The Guardian*, 4 November 2002).

However, some 'Blairites' suspected that Brown's stance on such issues was partly an attempt by the Chancellor to ingratiate himself with those Labour backbenchers and trade unions who were anxious about Blair's evident penchant for involving the private sector in the public services, in order to consolidate, or increase, his support when the time came to elect Blair's successor.

Certainly, some of the reported tension between Tony Blair and Gordon Brown is ascribed to frustrated leadership ambitions on the Chancellor's part. It has variously been rumoured that when John Smith died in May 1994, Blair persuaded Brown not to stand against him in the ensuing election for the Labour Party leadership, in return for a pledge by Blair that he would stand down halfway through a second term as Prime Minister, and pass on the premiership to Brown. While this author is sceptical about the veracity of such a deal – back in 1994, neither man (nor anyone else) could have been sure that Labour would win one general election, yet alone two in succession, and besides, Blair could not simply 'hand over' to Brown; the latter would have to be elected as leader via Labour's electoral college – numerous commentators (often claiming to have good 'inside' information) maintain that Brown believes that such a deal was made, and that Blair is now reneging on it, by showing absolutely no desire or intention to resign. On the contrary, as the half-way stage of New Labour's second term of office approached, Blair was hinting that he envisaged a third term as Prime Minister, because he felt that there remained so much work still to be done.

What has since been confirmed, however, about Brown's standing aside to give Blair a clear run at the Labour Party leadership in June 1994, was the former's insistence that in so doing, he expected Blair to allow him considerable latitude in shaping the next Labour government's economic, social and welfare policies. The confirmation came with the publication, in June 2003, of a single sheet of A4 paper, containing just 300 printed words and a significant hand-written amendment. The paper – obtained and published by *The Guardian* (6 June 2003) – revealed Brown's insistence that Blair 'guaranteed' to pursue an agenda outlined by Brown himself, 'the fairness agenda – social justice, employment opportunities and skills – which … should be the centrepiece of Labour's programme'. This paper apparently provided the basis of Brown's agreement, at Islington's *Granita* restaurant on 31 May 1994, not to stand against Blair in the imminent Labour leadership contest, and casts considerable light on how Brown has been able to exercise so much policy influence since 'New Labour' won the May 1997 election.

Irrespective of potential personal rivalries and frustrated ambitions, the relationship between any Prime Minister and Chancellor can enshrine tensions, due to the somewhat different perspectives fostered by each post. Whereas a Chancellor will invariably be first and foremost concerned with the economic implications or efficacy of a particular policy, and how the policy will be viewed by the 'the City' and financial markets, the Prime Minister will usually be somewhat more interested in the political or electoral ramifications of an initiative. Certainly, while Tony Blair has been 'most concerned with the government's popularity and always kept his ear to the heartbeat of the swing voter', Gordon Brown, as Chancellor, has 'wanted to maintain his good notices in the City', where he has enjoyed a respect not traditionally enjoyed by Labour Chancellors (Rawnsley, 2001: 156). Such differing perspectives, therefore, provide a further source of occasional tension between Prime Ministers and their Chancellors.

Yet while occasional conflicts, be they derived from ideological disagreements, policy disputes, personality clashes or rival leadership ambitions (any of which may also overlap or be interlinked), are unavoidable within the core executive – indeed, in virtually any social or political organization – the individuals and institutions collectively comprising the core executive are nonetheless bound together for the most part, if not always by shared policy goals, then certainly by mutual dependency, and the need to exchange or share resources in order to achieve their particular policy goals. Just as power itself is variable, shifting and shared between policy actors according to the issues and personalities involved, and the wider political environment or circumstances, so too do relations within the core executive vary somewhat, according to the policy actors and policy issues involved. Ministers disagreeing over one policy proposal might find themselves in agreement over another, thereby reflecting the manner in which relations within the core executive are often subject to shifting alliances and 'coalitions' between the actors involved. Ultimately, whatever disputes or disagreements occasionally arise, the policy actors who comprise the core executive recognize that they need the support and cooperation of others in order to achieve their own policy objectives. Constant conflict would merely ensure that no one achieved anything.

The 'Europeanization' of the core executive

Given the central importance of the core executive with regard to policy making in Britain, it is here that the need to adapt to the increasing policy competences and jurisdiction of the EU has been greatest. Consequently, a variety of institutional arrangements and processes have been developed in order to assist the core executive and its policy actors in dealing with EU initiatives and obligations which affect Britain. Yet it is also the case that the core executive has avoided radical restructuring in responding to the EU and its impact on Britain, by ensuring that 'European integration has been absorbed into the "logic" of the Whitehall machinery', so that 'while change has been substantial, it has been more or less in keeping with British traditions', developing in 'a largely accretive manner … simply absorbed into the existing institutions, and into the characteristics, methods, procedures and culture of Whitehall' (Bulmer and Burch, 1998: 606, 603, 613). Similarly, Kassim notes that 'the administrative norms and values that characterise Whitehall have been projected into the UK's management of EU matters' (2000: 27). Even the Europeanization of Britain's core executive, it would seem, has been conducted generally on the basis of incrementalism and piecemeal adaptation of existing institutional machinery, rather than the creation of specific bodies or Ministries *sui generis*.

Cabinet Committee on European Policy

This 22-member committee comprises most Cabinet Ministers, along with a Minister of State from the Foreign and Commonwealth Office, and the Attorney-General. Other ministers may be invited to attend if a particular policy or issue is to be discussed for which they are directly responsible. Also invited to attend is the UK Permanent Representative to the EU. The committee's remit is to determine the UK's policies with regard to European issues, and to consider its relations with other member states.

Cabinet Committee on European Union Strategy

Comprising 10 Cabinet Ministers, including the Prime Minister (who chairs it), Deputy Prime Minister, the Chancellor of the Exchequer, Foreign Secretary and Secretary of State for Trade and Industry, this committee, as the name suggests, is concerned with determining the government's overall strategy towards the EU, 'including preparations for UK entry into the single currency ... and the presentation of the Government's European policy' (www.cabinet-office.gov.uk/cabsec/2003/cabcom/eus).

The European Secretariat (in the Cabinet Office)

Rather than establish a separate Department for European Affairs, British governments have opted to coordinate EU policies through a European Secretariat within the Cabinet Office. As we noted above, the Cabinet Office and its various Secretariats play a major role in coordinating policies within the core executive, and supervising their implementation by the relevant department. In this context, the Cabinet Office's European Secretariat seeks to ensure not only that departmental policies are in accordance with EU obligations and objectives, but that in pursuing these obligations, departmental policies either do not impinge upon those of other departments, or, alternatively, in the case of 'cross-cutting' policies, that there is adequate coordination between the relevant departments.

On Friday mornings, there is a meeting involving the Head of the European Secretariat, the Foreign Office, relevant government departments, and UKREP (UK Permanent Representation). The latter, headed by a career diplomat of ambassadorial rank, is the cadre of officials from various government departments – but with Foreign Office, Department of Trade and Industry, and Treasury officials often prominent among its membership – and is a vital conduit between British and EU policy makers, both promoting and defending British interests in EU-level decision-taking areas, while also keeping relevant domestic core executive policy actors informed of imminent developments and policy initiatives. The latter role means that UKREP can 'alert the national capital of impending or possible legislative action', thereby enabling the relevant policy actors 'to intervene in the [EU] policy process at an early stage', reflecting a recognition that, just as in domestic policy making, 'early intervention in the initial technical phases of the policy process ... is the most effective way of influencing the final outcome' (Kassim, 2000: 40).

These Friday meetings are a vital part of the coordination process concerning European policies, ensuring that the relevant departments and their officials are kept informed of recent EU policy initiatives, and how these will impact on domestic policies and ministries. At the same time, however, these meetings are also a vital means of facilitating a considered and consistent British response to forthcoming EU initiatives and meetings, particularly by UKREP, who will usually have been able to indicate the likely stance of other member states and their representatives on specific issues, while also highlighting the extent to which various policy proposals are negotiable (Kassim, 2000: 41; Bulmer and Burch, 1998: 615).

The Foreign and Commonwealth Office

Of all the government departments in the core executive, the Foreign and Commonwealth Office (FCO) has consistently been the most regularly and actively involved in developing and coordinating Britain's relationship with Europe (a fact which is grist to the mill of those Right-wing Conservatives who have long viewed the FCO as 'the foreigner's friend', consistently 'selling-out' Britain's interests to 'Johnny Foreigner', in the name of international diplomacy). The FCO is said to have enthusiastically embraced British membership of the (then) EC from the outset, partly because this offered the department a vital new role following the decline of the empire and commonwealth (Buller and Smith, 1998: 175–6).

The FCO, along with the Cabinet Office's European Secretariat and UKREP, has been central to the coordination of European policy proposals within the core executive, although it is sometimes suggested that as other departments develop their own 'European Units', send their own officials to work in UKREP, and increasingly liase with their counterparts in other member states, then the FCO's coordinating role will diminish somewhat. An alternative view, though, is that these other departmental linkages will render the coordinating role of the FCO Office (in partnership with the European Secretariat of the Cabinet Office, and UKREP), more important than ever. Certainly, Burch and Holliday are convinced that these three institutions, along with 10 Downing Street, have developed into 'the core of the European network' in Whitehall (1996: 88). Kassim, meanwhile, believes that while the FCO's 'relative importance has been in decline' since Britain formally became a member of the (then) European Communities in 1973, it 'remains a core actor in the making and coordinating of the UK's EU policy' (2000: 37, 39).

The FCO enshrines three policy divisions *vis-à-vis* the EU, namely the European Union Division Internal, the European Union Division External, and European Union Bilateral Relations. A fourth, the European Union Division Presidency, is established when Britain hosts the UK Presidency. Each of these divisions reports to the FCO's Director for Europe (Kassim 2000: 38).

The Foreign Office has therefore 'occupied a central position in the UK's EU policy making system' (Kassim, 2000: 37), particularly as it 'provides the institutional framework for the day-to-day coordination of EC [EU] policy through the Permanent Representatives in Brussels' (Spence, 1993: 60). Without the strong coordination and central supervision provided by the FCO and its partners in the Whitehall 'European network', there is a danger that the trend towards policy subsystems, inter-departmental fragmentation and competition, and clientelistic relations with privileged organized interests which has manifested itself in the core executive will, over time, become replicated, to varying degrees, at EU level.

Other government departments

As neither the EU nor Whitehall are monolithic entities, the impact of the former on the latter has varied from one policy subsystem and department to another. In other words, some government departments and policy areas have become more 'Europeanized' than others. Furthermore, while some departments will view 'Europeanization' as a threat, to be resisted as far as possible in order to defend departmental autonomy, others will consider closer European integration in their policy subsystem as an opportunity: a means of achieving policy goals which would otherwise be difficult to attain from a position of relative autonomy.

Two inextricably linked factors have shaped the overall attitudes of government departments towards the EU. First, whether or not the department was closely involved in, or directly affected by, Britain's joining of (what was then) the European Communities in 1973. Second, the implications of subsequent EU policy developments and competencies on the department's own policy objectives and responsibilities.

According to Buller and Smith (1998: 172–7), departments which were closely involved with Europe from the outset have tended to evince a more positive perspective, whereas departments which have only subsequently, in the 1980s and 1990s, become increasingly affected by the EC/EU's expanding policy jurisdiction, have generally been rather less comfortable with this perceived incursion into their policy subsystems.

Apart from the Foreign Office, discussed above, the two departments identified by Buller and Smith as having generally been the most positive in their attitudes towards EC/EU membership, are the Ministry of Agriculture, Fisheries and Food (MAFF) – until its abolition in 2001 – and the Department of Trade and Industry (DTI). MAFF (perhaps in a manner somewhat similar to the FCO) was arguably given a new lease of life by Britain's accession to the European Communities in 1973, not least because of the role it bestowed upon departmental officials in defending agricultural subsidies via the Common Agricultural Policy (CAP), particularly during much of the 1970s and 1980s, when recession, fiscal retrenchment and political changes were prompting cutbacks in public expenditure and reductions in subsidies to other industries. What further enhanced the role of MAFF officials *vis-à-vis* the EU was the rather specialist, and sometimes scientific, nature of many aspects of agricultural policy, leading to Kassim's observation that: 'Some departments have a monopoly over technical expertise which may make it difficult for other actors to challenge their positions' (Kassim, 2000: 28). Indeed, shortly before the summer 2001 abolition of MAFF, and its replacement by DEFRA, it was suggested that 'Europe has given … MAFF … an important *raison d'être* without which [it] might have disappeared' (Marsh et al., 2001: 217). What might now be said is that without Britain's membership of the EC/EU, MAFF might have disappeared rather sooner.

The DTI, meanwhile – particularly the Trade 'division' – has discerned a clear congruence between many of the economic objectives of the EC/EU and its own, the more so following the implementation of the Single European Act. Certainly, the DTI's Trade division's belief in free trade has been reflected in many of the EC/EU's policies concerning the single market, monopolies and mergers, (de)regulation, competition, etc., and hence the DTI has tended to hold a positive view of Europe. Indeed, according to one departmental official 'in the areas that are core to the DTI, trade policy and Single Market policy, we are closer to the Commission probably than any other member state' (quoted in Buller and Smith, 1998: 174), while another DTI official acknowledges that the department has generally been in favour 'of a strong Commission which is capable of policing a single market, policing state aid, and which is capable of devising and seeing through an effective liberal trade policy' (quoted in Marsh et al., 2001: 220).

What has also enhanced the DTI's role in the EU policy process has been the highly technical character of certain policy issues, such as those pertaining to energy, and telecommunications, for example, reflecting the above point about technical expertise enhancing a department's influence, while also fostering a generally more positive stance *vis-à-vis* the EU. In the case of the DTI, the latter has been encouraged further by virtue of the clear orientation of EC/EU economic and trade policies towards extending free trade and fostering greater competition since the 1980s, as symbolized by the Single European Act. In this respect, rather than have to respond reluctantly to an EU-driven policy agenda, the DTI found that the EU's orientation was commensurate with the Trade Division's own commitment to facilitating free trade and promoting liberalization (Buller and Smith, 1998: 174; Kassim, 2000: 30; Marsh et al., 2001: 220).

This, in turn, indicates that 'Europeanization' is not simply a one-way, top-down process – as Eurosceptics tend to imply – but a two-way process, whereby on certain policy issues or in certain policy subsystems, domestic policy actors can seek to shape the EU policy agenda, or at least skillfully exploit that agenda to further their own policy objectives.

By contrast, Buller and Smith depict the DSS, and the Home Office, as the two departments whose stance towards Europe has been somewhat ambivalent, or even resentful at what is perceived to be a steady loss of autonomy due to increasing European integration. The DSS, for example, 'continually finds the EU is adding both legislative and expenditure burdens as a result of the Commission's attempts to harmonize social policy', whereas the Home Office 'is still concerned with limiting EU competence, maintaining sovereignty, and protecting perceived national interests', and thus seeks to retain 'control of immigration, law and order, or criminal justice issues' (Buller and Smith, 1998: 176; Marsh et al., 2001: 222–3).

The Treasury, meanwhile, has tended to evince a cautious, even slightly sceptical, stance towards the EC/EU, clearly concerned not only about the major implications of economic and monetary union, but also about the domestic expenditure consequences of particular EU policies and initiatives, such as 'match-funding' and 'additionality' *vis-à-vis* structural funds administered via the EU.

Virtually all departments, though, have established their own European directorates, divisions or units directly concerned with the impact or implications of EU directives and regulations on their policy subsystem(s). For example, one study suggested that the Department of Trade and Industry's European Directorate comprised 60 staff organized into five discrete units, dealing with the single market, state aid, industrial policy, energy and EU enlargement. The Home Office, by contrast, enshrines an EU and International Unit comprising about 15 staff (Kassim, 2000: 30, 31).

Although the EU thus impacts upon departments to different degrees, and in different ways, it is possible to identify a general paradox overall. In one sense, it clearly places certain constraints and obligations on departments, thereby impinging on their departmental autonomy. Yet it can also be argued that in another sense, the EU offers some departments the chance to defend their autonomy *vis-à-vis* other departments, by enabling them to claim that they need to pursue certain policies, or administer certain forms of expenditure, in order to meet their EU obligations. In other words, departments can occasionally invoke the EU as an ally if they are in dispute with other departments and/or the Treasury. Once again, therefore, we emphasize that 'Europeanization' should not be viewed as a simple, one-way, top-down process, but is, rather, something of a two-way, 'bottom-up' process, and as such, somewhat dialectical and sometimes contradictory.

Furthermore, as European integration continues apace, various departments and the EU – particularly via the Commission – are likely also to develop an increasing range of exchange relationships and forms of resource dependency, as departments and the Commission look to each other to facilitate the attainment of various policy objectives.

Conclusion

It is apparent that the individuals in the core executive, identified in the previous chapter, are both supported and constrained by the institutions of that core executive; they are simultaneously empowered and enmeshed by it. The institutions of the core executive enshrine a vital array of resources necessary for the formulation, development and implementation of public policy in Britain, but as with individual actors in the core executive, the relationships should be comprehended in terms of resource dependency and exchange relationships, rather than attempting to identify the 'most important/powerful' institution, even though one particular policy actor might appear to be prominent with regard to one particular issue at one particular moment in time.

Consequently, while there are certainly centrifugal tendencies within the core executive which foster fragmentation and interdepartmental suspicion or rivalry, these are necessarily countered by centripetal trends which – normally – prevent complete disintegration and ensuing policy paralysis. In this respect, the Policy Directorate in the Prime Minister's Office, and the Cabinet Office, both play vital coordinating roles, aiming to provide strategic oversight, and brokering agreements between conflicting departments or their ministers. Yet the Cabinet Office and Policy Directorate are both heavily dependent on departments, either for policy advice and expertise, or for compliance in the implementation of policies.

Ultimately, therefore, on most issues at least, the institutions of the core executive are obliged to work together, if only for reasons of enlightened self-interest. Different institutions in the core executive possess, or enjoy ready access to, particular resources, such as expertise, the 'right contacts', political authority, the support of 'client' groups, etc., and hence much policy making necessarily entails a process of mutually beneficial bargaining and brokering of deals.

This provides a further refutation of claims about 'prime ministerial government' or 'new presidentialism' because, like his predecessors, Tony Blair has 'gradually discovered ... how hard it is to implement change', for while: 'A Prime Minister may say what he wants, and can make a difference on a few important issues … Departments remain in charge of implementation and details, and they, in turn, are dependent on attitudes on the ground' (Riddell, 2001: 36).

Within the core executive, therefore, the mutual dependence which characterizes the relationships, resources, responsibilities and roles of individual policy actors is replicated between the institutional policy actors. In turn, of course, the individuals and institutions of the core executive are themselves mutually dependent. The core executive overall, meanwhile, is itself dependent upon, or constrained by, wider domestic and international (endogenous and exogenous) circumstances and events, of an economic, political or social nature.

Recommended texts

1   Peter Hennessy (2001b) *Whitehall*, London: Pimlico.

Voluminous, but highly readable, text, incoporating a wealth of empirical evidence and examples, and written in Hennessy's wonderful, inimitable style.

2   Simon James (1999) *British Cabinet Government*, 2nd edition, Routledge.

Well written and informative overview of the role and structure of the contemporary Cabinet, including chapters on the role of Cabinet Ministers, the Prime Minister, and collective decision making, as well coverage of the individuals and bodies which support or serve ministers and/or the Cabinet.

3   J.M. Lee, G.W. Jones and June Burnham (1998) *At the Centre of Whitehall*, Basingstoke: Palgrave.

A superb in-depth and very detailed study of the bodies which service and support the Prime Minister and the Cabinet, particularly the Prime Minister's Policy Unit (Directorate), and the Cabinet Office (and its various secretariats).

4   Dennis Kavanagh and Anthony Seldon (1999) *The Powers Behind the Prime Minister: The Hidden Influence of Number Ten*, HarperCollins.

A highly contemporary and incisive analysis of the support network – especially the Prime Minister's Office, and its staff – which serves British Prime Ministers. Particular emphasis on the period from 1970 through to Tony Blair's first premiership.

5   David Richards and Martin J. Smith (1997) 'How Departments Change: Windows of Opportunity and Critical Junctures in Three Departments', *Public Policy and Administration*, *12*.

Informative article detailing how, why and when departmental philosophies and established approaches to policy are challenged, thereby enabling policy change to be introduced.

6   Martin J. Smith (1999) *The Core Executive in Britain*, Basingstoke: Macmillan

Clear and concise text providing a very good analysis of the core executive, drawing particular attention to the interdependency and exchange relations between the various individuals and institutions involved.

7   Martin J. Smith, David Marsh and David Richards (1995) 'Central Government Departments and the Policy Process' in R.A.W. Rhodes and Patrick Dunleavy (eds) *Prime Minister, Cabinet and Core Executive*, Basingstoke: Macmillan.

Useful essay emphasizing the extent to which much detailed policy determination is conducted within departments, thereby placing a premium on coordination to ensure that departmental interests do not undermine the government's overall goals and strategy.

8   Simon Bulmer and Martin Burch (1998) 'Organizing for Europe: Whitehall, The British State and European Union', *Public Administration 76*: 4.

Useful article examining how the core executive has adapted to Britain's membership of the EC/EU, noting how adaptation has been achieved relatively smoothly, in a piecemeal, largely accretive manner.

5 Organized Interests and Policy Networks

Along with the core executive, organized interests have been widely recognized as central to policy making in Britain. Indeed, debates about the strength and influence of certain organized interests underpinned a wider discussion in the 1970s about the character of the British political system in general, with some academics warning that Britain was drifting towards corporatism (Pahl and Winkler, 1974), while others, such as Anthony King (1975) spoke of an 'overload of government', due largely to the number of organized interests lobbying ministers and civil servants to pursue – or avoid – particular policies. The New Right, in similar vein, alleged that some organized interests – most notably trade unions – had become too powerful, to the extent that their sectional interests were selfishly jeopardizing the 'national interest', impinging upon governmental autonomy in policy making, and undermining the formal role of Parliament (Raison, 1979). Certainly, by 1979, some political scientists not associated with the New Right were nonetheless observing that the role of organized interests had become so extensive and pervasive that Britain had effectively become a 'post-parliamentary democracy' (Richardson and Jordan, 1979).

Organized interests and policy making in historical context

Keith Middlemas originally used the term 'corporate bias' to refer to the increasingly close links between ministers, civil servants and key organized interests in Britain, and traces the process back to at least the second decade of the 20th century, although he acknowledged that it developed apace after World War II. Middlemas explains how the 20th century, up until 1979, witnessed two parallel trends: first, the emergence of large or powerful organized interests, particularly in the industrial and economic arenas of British society, and second, increasing government intervention in the economy and civil society, whereby the traditional (liberal) distinction between the public and private spheres, or between the state and the market, became blurred.

The combined effect of these two trends was that politicians and leaders of key organized interests developed an increasingly close, mutually supportive, relationship with each other. As the era of Victorian *laissez-faire* receded, and government intervention both widened and deepened during the course of the 20th century (particularly after 1945), so the state increasingly became the focus for organized interests seeking the pursuit – or, sometimes, the avoidance – of particular policies and legislation. Yet at the same time, increasing state intervention rendered governments increasingly dependent upon the advice and assistance of various organized interests. A symbiotic relationship between policy makers and leaders of key organized interests often developed as a consequence.

This, Middlemas notes, was particularly prevalent in the economic and industrial spheres of policy, where trade unions and employers' associations (or their national-level officials and leaders) enjoyed regular and routine contacts with government ministers and senior civil servants (Middlemas, 1979; Dorey, 1993a; Perkin, 1990: Chapter 7), thereby giving rise to the notion of 'tripartism', a three-way partnership between the representatives of organized labour, the business community, and senior politicians.

The institutional embodiment of this tripartite system was the National Economic Development Council (NEDC), which was launched in 1962, and comprised representatives from the 'two sides of industry' and various ministers. Sometimes referred to colloquially as 'Neddy', the NEDC met on a regular, often monthly, basis, to discuss issues pertaining to a range of economic and industrial policies, but with a particular remit to obtain faster economic growth. The NEDC also spawned a number of subsidiary bodies, widely known as 'little Neddies', concerned with specific industries or sectors of the economy (Middlemas, 1983). During the 1980s, however, the NEDC met with diminishing frequency, and with civil servants and junior ministers increasingly attending instead of Cabinet Ministers (Secretaries of State), reflecting the Thatcherite distaste for such tripartite discussions and decision taking, and their view that the trade unions had no legitimate role in economic policy making, and should therefore be excluded. When the NEDC was finally abolished at the end of 1992, the only surprise was that it had not been disbanded sooner.

However, not all organized interests enjoyed such a close relationship with ministers and civil servants, and they were therefore obliged to use other channels in order to exert influence on policy making. It was this 'dual system' which led political scientists such as Wyn Grant to develop a new typology for understanding the relationship of organized interests to policy makers.

Insiders and Outsiders

Grant classified organized interests in terms of their proximity to particular parts of the political system, and also the strategies they deployed in seeking to exercise influence. This yielded a distinction between 'insiders' and 'outsiders', with the former generally enjoying a close and constructive relationship with government departments, ministers and civil servants, and the latter normally obliged to pursue their campaigns via Parliament, and various public campaigns, including recourse to the media. It also implied that 'insider' groups are concerned primarily with the institutional policy agenda, whereas 'outsiders' are mainly part of the systemic agenda (Grant, 1989: 14–21).

'Insider' strategies by organized interests

It was those organized interests enjoying regular and routine access to policy makers which were deemed by Grant to enjoy 'insider' status, and who therefore tended to possess the greatest potential for influencing policies and legislation. As we discussed in Chapters 3 and 4, the 'core executive' is the key site of national-level policy making in Britain, and it is 'insider' groups who normally benefit from privileged access to the personnel and institutions of the core executive. Or as Wilson expresses it, because 'those really in power are to be found in the executive branch of government ... It follows that the most important decisions for interest groups to influence are inside the "black box" of decision-making which takes place between ministers and civil servants' (1990: 81).

These 'insider' groups or organized interests invariably possess a number of attributes which bestow this privileged access to elite-level policy makers within the core executive:

First, they possess professional or technical expertise which policy makers – ministers, government departments, and senior civil servants – require in order to formulate public policy and draft legislation. As Britain has become a more complex society since the beginning of the 20th century, so policy makers have increasingly required and relied upon the specialist advice which key organized interests have been able to offer. Thus was the British Medical Association (BMA) regularly consulted over various aspects of health policy after the establishment of the NHS in 1946. Indeed, one historian of the NHS asserted that:

> What the BMA had been denied during the drafting of the NHS Bill, it got immediately after its enactment ... What was granted, in effect, was the right to argue a case rather than merely to present it, and assurance that agreement with the [medical] profession would be earnestly sought, not just that its views would be taken into consideration.
>
> (Eckstein, 1960: 101–2; see also Abel-Smith, 1975: 248; Ham, 1999; Jones, 2005; Perkin, 1990: 347–8)

The BMA did find itself temporarily marginalized somewhat during the late 1980s and 1990s, though, when the Conservative governments of Margaret Thatcher, and then John Major, sought to reform the NHS in the face of opposition from the BMA.

Second, they occupy a structurally important position in the socio-economic order, such that their acquiescence or cooperation is almost essential for the successful implementation of public policy. If an organized interest has been deemed important enough to warrant being consulted over the formulation of public policy, due to its specialist knowledge or expertise, then it is also likely to be of vital importance in aiding the administration of the ensuing policy. If an organized interest usually enjoying 'insider' status is not consulted over a particular policy proposal, or a policy is pursued after it has articulated strong objections, then the aggrieved organized interest might seek to hinder the implementation of the policy. Alternatively, it might seek redress through the courts, with a view to instigating a legal challenge against the policy, or a particular aspect of it. Clearly, most policy makers, for most of the time, will wish to avoid fuelling such opposition and obstruction, thereby reinforcing the tendency to consult key organized interests, and secure their support, or at least their acquiescence.

Third, they are 'representative' of an important – numerically or strategically – section of British society, to the extent that policy makers deem it unwise to disregard their views. Such organized interests can claim to speak authoritatively on behalf of the majority of individuals in that particular occupation or profession, thereby imbuing the views so expressed with greater credence and credibility. For example, about 90 per cent of farmers in Britain have traditionally been members of the National Farmers Union (NFU), while a clear majority of police officers have usually belonged to the Police Federation, thereby enabling both bodies to claim that they are 'representative' of farmers and police officers respectively. This, in turn, will normally mean that policy makers will take their views and grievances more seriously when consulting them over the development of policy in their particular domain.

Fourth, they are considered (by policy makers) to be moderate and 'responsible', not only in their aims and objectives, but also in their methods. 'Insider' organized interests tend, in most cases, to seek either the continuity of existing policies, or only relatively minor piecemeal adjustments to them, as opposed to extensive, root-and-branch reform. This will usually endear them to policy makers, particularly senior civil servants, for whom relative continuity or only incremental change are usually highly valued, compared with root-and-branch reform of long-established policies. Furthermore, these 'insider' organized interests will be viewed as 'responsible' by virtue of their usual willingness to abide by the 'rules of the game', whereby negotiation (usually behind closed doors), confidentiality and willingness to compromise are the normal means of effecting influence or securing agreement *vis-à-vis* public policy. By contrast, 'going public', in the form of demonstrations or other forms of direct action, is generally viewed as the characteristic of an organized interest which is either less responsible and moderate than traditional 'insiders', or has failed to achieve its policy objectives through the normal processes of consultation and bargaining: public demonstrations often imply the failure, or even absence, of elite-level dialogue with formal policy makers.

In terms of the agendas identified in Chapter 2, 'insider' groups are normally concerned first and foremost with the institutional agenda, that is, with influencing policies concerning issues and problems which policy makers have already accepted as worthy of their attention. There will be occasions, though, when 'insider' organized interests will involve themselves in the systemic agenda also, just as their direct and regular access to senior civil servants and policy makers does not preclude them from seeking to exert additional influence via Parliament too.

Indeed, the assumption that 'insider' organized interests, by virtue of their privileged access to senior civil servants and ministers, would not concern themselves with Parliament was emphatically rejected by the publication of *Parliament and Pressure Politics* in 1990. Edited by Michael Rush, the book was based on a multiauthored study (by members of the prestigious Study of Parliament Group), involving more than 250 organized interests, which examined the extent to which such bodies sought to exert influence via Parliament, and the specific aspects of parliamentary activity which they focused on. One of the most surprising findings of this major study, as illustrated by Table 5.1, was the extent to which 'insider' groups simultaneously maintained or developed links with Parliament in addition to their regular links with senior civil servants and ministers. Indeed, Table 5.1 indicates that 'insider' groups actually make more use of Parliament than 'outsider' groups (discussed below), this usage clearly supplementing their regular contacts with the core executive. In pre-empting the obvious question as to why 'insider' groups feel it worth lobbying Parliament when they already enjoy regular access to the core executive, Judge draws attention to the fact that, as we note in the next chapter, Parliament is a key forum for *legitimating* public policy, so that while:

Table 5.1   Parliamentary contact by organized interests (%)

Type of contact	Insiders	Outsiders
Regular contact with MPs	85.8	66.7
Regular contact with peers	64.1	54.7
Written evidence to a Select Committee	83.0	53.1
Oral evidence to a Select Committee	73.6	31.8
Contacts with All-party groups	51.9	14.5
Contacts with Party Subject Groups	54.7	30.8

Source: Judge, 1990: 36

> Parliament may neither be routinely nor actively involved in policy discussions ... it impinges upon this process generally in delimiting the independence of any single policy community [discussed below], and also in factorising into the closed world of Whitehall a requirement to consider wider partisan/parliamentary/public concerns – even if only in the limited sense of seeking to anticipate or to forestall possible future public criticism in Parliament.
>
> (1990: 33; see also Norton, 1993a: 203–4)

Clearly, therefore, while 'insider' groups fully recognize that the core executive is the most important policy making arena overall, they are also cognizant that Parliament is also part of the policy process, even if a predominantly reactive, policy-modifying one. At the very least, 'insiders' can generally choose how much attention to devote to seeking to influence Parliament in tandem with their routine access to the ministers and civil servants. In contrast, for 'outsider' groups, such choice is rarely available, for Parliament is usually the primary locus of their lobbying activities.

'Outsider' organized interests

'Outsiders' are those organized interests which do not enjoy regular or close links with national-level policy makers, and who have therefore been obliged to pursue other strategies and channels in seeking to influence public policy. Indeed, strictly speaking, it might be argued that not all 'outsiders' should be deemed organized *interests* anyway, because various of them are more concerned with social or moral values, or the welfare of other people or even animals, rather than the material interests of the members themselves. It might also be suggested that some of these 'outsiders' are only loosely organized (whereupon they might sometimes be classified as 'social movements'). Yet while acknowledging these two points, we would suggest that such bodies are still collectivities which seek either to shape public policy in a manner which is beneficial to those 'interests' or sections of society, or to influence the systemic agenda, in order to raise public awareness of what they deem to be an undesirable or unjust state of affairs.

There are a number of reasons why some organized interests do not enjoy privileged or regular access to elite-level policy makers, and are thus consigned to 'outsider' status:

- Their 'demands' or objectives are considered (by policy makers) extreme, or irresponsible. Groups campaigning for an end to *all* experiments on animals or the renunciation of *all* nuclear weapons, for example, are likely to be viewed by policy makers as 'unrealistic' or 'unreasonable' in their demands, and thus not taken seriously. Indeed, the objectives of some such organized interests might well be viewed as a direct challenge to the 'dominant ideology' or value system of society, and thus further disregarded. Campaigners against poverty or low pay have often encountered this problem, for in a capitalist society and market economy such as Britain, socio-economic inequalities are widely viewed as inevitable and necessary, and even desirable (to provide incentives, rewards, etc.), so that those seeking to eradicate low pay or poverty are effectively challenging the values and processes upon which Britain's economic system is based.
- The policy being canvassed is ideologically incompatible with the institutional agenda, particularly the government's own political priorities or objectives. For example, the Campaign for Nuclear Disarmament (CND) was viewed with contempt and derision by Conservative ministers during the 1980s because those ministers were committed to *strengthening* Britain's nuclear capacity, and permitting the USA to place cruise missiles on British soil, as part of the 'special relationship' between the two countries.
- Their tactics or methods are similarly viewed as extreme or irresponsible, with groups such as the Animal Liberation Front (ALF) and Hunt Saboteurs, for example, unashamedly, even enthusiastically, engaging in direct action.
- The issue(s) which they are promoting are not considered important by policy makers; they are addressing matters considered to be of 'low political salience'. Of course, as part of the 'systemic agenda', such interests will be aiming to persuade policy makers that their issue *is* important, or ought to be recognized as such, and thus placed on the institutional agenda.
- Following on from this last point, 'outsiders' will not generally possess the expertise or specialist knowledge which policy makers require to formulate policies.
- The issue they are seeking to promote or raise awareness of does not correspond to a particular policy area or 'subsystem', and may, therefore, not come under the jurisdiction of a particular government department. This might make it difficult for an organized interest to promote awareness of an issue, even if it affects a relatively large number of people. For example, there have always been a plethora of groups concerned with the issue of poverty, but no one single policy subsystem or department can be deemed responsible for eradicating poverty (quite apart from the fact that policy makers might either deny the existence of poverty, or acknowledge it, but claim that the poor themselves are the authors of their own misfortune, so that political action is inappropriate). The DSS might claim that better educational opportunities and skills training would be more effective than increasing the levels of welfare benefits, and thus suggest that the issue is one for the Department For Education and Skills to address. The Department For Education and Skills, however, might suggest that the best means of tackling poverty is to ensure stable economic growth so that prosperity increases, thereby linking the issue to the Treasury's macro-economic strategy. The Treasury, in turn, might claim that continued economic expansion depends upon maintaining competitiveness, pursuing further liberalization, and reducing 'red tape' for companies and employers, thus passing responsibility to the DTI. Where a particular issue or problem (assuming it is even acknowledged as such) transcends the boundaries of several policy subsystems, and the issue is not part of the institutional agenda, each of the departments potentially involved can simply 'pass the buck'.

- Following on from the above example, an issue such as poverty might be confined only to the systemic agenda because there are several organized interests seeking to raise awareness of particular aspects of the alleged problem. The issue of poverty might well be addressed by SHELTER, linking poverty with homelessness, while Age Concern will seek to highlight the scale of poverty among the elderly who are struggling to survive on paltry state pensions. Meanwhile, the National Union of Students (NUS) might attempt to highlight poverty among many students since the abolition of maintenance grants, while the Child Poverty Action Group (CPAG) will focus on the plight of children living in low-income households, and Gingerbread draws attention to the poverty endured by many lone parents. The plethora of organized interests concerned with the issue of poverty, far from persuading policy makers to take the issue more seriously, and acknowledge that it is indeed a significant problem, may well enable those policy makers to adopt a dismissive stance towards the apparently incoherent and inconsistent character of the 'demands' being made by the various groups. Indeed, policy makers might even occasionally be tempted to play 'divide and rule', thereby fuelling friction, resentment or suspicion between the various organized interests.

- Some organized interests are 'outsiders' because they are not deemed 'representative' of the people they purport to be campaigning on behalf of. This is sometimes rather ironic, for while the predominantly middle class or professional socio-educational background of many organized interest members normally enables them to be treated more seriously and respectfully by policy makers (who themselves usually emanate from similar backgrounds), some groups, precisely because their members are predominantly from such backgrounds, are thereby deemed 'unrepresentative'. According to Whiteley and Winyard, this was a problem experienced by the 'poverty lobby' (quite apart from the other problems we have just identified), whereby the organized interests campaigning on behalf of the poor were often taken less seriously by senior civil servants precisely because the members – particularly the senior members or full-time leadership – were not themselves 'poor' or living in poverty (1987: 132; see also McCarthy, 1983: 220).

- A final reason why some organized interests endure 'outsider' status is that their active involvement is not considered necessary (by policy makers) in policy implementation. For example, ministers and civil servants do not really require the assistance of the elderly in administering pensions policies, or the active involvement of the low-paid in determining social security entitlement, and hence this will further reinforce the outsider status of groups representing (or purporting to represent) the elderly or the poor. In some respects, this follows on from the previous point, for by virtue of being 'unrepresentative', groups such as those constituting the poverty lobby 'are unable to deliver their clientele; they do not have sanctions such as non-cooperation with a new government policy' (Whiteley and Winyard, 1987: 133).

Denied regular access to policy makers in the core executive, 'outsider' groups generally seek to influence public policy either through Parliament, or by raising public awareness of an issue, in the hope that policy makers will then respond to the ensuing shift in public opinion. In this respect, 'outsiders' are again very much part of the systemic agenda.

'Outsiders' and Parliament

For many 'outsider' groups, therefore, exclusion from regular access to the core executive obliges them to focus a significant degree of their activity on Parliament. For such groups, the House of Commons (and, to a lesser extent, the House of Lords) affords a number of opportunities – as we will discuss a little more fully in the next chapter – to 'outsider' organized interests (although as noted above, many 'insiders' also avail themselves of such channels), most notably:

- Lobbying backbench MPs with the aim of persuading them to develop an interest in a particular issue, whereupon they might pursue it via Ministerial Question Time, correspondence with the relevant minister(s), raise the issue in an Adjournment Debate, sign an Early Day Motion, or introduce a Private Members' Bill.
- Persuading MPs to table amendments to a Bill during standing committee stage, when a Bill's clauses and provisions are examined in detail.
- Submitting evidence to a select committee inquiry into a relevant topic. The evidence might be in the form of a written submission, but it might also involve a representative of the organized interest being invited to appear before the select committee in order to answer questions from the MPs concerned.
- Establishing links with a relevant backbench subject or all-party committee.

As noted earlier, in Table 5.1, two-thirds of 'outsider' pressure groups surveyed were in regular contact with backbench MPs, and over half had submitted written evidence to a select committee, while almost one-third had tendered oral evidence. A similar number also had contacts with the various backbench subject committees found in the parliamentary parties (discussed in the next chapter).

'Outsiders' and extra-parliamentary activities

'Outsider' organized interests might also engage in extra-parliamentary activity, either as an adjunct to the above channels, or as an alternative if the above are either unavailable, or are deemed inappropriate. Extra-parliamentary activities which 'outsiders' might pursue include:

- Demonstrations, marches and rallies, to raise public awareness and thereby influence public opinion, which might in turn persuade policy makers to give the issue more serious consideration.
- Organizing petitions, which may then be submitted to 10 Downing Street, as an indication of the breadth or depth of public feeling on a particular issue.
- Placing adverts in newspapers, highlighting a particular issue, and possibly encouraging 'concerned citizens' to write to their MP, or a relevant Minister.
- Pursuing legal action, by challenging, via the courts, the legality or justice of a decision or policy. The courts might decree that a particular policy is discriminatory, for example, or that a minister has acted *ultra vires* (exceeded their legal powers). Recourse to the courts is likely to increase in the context of the 1998 Human Rights Act.
- Following on from the last point, legal action might be pursued at European level, either through the European Court of Human Rights (which is *not* part of the EU), or via the EU's Court of Justice.

In pursuing these courses of action, 'outsider' organized interests will often be seeking to influence the *systemic* agenda by raising the profile of a particular issue which they believe policy makers ought to be addressing.

Some 'outsiders', though, actually choose to avoid such peaceful, parliamentary or judicial channels, having no desire to be incorporated into the established political system or policy process. Such groups are termed by Grant as 'ideological outsiders' (1989: 18), or 'outsiders by choice' due to their hostility towards established politics and 'anti-system' stance. For such groups, of which the ALF and Hunt Saboteurs are clear contemporary examples, their 'outsider' status is a conscious choice, reflecting their determination not to be 'compromised' or 'corrupted' by involvement in 'bourgeois' political processes. For these 'ideological outsiders', direct action provides a far more effective means of achieving their policy objectives than any number of talks with 'establishment' politicians and civil servants, for such talks, these groups suspect, would merely place them under pressure to 'sell-out' their non-negotiable principles.

One particular advantage of Grant's insider/outsider typology is that it drew attention to temporal changes in the policy roles of certain groups, whereby the relationship of an organized interest to the core executive, for example, might change in certain circumstances. This was certainly the case during the 1980s, when the trade unions were transformed from classic 'insider' groups to outsiders, due to the Thatcher governments' antipathy to organized labour (Dorey, 2002a). Slightly more surprising, though, was the Confederation of British Industry's (CBI) overall loss of 'insider' status during the 1980s, their place being taken by the Institute of Directors, whose ideological instincts and policy preferences were rather closer to those of Margaret Thatcher herself than those of the CBI. Since 1997, though, under Tony Blair's premiership, the CBI has regained much of its former 'insider' status, certainly more so than the trade unions.

While Grant's typology has proved very useful in distinguishing between organized interests in terms of their strategies for seeking to influence public policy and/or agenda setting, other writers have sought to develop a model of organized interests which reflects the extent to which much policy making in Britain, and particularly within the core executive, is sectoral, based on particular policy subsystems. Or to put it another way, while the 'insider' versus 'outsider' distinction provides a useful account of the role of organized interests at the 'macro' level, which reflects 'broader questions concerning the distribution of power within contemporary society', some writers sought to develop a 'meso-level concept' to explain the role of organized interests, and their relationship with the relevant government department, in a particular policy area or subsystem. This yielded the notion of policy networks, an approach which not only 'emphasises the need to disaggregate policy analysis and stresses that relationships between groups and government vary between policy areas', but also recognizes that 'in most policy areas, a limited number of interests are involved in the policy-making process' (Rhodes and Marsh, 1992: 1, 4).

In particular, the policy networks approach suggested a continuum which drew attention to the existence of two sharply contrasting types of relationship between organized interests and policy makers in a particular policy subsystem, ranging from policy communities at one end, and issue networks at the other. As will become apparent, it has been policy communities which have exerted the greatest influence on policy making in Britain, or as Grant himself expressed it, the concept 'clearly provides a good fit with the available empirical evidence on how decisions are made in British government' (2000: 50), so it is to policy communities that we now turn our attention.

Policy Communities

In the earlier chapters on the core executive, we noted the extent to which some departments enshrined a particular departmental philosophy or perspective which strongly influenced their policy proposals. These departmental perspectives often partly reflect – and are then reinforced by – the close links which specific departments develop with key organized interests operating in their policy subsystem. As Richardson and Jordan once noted: 'The policy-making map is in reality a series of vertical compartments or segments – each segment inhabited by a different set of organised groups, and generally impenetrable by "unorganised groups" or the general public' (1979: 174). This led to the notion of policy communities, which, according to two of the academics most associated with the concept are 'networks characterised by stability of relationships, continuity of a highly restrictive membership, vertical interdependence based upon shared delivery responsibilities and insulation from other networks and invariably from the general public (including Parliament)' (Rhodes and Marsh, 1992: 13).

Similarly, Grant acknowledges that 'policy communities are generally organised around a government department and its network of client groups', whereby the 'real divisions are between the different policy communities, rather than within the communities themselves' (2000: 50).

The main characteristics of policy communities are summarized in Table 5.2.

Limited membership. A policy community comprises a very small number of policy actors, often with just one key organized interest involved with senior civil servants, the relevant government department, and the appropriate minister (s). In this respect, a policy community both reflects and reinforces a rather closed and elitist style of decision taking and policy making in Britain, although as we will note below, and again in Chapter 9, some policy communities have been weakened somewhat since the late 1980s and 1990s, thereby rendering them a little more open to other organized interests.

Functional or professional membership. The organized interest which comprises part of a particular policy community often has a membership based on the role(s) performed by

Table 5.2   Main characteristics of policy communities

Attributes	Policy community
Scope of membership	Very limited and closed
Criteria of membership	Functional or professional
Potential/actual membership	High
Linkages with policy makers	Close and regular
Continuity	High
Consensus	High–shared values
Resources	Rich in resources
Resource relationship	Shared and exchanged resources
Interaction	Bargaining and negotiation
Internal structure	Hierarchical/disciplined
Implementation role	Considerable/important

Source: Adapted from Marsh and Rhodes, 1992a: 251; Rhodes, 1997: 44

its members, either economically or professionally. In this respect, its membership is usually 'sectional', in the sense that it is derived from a particular section of British society, based on occupation or socio-economic function. Furthermore, this membership will be considered highly important, either in terms of status, strategic position in British society, or the societal functions fulfilled.

Actual membership vis-à-vis potential membership is high. The key organized interest which is part of a policy community is invariably able to claim that it is 'representative' by virtue of its high ratio of actual members *vis-à-vis* potential members. The NFU, for example, has usually comprised more than 90 per cent of British farmers, and has therefore been able to claim that it alone speaks authoritatively on behalf of the farming industry, a claim long accepted as justified by policy makers themselves (Grant, 1983). The more an organized interest is able to claim that the majority of those eligible to join it have actually done so, the more it can claim to be representative of a particular profession, industry, occupation or other strategically important sector of British society. This will often ensure that it is taken more seriously by policy makers, and incorporated into the policy-making arena, so that its views can be elicited while policy is being formulated.

Close, regular links with policy makers. Organized interests which are part of a policy community will enjoy regular access to policy makers, and be included in discussions over policy (or policy proposals) on a routine basis. Indeed, the relationship between the key organized interests and policy makers will be both close and closed, so that while the senior representatives of these interests normally enjoy an 'insider' relationship with senior civil servants, the relevant government department and its minister, such access is generally denied to other organized interests.

High level of continuity. With such close and regular links between the policy actors, a policy community normally evinces considerable continuity in terms of its composition and membership. Even though individual members will obviously change from time to time, the institutions and organizations that collectively comprise the policy community will generally remain the same. This, in turn, enables new individuals in the policy community (a new leader of a key organized interest or a recently promoted senior civil servant, for example) to be socialized into the extant dominant values or 'paradigm' of that policy community, thus further contributing to overall stability.

High degree of shared values. A policy community will usually be characterized by a high degree of shared values between the policy actors involved. There will normally be considerable agreement on their interests and objectives, and a similar degree of agreement on what issues are worthy of their attention at any particular time. Consequently, policy communities are often intimately bound up with *institutional agendas*, and play a central role in managing and processing the policy agenda. In this respect, Jordan has noted how 'a policy community exists where there are effective shared 'community' views on the problem. *Where there are no such shared views, no community exists*' (Jordan, 1990: 327, original emphasis). With regard to the health policy community, for example, Day and Klein (1992: 468) note how, the medical profession, prior to 1979 at least, 'achieved the ability to veto policy change by defining the limits of the acceptable and by determining the policy agenda'. Furthermore, policy communities will often broadly agree on the most appropriate or feasible response to particular problems, in the context of their shared values and objectives.

Rich in resources. The actors in a policy community will possess considerable and valuable resources, not necessarily in terms of money (although this will sometimes be the case too), but in the form of experience, expertise, specialist knowledge, technical understanding, etc.

Shared and exchanged resources. These particular resources will frequently be extremely valuable, if not vital, to other members of the policy community, and so there is a mutually beneficial process of exchange emerging from the process of bargaining and negotiation (noted below). As one writer has explained:

> The administrative agency [or government department] depends upon the pressure group for information, advice, prior clearance of policy decisions, and ... for political support in its competition with other agencies for the scarce resources within government. The pressure groups, on the other hand, depend on the agency for access to decision making and ultimately for favourable decisions on certain policies. For both sides, the ... relationship serves to regularize the political environment and to develop friendships in what might otherwise be a hostile political world.

(Peters, 1984: 158)

Bargaining and negotiation. Due to the resources which the policy actors possess, and the exchange relationships these entail, a policy community is notable for the degree to which decisions arise out of bargaining and negotiation between the leader(s) of the key organized interest and the government department involved. With bargaining and negotiation, there is a continual process of 'give-and-take', deriving from each actor's possession of (or ready access to) resources needed by others within the policy community. The relative parity of power, derived from the possession of (or ready access to) key resources, means that no one policy actor can usually impose its wishes or interests on the other members of that policy community, not least because it will probably then be deprived of resources, possessed by the other actors involved, which it itself wishes to gain access to, or benefit from. Consequently, policy communities are often characterized by 'positive-sum' (rather than 'zero-sum') relationships between their constituent members. In any case, because of the generally shared values and objectives of the policy actors, any disagreements are usually over particular details or technicalities, rather than fundamental issues or goals, and as such, more readily resolved through the compromises and mutual concessions which bargaining and negotiation usually yield.

Hierarchical and disciplined. The organized interests prevalent in any particular policy community are not only 'representative' (as noted above), but are normally able to ensure that their members abide by decisions reached between their leaders and senior civil servants and/or relevant minister. This ensures that the leaders can speak authoritatively on behalf of their organized interest and its members, while also ensuring that they can usually 'deliver' the compliance of their members. This is crucial, because without the ability to 'deliver' in this way, departmental officials and ministers are unlikely to consider it worthwhile bargaining, negotiating and entering into policy agreements with the leadership of the organized interests concerned.

Considerable implementation role. As a result of the above characteristics, organized interests in policy communities tend to play an important role in the implementation of public policies. By virtue of their high membership, and their claim to be the primary or sole institutional representative of those employed in a particular policy subsystem, policy communities can usually be relied upon by ministers and senior civil servants to play a key role in the implementation of agreed policies in their particular subsystem.

These characteristics reflect a key feature of central government in Britain, namely that while Britain was – prior to recent devolution initiatives – widely deemed a unitary state (although some writers have preferred to characterize Britain as a 'union state', given the distinctiveness of Scotland and Wales), it has also long been characterized by internal fragmentation into a series of semiautonomous policy subsystems. Indeed, this 'sectorization' has been identified as one of the key features of what Jordan and Richardson (1982) termed a 'British policy style', to which we return in Chapter 9. In the context of policy communities, the significance is that 'different professional or producer groups and different sections of government departments or government agencies dominate in different policy areas' (Marsh and Rhodes, 1992a: 264), as illustrated in Table 5.3.

Although the core of a policy community is generally based on the relationship between a specific government department and (usually) one particular organized interest, there are sometimes one or two 'secondary' groups in the policy sector whose views might occasionally be elicited on particular issues (Marsh and Rhodes, 1992a: 255–6; Smith, 1993: 61). The involvement of these secondary groups is, therefore, rather *ad hoc* and certainly not routine and regular as is the case for the primary organized interests. Examples of policy communities which existed for much of the postwar period in Britain are illustrated in Table 5.3.

Indeed, there are some highly specific divisions within particular policy subsystems themselves, such as the tobacco policy community, which might be viewed as a division of the trade and industry policy domain. Certainly, as Read's study has shown, a close relationship has often existed between the DTI and the tobacco industry, represented via the

Table 5.3 Key policy communities in contemporary Britain

Policy sector/subsystem	Department	Primary organized interests	Secondary organized interests
Agriculture	Ministry of Agriculture, Fisheries and Food[1]	National Farmers Union	Country Landowners Association
Health	Department of Health	British Medical Association	Royal College of Nursing
Law-and-Order	Home Office	Association of Chief Police Officers	Police Federation
Tobacco	Department of Trade and Industry	Tobacco Advisory Council	Advertising Association
Transport	Department of Transport	British Roads Federation	Society of Motor Manufacturers and Traders

[1]Replaced in 2001 by the Department of the Environment, Food and Rural Affairs (DEFRA)

Tobacco Advisory Council, which, since its formation in 1978, 'has established itself as the authoritative voice of the industry' (1992: 128).

What these policy communities indicate is that, just as relationships within the core executive, between the Prime Minister and ministerial colleagues, as well as between ministers and senior civil servants, are not zero-sum, but are based on resource dependency and exchange relationships, so too are relations within policy communities similarly symbiotic. Governments and relevant departments provide political authority, legislative endorsement, an appropriate policy framework and overall legitimation, while the key organized interest(s) provide specialist knowledge and expertise, technical or professional advice, and assistance in implementing agreed policies.

The impact of policy communities on public policy

The above attributes of policy communities have had significant implications in terms of their impact and influence on public policy in Britain since 1945. The most important of these has been a tendency towards overall stability and continuity of public policy in their particular policy subsystem (although there has been somewhat greater instability since the late 1980s, as we will note below, and again in Chapter 9). Policy communities are commonly characterized by the durability of existing policies, and their resistance to change, especially in the short term. This (small 'c') conservatism is not really surprising, for existing policies in their particular policy subsystem will usually have been the outcome of previous bargaining and negotiation between the key organized interest(s), senior civil servants inside the relevant government department, and the appropriate minister, these negotiations having yielded a compromise or consensus. As a result, the members of the policy community will be reluctant subsequently to change the agreed policy or strategy unless there are compelling arguments for doing so. Hence Marsh and Rhodes' observation that: 'the existence of a policy network/community is a key cause of ... continuity' and that 'the existence of a policy network or community acts as a major constraint upon the degree of policy change ... fosters incremental changes, thereby favouring the *status quo* or the existing balance of interests in the network.' However, because some changes are inevitable over time, policy networks will normally seek 'to contain, constrain, redirect and ride out such change, thereby materially affecting its speed and direction ... a *dynamic* conservatism' (1992a: 261–3). Similarly, Jordan and Richardson have noted that the 'logic of negotiation' intrinsic to a policy community tends to ensure that: 'policy makers in both government and groups will share an interest in the avoidance of sudden policy change. Working together, they will learn what kind of change is feasible, and what would so embarrass other members of 'the system' as to be unproductive' (1982: 93–4).

Consequently, the strength of a policy community has often been such that new ministers keen to promote new ideas and initiatives have met with considerable scepticism and resistance, and frequently been persuaded that their proposals are not really feasible or practicable. While some ministers may persevere with their initiatives, many have either been persuaded of the arguments against a particular policy proposal, or simply accepted that the resistance is likely to be so pronounced that perseverance will consume too much of their time and energy: some battles are simply not worth fighting.

As noted above, policy communities are often an important aspect of agenda management, seeking, as far as possible, to regulate the institutional agenda (along with ministers and senior civil servants) and thereby keep off issues from the systemic agenda which might challenge both their interests, and existing policies. Indeed, the relationship, between policy communities and institution agendas corresponds closely to Bachrach and Baratz's 'second' or 'hidden' face of power and their concept of 'non-decision-making', which (as we noted in Chapter 2) is 'exercised by confining the scope of decision-making to relatively safe issues', whereby 'demands for change in the existing allocation of benefits and privileges in the community can be suffocated before they are even voiced; or kept covert; or killed to prevent access to the relevant decision-making arena' (1970: 7). Or as Marsh and Smith have more recently expressed it, 'tight policy networks persist, in large part, because they are characterised by a large degree of consensus … on [the] policy agenda, the boundaries of acceptable policy' (2000: 6).

In this respect, policy communities, and their degree of control over the institutional agenda, exemplify Schattschneider's concept of the 'mobilization of bias' (also noted in Chapter 2). He emphasized how some issues are organized into politics, while others are excluded, and that the ability to determine the latter is central to politics: 'the definition of the alternatives is the supreme instrument of power' (1960: 69). This illustrates the veracity of Smith's observation that in a policy community, the ideological framework and the institutional structure are inextricably linked and mutually reinforcing:

> If there is a dominant set of beliefs, it protects the institutions by justifying the inclusion of certain interests and preventing the conceptions of alternatives. The institutional structures protect the ideology by preventing the access of groups which could suggest new ideas and policies … If groups do arise which question the agenda, then the institutional means can be used to keep them out.
>
> (1990: 45–6)

Issues or organized interests which might challenge the existing goals, policies or resources within a particular policy community are likely to be met with resistance, often in the guise of being labelled 'unrealistic' or 'irresponsible'. Resistance might also manifest itself through casting aspersions on the motives of those who are perceived to constitute a potential challenge to the actors in the extant policy community, thereby seeking to discredit them, and undermine their legitimacy. One way to do this, ironically, might be to imply that the 'outsiders' are motivated by self-interest and the selfish pursuit of power or their own ends, thus depicting them unfavourably with the professed 'responsibility' of those actors who comprise the policy community.

With particular reference to the health policy community, for example, Smith observes how the key policy actors, namely the Department of Health (DOH) and the BMA:

> excluded other actors who did not share their perceptions of health policy. This exclusion occurred through institutional arrangements – when making policy the Ministry gave formal recognition to the doctors – and through ideology – the notion of clinical autonomy meant that it was the doctors alone who had responsibility for health policy in the last instance.
>
> (1993: 175)

Certainly, if challenged, the key actors in a policy community might seek to change the terms of debate to undermine their critics. For example, the tobacco policy community, faced since the 1970s with campaigns from groups pointing out the health risks of smoking, and calling for curbs either on tobacco advertising, or on smoking in public places, has responded by depicting smoking as an issue of individual liberty in a free society, in which smokers need to be defended from the encroaching 'nanny state'. That said, the tobacco policy community has been forced onto the defensive since the 1970s, and consequently obliged to accept curbs on advertising, as well as increasing statutory restrictions on smoking in public places. Indeed by autumn 2004, an increasing number of pubs and restaurants were designating themselves 'no smoking' establishments, a trend which would have been unimaginable 20 years ago.

This last point suggests that while policy communities are, by definition, generally characterized by organizational stability and relative policy continuity, they are not entirely static, for changes do occasionally occur. We therefore need to consider how and why a policy community might be challenged, possibly resulting in more significant policy change. Certainly, in Britain since the late 1980s, a number of policy communities seem to have experienced varying degrees of destabilization.

How policy communities change

Policy communities are occasionally destabilized or disrupted by the introduction of a new policy, although as previously noted, the key actors will normally seek to resist policies which they deem inimical to their interests, or which conflict with their shared values. Sometimes, though, a new policy will be introduced as a consequence of the destabilizing of a particular policy community. In this respect, the notion of 'policy streams' (discussed in Chapter 2) is pertinent, for the flowing together of the three streams, identified by Kingdon, opens a policy window, and thereby enables a new policy to be introduced.

Precisely how a policy community responds to such circumstances depends, of course, on the nature of the problem which has led to policy change, and whether new political or policy actors have established themselves as a consequence.

The main challenges to an extant policy community emanate from five main sources or circumstances:

1 Significant changes to the dominant ideological framework or political climate, resulting in a 'paradigm shift' (the third of the policy streams delineated by Kingdon (1995)).
2 Crises.
3 The emergence of new, possibly scientific, evidence and knowledge.
4 The loss of 'representativeness' by the hitherto dominant organized interest.
5 Successful use of alternative channels of access or influence by actors excluded from the policy community.

These five sources are not mutually exclusive, for any combination of them might become interlinked on occasion and reinforce each other. For example, a crisis often provides the impetus for an official inquiry, which then reveals new evidence concerning the cause or origins of the problem.

Changes in the dominant ideological framework or political climate

This particular account of how policy communities can be destabilized or disrupted is normally cited with direct reference to the election of Margaret Thatcher's first Conservative government in 1979. Subsequently Prime Minister for the next 11 years, Thatcher, along with many of her closest ministerial colleagues (and further encouraged by various Special Advisers), consciously sought to challenge a number of 'vested interests' who were deemed resistant to the New Right philosophy, and many of the policies which the Thatcher governments wished to implement. Thatcherites fully recognized the inherent conservatism of many actors in various policy subsystems – a wonderful irony that a series of Conservative governments berated other institutions for being too conservative – and thus sought to challenge their role and dominance, in order to effect change in a neo-liberal or consumer-orientated direction. Much of the New Right's rhetoric was condemnatory of 'producer interests' who jealously and selfishly defended their perceived interests and privileges against those of their 'clients', consumers, or society in general.

Whereas many policy communities had originally become established in the context of the postwar social democratic consensus, with its emphasis on industrial partnership, political stability and social harmony, Thatcher proudly proclaimed herself to be a 'conviction politician', and as a result, throughout the 1980s, her governments explicitly aimed to challenge some of these policy communities and the allegedly self-serving policy continuities which they entailed.

At a general level, the post-1979 promotion of economic liberalization and market-based solutions to social problems provided a notable challenge to the relatively closed, conservative and consensual world of many policy communities. Thatcherites drew a clear distinction, often in a highly populist manner, between selfish and self-serving 'producer interests' on the one hand, and either the 'national interest', or 'the interest of the consumer' on the other, with Thatcher and her ministerial colleagues clearly on the side of the latter two and against the first.

At this macro level, the Thatcherite promotion of economic liberalism, and the lauding of 'market forces' as the prime determinant of economic activity, resulted in the increasing marginalization and exclusion of the trade unions from economic and industrial policy making. As previously noted, this was most apparent in the downgrading, and eventual abolition (in 1992), of the NEDC, which had previously entailed senior trade union representatives meeting monthly with employers' representatives and Cabinet Ministers jointly to discuss a range of economic and industrial policies. Such neo-corporatist styles of policy making were anathema to Thatcher and her ministerial acolytes, and so from 1979 onwards, there was a clear attempt at moving away from such tripartite policy forums (Dorey, 2002a).

What this entailed at sectoral or policy subsystem levels was a restructuring of various policy-shaping arenas, whose composition and membership was changed, in order both to reflect and reinforce the ideological orientation and policy preferences of ministers. This was clearly the case with the Manpower Services Commission (MSC), which was replaced, in 1988, by Training and Enterprise Councils (TECs). Whereas trade unions had enjoyed parity of representation with employers on the MSC, union membership of the TECs was significantly reduced, to the extent that in 1992 only 5 per cent of places on the 82 TECs (in England and Wales) were allocated to trade union officials (McIlroy, 1995: 207), while the overwhelming majority of seats were filled by employers and other representatives from the business community. Indeed, the operating agreement of the TECs clearly states that at least 66 per cent of TEC 'directors' must 'hold the office of chairman or chief executive of a company or top level operational manager at local level of a company, or a senior partner of a professional partnership within (in each case) the private sector' (quoted in Graham, 1995: 275).

Elsewhere, in the sphere of secondary education, the 1988 Education Act transferred the responsibility for the management of schools from Local Education Authorities (LEAs) to schools' own governing bodies, while also permitting schools to 'opt-out' of LEA control, and become grant-maintained instead. These particular measures (the Act enshrined several others, including the National Curriculum) not only sought to diminish the role of LEAs and local authorities in the provision of secondary education, but also to reduce the role of the teaching unions, thereby serving to weaken the education policy community, particularly as the governance of education was increasingly transferred to sundry 'quangos' and agencies.

The distaste with which some Conservative ministers viewed the education policy community was clearly articulated by Kenneth Baker, the Secretary of State for Education who had introduced the 1988 Education Act. Baker opined that: 'the DES represented perfectly the theory of "producer capture", whereby the interests of the producer prevail over the interests of the consumer … the Department [was] in league with the teacher unions, university departments of education … and local authorities' (1993: 168).

Similar views were expressed by one of Baker's successors, John Patten (1995: 196–7). Indeed, the unconcealed contempt which such ministers harboured towards the education policy community led a retired Senior Chief Inspector of Schools publicly to complain about the Conservative governments' inclination to elicit the views of ideologically sympathetic individuals and think tanks, and thereby ignore the views and experience of those who actually worked in schools (cited in Chitty and Simon, 1993: 15).

Similarly, in 1989, the BMA experienced a challenge to its central role in the health policy community, when the third Thatcher government launched a review of the NHS (Baggott and McGregor-Riley, 1999: 71–2; Burch and Holliday, 1996: 232–8; McGregor-Riley, 1997). Partly in order to control escalating costs and secure greater efficiency in the deployment of resources, and also to introduce greater managerial rigour and coherence into the NHS, the Thatcher governments found it necessary to confront the BMA, which had hitherto enjoyed considerable autonomy and influence within Britain's health service. The reforms simultaneously promoted organizational restructuring, entailing a more hierarchical system of management in the NHS, coupled with the promotion of 'consumer power' in the form of greater choice and rights for patients. These two aspects, coupled with the introduction both of cash limits and of internal markets, entailing a purchaser-provider demarcation within the NHS, constituted a clear challenge to the BMA in particular, and the health policy community more generally. For example, 'it was general managers, not the clinical trades, who were now to decide on the division of labour, on the training, on the structure and the measures that were needed, on appropriate individual performance' (Strong and Robinson, 1990: 23).

Thus, as Smith observes: 'It was clear that in reforming health policy, and in changing the management structure, the Thatcher governments were preparing to challenge the existing policy community', so that with the introduction of the reforms, 'relations between doctors and the government ... deteriorated' (1993: 182–3; Wistow, 1992: 71). The most obvious public manifestation of the breakdown in relations between the medical profession and ministers was the former's national advertising campaign – 'What do you call a man who won't listen to medical advice? Kenneth Clarke' (the then Health Secretary) – attacking the reforms. For a traditional 'insider' group and core policy community member to resort to such public campaigns and personalized criticisms clearly reflected a serious breakdown in the relatively closed and consensual relationships which generally characterize policy communities.

In the above examples, the detrimental impact which the changed ideological climate wrought on the policy communities was often compounded by the attitude or personality of particular ministers. Both Norman Tebbit and Nigel Lawson, for example, made clear their low opinion of the NEDC, and considered its meetings a waste of their time (Tebbit, 1988: 193; Lawson, 1992: 713–14). Meanwhile, both the BMA and the teaching unions found themselves being treated with a notable (and very public) lack of respect by the pugnacious Kenneth Clarke, who served as Minister of Health in the late 1980s, and then, as just noted, Secretary of State for Education during the early 1990s.

Some writers have therefore suggested that ideological change might be imposed or reflected by 'despotic power' (Smith, 1993: 95–6), whereby ideologically-motivated political actors resolve to break up, or at least destabilize, an extant policy community, either by marginalizing the previously dominant organized interests and/or permitting the involvement of other groups with an expressed interest in that particular policy subsystem, or by altering the institutional agenda, so that new issues or objectives are prioritized. The Thatcher governments of the 1980s provide the clearest examples of such 'despotic power', harnessed to ideologically-driven change, *vis-à-vis* a number of former policy communities.

The second Blair government meanwhile, abolished the Ministry of Agriculture, Fisheries and Food in 2001, replacing it with a new Department of the Environment, Food and Rural Affairs (DEFRA), which seemed to herald a further downgrading or destabilizing of the NFU's former role in the agricultural policy subsystem. Not only does DEFRA exclude 'agriculture' from its name, it also makes clear that farming is just one aspect of 'rural affairs'. When these, in turn, are placed alongside environmental and food issues within one huge department, it is immediately apparent that the NFU is highly unlikely to enjoy the same degree of input into the policy process as it did when it enjoyed an almost exclusive relationship with MAFF (although even MAFF formally distinguished between farming and food). How the NFU has responded to this major institutional change, and the extent to which it has now been displaced by other rural or consumer-orientated organized interests, are issues which offer ample scope for research.

Crises

Occasionally, a disaster, epidemic or catastrophe can draw instant and widespread attention either to a new issue, or to a problem whose seriousness, scale and significance had not previously been acknowledged. When a major event suddenly pushes the issue towards the top of the institutional policy agenda, policy makers will feel obliged to act immediately, or at least be seen to act. On such occasions, the consequent policy response might well downgrade or abandon traditional negotiations with the dominant organized interest in the relevant policy subsystem, either because of lack of time – this quite likely being a situation warranting crisis management – or because the dominant organized interest in the relevant policy community might, on this occasion, be deemed part of the problem. As such, a crisis can result in a rupture within the traditional policy community, sometimes temporary, but occasionally longer lasting. For example, the agricultural policy community seems to have been weakened somewhat by various crises since the later 1980s, most notably the 'salmonella in egg production' crisis (Smith, 1991), the BSE crisis (Grant, 1997; Greer, 1999) and the 2001 foot-and-mouth epidemic (McConnell and Stark, 2002; Parry, 2003). Certainly, crises often prompt the inquiries which elicit new evidence and knowledge which, in turn, can challenge some of the norms and shared values upon which the policy community was based.

New evidence or knowledge

In Chapter 2, we noted briefly how new evidence and knowledge can exercise an influence on public policy and constitute a source of policy change. New evidence or knowledge can serve to destabilize or disrupt extant policy communities, by challenging the core principles or values upon which they have hitherto been based. Furthermore, new evidence and knowledge can lead to problem identification or definition, and thereby shape the policy agenda in a manner which has significant implications for existing policy actors and the relationships between them. It is in this respect that new evidence or knowledge can occasionally pose a challenge to an extant policy community, and reshape the institutional agenda.

In Britain, the three policy communities which have experienced the most notable challenges to their principles and prevalence, in large part as a consequence of new evidence or more advanced knowledge, are those of agriculture, transport and tobacco. The three crises (noted above) which have affected the agriculture policy community since the late 1980s also yielded new scientific evidence and knowledge which, in turn, raised serious questions about certain farming practices, thus exposing the farming industry to unprecedented critical scrutiny. The allegation, in December 1988, by the then Health Minister, Edwina Currie, that 'most of the egg production of this country, sadly, is now affected with salmonella', prompted an immediate slump in egg sales, and a furious response by the NFU, who not only demanded Currie's resignation, but compensation from the government for the lost revenues caused by the dramatic decline in egg sales.

Both of these demands were met, but while this implied a total victory for the agricultural policy community – having their two demands met so readily seemed to provide the clearest possible example of the strength of the agriculture policy community – its position had nonetheless been weakened somewhat in the longer term, for farming practices in general, and food production in particular, henceforth became subject to rather greater scrutiny and 'politicization'. As Smith (1991) notes (in his excellent study of the impact of the 'salmonella in egg production' episode) while organized interests can sometimes challenge or penetrate an extant policy community, 'there has to be a means for these groups to enter', and one of these means is provided when 'new issues or information cut across the policy community and create new problems with which the community cannot cope (Smith, 1991).

Part of that debate which followed the 'salmonella in egg production' furore, concerned the various forms of agrichemicals and pesticides which many farmers use to maximize their production of meat or crops. Indeed, the new evidence and expertise have emanated from both the medical profession and environmentalists, the former identifying various health risks associated with 'chemically-enhanced' methods of food production, and environmentalists drawing public attention to the impact of intensive farming methods and the use of agrichemicals and pesticides on wildlife and the countryside generally. For example, Smith cites a late 1980s study which revealed that out of 426 pesticides approved by the MAFF, 124 were suspected of being linked to cancer (1991: 249). Also, since the late 1970s, medical evidence has indicated links between certain forms of dietary intake and food consumption, and health problems, such as heart disease (Centre for Agricultural Strategy, 1979; Mills, 1992). Food production (and, by implication, farming) has been further 'politicized' as a policy issue by the concerns which some medical experts and nutritionists have raised about the longer-term health impact of additives used to improve the appearance, flavour or 'freshness' of certain food products.

Elsewhere, scientific evidence has highlighted the way in which various chemicals, sprayed on farmland to maximize crop production or eradicate weeds, are eventually washed, by rain, into neighbouring rivers, thereby poisoning fish (which then affects other wildlife which feed on the fish).

The development of such medical and scientific evidence, and the extent to which it entered the public consciousness – greatly assisted by the various crises alluded to above – served to 'politicize' farming as an issue, and thereby focus critical attention on the principles and practices of the agricultural policy community. The politics of food production ceased to be a predominantly technico-administrative issue jointly and privately determined between MAFF and the NFU, but became subject to a rather more open and public debate in which sundry other organizations and interests contributed, not least medical experts and the BMA, the Department of Health, nutritionists and consumer groups (Smith, 1991: 251).

One particular reason why the above agricultural crises and the concomitant medical or scientific evidence concerning farming methods and food production have had such a discernible impact on the agricultural policy community, derives from the fact that such crises and discoveries not only made the issue highly visible or readily understood by much of the public, but also because consumers could 'relate' to the problems, through concern about how they and their families might be affected. In other words, the issue enjoyed 'specificity' and 'comprehensiveness' (Solesbury, 1976, as noted in Chapter 2), and consequently moved beyond the purely scientific or technical, attracting the concern of an anxious public who sought swift assurances that remedial measures were being invoked by policy makers.

Both the 'salmonella in eggs' issue, and the implications for meat consumption engendered by the BSE epidemic, evinced 'specificity', in that there was a clear or highly visible focus to the issue, and 'comprehensiveness', in the sense that anyone who consumed eggs, and/or ate meat, could feel that the issue affected – or could affect – them. Or as Smith remarks, 'food issues, like heart disease, additives and food poisoning touch people much more directly than agricultural support prices' (Smith, 1991: 253).

Elsewhere, the transport policy community has found itself subject to challenges from both environmentalists and health experts since the late 1980s, due to increasing evidence about the detrimental impact which increased traffic and associated exhaust fumes are having both on the environment in general (the greenhouse effect, depletion of the ozone layer, global warming, etc.), and on people's health in urban areas (especially with regard to increasing cases of asthma). These developments are addressed by Robinson (2005) in his chapter in this book's companion text, *Developments in British Public Policy*.

Meanwhile, Read's (1992) aforementioned case study shows how the tobacco policy community was forced onto the defensive when, in the 1970s, medical evidence established a clear link between cigarette smoking and various respiratory diseases, most notably lung cancer. Since then, further medical research has suggested that 'passive smoking' (inhaling smoke from other people's cigarettes) can itself increase the likelihood of developing respiratory illnesses. The tobacco policy community has thus been obliged to accept increasing statutory restrictions on cigarette advertising, and, more recently, a growing number of 'no-smoking' zones in public arenas, such as pubs and restaurants, as well as on most modes of public transport. These restrictions are in addition to the longstanding legal obligation on tobacco companies to place a prominent health warning on cigarette packets.

In these respects, therefore, we can see that the tobacco policy community is no longer as dominant as it once was, and has increasingly had to respond to new issues and evidence being placed on the policy agenda by other policy actors and experts. In this regard, the tobacco policy community has found itself seeking to define smoking in terms of 'individual liberty', against a range of other actors who have increasingly defined smoking as an issue of public health. In this respect, the tobacco policy community has lost some of its hitherto control over the institutional agenda, as new evidence and organized interests have made some headway.

Loss of 'representativeness' by a hitherto dominant organized interest

Loss of (or reduced) 'representativeness' can take three main forms. First, the previously dominant organized interest may experience a decline in membership – or density of membership – and thus be less able to claim that it is the authoritative or legitimate voice of those working in a particular policy subsystem.

This scenario may well involve the emergence of rival groups within the policy subsystem, which claim to represent better the interests of those employed within it. In other words, the policy subsystem becomes more fragmented, and somewhat more pluralistic. Ironically, it might be the very closeness and consensual nature of the hitherto dominant organized interest's relationship with policy makers that enables others within the policy subsystem to claim that the leadership has become 'out of touch', and is failing to represent accurately or adequately the material interests of the wider membership.

This has partly been the case in the agricultural policy community in Britain, where more militant farmers' groups – such as Farmers for Action – have criticized the 'cosy' relationship between the NFU and the (former) MAFF, alleging also that the NFU does not adequately represent the interests of small or family farms, compared with large farms and agricultural businesses (Parry, 2003).

The second main way in which the previously dominant organized interest in a policy subsystem may find its 'representativeness' being undermined is when that policy subsystem experiences a process of diversification, leading to divergent or even conflicting interests within it. Once again, the agricultural policy community provides a good example of this, for the farming industry has witnessed increasing specialization and 'niches' since the late 1980s, such as the emergence of organic farming, which further inhibits the NFU's ability to claim that it is *the* representative voice of all farmers in Britain. Similarly, hill farmers in north Wales might have rather different interests to the so-called 'barley barons' of East Anglia, thereby leading to concern within the farming 'community' about how effective the NFU is in representing increasingly diverse interests among farmers.

The third main way in which the hitherto 'representativeness' of a dominant organized interest in a policy community is challenged is when other, alternative interests gain access to the policy subsystem, and thereby start to shift the terms of debate, and themselves shape the institutional agenda. Another of the ways in which the agricultural policy community has been weakened since the late 1980s concerns the emergence, or increased power, of other actors with a strong interest in food production, most notably food retailers and supermarkets, along with organized consumer interests (Smith, 1990). Trends towards semi-monopolization of the food retail industry by a relatively small number of supermarkets (Tesco, Sainsbury, Asda and Safeway account for 75 per cent of grocery sales in Britain), for example, has served to increase their influence *vis-à-vis* the farming industry when meeting relevant departmental ministers or officials, particularly as food retailers can often cite consumers' concerns over such matters as food safety. Indeed, such matters have resulted in the DOH becoming much more involved in issues pertaining to food safety, nutrition and dietary issues, thereby further challenging aspects of the agricultural policy community. At the same time, the rise of environmentalism has further added to public concern over the health implications of certain farming practices and methods of maximizing food production (quite apart from the more general concerns about the impact of agrichemicals and pesticides on wildlife in the countryside).

Use of alternative channels by other policy actors

Occasionally, a policy community might be destabilized or disrupted by 'alternative' or 'outsider' organized interests skilfully exploiting other channels of influence. We noted above the existence of a relatively long-standing transport policy community, comprising the Ministry of Transport, the British Road Federation and highway engineers. Yet on various occasions since the 1970s, the transport policy community has been challenged by what Dudley and Richardson term an 'adversarial policy community' (1996: 64), primarily comprising organized environmentalists, who have exerted influence through other policy-influencing arenas. This has sometimes served to constrain the trunk road building programme which the transport policy community had traditionally promoted as the solution to increasing car ownership, and consequent congestion on Britain's roads. Indeed, the 'adversarial policy community' of antiroad-building environmentalists can be said, particularly since the 1990s, to have prompted some questioning of the whole premise that building more roads will reduce traffic congestion, rather than actually encouraging even more road transport (quite apart from the concomitant pollutant impact of yet more cars and lorries on yet more roads).

Although this antiroad-building 'adversarial policy community' was undoubtedly aided by a more favourable exogenous climate, operating as it was in the context of attempts by the Treasury to curb increases in public expenditure (spending on infrastructure is invariably viewed as a 'soft' target in times of fiscal retrenchment), coupled with growing awareness of the scale and impact of environmental pollution (as exemplified above with regard to new evidence or scientific knowledge), what really enabled the antiroad-building lobby to exert influence, on occasions, from the late 1970s onwards, has been its use of public inquiries to present arguments and evidence against proposals to build more roads. Had it relied solely on direct action, it is highly unlikely that it would have enjoyed nearly as much success, for as we know, direct action is usually viewed as 'irresponsible' or 'extreme' by policy makers, and much of the media.

However, by participating in the public inquiries which have frequently followed planning applications to build new roads, environmentalists have not merely been able to enhance their own credibility and legitimacy as 'responsible' policy actors, they have been able to marshal evidence and arguments against particular road-building schemes and applications. As Dudley and Richardson note 'even though it was not strongly represented within the traditional core policy making community, the environmental lobby had discovered the appropriate arena for its pressure'. As such, they emphasize that:

> It is of crucial importance, therefore, to recognise that, although an interest may be apparently excluded from a core policy community, by selection of the correct arena for its activity, and effective transmission of its message, it may, by indirect means, have a significant effect on the policy network and policy itself.
>
> (1996: 75)

Of course, another, alternative channel of influence which an increasing number of organized interests have pursued is the EU, a development considered more fully below.

Certainly, since the 1980s, various policy communities in Britain have been affected by the above trends and developments, to the extent that a number of writers – including some who were previously closely associated with the concept – now suggest that policy making 'is often much more fluid and unpredictable – and less controllable' than policy community theorists previously assumed. Policy communities remain in various policy domains and subsystems, but they are nonetheless more susceptible to 'counter-tendencies which lead to lack of control, policy instability and unpredictable outcomes' (Richardson, 2000: 1008). Policy communities seem to have become more vulnerable to various challenges since the 1980s, so that those which remain do so in a less stable political and institutional universe, and consequently find it more difficult to retain control over the institutional policy agenda.

Outcomes of challenges to policy communities

When policy communities are challenged, there are usually two main potential outcomes. One is that the policy community is reconstituted, with a new organized interest at its core, in place of the group which had previously been hegemonic in that policy subsystem. This was evidently the case with training policy, as noted above, when the trade unions' representation on the TECs was permanently downgraded and diminished, and that of employers correspondingly increased. In this context, an organized interest which is more ideologically compatible with the government is admitted to the policy community, or granted greater prominence and influence within it, in place of an organized interest which has become viewed as 'off-message'.

The second possible longer-term outcome – and generally the more likely one – is that the destabilizing of a policy community is followed by a partial reconciliation, albeit on terms which are somewhat less favourable to the key organized interest(s) than previously. The dominant organized interest(s) might seek, or be offered, a *rapprochement*, although this will invariably require that they broadly accept the new policy which disrupted the policy community in the first place.

At the same time, though, the formerly dominant organized interest in a particular policy community might also find that it has to accept the incorporation of other groups who were previously excluded. In the latter scenario, of course, the policy community itself will be somewhat looser, and prone to further instability on subsequent occasions. For example, given that MAFF was replaced, in the summer of 2001, by DEFRA, the NFU has since found itself having to accept the involvement of various environmental and consumer groups in the policy domain(s) covered by the new department. In such situations, some policy communities 'may become linked to a rather messy and unpredictable chain of actors, who do not know each other well and do not speak the same language' (Richardson, 2000: 1008). Of course, this begs the question of whether they can still be meaningfully characterized as policy communities.

Some previously privileged organized interests might conclude that their involvement in these slightly looser 'policy communities' is still worthwhile, in order to retain or regain at least some influence and credibility, either in the eyes of the other policy actors in 'their' subsystem', or in the eyes of their members: some, reduced influence or input, might well be judged better than no influence or input at all. For their part, meanwhile, ministers might recognize the value of securing the cooperation of the relevant organized interests with regard to the implementation of the new policy. At this stage, the groups might be 'brought in from the cold' to be consulted on the practicalities of administering the new policy. Or as Richardson observes, in several policy areas and subsystems during the 1980s and early 1990s:

> The destabilisation of policy communities ... was almost invariably followed ... by a return to the accepted values and norms of the policy process. Thus, once a sector has been 'shaken and stirred', the affected interests were then soothed by being invited back into the inner circle of negotiations with government. The new policy style was ... to insist that the principles underlying the reforms should be maintained, but literally to negotiate the implementation with the affected interests and to make significant concessions in that process.

(1993: 97–98)

This seems to have been the case with regard to both the teaching unions and the medical profession, in the cases cited above, for during the 1990s, once the decisions concerning health and education reforms had been taken, and the relevant legislation enacted, the professions were consulted over precisely how best to implement the reforms. This can reflect enlightened self-interest on the part of ministers, for with regard to the post-reform consultation of the medical profession and health practitioners, it has been noted that: 'Following the confrontational crisis, it was in the self-interest of government to be conciliatory and to revert to administering policy through the medical profession' (Day and Klein, 1992: 475).

Similarly, the disruption caused to the education policy community by the Thatcher governments' determination to introduce major reforms of secondary education was eventually followed, in the 1990s, by a somewhat more emollient approach to the teaching unions under John Major's premiership. The government appreciated that while it had been able to develop a new education policy in spite of the hostility of teachers' unions (which were, therefore, largely excluded from the policy initiation and formulation stages), the cooperation of the teaching profession was vital to the successful implementation of the reforms. Consequently, teaching unions were permitted to express their concerns and views, not on the substance or objectives of the reforms, but on the practicalities and administrative aspects of operating the new policy.

Clearly, then, many policy communities have been destabilized since the 1980s, and even when subsequently reconstituted, have been less closed and tightly-knit than previously. Certain policy subsystems remain dominated overall by a close relationship between a key organized interest and the relevant government department, but even these linkages appear to be somewhat looser than prior to the 1980s, with ministers somewhat more willing either to use 'despotic power' to impose change, or to consult a somewhat wider range of organized interests.

Meanwhile, some organized interests have never enjoyed the privileged position of belonging to a policy community, and have therefore been part of an 'issue networks' universe.

Issue networks

If policy communities represent one end of a 'policy networks' continuum, based on close and closed relations and interaction between policy makers and organized interests, then issue networks constitute the other end, the polar opposite. In an issue network there is, potentially or in actuality, a relatively large and diverse membership, with a plethora of organized (sometimes loosely organized) interests and several government departments, reflecting the diverse or multifaceted nature of the policy issue involved (Table 5.4). Yet this eclecticism militates against the development of permanent and stable relationships, either between the organized interests themselves, or between them and the government departments. This instability both reflects and reinforces the absence of a clear consensus in an issue network, over both the underlying cause of a problem and with regard to who should accept responsibility for solving it, quite apart from the question of *how* it should

Table 5.4   Characteristics of an issue network

Attributes	Issue network
Scope of membership	Wide ranging and open
Criteria of membership	Usually social or moral
Potential/actual membership	Low
Linkages with policy makers	Loose and sporadic
Continuity	Considerable fluctuation
Consensus	Low(er) – value conflict
Resources	Limited/uneven resources
Resource relationship	Less valuable resources
Interaction	Consultation
Internal structure	Looser/leaders often weaker
Implementation role	Limited/non-existent

Source: Adapted from Marsh and Rhodes, 1992a: 251; Rhodes, 1997: 44; Daugbjerg, 1998: 44

be solved. As Smith elaborates, in an issue network, 'the sheer number of groups means that consensus is practically unachievable … because so many groups' various different problems and solutions exist within the policy domain'. The number of government departments involved further compounds the problem of 'conflict over who is responsible for a policy or issue, who should be involved and what action should be taken' (1993: 63; see also Rhodes and Marsh, 1992: 14).

Open membership. In terms of membership, issue networks are usually characterized by considerable eclecticism, whereby several policy actors can be, and often are, involved. No single organized interest normally prevails, but, instead, several interests might be involved in seeking to influence public policy. Furthermore, the policy issues involved might not be readily attributable to one particular government department, but, instead, transcend several department boundaries, thus making it more difficult for the organized interests to focus on one specific 'target'. Departments might even 'pass the buck', or play the groups off against each other, in a form of 'divide and rule'. Certainly, responsibility for some policy issues, such as poverty or the environment, is difficult to ascribe to one particular government department, thereby adding to the difficulties of organized interests in an issue network in pursuing a clear, coherent and focused campaign, and ensuring that the issue moves from the systemic agenda to an institutional agenda. As Jordan has noted: 'Issue networks are fragmented, open and extraordinarily complex, and are ill-structured for resolving conflicts and reaching authoritative decisions.' In so doing, Jordan explicitly draws attention to the characteristic of 'fragmentation', which clearly contrasts with the 'segmentation' to be found in a policy community (1981: 95–6).

Social or moral basis of membership. In an issue network, the organized interests involved are often concerned with social or moral issues, reflecting normative assumptions about what constitutes a 'good society', or deriving from concern for the welfare of others (be they people or animals). While such organized interests might reflect considerable altruism on the part of their members, they are often less likely to be considered important to policy makers, unless the values being espoused happen to coincide with an occasional 'moral crusade' being pursued by a prominent politician, or a 'moral panic' being fuelled by the media, usually the tabloid press.

Actual membership vis-à-vis potential membership is low. The social or ethical concerns of many organized interests in an issue network mean that however popular their 'cause' might be at any particular time, their membership is invariably likely to be relatively low, for only a proportion of potential members (every adult in Britain!) are actually likely to acquire membership. Again, unless an organized interest is campaigning on an issue which policy makers or prominent politicians wish to place on the institutional agenda, they are likely to be perceived or portrayed as 'unrepresentative' by policy makers. For example, while the CND claimed up to 250,000 members during much of the 1980s, Margaret Thatcher (and her supporters) could retort that out of a population of about 56 million people, CND's membership represented just 0.45 per cent of people in Britain! Not dissimilarly, following a highly publicized (and favourably reported by many newspapers) protest march through London by the Countryside Alliance in September 2002, apparently attended by 400,000 people, a Labour minister dismissed its significance by asserting that less than 1 per cent of British people had bothered to take part.

Loose and sporadic linkages with policy makers. The organized interests in an issue network generally have rather looser and fewer contacts with policy makers. There might be occasional, infrequent contacts, or perhaps *ad hoc* meetings with policy makers on a particular issue. Some organized interests, however, will not be consulted at all, either because their objectives (or tactics) are not compatible with those of policy makers – it is difficult to envisage senior civil servants or a government minister discussing animal welfare policy, over coffee and biscuits, with representatives of the ALF, for example – or because they do not possess relevant or valuable information needed by policy makers. The sporadic nature of linkages between the policy actors in an issue network also means that they do not normally develop the close rapport or strong professional relationship which more regular and frequent contacts would foster.

Considerable flexibility and fluctuation of membership. Unlike organizations whose membership is based on occupation, profession or socio-economic function, the organized interests in an issue network tend to be characterized by much greater fluidity of membership, both between and within the groups involved. There are often several organized interests involved in a particular policy area, but some of these will disband, change their names, or perhaps be displaced by a new group campaigning on a similar issue. At the same time, though, many organized interests in an issue network will find it difficult to retain members on a long-term basis, for various reasons. For example, the limited or only occasional policy influence of many such organized interests can engender a sense of disillusion among some members, who may therefore let their membership lapse. Other members may become less actively involved, or even discontinue their membership, because work or family commitments become more important or time consuming.

Limited shared values. The organized interests in an issue network will often have somewhat diverse aims and objectives, which means that they will find it more difficult to establish common ground with each other. Even under the rubric of 'animal welfare' or 'environmentalism', there may well be a plethora of organized – and quite possibly some less well-organized – interests, each focusing on a particular aspect or dimension of the broad issue. Even more important, though, is likely to be a relative lack of shared values with policy makers themselves, especially if the aims of the organized interests are incompatible with the dominant aims or interests of policy making elites. In other words, organized interests in an issue network will often find that their values are at odds with those prevalent on the institutional agenda.

Limited or uneven resources. The organized interests in an issue network also tend to suffer from a relative lack of resources. This might well entail limited finances, reflecting limited or fluctuating membership, or the fact that subscription fees need to be kept low in order to retain existing members and/or recruit new ones. However, in an issue network, the organized interests will also tend to lack other resources vital to policy makers, most notably technical knowledge, specialist information and expertise of various kinds. This lack of resources, of course, will be compounded by the issue networks' lack of value compatibility with the objectives prevalent on the institutional agenda.

Resources are of limited value or utility. The resources which might be possessed by organized interests in an issue network are often of little value or interest to policy makers, for the reasons alluded to directly above. For example, antinuclear groups and campaigners in the 1980s would not have possessed resources needed by ministers committed to increasing Britain's stockpile of nuclear weapons, and expanding nuclear power as a source of fuel. The knowledge which such groups did possess, concerning the environmental, health and safety risks involved in developing nuclear weaponry and power, was not really needed by those committed to nuclear weapons and power (quite apart from the ideological incompatibility between such groups and Conservative ministers during this decade).

Consultation. The generally limited utility to policy makers of organized interests in an issue network ensures that contacts between them are not only relatively sporadic and infrequent, but also consultative. By virtue of not possessing valuable resources, nor occupying an important socio-economic or high status position in British society, organized interests in an issue network do not normally possess the power necessary to engage in a process of bargaining and negotiation. Instead, while they might be consulted on certain issues, this will be very much at the discretion of policy makers, who may also decide to disregard the views or arguments advanced by representatives of the organized interest(s) involved. While this will not always be the case, the process of consultation might be pursued by policy makers primarily as a means of legitimizing a preferred policy initiative, for it can subsequently be claimed that 'interested parties' were consulted, and had the opportunity to express their views, even if they did not approve of the policy outcome. Meanwhile, from the perspective of the organized interests involved, it is better to participate in consultative exercises anyway, because the possibility of occasionally exerting an influence on policy makers is clearly preferable to not taking part at all, and thus having absolutely no chance of exercising any influence whatsoever. Furthermore, the organized interests may envisage that if they can present persuasive arguments concerning a particular proposal, they might be taken more seriously in the future, acquire greater credibility, and thus begin to develop closer or more regular linkages with policy makers. This has evidently been the experience of the environmental group, Friends of the Earth, since the 1990s.

Looser or less hierarchical structure. Many individual organized interests in an issue network are generally more loosely organized than the 'insider' groups in a policy community. This looser, less hierarchical structure derives largely from the more disparate aims of 'outsider' groups, and the greater fluidity of their membership. It can also, occasionally, reflect a hostility to traditional top-down patterns of authority, hierarchy and leadership, and a concomitant belief in egalitarianism or 'group democracy'. Consequently, control by the central- or national-level leadership is often much more difficult, which clearly has serious implications for its ability to 'deliver' its members (i.e. ensure their compliance) in the event of entering into a agreement with policy makers to assist in implementation. This loose or less hierarchical power structure is therefore a further reason why certain groups are part of an issue network, and only occasionally – if ever – consulted by policy makers.

Implementation role. In an issue network, organized interests normally play only a limited role, if any, in assisting policy makers with the implementation of public policy. Senior civil servants and ministers are not normally dependent upon the cooperation or compliance of such organized interests in administering policies, partly because such interests (by definition, as noted above) do not generally occupy an important socio-economic or structural position in British society, partly because of the relative fluidity of their membership, and also because of their less hierarchical power structure. As a result, while the leadership is less able to ensure the compliance of their members, those members themselves are less able to obstruct the implementation of policies with which they disagree. Indeed, attempts at outright obstruction might involve the members coming into conflict with the law, and thereby further confirm the group's 'outsider' status and lack of 'responsibilty'.

A clear example of an issue network is the 'poverty lobby', a term commonly used to characterize those organized interests campaigning about low incomes and those who are effectively marginalized from mainstream society due to lack of material resources. Below are just a few of the organizations (including charities) that might be said to form part of Britain's 'poverty lobby'.

- Age Concern
- Big Issue Foundation
- Centre Point
- Child Poverty Action Group
- Christian Aid
- Credit Unions
- Family Welfare Association
- Gingerbread
- Low Pay Unit (abolished 2003)
- National Council for One Parent Families
- National Housing Federation
- National Union of Students
- Peabody Trust
- Runnymede Trust
- Salvation Army
- Save the Children
- Shelter
- War on Want
- War Widows Association
- Women's Aid.

Of course, some of these organizations would insist that they are *not* first and foremost antipoverty bodies, but campaign against low pay and inadequate incomes only insofar as these underpin or compound the other problems experienced by their 'clients'. This being the case, we can immediately see how in an issue network, the greater number of organizations also reflects a greater divergence of interests and objectives. For example, while

Gingerbread might sometimes draw attention to the poverty in which many single parent families live, it is also concerned with a range of issues and problems encountered by such families, of which poverty is but one (albeit a highly significant one).

Furthermore, the very fact that there are so many organized interests involved in the 'poverty lobby', and that they 'represent' such diverse sections of society deemed to be affected by poverty, is a major source of weakness in terms of influencing public policy. For example, many elderly people, homeless people, single parents, students, and the unemployed experience varying degrees of poverty, but they would probably not identify with each other, and believe that they shared a common cause. On the contrary, measures to alleviate the poverty of one section of society might merely fuel resentment among other 'poor' sections of society. Besides, the underlying cause of poverty among these different sections of society varies markedly, making it even less likely that one particular policy would tackle the problem.

As we noted when discussing 'outsider' pressure groups, one particular problem affecting the 'poverty lobby', and thereby rendering it very much an issue network, is the range of departments which might be considered to have a role to play in tackling either the causes or the consequences of poverty. Precisely because poverty emanates from a variety of sources and causes, it is a 'problem' (the parentheses are to recall the point made in Chapter 2, about the way that problems are often socially constructed or ideologically contested, and therefore might not always be publicly acknowledged as problems warranting action from policy makers) which no single department is likely to accept primary responsibility for remedying. For example, as we noted above, poverty might be attributed to inadequate benefits, and therefore deemed a Department of Work and Pensions matter, or to low educational attainment, and thus be viewed as a Department of Education and Skills issue, due to the low educational attainment or achievements of many who are economically inactive or/and 'socially excluded'. In this sense, the multicausal nature of poverty makes it extremely difficult for the groups involved either to develop a clear and coherent strategy, or to coalesce effectively around one particular department. These problems are quite apart from those deriving from the general inability of the 'poverty lobby' to play a meaningful role in either the formulation or implementation of any antipoverty policies which might otherwise be adopted. This is not to say that such groups will *never* be consulted – some of them certainly seem to have been granted a more receptive ear by the Blair governments, committed as they have been to tackling social exclusion – but that any such involvement in the policy process will be *ad hoc* or limited, and very much dependent on whether ministers and civil servants wish to elicit their views: they would not normally *need* to.

Of course, the multicausal origins of poverty, and the multi-departmental character of eradicating it, are a major reason why the Blair governments (as noted in Chapter 4) have established a Social Exclusion Unit within the Cabinet Office, with a view to developing and coordinating an interdepartmental strategy for tackling the problem (although note the use of the term 'social exclusion' in preference to the narrower or possibly more contentious term 'poverty'), which, in turn, further reflects the professed desire for 'joined-up government'.

Another policy area which, until the 1990s at least, was characterized by an issue network (as opposed to a policy community) was that of the environment. A range of organized interests campaigned on various aspects concerning the environment including:

- Council for the Protection of Rural England
- Friends of the Earth
- Greenpeace
- National Trust
- Nature Conservation Council
- Royal Society for the Protection of Birds
- Transport 2000.

As with the 'poverty lobby', the environment issue network enshrined an eclectic array of organized interests, and the diverse character of their particular concerns – even within the policy subsystem of the environment – meant that they rarely occupied much common ground, or developed a coherent and unified campaign. Or as Ball and Millward have observed, 'environmental groups ... range over such a wide spectrum that it is difficult to generalise about common objectives, ideology and membership' (1986: 166).

Occasionally, perhaps, they could coalesce around a specific issue, such as the 1990s opposition to the Major governments' road-building programme, but they did not, and could not – for both organizational and ideological reasons – become anything even remotely akin to a policy community: their opposition to the building of more roads and by-passes stemmed from differing underlying concerns and objectives. Furthermore, this oppositional stance obviously placed them at odds with the government itself, even if individual groups, such as Transport 2000, found themselves being consulted by policy makers more regularly than hitherto (see Robinson, 2000: 120–1; 2005). By contrast, the government enjoyed the support of the transport policy community, leaving some of the antiroad-building campaigners to resort to direct action in an attempt physically to obstruct the road-building work. Not only did this render them even more at odds with the government, it also led to further fragmentation within the environment issue network, due to the unease which more respectable or conservative environmental groups felt at the use of direct action, often of an illegal nature, and mostly perpetrated by self-styled eco-warriors (Robinson, 2000: 132–51).

Apart from the example of opposition to road building, the environment issue network, like the 'poverty lobby', finds itself confronted by a range of departments which might be targeted, and any one of which is likely to respond by passing the buck, by suggesting that environmentalists would be better served by approaching the department of *y* or the ministry of *z*. For example, the former Department of the Environment, in spite of its name, had only a very limited interest in environmental matters *per se*, most of its work having been concerned with local government and housing. The Department of Transport, meanwhile, as we noted in Chapter 4, was characterized by a discernible pro-private transport philosophy, and would therefore generally be strongly in favour of road building. Elsewhere, the DTI would be unhappy about 'excessive' antipollution measures being imposed on firms, doubtless arguing that these would add to their costs, increase their bureaucratic burden, and ultimately undermine their competitiveness, whereupon the Department of

Employment (as was) might well have added its voice, pointing out the likely impact in terms of job losses in the construction industry.

Unlike the organized interests in a policy community, therefore, those in the environment issue network do not have just one specific department which can be deemed solely responsible for that particular policy subsystem. Instead, the multifaceted nature of the issue ensures that different departments might be considered responsible for particular aspects of the issue, but never for the whole of it. In other words, the divergent concerns which might be enshrined within the environment issue network are generally matched by the range of government departments and ministries which could be said to have (at least, partly or potentially) an environmental aspect to part of their remit, or within their policy subsystem.

Even if there were a specific department to which the organized interests in an issue network might want to focus their attention, it is unlikely that the department itself would need to seek the advice or cooperation of those groups. Not only would their disparate character normally prevent them from articulating a coherent perspective, and effectively speaking with a single voice, they would probably not be needed by policy makers for implementation purposes. For example, it was the DSS (now the Department of Work and Pensions) which administered Income Support and Old Age Pensions, not the Child Poverty Action Group, Gingerbread or Age Concern.

Ultimately, therefore, the organized interests in an issue network will usually enjoy only limited or sporadic consultation with policy makers – and even this may be purely cosmetic or presentational from a government's point of view – and little, if any, role in implementing public policy. Hence the tendency for organized interests in an issue network to focus more on influencing the systemic agenda, in the hope of highlighting issues which will subsequently be addressed by those with greater political power and policy influence, or which might even enable the interests concerned to become at least partly incorporated. Alternatively, or additionally, of course, the organized interests might seek to exercise influence *vis-à-vis* public policy via the EU.

Organized interests and the European Union

Irrespective of whether they are 'insiders' or 'outsiders' in Britain, and normally part of a policy community or issue network, an ever-increasing number of Britain's organized interests have turned their attentions towards the EU, viewing it as an additional, or possibly alternative, arena in which they can seek to shape policy agendas and influence policy outcomes.

There are generally four discrete ways in which British organized interests can seek to influence policy making in the EU: lobbying national representatives prior to meetings in Brussels; developing regular linkages, most notably with the European Commission itself, by maintaining an office in Brussels; forming alliances with similar organized interests and counterparts in other member states; and taking cases to the European Court of Justice.

Lobbying national representatives

The main focus of such lobbying would be the relevant minister prior to a meeting of the Council of Ministers, whereby the organized interests would seek to persuade them why he/she ought either to support or oppose a particular policy proposal in the Council. However, it is unlikely that ministers would normally be swayed by such lobbying, due mainly to the extent that other factors will normally determine their approach, such as departmental interests, the Cabinet's previously agreed line, the briefings provided by the Cabinet Office's European Secretariat, and/or the advice offered by UKREP.

Developing regular linkages in Brussels itself

Just as the most effective institutional focus of lobbying in Britain is usually the core executive, particularly the relevant government department, so the primary target of most organized interests at EU level has been the European Commission, and its Directorates-General. This is hardly surprising, given the role (noted in Chapter 8) of the Commission in formulating EU policies, for as is the case at domestic level, the earlier in the policy process that an organized interest can acquire access to policy makers, the more chance it will have of exercising at least some influence over the subsequent policy. Indeed, those organized interests who are deemed sufficiently important or knowledgeable in a particular policy area are likely to have their views and advice sought by the European Commission anyway; the Commission is as likely to approach the organized interest(s) as vice versa when formulating policy, or even before it has decided to develop a new policy.

In this respect, most of the characteristics which bestow 'insider' status on organized interests in Britain are equally valued by the European Commission, namely relevant specialist knowledge and expertise, responsibility in their methods and behaviour (thus accepting of the 'rules of the game'), reasonable or realistic in their policy objectives, compatibility with the policy goals of those they are seeking to influence, representative of their particular policy subsystem and/or members, and well resourced, with a permanent core of full-time, professional staff, with whom regular contact and consultation can be maintained.

To seek or maintain regular linkages with the European Commission, many organized interests now have a permanent office or headquarters in Brussels, often within walking distance of the Commission. However, it is also recognized that, hitherto, the European Commission has often been more open, accessible and receptive to a wider range of organized interests than the core executive in Britain (especially the senior civil service), although as the EU extends its policy jurisdiction, and policy making becomes increasingly technical or administrative, then the Commission itself may similarly seek greater order and stability by regularizing the number and nature of the organized interests with which it conducts regular consultation. Indeed, Mazey and Richardson believe that this process has already begun, although it is far from complete, so that there remains scope for a wider range of organized interests to seek a policy input (1996: 42).

One way in which the European Commission is likely to seek greater order and stability into EU policy making is to place increasing importance on those organized interests which can claim to be representative of a particular policy sector or subsystem at European, rather than purely national, level. As such, British organized interests are likely to respond accordingly – indeed, many have already done so – by forming or joining alliances with their counterparts in other EU member states.

Forming alliances with similar organized interests in European Union member states

Many British organized interests have attempted to influence EU policy making by forming alliances with their counterparts in other member states. Certainly, the number of Euro-level groupings has increased significantly, from about 430 in 1980 to over 700 in 2004 (for the full list, see www.europa.eu.int/comm/civil_society/coneccs), meaning that most policy sectors or subsystems will be represented at EU level via a transnational alliance of the relevant organized interest from a particular policy subsystem in each member state. Table 5.5 shows some examples of the 'Euro-groups' which British organized interests belong to for the purpose of EU lobbying. While some national level organized interest groups might feel that various of their interests are somewhat different to those of their European counterparts, they are still increasingly likely to recognize that their overall interests are best served by seeking to work with similar organized interests in other member states. Or as Mazey and Richardson observe:

> Europeanization of policy-making in Western Europe may already have achieved a critical mass and momentum to convince most organized interests that Brussels is a permanent and increasingly important feature of their organizational environment ... recognition of the over-riding need for Euro-level solutions to their members' problems may prove an effective counterweight to their centrifugal tendencies. As Europeanization accelerates, most policy actors recognize that some means has to be found of regularizing and institutionalizing such activity.
>
> (1996: 44–5)

Yet Mazey and Richardson also point out that this is a dual process, for:

> Officials in Brussels know, as do officials at the national level, that interest associations can be simultaneously a source of help and trouble. It makes sense to bring those interests together in some *ad hoc* or permanent structure in order to define problems, devise possible solutions and mobilize support from those who 'matter' for successful implementation.
>
> (1996: 48)

In other words, just as certain organized interests have variously been 'incorporated' into the policy process in Britain, at both formulation and implementation stages, so too have certain organized interests been co-opted by the European Commission to assist in the development and administration of EU policies. Indeed, Greenwood notes how the European Commission itself has sometimes encouraged and facilitated the formation of Euro-level groups (2003: 14–16).

Organized interests and the European Court of Justice

It is also important to note that the European Court of Justice offers Britain's organized interests a means of ensuring that EU policies are properly implemented by British governments. With the European Court of Justice responsible for ensuring that member

Table 5.5   Examples of Euro-groups to which British organized interests belong

Policy sector	British organized interest	Euro-group
Agriculture	National Farmers' Union	Committee of Professional Agricultural Organizations
Banking and Finance	British Bankers' Association Building Societies Association/Council of Mortgage Lenders	European Banking Federation European Federation of Building Societies
Chemicals	Chemical Industries Association	European Chemical Industry Council
Civil Engineering	Institution of Civil Engineering	European Council of Civil Engineers
Construction	Federation of Master Builders British Cement Association	European Builders Confederation European Cement Association
Dairy industry	Dairy Industry Federation	European Dairy Federation
Dentistry	British Dental Hygienists Association	European Liaison Committee for Dental Hygiene
Employment (Protection and Rights)	Trades Union Congress (TUC)	European Trade Union Confederation
Food and Drink	Food and Drink Federation	Confederation of the Food and Drink Industries of the European Union
	Ice Cream Federation	Euroglaces (Association of the Ice Cream Industries of the EEC)
	Seasoning and Spice Association	European Spice Association
Law	Law Society	International Bar Association
Media	National Union of Journalists	European Federation of Journalists
Paper	Paper Federation of the United Kingdom	Confederation of European Paper Industries
Small Businesses	Federation of Small Businesses	European Small Business Alliance
Timber	Timber Trade Federation	European Timber Trade Association
Tobacco	Tobacco Manufactures' Association	Confederation of European Community Cigarette Manufacturers
Tourism	British Tourist Authority	European Travel Commission
Transport	Association of Train Operating Companies	Community of European Railways
	British Ports Association	European Sea Ports Association
Veterinary	British Veterinary Association	Federation of Veterinarians of Europe

Source: www.europa.eu.int/comm/civil_society/coneccs

states comply with EU law, organized interests will occasionally take a case to the court if they believe that a British government is failing to implement an EU law which would be beneficial to their membership, or the section of society which they represent. For example, one mid-1990s survey revealed that about 30 per cent of British cases concerning equal pay and equal treatment at work, which were taken to the European Court of Justice, had been pursued or funded by the Equal Opportunities Commission (Barnard, 1995: 254).

The EU has therefore provided British organized interests with an increasing range of options and opportunities to seek to influence public policy, reflecting the fact that 'the EU policy process is best characterised as a multi-level, multi-arena, multi-venue game' which 'provides a multitude of access points for policy professionals and interest groups of all kinds'. Indeed, with reference to the earlier point about organized interests exerting influence thorough 'alternative arenas', the EU has provided such interests with 'some very effective alternative arenas or venues in which to play', particularly for organized interests 'excluded … from national policy communities' (Richardson, 2000: 1013). However, even organized interests enjoying 'insider' status or policy community membership have increasingly pursued a dual strategy, whereby the domestic policy linkages and participation are supplemented by involvement in the policy process at EU level.

The involvement of an increasing number of British organized interests in the EU policy process therefore also reflects the manner in which some extant policy communities have been partly destabilized or reconstituted since the 1980s, thereby leaving organized interests to seek either alternative, or additional, 'arenas' in which to seek to influence public policy. This, in turn, is likely to increase the vulnerability of those policy communities which have hitherto remained relatively intact.

Conclusion

Organized interests remain a key component of the policy process in Britain. While the 1980s and 1990s witnessed various changes in the involvement of organized interests, either in terms of which groups were granted 'insider' status, or alternatively, in the sense of experiencing a restructuring of their particular policy community, organized interests still played a crucial role in providing advice and assistance in the formulation and implementation of public policy. Even those organized interests which do not enjoy regular access to policy makers can play a significant role in seeking to shape the systemic policy agenda, or raise sufficient awareness of a problem that it becomes part of the issue attention cycle.

Even when particular organized interests were partially or wholly excluded from policy making during the 1980s and 1990s, they were usually consulted when implementation problems subsequently manifested themselves – which they sometimes did precisely because the knowledge which these groups possessed had not been solicited at the outset, when they might otherwise have highlighted probable problems of practicability. Similarly, although various policy communities have been destabilized and/or restructured since the late 1980s, many policy subsystems or domains continue to be characterized by a close – if not quite as closed as previously – relationship between the relevant department and particular organized interests.

Meanwhile, the organized interests 'universe' has itself been 'Europeanized', with many, if not most, national-level (as opposed to purely local) organized interests seeking to exercise influence through the EU, either as an adjunct to their domestic lobbying, or as an alternative when they have been marginalized. Just as some government departments have arguably been reinvigorated by Britain's membership of the EC/EU (as we noted in Chapter 4), so too have some organized interests discovered additional or alternative opportunities for policy influence via the EU.

Organized interests undoubtedly now compete with think tanks and policy advisers in attempting to influence public policy and shape either the systemic or institutional policy agendas, but they nonetheless remain key components of the policy process, and are likely to do so. Since the 1980s, their 'universe' has clearly been subject to reform, reordering and restructuring, but the organized interests themselves have not been rendered redundant.

Recommended Texts and Further Reading

1   Wyn Grant (2000) *Pressure Groups and British Politics*, London: Macmillan.

Good overview of the types and activities of organized interests, and the various ways in which they seek to influence politics and policy making in Britain.

2   David Marsh and R.A.W. Rhodes (eds) (1992a) *Policy Networks in British Government*, Oxford: Clarendon Press.

Seminal text on this topic, commencing with a conceptual overview before providing a series of case studies, written by appropriate experts, spanning a range of policy areas and subsystems.

3   Jeremy J. Richardson (1993) 'Interest Group Behaviour in Britain: Continuity and Change' in J.J. Richardson (ed.) *Pressure Groups*, Oxford: Oxford University Press.

Essay examining the role of organized interests following the downfall of Margaret Thatcher in 1990. Argues that in spite of being excluded at the formulation stage of various policies, many pressure groups were subsequently reincorporated into the policy process, particularly as implementation problems emerged.

4   Jeremy. J. Richardson, (2000) 'Government, Interest Groups and Policy Change', *Political Studies*, 48:5.

Excellent article examining how various policy communities were destabilized during the 1980s and 1990s. Notes, though, that many organized interests responded by seeking new arenas and channels of influence, with the EU especially offering new opportunities for involvement in the policy process.

5   Martin J. Smith (1993) *Pressure, Power and Policy: State Autonomy and Policy Networks in Britain and the United States*, Hemel Hempstead: Harvester Wheatsheaf.

Highly informative and well written discussion about the concept of policy networks, illustrated by good use of empirical examples, and noting the implications for policy making. Also considers how policy networks (and hence policies) change.

6   Parliament and Public Policy

It has long been widely accepted that Parliament plays only a limited, indirect, role in policy making in Britain, not least because of the extent to which policies are largely predetermined via the core executive and policy communities (as noted in the previous three chapters). This factor, along with the relatively high degree of party cohesion, especially in the House of Commons, means that once public policy is presented to Parliament, often in the form of a Bill, there are likely to be few significant changes to it. As Philip Norton (1993a), one of Britain's leading academic experts on Parliament (and himself now a Member of the House of Lords) has suggested, Parliament is a policy-modifying body, rather than a policy-making one. Parliament has been further constrained by Britain's membership of the EU, whereupon European law takes precedence over domestic law.

Yet to suggest that Parliament has become completely irrelevant to the policy process in Britain today would be to overlook a range of other functions which it fulfils, other than that of passing legislation, and through which it can exert an indirect influence on public policy. For example, Ministerial Question Time is a major means by which ministers and their policies are formally rendered accountable, as are the departmental select committees. These functions, along with others – such as Debates on the Floor of the House – collectively serve to imbue public policy with legitimacy. Indeed, some academic experts on the role of Parliament maintain that *legitimation*, rather than legislation, is probably Parliament's most important role. Failure to appreciate the significance of this role, it is suggested, underpins many of the claims about the decline or irrelevance of Parliament (Judge, 1993: 2, 130–1; Norton, 1993a: 131–46, 202–6).

The legislative process in the House of Commons

There are three types of Bills variously considered by Parliament (especially the House of Commons), namely Public Bills, Private Bills and Private Members' Bills, each of which will be briefly discussed.

Public Bills

These are Bills which are introduced by the government, via a senior minister (deemed to be 'sponsoring the Bill'), and invoke legislation which is applicable to all citizens or institutions in Britain – in effect, general law – unless explicitly specified otherwise. Public Bills constitute the overwhelming majority of legislation considered by the House of Commons,

Figure 6.1   Parliamentary stages of a Public (Government) Bill starting in the House of Commons

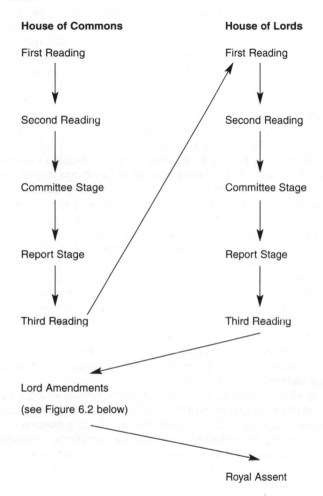

consuming about 30 per dent of the House's time each session. For example, in the 2001–2 Parliamentary Session, out of the 1,540 hours during which the House of Commons sat in total (excluding the 474 hours of parallel sittings in Westminster Hall), just under 476 hours were devoted to Public Bills. These Public Bills follow a clear sequence when proceeding through Parliament, as indicated in Figure 6.1.

Although this illustrates the stages of a Public Bill introduced in the House of Commons before proceeding to the House of Lords, such Bills can be launched in the House of Lords, and then proceed to the House of Commons. In either case, the sequence of stages that a Bill passes through is identical. In general, the Public Bills which commence in the House of Lords are those that are less partisan or politically controversial, or perhaps more 'technical'.

Each stage of a Bill's passage through Parliament serves a different purpose.

- *First Reading* – this simply entails the title of the Bill being read to the House of Commons (or Lords) by the Clerk, and a 'dummy' copy of the Bill placed on the Table.
- *Second Reading* – this stage is concerned with the principles and purpose of a Bill, and usually entails parliamentary Debate lasting 3–6 hours, although very occasionally, in the case of a particularly major or controversial Bill, the Second Reading Debate may take place over 2–3 days. At the end of the debate, there is a division (vote) on the Bill, and if it is supported by a majority of MPs, then the Bill is said to have been given its Second Reading.
- *(Standing) Committee Stage* – this is where a Bill is examined in detail, line-by-line, clause-by-clause. Standing Committees examining a Public Bill will normally comprise between 16 and 25 MPs, with the composition reflecting the balance of the parties in the House of Commons. Having a relatively small membership enables a much more detailed discussion of the Bill to take place, for at Standing Committee stage, it is the technical details and minutiae of a Bill which are the primary focus. Hence the Standing Committee scrutinizes the Bill in an attempt at identifying specific problems or inconsistencies. It is at Standing Committee stage that amendments to a Bill will be put forward ('tabled'), often of a rather specialized or technical nature. Each amendment may be subject to a vote in which case there will be a division between 'ayes' and noes', just as there is on the Floor of the House of Commons. Crucially, however, no amendments can be tabled which would affect or alter the overall principles or objectives of the Bill, for these have already been affirmed via its Second Reading. However, as the government has an in-built majority on a Standing Committee, 'hostile' or 'wrecking' amendments are rarely approved. Nonetheless, the Standing Committee stage of a Bill is when Parliament plays the most active or thorough role in the legislative process.
- *Report Stage* – having been through standing committee, an amended Bill is 'reported back' to the House, whereupon further debate on the revised Bill takes place, and additional amendments may be proposed.
- *Third Reading* – this represents a final debate on the Bill before it goes to the House of Lords, or to the House of Commons if the Bill was actually first introduced in the Second Chamber. At this stage, no further amendments are usually made and Third Readings are usually a formality, dispensed with fairly swiftly, sometimes in less than an hour.
- *House of Lords* – when a Bill has completed these stages in the House of Commons, it is then sent to the House of Lords (usually referred to by MPs, in parliamentary parlance, as 'another place'), where it undergoes the same stages as in the Commons.
- *Lords' Amendments* – after a Bill has gone through its stages in the House of Lords, it is returned to the House of Commons, where MPs debate whether to accept the amendments made by peers in the Second Chamber. If they are willing to accept these amendments then it can finally receive its Royal Assent (see below).

However, if ministers are not happy about the manner in which a Bill has been amended by the House of Lords, then one of four options is available to them, as illustrated by Figure 6.2.

In the first of the above scenarios, the government will send 'a Message' to the House of Lords, explaining why it is unhappy with the amendment(s), whereupon the House of Lords declines to insist on its amendment(s), and thereby allows the Bill, as originally approved by the House of Commons, to proceed to its Royal Assent.

In the second scenario, while unhappy with the House of Lords amendment(s), the government offers further amendments of its own, with a view to securing a compromise

Figure 6.2   Options when a government is unhappy with House of Lords amendments to a Bill

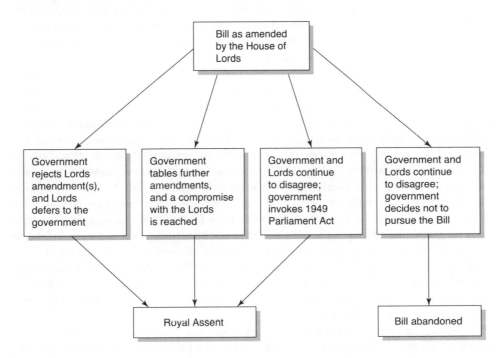

with the House of Lords. If the House of Lords agrees to the new amendments, then the Bill can proceed to its Royal Assent.

In the third scenario, neither the government nor the House of Lords are able, or willing, to agree; the government rejects the House of Lords amendments, but the Lords insists on their retention. Assuming that the government is determined to pursue the Bill, it will invoke the 1949 Parliament Act, which allows for a 'disputed' Bill to be passed in the following Parliamentary session, without the approval of the House of Lords. In such cases, the reintroduced Bill must be identical to the original. Usually, neither the government nor the House of Lords will want to push their disagreements this far, and so invoking the 1949 Parliament Act is very rare. A recent example of this scenario, though, concerned the 1998 European Parliamentary Elections Bill, which was only enacted by invoking the 1949 Parliament Act to over-ride the House of Lords' objections to aspects of the Bill. The Blair government has also invoked the 1949 Parliament Act to overcome continued House of Lords opposition to the Bill to ban foxhunting.

The most extreme scenario in Figure 6.2 is the fourth option, where neither the government nor the House of Lords are willing to 'back down', but ministers are not inclined to persevere with the Bill to the extent of invoking the 1949 Parliament Act. In this extremely rare scenario, the Bill is likely to be abandoned altogether.

Once a Bill has been approved by both the House of Commons and the House of Lords, it then proceeds to receive its *royal assent*. This reflects the fact that, strictly speaking, Parliament comprises not only the two Houses, but also the Monarch ('the Queen-in-Parliament'), so that only after the Royal Assent has been given can it constitutionally be claimed that Parliament has consented to a particular Bill. The Royal Assent is a formality – no Monarch has refused to grant it since 1707.

The overwhelming majority of Public Bills do reach the statute book, and the fact that governments are so rarely defeated over their legislative proposals and programme strongly underpins the view that Parliament is a weak body, largely subordinate to the (core) executive. For example, only three Public Bills failed to secure their Second Reading during the 20th century, namely the 1924 Rent Restrictions Bill, the 1977 Reduction of Redundancy Rebates Bill, and the 1986 Shops Bill. The latter was particularly noteworthy, because whereas the governments in 1924 and 1977 lacked a clear parliamentary majority (and were therefore more vulnerable to defeat), the Thatcher government in 1986 had a 140+ majority in the Commons, yet a sufficient number of Conservative MPs were so opposed to the Bill's objective of legalizing Sunday trading, that by entering the 'no' Lobby alongside Opposition MPs, they were able to deny it a Second Reading, thereby securing its abandonment (for case studies of the parliamentary defeat of the Shops Bill, see Brown, 1990; Regan, 1988).

Meanwhile, in the 2002–3 Parliamentary Session, of the 36 Public Bills introduced by the Blair government, 33 received the Royal Assent. Of the three 'failures', two ran out of time, but were carried over to the next session, while one – to outlaw fox hunting – was opposed by the House of Lords.

However, the rarity of governmental defeats does not necessarily constitute incontrovertible evidence that Parliament is a weak institution which lacks influence over government or public policy. It is reasonable to assume that governments will normally only introduce Bills which they are confident will be supported by the majority of their backbench MPs, thereby minimizing the likelihood of defeat at Second Reading stage. Ministers will either make judgements about 'anticipated actions' (or reactions) before deciding to proceed with the introduction of a Bill, or they will elicit the views of their backbench colleagues. As we note below, each of the main parties has a range of backbench subject committees, covering various policy areas or matching the key departments, and these will sometimes invite the relevant minister to speak, or answer questions. Such interaction will enable ministers to gauge the views of their backbenchers, and ascertain what they will – and will not – support in the division lobbies.

Even when ministers do not attend meetings of backbench subject committees, a party whip will usually do so, and he/she will, in return, keep the Chief Whip informed about the views of backbench MPs. The Government's Chief Whip, in turn, is a member of the Cabinet, and can therefore offer advice to ministers about what their backbench colleagues are likely to support or oppose in the Commons (Dorey, 1992). If the Chief Whip reports to the Cabinet that a sufficient number of the government's own backbenchers are likely to vote against a proposed measure or Bill, ministers may well decide to defer or drop the proposal, rather than be publicly defeated on the Floor of the House. Viewed from this perspective, the rarity of government defeats in the House of Commons suggests, not so much the almost invincible power of the (core) executive over Parliament, but the latent power of governmental backbenchers. If governments invariably secure parliamentary approval for their legislative proposals, it is likely to be because they usually pursue legislative proposals which they are confident will be endorsed. Of course, there will occasionally be claims by government back-benchers that the party's whips have coerced or blackmailed them into voting for certain measures to which they were opposed, but the government's business managers know that there are limits to how far they can repeatedly secure compliance through compulsion.

Another way in which ministers keep themselves appraised of the views and anxieties of their backbench colleagues is through occasional attendance at meetings of their par-liamentary party. For example, the Parliamentary Labour Party (PLP) meets weekly, and provides an opportunity for Labour MPs to ask a range of questions, and raise a variety of issues, concerning aspects of government policy and strategy. Such meetings offer another means by which ministers may be informed that a proposal will be opposed by a large number of the government's backbenchers, or only supported if it is substantially modi-fied before being formally introduced. For example, Charles Clarke, Labour's former Education Secretary, felt obliged to offer a number of concessions, and make a number of changes, to the Blair government's Bill for introducing university top-up fees, after encountering widespread opposition at meetings of the PLP (this opposition also expressed via the large number of Labour MPs who signed Early Day Motions[1] condemning the initial proposals).

One final reason why so few Public Bills are defeated at Second Reading stage is that even if government backbenchers harbour reservations about certain details, most of them are likely to endorse the broad principle(s) on which the Bill is based, or the broad objec-tives it is intended to achieve. After all, the Cabinet which has formally ratified a legisla-tive proposal comprises ministers from the same party, so it is unlikely that the majority of the government's backbenchers will be so strongly opposed to a Bill approved by their own Cabinet colleagues that they feel compelled to vote against it.

Besides, if the Second Reading debate does reveal that the government's backbenchers are unhappy about a particular aspect or detail, the minister 'sponsoring' the Bill is likely to promise that the government will accept the tabling of appropriate amendments during the Bill's (standing) committee stage. Such a ministerial pledge will usually be sufficient to pacify the government's backbenchers, and thereby persuade them to give the Bill its Second Reading.

A more general reason for the degree of success enjoyed by Public Bills is simply that the government has overall control, and enjoys the lion's share, of the allocation of time in the House of Commons: 'the Government dominates the timetable' (Norton, 1993a: 54). For example, in the 2002–3 Parliamentary session, out of the total 1,287 hours of business con-ducted on the Floor of the House of Commons, 412 hours were taken up by Government

---

[1]An Early Day Motion (EDM) is a motion tabled by MPs calling for a debate about a topic 'on an early day'. MPs who agree with an EDM are likely to add their signature, and in this respect, EDMs can provide a general indicator of backbench opinion on an issue. However, EDMs are not usually debated directly, and MPs signing them do not seriously expect them to be. Very occasionally, though, a large number of signatories might elicit some kind of conciliatory response from the gov-ernment, as was the case when large numbers of Labour MPs signed EDMs condemning top-up fees.

Table 6.1 Selected Private Bills introduced in the 2002–3 Parliamentary session

Title	Organization(s)	Purpose
Mersey Tunnels Bill	Merseyside Passenger Transport Authority (aka Merseytravel)	To amend existing statutory provisions concerning the levying of tolls, and to remove certain restrictions concerning the manner in which these revenues are subsequently spent.
Hereford Markets Bill	Hereford District Council	To empower the council to relocate existing markets, whose location and operation are laid down by a Royal Charter dating back to 1597.
Nottingham City Council Bill	Nottingham City Council	To empower the Council to regulate the activities, and require the registration of, second-hand goods dealers and 'squat traders'.
London Local Authorities and Transport for London Bill	Westminster City Council (on behalf of London Borough Councils) and Transport for London	To empower London Borough Councils and Transport for London to impose fixed-penalty fines on motorists who contravene road traffic regulations (thereby rendering such contraventions civil, rather than criminal, offences).

Source: House of Commons, 2003

(Public) Bills. By contrast, Private Members' Bills consumed just 63 hours of Commons' time. During the same session, the 20 Opposition Days (when the Opposition parties are permitted to select a topic for debate) totalled 130 hours.

Private Bills

Private Bills are concerned with a request by private or public organizations, or occasionally an individual, for certain, specified statutory powers: they wish to pursue a course of action which they are not otherwise legally empowered to undertake, and for which, therefore, special legislative provision has to be enacted. Private legislation is most commonly concerned with providing local authorities or public bodies with specific statutory powers to undertake a specific course of action, as is indicated by the examples in Table 6.1, which are taken from the 2002/3 Parliamentary Session.

In the autumn of 2004, meanwhile, a number of local authorities were planning to pursue Private Bills to empower them to ban smoking in public places in their respective districts.

Private Members' Bills

Private Members' Bills are introduced by backbench MPs, and represent one of the very few opportunities available to backbenchers to initiate legislation (rather than responding to the government's legislative initiatives). Each year, at the beginning of the new Parliamentary session in November, a ballot is conducted in the House of Commons, in which the first 20 backbench MPs to be drawn are entitled to introduce a Bill. In practice, though, only the first 12 MPs, at most, are likely to be granted sufficient parliamentary time, due mainly to the fact that Private Members' Bills are usually debated on Fridays, with the rest of the week being consumed by Public and Private Bills, debates, various other government business, and the 20 'Opposition Days', when the Opposition parties are entitled to select a topic for debate. Indeed, it has been calculated that whereas the House of Commons spends about 33 per cent of its time debating Public Bills, only about 5 per cent of its time is devoted to discussion of Private Members' Bills (Norton, 1990b: 200). Or put another way, in the 2001–2 Parliamentary Session, out of the 1,540 hours for which the House of Commons sat, and compared with the 476 hours devoted to Public (Government) Bills, a total of just under 77 hours were expended on Private Members' Bills.

Subject to the proviso that their proposed legislation does not involve additional public expenditure – unless the Treasury has costed and approved any such increase beforehand – Private Members' Bills can, in principle, be used by MPs to introduce legislation on almost any issue they wish. An MP may opt to introduce a Bill on a policy issue which he/she feels strongly about, or on behalf of a section of British society which they believe is disadvantaged or discriminated against. Some Private Members' Bills may also be suggested to backbench MPs by the government itself, if it is keen to introduce legislation but has no spare time in its own parliamentary timetable.

Private Members' Bills also attract considerable attention from numerous organized interests, for such legislation is seen as a valuable means by which 'outsider' pressure groups especially can influence public policy in Britain, or at least seek to push an issue onto the policy agenda. As such, the interest displayed by such groups tends to be both 'intense' and 'broad' (Norton, 1990b: 201). Each November, immediately following the ballot of MPs conducted at the beginning of the Parliamentary Session, the 20 successful backbenchers will often be inundated by suggestions or even draft proposals for legislation by a plethora of organized interests, particularly those who neither enjoy close or regular contact with the core executive nor form part of a policy community. An oft-cited example is that of the Labour MP, Austin Mitchell, who came sixth in the ballot for the 1983–4 Parliamentary Session, whereupon: 'Letters, draft Bills, ideas and invitations poured in.' Before too long, Mitchell 'had fifty suggestions, twenty possible Bills (three in draft) and five front runners' (1986: 2).

Rather more recently, when introducing the Second Reading of her Female Genital Mutilation Bill (to prohibit parents from sending, or taking, their daughters abroad, for such operations, most notably female circumcision; these operations having been outlawed *in* the UK since 1985), Ann Clwyd briefly explained why she chose this particular Bill 'over the many hundreds of others that were suggested to me' (House of Commons Debates, 21 March 2003, col. 1190).

The Private Members' Bills which have, historically, tended to receive the most attention, have been those addressing so-called moral or conscience issues, with the classic examples provided by the 'permissive' legislation of the latter half of the 1960s, when Private Members' Bills heralded the legalization of homosexuality (Richards, 1970: 75–84),

Table 6.2 MPs successful in the ballot for Private Members' Bills in the 2003–4 Parliament, and title of their Bill

Name of MP	Party	Title of Bill
Andrew Stunell	Lib Dem	Sustainable and Secure Buildings
Hywel Francis	Labour	Carers (Equal Opportunities)
Jim Sheridan	Labour	Gang-masters (Licensing)
Julian Brazier	Conservative	Promotion of Volunteering
Dari Taylor	Labour	Cardiac Risk in the Young (Screening)
Kevan Jones	Labour	Christmas Day (Trading)
Eric Martlew	Labour	Protection Headgear for Young Cyclists
John Maples	Conservative	Constitution for the European Union (Referendum)
Adrian Flook	Conservative	Retirement Income Reform
Gordon Prentice	Labour	Referendums (Thresholds)
Eric Pickles	Conservative	Town and Country Planning (Enforcement Notices and Stop Notices)
Lembit Opik	Lib Dem	Wild Mammals (Protection Amendment) (No. 2)
Andy King	Labour	Performance of Companies and Government Departments (Reporting)
Andrew Robathon	Conservative	Property Repairs (Prohibition of Cold-calling)
Hugh Robertson	Conservative	Illegal Hare-coursing (Enforcement of Prohibition)
Michael Foster	Labour	Highways (Obstruction by Body Corporate)
Gregory Baker	Conservative	Genetically Modified Organisms
Richard Spring	Conservative	Town and Country Planning (Telecommunications Masts)
Gerald Howarth	Conservative	Trespassers on Land (Liability for Damage and Eviction)
Ian Lucas	Labour	Older People's Commissioners

Source: www.parliament.uk/faq/ballot_faq

the liberalization of the laws concerning divorce (Lee, 1974: Chapter 7; Richards, 1970: 137–58) and abortion (Richards, 1970: 98–112), and the abolition of the death penalty (Richards, 1970: 52–62). However, many such Bills were preceded or accompanied by some kind of formal inquiry or (Royal) commission, the reports of which then endorsed or legitimized the proposed legislative reforms: 'It seems probable that no (controversial moral) Private Members' Bill could succeed without some preliminary inquiry of some kind' (Richards, 1970: 200; see also Richards, 1979).

An indication of the eclecticism of Private Members' Bills is indicated by Table 6.2, which lists the 20 MPs who were successful in the ballot for Private Members' Bills in the 2002–3 Parliamentary Session, and the title of their proposed Bill.

MPs who have not been successful in the ballot at the start of the Parliamentary Session may subsequently seek to introduce a Private Members' Bill via Standing Order No. 23, more commonly known as the Ten Minute Rule. The Standing Order permits an MP – subject to them having provided prior notification of their intention – to ask the House of Commons for leave to introduce a Bill on a particular topic or issue. If the House consents to this request (a division is not always necessary at this stage), then the Bill is deemed to have been granted a First Reading, and a date will be set for its Second Reading.

For example early in 2003, a Labour backbencher, James Purnell, was granted permission to introduce a 'Ten Minute Rule Bill' which would ensure that when an unmarried, but 'cohabiting', public sector employee died, their partner was entitled to receive appropriate pension payments or 'survivor benefits', these having often only been payable to married partners (House of Commons Debates, 21 January 2003, cols 185–6). Less than three months later, another Labour backbencher, Gareth Thomas, was 'given leave' – by 115 votes to 43 – to introduce a Ten Minute Rule Bill 'to prohibit smoking in cafés and restaurants' (House of Commons Debates, 14 April 2003, cols 647–50).

The parliamentary stages for a Private Members' Bill, irrespective of whether it is a 'Ballot' or a Ten Minute Rule Bill, are similar to those for a Public (Government) Bill (for a more detailed overview, see: Blackburn and Kennon, 2003: 539–62; Marsh and Read: 1988: Chapter 1). However, unless backed by the government, many Private Members' Bills fail to proceed past the Second Reading stage. This is mainly because most Private Members' Bills are debated on Fridays, thereby limiting the time available for such bills. As such, some Private Members' Bills only reach the statute book because sympathetic ministers make government time available in order to expedite the bill's passage (Marsh and Read, 1988: 54–61).

Just how difficult it is for Private Members' Bills to reach the statute book is illustrated by Table 6.3, which shows that while 'balloted' Private Members' Bills tend to be more successful than Ten Minute Rule Bills, this success remains limited. For example, between 1990–1 and 1999–2000, there were only three Parliamentary Sessions in which more than 10 of the (20) Balloted Private Members' Bills actually reached the Statute Book, while in the 1999–2000 session, only five were similarly successful. Similarly, in the 2001–2 session, only five balloted Private Members' Bills actually reached the statute book. Overall, therefore, the overall success rate (in terms of actually receiving Royal Assent) of Balloted Private Members' Bills is rather less than half.

Ten Minute Rule Bills, though, are clearly even less successful, with a paltry four reaching the statute book between 1980–1 and 1989–90, for example. More recently, in the 2001–2 Parliamentary Session, out of the 66 Ten Minute Rule Bills which backbench MPs sought to introduce, a mere two actually became law.

That said, even though the majority of Private Members' Bills do not reach the statute book, they are not necessarily a waste of political or parliamentary time. For either the backbench MP personally, or an organized interest on whose behalf an MP is acting, merely introducing a Private Members' Bill can be a useful means of generating public awareness of an issue, thereby possibly raising its status or profile on the systemic agenda, which, in turn, might help to move it, eventually, onto an institutional agenda. Indeed, Private Members' Bills have occasionally been withdrawn following a ministerial pledge that the government itself would introduce a (Public) Bill to address the particular policy issue, thereby obviating the need to persevere with the Private Members' Bill. In this respect, the fact that a Private Members' Bill does not actually reach the statute book does not necessarily signify complete failure.

Table 6.3 Number of Private Members' Bills reaching the statute book since 1970–1, according to category

Parliamentary Session	'Balloted' Private Members' Bills	Ten Minute Rule Bills
1970–1	7	0
1971–2	7	0
1972–3	7	3
1973–4	0	0
1974–5	12	0
1975–6	12	0
1976–7	6	0
1977–8	6	0
1978–9	0	0
1979–80	5	0
1980–1	7	1
1981–2	7	0
1982–3	5	1
1983–4	10	0
1984–5	11	2
1985–6	13	0
1986–7	7	0
1987–8	9	0
1988–9	6	0
1989–90	8	0
1990–1	11	0
1991–2	8	0
1992–3	6	2
1993–4	8	0
1994–5	9	3
1995–6	12	1
1996–7	14	1
1997–8	5	1
1998–9	7	0
1999–2000	5	0
2000–1*	0	0
2001–2	5	2
2002–3	12	0

*Short Parliamentary Session due to general election in June 2001. No Private Members' Bills reached the statute book in this short Parliament.
Source: House of Commons Information Service, 2003: 2

Parliamentary committees and public policy

Apart from the standing committees which, as we noted above, examine Bills in detail following Second Reading, there are various other parliamentary committees which play at least an indirect role in shaping or influencing public policy in Britain, although it will also become apparent that they also suffer from notable limitations or weaknesses in fulfilling such a role.

Departmental Select Committees

Undoubtedly the most important, and potentially influential, of these parliamentary committees are the Departmental Select Committees, most of which were established in 1979. Previously, select committees had been established on an *ad hoc* basis, with a view to examining a particular policy area or topic. This was the case in the latter half of the 1960s, for example, when the then Labour government, led by Harold Wilson, experimented with the creation of a small number of select committees to investigate specific issues on a generally 'one-off' basis. Although the experiment was viewed as something of a mixed success, it certainly whetted the appetite of those backbench MPs who favoured a more systematic means of investigating public policies, and of holding departments and their ministers more fully to account. For such MPs, if the experiment had proved only partly successful, the answer was not to abandon the principle of select committees, but to devise a more rigorous and coherent system, whereby such committees could play a more regular and meaningful role in the parliamentary scrutiny of public policy.

Thus it was that in 1979 – the time-lag itself indicative of the often slow or incremental character of many new policy initiatives in Britain for much of the postwar period, even in Parliament itself – a new system of select committees was established (in spite of the fact that Margaret Thatcher herself was less than enthusiastic about this potential empowerment of backbench MPs *vis-à-vis* the executive), each of which corresponded to a particular government department. Originally, it had been intended that 12 such select committees would be created, but following the failure of the out-going Labour government's devolution measures, two further select committees were established – one on Scottish Affairs, and the other on Welsh Affairs – thereby yielding a total of 14 (for an overview of their introduction and early operation, see: Drewry, 1989; Englefield, 1984; Johnson, 1988; Rush, 2000: 120–7).

Since then, prime ministerial restructuring of the core executive after the 1992, 1997 and 2001 general elections has resulted in the abolition or merger of some government departments, as well as the occasional creation of new ministries, which has, in turn, yielded corresponding changes to the Departmental Select Committees during this period, to the extent that there are now 18. The manner in which the Departmental Select Committee system has changed since its inauguration in 1979 is indicated in Table 6.4.

Most of these select committees comprise 11 MPs, with the government allocated 6 or 7 MPs (depending on how many seats it has overall in the House of Commons) and the remaining 4–5 MPs drawn from the Opposition parties. On the Environment, Food and Rural Affairs Select Committee, however, there is a total of 17 MPs, with 11 Labour MPs, 4 Conservatives, 1 Liberal Democrat and 1 Ulster Unionist. The Northern Ireland Committee, meanwhile, comprises 13 MPs, of which 7 are Labour MPs, 2 are Conservatives, 2 are from the Ulster Unionist Party, 1 from the Democratic Unionist Party and 1 from the Social Democratic and Labour Party.

The primary role of the Departmental Select Committees is to 'examine the expenditure, administration and policy of the principal Government Departments … and associated

Table 6.4 Departmental Select Committees in 1979, 1992 and 2004

1979	1992	2004
1. Agriculture	1. Agriculture	1. Constitutional Affairs
2. Defence	2. Defence	2. Culture, Media and Sport
3. Education	3. Education	3. Defence
4. Employment	4. Employment	4. Education and Skills
5. Environment	5. Environment	5. Environment, Food and Rural Affairs
6. Foreign Affairs	6. Foreign Affairs	6. Foreign Affairs
7. Health	7. Health	7. Health
8. Home Affairs	8. Home Affairs	8. Home Affairs
9. Scottish Affairs	9. National Heritage	9. International Development
10. Social Security	10. Science and Technology	10. Northern Ireland
11. Trade and Industry	11. Scottish Affairs	11. Office of the Deputy Prime Minister*
12. Transport	12. Social Security	12. Science and Technology
13. Treasury and Civil Service	13. Trade and Industry	13. Scottish Affairs
14. Welsh Affairs	14. Transport	14. Trade and Industry
	15. Treasury and Civil Service	15. Transport
	16. Welsh Affairs	16. Treasury and Civil Service
		17. Welsh Affairs
		18. Work and Pensions

*Covers housing, planning, local government and the regions.

public bodies'. To this end, Departmental Select Committees are entitled to 'send for persons, papers and records ... and adjourn from place to place'. The last aspect refers to the occasional practice of conducting visits to other parts of the country – or even, occasionally, overseas – to conduct interviews or obtain further evidence, in connection with a particular inquiry.

The Departmental Select Committees enjoy considerable autonomy and discretion in determining their topics of inquiry. They are entitled to choose which aspect of their department's expenditure, administration or policy to investigate, and in so doing, can decide between a rather general inquiry, or a very specific one, perhaps examining a particular aspect of a specific policy in detail. Table 6.5 illustrates four inquiries conducted by each of the main Departmental Select Committees since 2001. It can be seen, for example, that the Select Committee on Culture, Media and Sport has investigated the British tourism industry on the one hand, and the future of Wembley stadium on the other, while the Foreign Affairs Select Committee has undertaken investigations into such topics as Anglo-American relations, and the future of Gibraltar, as well as how the government took the decision to go to war with Iraq in 2003. Such examples indicate both the breadth and the depth, as well as the generality and specificity, of topics which Departmental Select Committees choose to investigate.

Table 6.5 Examples of inquiries conducted by Departmental Select Committees since 2001

Select committee	Topic of inquiry
Culture, Media and Sport	1. National Museums: Funding and Free Admission 2. British Tourism Industry 3. Future of Wembley Stadium 4. Privacy and Media Intrusion
Defence	1. European Security and Defence 2. Threat from Terrorism 3. Future of NATO 4. Defence Procurement
Education and Skills	1. Qualifications and Curriculum Authority 2. General Teaching Council 3. The Work of OFSTED 4. A-Level Standards
Environment, Food and Rural Affairs	1. The 2001 Foot-and-Mouth Epidemic 2. Reform of the Common Fisheries Policy 3. Rural Payments Agency 4. Poultry Farming in the UK
Foreign Affairs	1. Future of Gibraltar 2. Anglo-American Relations 3. EU Enlargement 4. Decision to go to war in Iraq
Health	1. Handling Clinical Negligence Claims 2. Sexual Health 3. Role of the Private Sector in the NHS 4. Provision of Maternity Services
Home Affairs	1. Police Reform 2. Government's Drugs Policy 3. Prison Overcrowding 4. Removal of Asylum Seekers
International Development	1. Afghanistan: Further Developments 2. The Humanitarian Crisis in Southern Africa 3. Tackling World Poverty and Debt 4. Humanitarian Aspects of Military Action in Iraq
Northern Ireland Affairs	1. Control of Firearms in Northern Ireland 2. Parades Commission 3. Northern Ireland Human Rights Commission 4. Illegal Drugs Trade in Northern Ireland
Office of the Deputy Prime Minister*	1. Affordable Housing 2. Reducing Regional Disparities in Prosperity 3. Sustainable Communities in the South East 4. The Evening Economy and Urban Renaissance

(Continued)

Table 6.5 (Continued)

Select Committee	Topic of inquiry
Science and Technology	1. Human Genetics and Embryology 2. Towards a Non-carbon Fuel Economy 3. Medical Research Council 4. Scientific Responses to Terrorism
Scottish Affairs	1. The Work of the Scottish Consumer Council 2. Future Skills Scotland 3. Employment in ship-building on the Clyde 4. Scottish Office Expenditure
Trade and Industry	1. Consignia 2. White Paper on Modernizing Company Law 3. Manufacturing Strategy 4. UK Biotechnology Industry
Transport	1. Urban Charging Schemes 2. Public Spaces 3. London Underground – The Public-Private Partnership 4. Overcrowding on Public Transport
Treasury	1. Financial Services Authority 2. Banking and Small Businesses 3. Economic and Monetary Union 4. The UK and the Euro
Welsh Affairs	1. Transport in Wales 2. Farming and Food Policy in Wales 3. EU 'Objective One' Funding for Wales 4. The Primary Legislative Process as it Affects Wales
Work And Pensions	1. Pension Service 2. Future of UK Pensions 3. Government's Employment Strategy 4. Childcare for Working Parents

*Established July 2002.

Having decided on its topic of inquiry, a Departmental Select Committee will normally invite written evidence from 'interested parties', that is, individuals or organizations which are in any way affected by, or knowledgeable about, the particular policy or problem chosen for investigation. Needless to say, the volume and range of written submissions can be considerable. For example, when the Home Affairs Select Committee launched its 2001–2 inquiry into 'The Government's Drugs Policy: Is It Working?', it received written submissions from an extremely wide range of organizations, an indication of which is provided in Table 6.6 below.

Table 6.6   Organizations submitting evidence to Home Affairs Select Comittee Inquiry into the Government's drugs policy, 2001–2

- Action on Hepatitis C
- Addiction
- ADFAM
- Alliance for Cannabis Therapeutics
- Association of Chief Police Officers
- Bradford Drugs and Alcohol Action Team
- Bristol Drug Action Team
- Burton Addiction Centre
- Centre for Addiction Studies
- Christian Institute
- Church of England Board for Social Responsibility
- Criminal Justice Association
- Dance Drugs Alliance
- Drug Education Forum
- DrugScope
- East Riding and Hull Drug Action Team
- Edinburgh Drug Action Team
- Ethnicity and Health Unit (University of Central Lancashire)
- Greater London Authority
- Green Party
- G. W. Pharmaceuticals plc
- Health Development Agency
- HM Customs and Excise
- Home Office
- Independent Drug Monitoring Unit
- Islington Drug and Alcohol Action Team
- Lancashire Drug Action Team
- Liberty
- Life Education Centres
- Local Government Association
- London Borough of Camden
- London Drug Policy Forum
- National Children's Bureau
- National Crime Squad
- National Drug Prevention Alliance
- National Schizophrenia Fellowship
- National Treatment Agency
- National Union of Teachers
- Netherlands Drug Policy Foundation
- Positive Prevention Plus
- Quaker Action on Alcohol and Drugs
- Redcar and Cleveland Borough Council
- Release
- Royal College of Physicians
- Royal College of Psychiatrists
- Royal Pharmaceutical Society of Great Britain
- Thames Valley Police
- Transform
- Turning Point
- UK Harm Reduction Alliance.

Meanwhile, among the individuals who submitted written evidence were a former British Ambassador to Colombia, General Practitioners (GPs), lawyers, senior police officers (including some who had retired), social workers and teachers.

As is apparent from the above example, organized interests are major contributors of written evidence to Departmental Select Committees, thereby providing an important linkage between such interests and Parliament. Indeed, in a major study of the links between Parliament and organized interests conducted in the late 1980s (unfortunately, there has been no similar or comparable study since), it was revealed that 65.6 per cent of organized interests had submitted written evidence to a Departmental Select Committee (Rush, 1990: 146).

Furthermore, the same study also found that no less than 69.2 per cent of organized interests believed that their evidence had 'some' impact on the relevant select committee and its report, with a further 16.3 per cent adjudging their evidence to have had a 'significant' impact. Only 4.1 per cent considered their evidence to have had no impact on select committees and their reports (Rush, 1990: 147).

Table 6.7 Number of appearances to provide oral evidence to Departmental Select Committees in 2002–3 session

Select Committee	Total number of meetings	Ministers	Civil servants	Agencies, public or Non departmental bodies	Other witnesses
Culture, Media and Sport	41	11	15	72	125
Defence	43	10	55	6	31
Education and Skills	54	10	11	22	79
Environment, Food and Rural Affairs	32	11	18	8	66
Foreign Affairs	48	13	42	0	33
Health	38	8	13	22	73
Home Affairs	39	13	28	4	42
International Development	52	18	32	8	101
Northern Ireland Affairs	38	8	24	22	76
Office of the Deputy Prime Minister*	42	10	34	34	180
Science and Technology	31	8	27	26	74
Scottish Affairs	21	3	11	27	18
Trade and Industry	56	11	21	34	165
Transport	37	8	25	50	181
Treasury	48	4	23	41	110
Welsh Affairs	35	5	12	20	73
Work And Pensions	35	5	20	16	55

*Covering housing, planning, local government and the regions.
Source: House of Commons, 2004

When the written submissions have been received, the Departmental Select Committee will then invite some of the respondents to appear in person, and give oral evidence. This takes the form of questioning by the MPs on the select committee, with a view to elicit further or more in-depth information.

Also periodically invited to give oral evidence on a particular topic are ministers themselves, as are senior civil servants in the relevant government department. Such ministerial appearances are a crucial means by which they are rendered accountable for their Department's policies, while simultaneously enabling Departmental Select Committees to scrutinize the executive (a key function of Parliament). Ministers may well be asked to explain or justify a policy initiative or decision, particularly if the policy has engendered problems. Similarly, senior civil servants from the relevant department will also routinely be invited to provide oral evidence.

Table 6.7 illustrates the number of appearances by ministers, civil servants and senior officials from relevant public or non-departmental government bodies, such as executive agencies (i.e. Prisons Agency, CSA, etc.), to give oral evidence to Departmental Select Committees during the 2002–3 Parliamentary session, while Table 6.8 provides examples of the type of agencies and sundry other public bodies which gave oral evidence to these committees during the Parliamentary session.

Upon completion of its inquiry, a Departmental Select Committee will publish its report, hoping, in many cases, that this will prompt at least some modification of existing policy or legislation, although Norton has suggested that: 'Most of the recommendations contained in [select] committee reports may be termed humdrum rather than major in policy terms' (1993a: 65). Yet it may be precisely because they tend to be 'humdrum' that governments may feel more inclined to accept various select committee recommendations, whereas ministers would probably be rather more dismissive of recommendations which were 'major in policy terms', not least because they might readily be construed as significant criticisms of governmental policy, or as entailing a major departure from the government's programme.

In the above example of the Home Affairs Select Committee's inquiry into the Government's Drugs Policy, its May 2002 Report enshrined 24 main conclusions and recommendations, and while it declined to endorse the decriminalization of 'soft drugs' such as cannabis, it did recommend that cannabis be reclassified, by downgrading it from a Class B to a Class C drug, with a corresponding reduction in the police's powers of arrest regarding possession of cannabis. This particular proposal was accepted by the Home Office, so that cannabis was indeed subsequently reclassified as a Class C (rather than more serious Class B) drug – although as if to counter anxieties or allegations that the government was 'going soft' on drugs, it was also proposed to increase maximum prison sentences, to 14 years, for those found guilty of importing or selling cannabis. There did appear to be some inconsistency here, of course, for if someone was in possession of cannabis, then someone is likely to have imported it and/or sold it to them!

Nearly a year later, a recommendation by the Transport Select Committee that motorists ought pay fees to drive on various roads, in order to reduce traffic congestion, was followed, just a couple of months afterwards, by a government announcement that it was indeed considering the introduction of 'congestion charges' on a national basis, as well as planning a road-widening scheme which might entail 12-lane motorways (*The Sunday Times*, 8 June 2003; *The Observer*, 15 June 2003).

Government departments are expected to reply, within 60 days, to each report published by 'their' Departmental Select Committee. At the very least, if no modification of policy is envisaged, the department will be expected to explain why it does not intend to act upon the recommendations of the select committee, and is thus intent on continuing with the existing policy.

In this respect, the select committee can still be said to have held the government department and its minister to account, obliging them publicly to defend and explain their policy stance. Furthermore, a few select committee reports will be debated on the Floor of the House of Commons each session, thereby providing other MPs with opportunities to question aspects of public policy, and compelling ministers to provide a further justification for their policies.

Table 6.8 Examples of agencies, public bodies and non-departmental Organizations giving oral evidence to Departmental Select Committees in 2002–3 Parliamentary session

Select committee	Agencies, public bodies and non-departmental Organizations
Constitutional Affairs*	Commission for Racial Equality; Legal Services Commission; Commission for Judicial Appointments
Culture, Media and Sport	Arts Council; BBC; British Film Institute; Channel 4; Museums Association; Natural History Museum; Tourism Alliance; UK Sport
Defence	Defence Procurement Agency; Warship Support Agency; Veterans Agency
Education and Skills	Higher Education Funding Council for England (HEFCE); OFSTED; Qualifications and Curriculum Authority; Teacher Training Agency
Environment, Food and Rural Affairs	Environment Agency; Forestry Commission; Office of Water Services
Foreign Affairs	None
Health	Association of Community Health Councils; Health Development Agency; NHS Trusts (various)
Home Affairs	Parole Board of England and Wales; Youth Justice Board
International Development	CDC Capital Partners
Northern Ireland Affairs	Police Ombudsman for NI; Probation Board for NI; NI Prison Service
Office of the Deputy Prime Minister**	English Nature; Government Office for the South West; Housing Corporation; Learning and Skills Council; North West Development Agency
Science and Technology	Health and Safety Executive; Highways Agency; Medical Research Council; Particle Physics and Astronomy Research Council; Royal Society
Scottish Affairs	British Waterways Scotland; Scottish Enterprise; Scottish Low Pay Unit; Citizens Advice Scotland
Trade and Industry	East Midlands Development Agency; Ofgem; Oftel; Radiocommunications Agency; UK Atomic Energy Authority
Transport (including Transport Sub-committee)	Civil Aviation Authority; Highways Agency; London Underground; Strategic Rail Authority; Sustainable Development Commission
Treasury	Bank of England; Financial Services Authority
Welsh Affairs	Children's Commissioner for Wales; Audit Commission in Wales; Strategic Rail Authority
Work and Pensions	Child Support Agency; Jobcentre Plus; Learning and Skills Council

*A Department of Constitutional Affairs was established in June 2003, and replaced the Lord Chancellor's Department.
**Covers housing, planning, local government and the regions.
Source: House of Commons, 2004

It is also likely that serving on a select committee enables MPs to acquire considerable expertise in a particular sphere of public policy. As MPs usually serve on a select committee for the lifetime – 4–5 years – of a Parliament (and often have their membership renewed for a further 4–5 years following a general election), they are able to immerse themselves in a specific area of public policy, and become highly knowledgeable about it. This might enable them to ask more probing or searching questions of those appearing before a select committee inquiry, and of the relevant minister(s) at Question Time on the Floor of the House of Commons. In other words, the expertise acquired through serving on a select committee for several years is likely to enhance MPs' ability or effectiveness in scrutinizing the executive and its policy decisions. This could also be viewed as another aspect of the 'professionalization' of MPs in Britain, and the rise of the 'career politician'. Indeed, some MPs seem to view service on a Departmental Select Committee as an alternative career to seeking ministerial office; for it enables backbench MPs to play a more active role in Parliament, and with the potential for exercising some influence on public policy, at least occasionally. Gerald Kaufman, for example, having been a minister in the 1974–79 Labour governments, has become a formidable and respected chair of the Culture, Media and Sport Select Committee since 1997, while Tony Wright, a prominent Labour 'modernizer', has similarly established himself as a highly-regarded chair, since 1997, of the Public Administration Committee (see below).

Evaluating the actual influence of Departmental Select Committees on public policies is methodologically difficult, not least because any subsequent policy change might well be influenced by factors other than the report or recommendations of a particular committee. It is therefore often difficult to attribute a particular policy change to a particular Departmental Select Committee. Consequently, academic commentators continue to disagree over the policy influence and impact of such committees, with Griffith and Ryle once asserting that: 'Select Committees have not made a general impact on government policies' (1989: 430). More recently, however, a leading academic expert on Departmental Select Committees, Michael Rush, has offered a more charitable view, citing statistics which, while not conclusive or clear cut, do suggest 'some influence and therefore impact on the part of the departmental committees' (2000: 124). Certainly, one commentator claims that since their inception in 1979, Departmental Select Committees 'have produced a number of coruscating reports, in which the incompetence, inadequacies and indolence of government have been laid bare' (Paxman, 2003: 186).

Of course, a condemnatory report might not necessarily yield a significant change of policy if ministers are convinced that the policy is the most appropriate one, and has been unjustly castigated by the select committee. Nor have select committees prevented various policy disasters or failures since 1979, but then, as their primary role has hitherto been to examine the implementation and impact of public policy *after* its enactment, they should not be criticized for 'failing' to prevent policy failures. What Departmental Select Committees can do when serious policy failures occur, though, is examine the causes or origins, and establish why policy makers failed to foresee the consequences. This, in turn, may reduce the likelihood of similar policy failures occurring in the future, by encouraging policy makers to consider more carefully the options available to them, and the likely consequences of pursuing them. It may also encourage policy makers to consult more widely, so that those with expertise in a particular policy subsystem, or who are likely to be affected by a proposed policy, can highlight potential risks or deficiencies in the draft proposals.

In these respects, Departmental Select Committees may have played a part in encouraging a recent trend towards both more 'rational' policy making, and in evidence-based policy making (as discussed in Chapter 2, and considered again in Chapter 9). Certainly, Departmental Select Committees are increasingly engaging in 'prelegislative scrutiny', whereby they conduct inquiries into draft Bills or White Papers (which usually herald the imminent introduction of legislation), with a view to evaluating the efficacy of legislative proposals, or identifying potential problems. In this respect, Departmental Select Committees – and thus, Parliament – can be said to be developing a more active, and proactive, role in the policy process in Britain today.

This, in turn, represents a further challenge to the simplistic top-down, linear model of the policy process which was discussed in Chapter 1. As we suggested then, although we can identify discrete 'stages' of policy making for analytic purposes – as, indeed, this book does – the reality is more complex and 'messy'. This is a theme to which we will return in Chapter 9.

Meanwhile, even if the Departmental Select Committees normally contribute only to relatively modest or technical policy changes – these might nonetheless be welcome or valuable to those affected by a particular policy – Departmental Select Committees are still an important institutional means whereby a government's public policies are subject to scrutiny, policy makers are obliged to defend and explain themselves, and the (core) executive overall is held to account by Parliament. Indeed, in 2002, Stephen Byers resigned as Secretary of State for Transport following serious criticism of the government's transport policies and strategy by the Transport Select Committee. Such a dramatic outcome is obviously rare, but it nonetheless indicates that in particular circumstances, a condemnatory report by a select committee – particularly if it is a unanimous one, whereby Government and Opposition MPs on the committee are in agreement – can have a notable impact. While such occurrences are infrequent, the potential is there.

Trends therefore seem to suggest that the importance and impact of Departmental Select Committees are likely to increase. Certainly, one academic expert on Parliament has argued that 'the longer-term impact on policy and administration is likely to be significant, especially as committees increasingly review earlier inquiries and return to particular policy areas' (Rush, 2000: 127).

Other types of investigative committees

While the Departmental Select Committees are probably the most well known of Parliament's investigatory committees, there are a couple of others which are also of considerable importance in contributing towards the scrutiny of governmental administration, expenditure and policy, even though they do not 'shadow' a specific department. These are the Public Administration Committee, and the Public Accounts Committee.

Public Administration Committee

The Public Administration Committee was established in July 1997, having previously been the Committee for the Parliamentary Commissioner for Administration (more commonly known as the Ombudsman). In this earlier guise, it was concerned primarily with examining the reports published by the Ombudsman, paying close attention to policy issues which had acquired particular prominence in these reports. Having become the Public Administration Committee, its remit has been widened to include administrative matters concerning the civil service. In its relatively short life to date, the Public Administration Committee has acquired considerable prominence and a formidable reputation. As mentioned above, it is chaired by the highly-respected Labour MP – and a former politics lecturer at Birmingham university – Tony Wright.

The Public Administration Committee has conducted a wide range of inquiries in recent years, reflecting its broadened remit. Furthermore, in 2002, it was announced that Tony Blair had agreed to be questioned, on a twice yearly basis, by the Public Administration Committee. Prime Ministers had previously been spared appearances in front of select committees, due to their lack of direct departmental responsibilities. The following are examples of inquiries undertaken by the Public Administration Committee since 2001:

- Appointment and Use of Special Advisers
- Civil Service Issues
- Freedom of Information
- Government by Appointment
- Government by Measurement (the use of targets)
- Ministerial Accountability and Parliamentary Questions
- Ministerial Patronage
- NHS Direct in England
- Ombudsman Issues
- Public Appointments and Patronage
- Public Services Reform
- Public Services Targets.

Furthermore, the Public Administration Committee often elicits oral evidence from a somewhat wider range of ministers and senior civil servants than the Departmental Select Committees, due to the much more eclectic choice of topics it investigates. This means that during the course of a Parliamentary Session, the work of more departments – along with the Cabinet Office – come within its purview. Similarly, the Public Administration Committee will tend to invite appearances from a wider variety of agencies, non-governmental bodies and other public organizations. For example, during its 41 meetings in the 2001–2 Parliamentary Session, the Public Administration Committee was presented with oral evidence from senior civil servants representing the Cabinet Office, Department of Transport, Local Government and the Regions, Home Office and the Treasury, as well as from representatives from the CSA, Commission for Racial Equality, Disability Rights Commission, Equal Opportunities Commission, and Legal Services Commission. Also appearing before the committee, of course, was the Parliamentary Commissioner for Administration, more commonly known as the Ombudsman.

Public Accounts Committee

The other main investigative committee is the Public Accounts Committee, which was established back in 1861, and as such, is the oldest of the Select Committees. The 16 MPs on the Public Accounts Committee examine the expenditure of government departments and agencies – thereby supplementing the examination of expenditure performed by the Departmental Select Committees – but have increasingly, since the 1980s at least, paid particular attention to the criteria of 'value-for-money', efficiency and effectiveness, in the way that departments have spent public funds. In performing this function of financial scrutiny, the Public Accounts Committee works very closely with the National Audit Office, and its chief, the Comptroller and Auditor General. The Public Accounts Committee has a formidable – even feared – reputation in Westminster and Whitehall, and reports which are critical of the way that public monies have been (mis)spent are normally taken very seriously. The following is a sample of the topics and issues which have been investigated by the Public Accounts Committee since 2001:

- Channel Tunnel Rail Link
- Collection of Fines in the Criminal Justice System
- Collection of the Television Licence Fee.
- Department of Trade and Industry: Regulation of Weights and Measures
- Fraud and Error in Income Support
- Improving Student Participation and Achievement in Higher Education (England)
- Income Tax Self-assessment
- Maintaining the Royal Palaces
- Ministry of Defence: Major Projects Report 2001
- NHS Waiting Lists
- Public-Private Partnership initiative for National Air Traffic Services
- Tackling Benefit Fraud
- Tackling Obesity in England
- Tackling Pension Poverty
- The PFI for the Redevelopment of the West Middlesex Hospital
- Tobacco smuggling.

The nature of its remit also means that the Public Accounts Committee obtains evidence from a wider range of departments and their senior civil servants than the Departmental Select Committees, as well as from a wide variety of agencies and other public bodies, as is illustrated by Table 6.9.

Other backbench parliamentary committees

There are two other types of parliamentary committee through which backbench MPs can seek to exert at least an indirect influence on public policy in Britain, namely the backbench subject committees, and the all-party committees.

Backbench subject committees

Backbench subject committees exist in both the Labour and the Conservative parties at parliamentary level, and are open to MPs in each party who have a particular interest in a specific issue or policy area (for an excellent historical overview of their development, see Norton, 1979: 32–49). These backbench subject committees, particularly in the governing

Table 6.9   Departmental civil servants and a sample of agencies and other public bodies appearing before the Public Accounts Committee during its 58 meetings in the 2002–3 Parliamentary session

Department	Number of appearances	Agencies and other public bodies	Number of appearances
Cabinet Office	0	Arts Council England	1
Culture, Media and Sport	3	Defence Procurement Agency	1
Defence	5	Environment Agency	3
Education and Skills	0	Food Standards Agency	2
Environment, Food and Rural Affairs	8	Health and Safety Executive	2
Health	15	HM Customs and Excise	3
Home Office	3	Inland Revenue	3
International Development	3	National Audit Office	64
Office of the Deputy Prime Minister	1	Office of Fair Trading	1
Trade and Industry	4	OFTEL	3
Transport	4	Passports Agency	1
Treasury	53	Social Services Inspectorate	1
Work and Pensions	14	Warship Support Agency	1

Source: House of Commons, 2004: 254–5

party, generally correspond to the main government departments, although with one or two additions or variations. For example, during the second Blair government's term of office, the Parliamentary Labour Party had 18 backbench committees, covering the following policy areas:

- Cabinet Office
- Culture, Media and Sport
- Defence
- Education and Skills
- Environment, Food and Rural Affairs
- Foreign and Commonwealth Affairs
- Health and Social Services
- Home Affairs
- International Development

- Legal and Constitutional Affairs
- Local Government and the Regions
- Northern Ireland
- Parliamentary Affairs
- Trade and Industry
- Transport
- Treasury
- Women
- Work and Penions.

The Conservative Party, on the other hand, its ranks seriously depleted by the scale of the 1997 and 2001 election defeats, had rather fewer, but broader ranging, parliamentary committees, namely:

- Agriculture, Rural Affairs and Environment
- Constitutional Affairs
- Culture, Media and Sport

- Defence and Foreign Affairs
- Economic Affairs, Enterprise, Pensions and Social Affairs
- Education
- Health and Social Services
- Home Affairs
- Transport, Local Government and Planning.

Unlike those in the Labour Party, the Conservative subject committees include the relevant Shadow Ministers (when the party is in Opposition), one of whom actually chairs 'their' committee. For example, Michael Ancram was (at the beginning of 2003) chair of the Conservatives' parliamentary Defence and Foreign Affairs Committee, while Dr Liam Fox chaired the Conservatives' Health and Social Services Committee. Clearly, then, when the Conservatives are in Opposition, their parliamentary committees are not merely backbench committees, due to the role played by the party's Shadow Ministers, but when the party is in office, the chairs of these committees are backbenchers, elected by their fellow party colleagues.

Although these backbench subject committees meet with varying frequency, they do provide a forum in which each party's MPs can exchange views and ideas about what their party is doing – or ought to be doing – with regard to a specific policy issue or problem.

To this end, a backbench subject committee will sometimes invite the relevant minister (or Shadow Minister if the party is in Opposition) to explain – and, by implication, defend or justify – the government's stance on a particular issue, or perhaps face a 'question-and-answer' session. As Brand points out, for a minister or Opposition counterpart, their party's backbench subject committee 'constitute a "public"', for it comprises 'the MPs on his (sic) own side which is particularly interested in his field, which will be particularly knowledgeable, and the most likely to provide informed, if friendly, criticism for his proposals' (1992: 54). On rare occasions, less-than-friendly criticism might even result in a particular policy proposal being abandoned by the minister concerned (Silk and Walters, 1998: 51), as was the case back in 1992, when the then Secretary of State for Trade and Industry (calling himself the President of the Board of Trade, though), Michael Heseltine, felt obliged to abandon an announced plan to close, almost immediately, a further 30 or so coal mines, resulting in the loss of thousands of mining jobs, following hostility expressed to the proposal at a meeting of the Conservatives' backbench Trade and Industry Committee. As such, in spite of the various constraints impinging upon backbench MPs generally, coupled with the crucial role played in policy making by both the core executive and policy communities, many backbench subject committees in both of the main parliamentary parties 'believe that they can contribute to policy making' (Jones, 1990: 122).

Another means whereby backbench subject committees can exert some influence on their party's policies is also noted by Brand, primarily with regard to the Conservative Party, where the chairs of its various subject committees are quite often consulted over the drafting of their party's election manifesto, a privilege not normally granted to those chairing Labour's subject committees (1992: 53).

Many backbench subject committees will also, to varying degrees, and with varying frequency, invite outside speakers, such as the leader of an organized interest, to provide first-hand information, or answer questions, about how a particular policy is impacting upon the section of society they purport to represent. Indeed, for some organized interests, backbench subject committees are a valuable means of parliamentary access and indirect or supplementary influence *vis-à-vis* public policy. Thus, in a major study, conducted in the late 1980s, of the relationship between Parliament and pressure groups, and edited by Michael Rush (1990), it was found that 61.2 per cent of organized interests considered backbench subject committees to be 'useful', whereas the all-party groups (discussed below) received a 47.9 per cent 'useful' rating (Jones, 1990: 130). Certainly, according to Jones, many party subject committees and organized interests are 'interdependent', with the 'parliamentary skills and political contacts of the backbenchers ... balanced by the research and information facilities made available by organized interests' (1990: 117–8).

All-party Committees

In addition to the subject committees operational in each of the two main parties, there are also many parliamentary committees open to MPs of any parliamentary party. These All-party Committees (or groups, as they are also termed) reflect areas of shared interest or concern between MPs from different parties, and indicate that on some issues – as with the Departmental Select Committees – MPs from different parties can develop a relatively strong degree of bipartisanship. In the 2002–3 parliamentary session, there were 238 All-party groups, and as the sample below illustrates, they are remarkably broad ranging in the topics they cover, some of them being concerned with traditional policy areas, while many others reflect the interest of some MPs in rather more esoteric issues or causes.

- AIDS
- Animal welfare
- Beer
- Breast cancer
- Compassion in dying
- Disability
- Domestic violence
- Education
- Epilepsy
- Food and health
- Football
- Fruit industry
- Gardening and horticulture
- Health
- Heart disease
- Human rights
- Internet
- Maternity
- Mental Health
- National Parks
- Opera
- Penal affairs
- Police
- Poverty
- Refugees
- Road safety
- Science
- Sex equality
- Sport and leisure
- Tourism
- Transport
- United Nations
- University
- Wildlife Protection
- Wine
- Youth affairs.

Like the party subject committees, these All-party Committees will meet with varying frequency, providing an arena for discussion and the exchange of views between back-bench MPs sharing an interest in the policy area. Similarly, the All-party Committees will occasionally invite a relevant minister to speak or answer questions.

Furthermore, many of these committees will establish linkages with relevant organized interests (or vice versa), thereby developing something of a symbiotic relationship: the orga-nized interest will hope to exert indirect influence via the MPs on the All-party committee, while the MPs themselves will welcome the specialist information which the organized inter-est can provide. As Jones has noted, the All-party groups 'have much to commend them-selves to organized interests seeking to influence Parliament', and as such, 'have long been regarded as a natural focus for pressure-group attention' (Jones, 1990: 125, 126).

In particular, the major study (cited above) of linkages between Parliament and orga-nized interests, found that whereas 'insider' pressure groups tended to consider the party subject committees more amenable, 'outsider' groups gravitated more to the All-party committees: 26.2 per cent of 'outsider' groups found contact with All-party committees 'very useful', whereas only 14.3 per cent of 'insider' groups were of this view. One of the main reasons for this divergence, Jones explains, is that 'outsider' groups – who tend to be concerned with social, moral or ethical issues – often wish to be considered as non-partisan or politically neutral, lest a close identification with one particular party will either alienate actual or potential members, or damage their chances of exerting influence when there is a change of government (Jones, 1990: 132).

Ministers' Question Time

Questions addressed to ministers by backbench MPs have long been a major means by which Parliament seeks to hold the (core) executive to account, obliging ministers to explain and justify their decisions and policies, and those of their departments. Through Ministerial Question Time, therefore, one aspect of the doctrine of individual ministerial responsibility is upheld, whereby ministers have to defend, in Parliament, their depart-ment's policies.

Ministers' Question Time is organized on a four-weekly rota, as illustrated in Table 6.10. The ministers (Secretary of State and their junior ministers) representing whichever gov-ernment department is scheduled for Question Time on a particular day, answer questions, at the Despatch Box in the House of Commons, usually for 30 minutes.

Although Ministers' Question Time is often an opportunity for political point-scoring, it nonetheless performs a vital function in ensuring that ministers regularly appear before MPs to explain and justify the policies of their departments, and *inter alia* the policies of the government itself. In this respect, Ministers' Question Time is a crucial means by which the legislature seeks to hold the (core) executive to account, and ensure that public policy is subject to scrutiny beyond the legislative process. This, in turn, can help to ensure that ministers themselves are made aware of particular problems concerning a policy, thereby possibly persuading them of the need to modify it. As John MacGregor, a former Conservative minister and Leader of the House (of Commons) has acknowledged:

Table 6.10   The departmental rota for Ministers' Question Time

1st Monday	1st Tuesday	1st Wednesday	1st Thursday
Culture, Media and Sport (2.30 – 3.00)	Transport (11.30 – 12.00)	Office of the Deputy Prime Minister (11.30 – 12.00)	Environment, Food and Rural Affairs (11.30 – 12.00)
Church Commissioners	Cabinet Office	Prime Minister (12.00-12.30)	
2nd Monday Work and Pensions (2.30 – 3.00)	**2nd Tuesday** Scotland (11.30 – 12.00)	**2nd Wednesday** Northern Ireland (11.30 – 12.00)	**2nd Thursday** Education and Skills (11.30 – 12.00)
	Lord Chancellor's Department	Prime Minister (12.00 – 12.30)	Solicitor General
	President of the Council/Leader of the House of Commons		
3rd Monday Home Office (2.30 – 3.00)	**3rd Tuesday** Health (11.30 – 12.00)	**3rd Wednesday** Wales (11.30 – 12.00)	**3rd Thursday** Trade and Industry (11.30 – 12.00)
		Prime Minister (12.00 – 12.30)	Minister for Women
4th Monday Defence (2.30 – 3.00)	**4th Tuesday** Foreign and Commonwealth Office (11.30 – 12.00)	**4th Wednesday** International Development (11.30 – 12.00)	**4th Thursday** Treasury (11.30 – 12.00)
		Prime Minister (12.00 – 12.30)	

questions sometimes draw to the attention of a Minister an aspect of policy, or of the working of his Department with which he was not familiar, and through the briefing that he gets, to pursue issues on that particular aspect of policy, and that does sometimes lead to changes.

(Quoted in Giddings, 1993: 134–5)

Or as Norton has noted: 'Questions may result in attention being given to an issue previously neglected by the Minister, and some consequent modification of departmental policy' (1993b: 111). In this respect, Question Time can play a role in agenda setting, with MPs raising awareness of an issue or problem, and thereby persuading the relevant minister and his/her department to place it on the institutional agenda.

Occasionally, persistent questioning on a specific issue, by MPs at Ministers' Question Time, might also prompt the modification or reform of an existing policy, particularly if it has also been subject to criticism by a Select Committee inquiry. This was the case following the 1993 launch of the CSA, whereupon Social Security ministers regularly faced questions citing various problems which the new body was either encountering itself, or causing for MPs' constituents who had dealings with it. Meanwhile, the Social Security Select Committee investigated the operation of the CSA on more than one occasion during the mid-1990s, subsequently issuing highly critical reports. The combined effect of regular, probing Questions to Social Security Ministers concerning the CSA – and the citing of specific cases concerning individual constituents who were being directly and detrimentally affected – in conjunction with strong, cross-party (bipartisan) criticism from the relevant Departmental Select Committee (as noted earlier), contributed towards subsequent reforms of the CSA, initially during John Major's premiership, and subsequently by the first Blair government (Dorey, 2000: 164–8).

Correspondence between MPs and ministers

Although Questions to Ministers remains a valuable, and highly visible, means by which MPs seek to hold ministers and their departments to account, and draw attention to particular policy issues, there is another important, but rather more hidden, linkage between MPs and ministers, namely that of correspondence, usually in the form of letters or, on occasions, personal meetings between a minister and an MP (or possibly a group of MPs).

The number of letters sent by MPs to ministers and their departments has increased considerably since the 1970s, reflecting both the greater willingness of constituents to report matters of concern to their local MP, and the greater 'activism' of many MPs themselves (perhaps seeking a more substantive role in influencing public policy, however indirectly or reactively, or maybe aiming to prove their value to their constituents, with a view to securing re-election). The volume of correspondence sent by MPs and peers to ministers, government departments and their main executive agencies each year is clear from Table 6.11.

Meanwhile, a 1990 survey revealed that altogether, ministers answered 250,000 letters each year, most of these sent by MPs (Elms and Terry, 1990; Norton, 1993a: 150). Certainly, when she was a Minister of State in the Department of Health, Edwina Currie recalls signing about 10,000 letters in the course of a year (Currie, 1989: 231–2). Meanwhile, on one occasion during his time as Secretary of State for Social Security during the mid-1990s, Peter Lilley had about 1,000 letters on his desk, awaiting his signature, concerning the controversial CSA (Channel 4, 1999).

Letters from an MP to a minister – either the constituent's original letter forwarded by the MP, or a letter written on the constituent's behalf by the MP explaining the problem or grievance – are given a high priority within government departments, and traditionally must be answered directly by the minister concerned, rather than by a senior civil servant (Norton, 1993a: 149), although with an increasing number of departmental responsibilities now performed by executive agencies, ministers have tended to delegate some of the replies to the chief executive of the relevant agency (Silk and Walters, 1998: 196). MPs may also

Table 6.11 Letters from MPs/peers received by government departments/agencies/ministers in 2002 and 2003

Department/agency	2002	2003
Culture, Media and Sport	4,767	5,460
Defence	5,381	5,565
Education and Skills	15,595	14,424
Environment, Food and Rural Affairs	11,241	10,410
Foreign and Commonwealth Office	15,535	30,168
Health	17,942	19,029
Home Office	26,053	37,153
International Development	2,612	3,676
Northern Ireland	501	503
Office of the Deputy Prime Minister*	5,523	8,737
Scottish Office	115	73
Trade and Industry	11,565	14,678
Transport	6,505	10,196
Treasury	4,647	4,036
Welsh Office	118	120
Work and Pensions	14,297	12,157

*Covers local government, housing and planning
Source: Cabinet Office, 2004: Annex A

arrange a personal meeting with the relevant minister to explain or discuss a constituent's problem more fully, if it is deemed serious enough, or is a matter affecting many of the MP's constituents.

Again, although it is almost impossible methodologically to measure the impact on public policy and policy change which such letters might exercise, it does not seem unreasonable to assume that several thousand letters from MPs on the same issue or problem might persuade the relevant minister of department to modify their stance. Certainly, the volume of letters received by the (former) DSS, in connection with the CSA, during the mid-1990s, was one of the factors which led to the policy's subsequent modification.

Parliament and the European Union

The House of Commons established a Select Committee on European Legislation in 1974, although it is now known as the European Scrutiny Committee. Consisting of 16 MPs, its remit is to assess the legal and/or political importance of each EU document (more than 1,000 per annum), and decide which of them should be debated by MPs. Most documents are technical or administrative in character, so that only a few are politically controversial. The committee also monitors the work of British Ministers *vis-à-vis* the Council of Ministers, and keeps EU developments – institutional, legal and procedural – under review. A Commons resolution passed in 1990 decreed that a British minister should not approve a policy proposal in the Council unless it had already been debated and approved

Table 6.12   Policy areas covered by House of Commons European Standing Committees

European Standing Committee A	European Standing Committee B	European Standing Committee C
Environment, food and rural affairs	Foreign and Commonwealth	Culture, Media and Sport
Transport, local government and the regions	Home office International development Treasury Work and pensions	Education and skills Health Trade and industry

by one of the European committees. If such approval or support is offered, the minister is expected to provide an explanation to the European Legislation Committee.

The House of Commons also has three European Standing Committees, in which debates take place on those documents which have been selected by the select committee. Unlike other Parliamentary Standing Committees, the European Standing Committees are permanent bodies, in that the 13 MPs serve for the duration of a Parliament (4–5 years), although other MPs may also attend debates, but not cast a vote. Each of the European Standing Committees covers particular policy areas, as indicated in Table 6.12, and may interview the relevant minister at the beginning of a meeting.

Through such means, therefore, the House of Commons can seek to ensure at least a modicum of Ministerial responsibility to Parliament for EU legislation, even though Qualified Majority Voting means that a British minister will be unable to prevent the Council of Ministers from adopting a particular policy if it is proffered support by enough ministers from other member states.

Like its Commons counterpart, the House of Lords' Select Committee on the European Communities was also established in 1974, and retains its original remit of examining proposals emanating from the European Commission, with particular reference to their potential or likely impact on public policy in Britain. However, given the broad nature of this remit, coupled with the legal or technical complexity of many EU documents and other matters, much of the committee's work is undertaken by six subcommittees, each specializing in specific areas of policy, as illustrated by Figure 6.3.

The House of Lords European Union Select Committee comprises 19 members, and is serviced not only by a clerk, but also a legal adviser. It has long enjoyed the reputation as being one of the House of Lords most respected select committees, although as Norton acknowledges, this reputation 'probably exceeds its impact' (1993a: 126). The subcommittees, meanwhile, have 11–12 members, and a clerk, each, with subcommittee E (Law and Institutions) also having its own legal adviser.

Conclusion

It is clear that while Parliament is not normally a policy-making institution *per se*, it still performs a number of important roles in the policy process. Indeed, those critics who refer

Figure 6.3   House of Lords Select Committee on the European Union

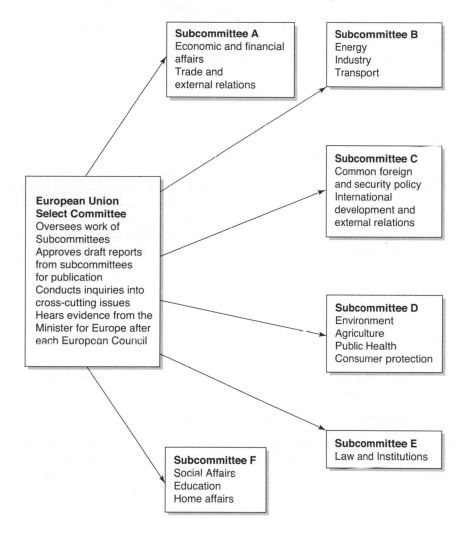

to the 'decline' of Parliament fail to appreciate that it has almost always been a body *reacting to* policy initiatives from above or beyond, so that executive dominance is not really a new phenomenon or recent trend. As noted at the outset, experts such as Norton categorize Parliament as a policy-modifying body, rather than a policy making one.

   Once it is understood that parliamentary activity entails more than just the formal passage of governmental legislation, one begins to appreciate the other means by which Parliament can seek to influence public policy, most notably through Parliament's plethora of backbench committees, and via Private Members' Bills (even though only a minority reach the statute book, those that do may make a notable difference to British society, or, at least, to certain sections of the populace). Meanwhile, even though Ministerial Question Time does not normally result directly in policy changes, it does oblige ministers to offer a public defence of their policies to MPs, thereby fulfilling the vital function of scrutiny of the executive.

Ultimately, Parliament's various debates (including those pertaining to the passage of Bills), investigative committees and other forms of scrutiny, are vital means of imbuing public policies with legitimacy, both 'manifest' and 'latent': 'As the body accepted by both mass and elites for legitimating measures of public policy, Parliament is a powerful body' (Norton, 1993a: 131–46).

Admittedly, since Norton made this claim, the British electorate has become more cynical about politicians and, indeed, much of the political process in general, but Parliament remains the main institutional forum in which government measures and public policies are regularly debated and examined by elected representatives, and which ultimately confers legitimacy on these policy outputs. For these reasons, and various others of a more normative nature beyond the remit of this study, if Parliament did not exist, it would almost certainly have to be invented.

Recommended Texts and Further Reading

1   Robert Blackburn and Andrew Kennon, *Parliament: Functions, Practice and Procedures*, 2nd edition (2003, Sweet & Maxwell), 1st edition written by John Griffith and Michael Ryle, published in 1989.

    An extremely comprehensive and detailed – almost encyclopedic – analysis of the internal workings and activities of Parliament.

2   David Judge, *The Parliamentary State* (1993, Sage).

    Examines Parliament's importance with regard to the wider British political system, including its 'legitimation' function. Insists that it is 'time to take Parliament seriously'.

3   Philip Norton, *Does Parliament Matter?* (1993a, Harvester Wheatsheaf).

    The most concise of Norton's many books on Parliament, this clearly shows how Parliament operates, and why the answer to the book's title is 'yes'. However, Norton readily acknowledges Parliament's deficiencies and limitations.

4   Michael Rush, 'Parliamentary Scrutiny' in Robert Pyper and Lynton Robins (eds) *United Kingdom Governance* (2000, Macmillan).

    Examines the methods and effectiveness of parliamentary scrutiny of government and public policies during the 1980s and 1990s.

5   Paul Silk and Rhodri Walters, *How Parliament Works*, 4th edition (1998, Longman).

    A useful account of the internal organization and day-to-day activities of Parliament.

6   Donald Shell, *The House of Lords*, 2nd edition (1992, Harvester Wheatsheaf).

A good, concise discussion of the functions and activities of the House of Lords *per se*, although another, updated, edition would be welcome.

7   Michael Rush (ed.) (1990) *Parliament and Pressure Politics*, Oxford: Clarendon Press.

Excellent and exhaustive survey of the linkages between Parliament and organized interests. Includes very informative essays on backbench committees and the legislative process.

7 The Implementation of Public Policy

It is only since the 1970s that implementation has become viewed directly and explicitly as a subject of policy analysis in its own right. Previously, implementation was assumed to be a relatively unproblematic, final stage in an apparently linear or 'stagist' policy process: agenda setting and problem recognition; policy formulation (involving the core executive and policy networks); policy endorsement and legislation (via Parliament); implementation, whereby the resultant policy was put into practice. Little academic attention was previously paid to the implementation 'stage'.

This linear, sequential or stagist model of the policy process also presupposed a top-down approach, whereby those responsible for implementing public policy simply acted in accordance with guidelines or instructions laid down by formal policy makers, thereby reflecting a clear, hierarchical chain of command.

Since the 1970s, however, these assumptions have been challenged by many writers, to the extent that implementation has become a topic of analysis in its own right, and thus worthy of a separate chapter in any book on policy-making. It was Pressman and Wildavsky's book, entitled *Implementation* (but with an exceptionally long subtitle!) published in 1973, which heralded a fundamental change in the approach to implementation. By studying the application of a particular policy – the Economic Development Administration program – in the US town of Oakland, in California, Pressman and Wildavsky drew academic attention to the manner in which the implementation 'stage' often determined the ultimate success or failure of public policy, and as such, was an aspect of the policy process which was far more important and influential than had previously been assumed. In so doing, Pressman and Wildavsky effectively challenged two of the tacit assumptions of traditional policy analysis. First, they drew attention to the inadequacy of orthodox linear models of the policy process. The clear implication of Pressman and Wildavsky's study was that rather than assuming a policy process with a beginning (agenda setting and problem recognition), middle (policy formulation and approval) and end (implementation), the policy process was circular and continuous. The apparent 'end stage' of implementation actually contributed towards policy making, for feedback arising from the identification of practical problems, such as unenforceability, unintended consequences, or administrative complexity, led to subsequent revisions of policy, or even the introduction of new policies. Or as Hill has expressed it, a policy decision often 'sets off a long and complicated chain – the implementation process – full of opportunities for things to go wrong' (1998: 233).

Seen from this perspective, there was no definite beginning, middle and end to the policy process, but instead, an ongoing process of refinement, readjustment and reform, arising from deficiencies identified during implementation 'stage'. In cases of serious policy failure, the issue which the policy was intended to ameliorate would probably move back up, or onto, the institutional agenda: the implementation stage did not represent 'closure'. Indeed, implementation can itself contribute to the process of policy learning, as policy makers recognize problems pertaining to practicability or enforceability, and subsequently seek to avoid them 'next time'.

The second tacit assumption of traditional policy analysis which was challenged by Pressman and Wildavsky's study was that concerning the role of the 'street level bureaucrats' who administered and applied public policy. The hitherto assumption had been that these 'street level bureaucrats' were effectively passive functionaries or line managers, simply applying regulations, or enforcing legislation, as laid down by their political or organizational superiors. This also reflected a simplistic top-down view of the policy process. However, a major consequence of Pressman and Widlavsky's work was the realization that 'street level bureaucrats' themselves often played a significant role in determining how public policies were actually applied, and in so doing, could shape policy outcome in ways which had not been envisaged or intended by policy-making elites. Far from being mere administrative automatons, 'street level bureaucrats' were actually key actors themselves in the policy process, to the extent that, by accident or design, by intention or inadvertence, they could shape the 'final' policy, even though ministers and senior civil servants (and maybe Special Advisers) assumed that what they had originally agreed represented the final policy.

Pressman and Wildavsky therefore served to galvanize wider academic interest in the implementation 'stage' of the policy process, prompting many other writers to devote attention to the dynamics of implementation, and the ways in which policies either failed at implementation 'stage', or the manner in which deficiencies in a policy only became apparent while it was being implemented, thereby returning the issue or problem back to the policy agenda.

The Prerequisites for 'Perfect Implementation'

To understand the importance of the implementation 'stage', and appreciate why it is at this stage that problems often arise or become apparent, various writers have identified the criteria which would need to be met in order to achieve 'perfect implementation'. Their objective has not been to offer a normative or prescriptive model of how policy *ought* to be implemented, but, instead, to provide a heuristic device (a social scientific model or paradigm used for illustrative purposes) against which empirical reality can be contrasted, and differences or discrepancies explained. If the reader's response to the list of criteria required to facilitate 'perfect implementation' is: 'They are unattainable in the real world', then he/she will readily understand why policies often unravel at implementation stage, or prove to be only partially successful.

Although it was Hood (1976: 6) who originally compiled a model of 'perfect implementation', other writers have refined the list of criteria on which the model was based, and so what follows constitutes something of a synthesis, extrapolating not only from Hood's work on this topic, but also from Gunn (1978), Hogwood (1987: 165–70), Hogwood and Gunn, 1984: 199–206), Pressman and Wildavsky (1973) and Sabatier (1986). The criteria for 'perfect implementation' are synthesized in the list below (although the eighth and final point has been added by this author) and then discussed more fully.

1   External agencies do not impose major constraints.
2   Dependency relationships are minimal.
3   There are a minimal number of 'decision points'.
4   Resources are adequate.
5   Policy is based on a valid theory of cause and effect.
6   The objectives are clear, coherent and consistent.
7   The objectives are fully understood and/or accepted by 'street level bureaucrats'.
8   That those to whom a policy is applied or targeted respond in the anticipated manner.

External agencies or events do not impose major constraints

This particular requirement would necessitate policies to be self-contained entities, operating independently of wider economic, political or social developments and events. Clearly, however, in an increasingly complex society, itself existing in an increasingly interconnected world, the chances of any policy benefiting from such autonomy are extremely unlikely. As such, almost all policies are at least partly contingent upon the behaviour of other actors, institutions and occurrences, which can seriously inhibit or undermine the efficacy or effectiveness of the original policy.

One of the most obvious and important constraints upon the effective implementation of public policy in this context is that of the economy, both at domestic level, and in an international or global context (which itself increasingly impinges upon the domestic economy, as we will discuss in Chapter 8). Not only are a Chancellor's macro-economic and fiscal policies based on assumptions and forecasts about a range of other economic trends and indicators, but, in turn, many of the government's programmes and policy goals, and departmental plans, are dependent on the level of economic growth and stability, and the extent to which predicted revenues (necessary to fund a large proportion of policies and programmes) are actually received by the Treasury.

Since at least the 1970s, however, the British economy has become increasingly vulnerable to economic events and developments in the wider world, and these have often had a detrimental impact on governmental expectations or projected targets concerning levels of consumer spending, inflation, investment, employment levels and trade. In the mid-1970s, for example, the 1974–9 Labour governments of Harold Wilson and then James Callaghan, were faced with serious economic problems, particularly extremely high levels of inflation (above 24% in 1975 and nearly 16% two years later), which effectively destroyed the government's commitment to maintaining full employment and expanding welfare provision.

A major contributory factor in fuelling these high levels of inflation during the mid-1970s was the 400% increase in the price of oil, imposed by OPEC countries in 1973, following the outbreak of the Yom Kippur war. As Britain's own North Sea oil was not 'on stream' at this time, the country was heavily dependent on importing oil from the Middle East, and hence the massive price increase had serious repercussions (other western European countries were also affected, to varying degrees) for the British economy.

In an attempt at curbing the ensuing inflation, the Wilson-Callaghan governments sought a series of incomes policies with the trade unions (having been elected in 1974 rejecting governmental interference in wage determination), in the hope that lower pay deals would help to slow down price increases, and, in turn reduce inflation. These ministerial attempts at securing pay restraint were increasingly resented by trade unions and their members, culminating in the notorious 1978–9 'winter of discontent', which effectively sounded the death knell for the Labour government, and heralded 18 years of Conservative rule.

At the same time, however, the economic repercussions of the OPEC price hike also resulted in the Labour Chancellor, Dennis Healey, seeking an IMF loan of £2.3 billion. The IMF granted this loan, but imposed a number of conditions, which obliged the Labour government to cut public expenditure, of which social security and welfare provision comprised a significant proportion. By this time, the Prime Minister, James Callaghan, had already announced the abandonment of full employment, explaining that in such economic circumstances, this was now beyond the government's control.

Here, then, was a government which had been elected in 1974 (there had been two elections, in fact, one in February, the other in October), and whose policy pledges included a rejection of incomes policies, maintenance of full employment, increased public expenditure and improvements in the 'social wage', and yet which, within two years, due to external economic developments and their impact on the British economy, abandoned all of these policies and commitments, thereby bitterly disappointing those who had voted for it, and incurring the Labour Party a reputation for economic incompetence which affected it for most of the next 18 years.

The Conservatives too have been seriously affected by such exogenous economic factors, for within months of winning the April 1992 election – having persuaded enough voters that the recession was due to a downturn in the global economy, beyond the government's control (and thus for which it should not be blamed) – John Major's re-elected government saw its own economic strategy dramatically affected by external circumstances. These occurred in the form of heavy selling of sterling by speculators in the currency markets, which led ultimately to Britain's enforced withdrawal from the EU's Exchange Rate Mechanism on 16 September 1992, since known widely as 'Black Wednesday' (for a full discussion of this episode, see Thompson, 1995: 248–74; 1996). Indeed, one academic declared that Britain's ERM withdrawal 'consigned to the dustbin the most important components of the Major Court's (sic) domestic and external governing strategies' (Bulpitt, 1996: 248). As it turned out, the Major government did hastily devise a new (or, some might say, returned to the pre-ERM) fiscal and monetary policy, including an inflation target of 2.5%, to be achieved by strict controls over both public expenditure and public sector pay awards. There were also various increases in indirect taxation. The damage, however, had been done to the Conservatives' hitherto reputation for economic competence, and in this context, the immediate loss of public and electoral popularity was subsequently compounded by the rises in indirect taxation, not offset by any visible corresponding improvement in Britain's public services and infrastructure. 'Black Wednesday' was to become the Conservative Party's equivalent of Labour's 'winter of discontent', to the extent that more than 10 years later, the Conservative Party was still struggling to win back the electorate's trust on the crucial issue of 'economic competence'.

However, having thus been re-elected in June 2001, the second Blair government also found external, exogenous events imposing constraints on its ability to 'deliver' promised improvements in public services, most notably health and education. By the beginning of 2003, with the economy growing at a slower rate than anticipated, which had serious implications for the generation of wealth and revenues which proposed increases in public expenditure were predicated on, the Chancellor, Gordon Brown, was apparently facing the dilemma of whether to impose (further) tax increases, which would probably prove electorally unpopular, and provide the Conservative Opposition with political ammunition against New Labour, or to scale down the proposed increases in public services 'investment'. This latter option would also be electorally unpopular, though, given how much of its reputation the Blair government had staked on improving public services and infrastructure during the second term.

For example, by the spring of 2003, it was becoming apparent that the Blair governments' commitment to reducing teachers' workloads, by employing more classroom assistants, was jeopardized by a funding crisis which left many schools without sufficient funds to appoint such assistants. Indeed, cash shortages meant that some schools were having to contemplate making both support staff and teachers redundant (*The Guardian*, 4 April 2003), a move which would also have a detrimental impact on the earlier goal of reducing class sizes through improving teacher-pupil ratios.

Major external events are by no means the only constraint which can impinge upon the successful implementation of a particular policy initiative. Domestic developments can sometimes serve to undermine a policy goal or strategy, even when they appear to be unrelated. For example, the Blair government has found that its goal of recruiting more public service employees – improving public services being a major overall objective of Blair's second term – has proved rather problematic in London and the south-east, due, in large part, to the phenomenal increase in property prices in recent years. While many teachers earn approximately £20-25,000 at most, and most nurses earn rather less, the price of a family home in London and the south-east is often rather more than £300,000. Clearly, unless a nurse or a teacher has a partner who is a high earner (or they have inherited a sizeable sum of money), they are unlikely to be able to afford to move to London or the south-east, even if they want to, and the government wants them to. Thus is the pursuit of one policy goal significantly undermined by 'external' social or economic developments which are theoretically entirely separate, but which have a serious impact in practice.

Dependency relationships are minimal

Ideally, the agency or policy actor(s) responsible for implementing a policy would enjoy maximum autonomy from others in the policy process, in order that they could administer the policy as intended, and without the need to seek the agreement or cooperation of others. Clearly, the more actors involved in the implementation of a policy, the greater is the potential either for communication problems or conflicts of interest, the latter invariably due to the actors seeking to pursue their own particular goals. Yet in practice, of course, it is almost inevitable and unavoidable that those actors or agencies implementing a policy will be at least partly dependent on the cooperation or compliance of others in the policy process. Indeed, as we will discuss in the next chapter, trends since the 1980s have increased significantly both the breadth and the depth of dependency relations between actors in many policy domains.

A major problem concerning the privatization of Britain's railways in 1996, for example, was precisely the extent to which the industry was broken up into more than 100 companies, not only in the sense of regional railway companies being established, with a subsequent lack of coordination between train services and timetables in different parts of the country, but also in a functional sense, with different companies having different responsibilities, such as actually operating the trains, or maintaining tracks and signalling, or catering, etc. The 25 regional train operators, therefore, have sometimes found that their ability to provide a punctual and reliable service has been undermined by the failure of those responsible for track maintenance – 19 rail engineering companies – to complete engineering works on time.

Similarly, the train operators lease rolling stock (carriages) from a small number of companies established to provide precisely this service, but the latter could be said, on commercial grounds, to have an interest in using existing rolling stock for as long as practically possible, thereby maximizing their financial returns, and thereby deferring investment in new, upgraded carriages which would provide rail 'customers' with more comfortable journeys (Haubrich, 2001: 322).

There are a minimal number of 'decision points'

One of the main findings to emanate from Pressman and Wildavsk'y study concerned the number of 'decision points' which occurred *after* a policy had been formally adopted. It was discovered that policies will often encounter a number of situations and stages where 'street level bureaucrats' need to consider how to proceed, or how to apply the policy in the particular circumstances facing them. The cumulative effect of such successive 'decision points' may well be to alter the policy in ways never envisaged or intended by those who formulated it originally, thereby impinging upon its effectiveness.

Certainly, the more decision points which arise during implementation, the more likely it is that a policy will be altered and amended (rather like the original message in a children's game of 'Chinese whispers'!), possibly to the extent of bearing little resemblance to the original policy introduced by 'core executive' and formally approved by Parliament. In such circumstances, disputes may arise, especially if the policy proves ineffective, between national level policy makers and 'street level bureaucrats', with the former alleging that the policy has been misinterpreted or poorly administered, and the latter retorting that the original policy was inherently flawed or inappropriate to the problem it was supposed to tackle.

Yet if central policy makers seek to overcome this problem by attempting to ignore or bypass subnational policy actors or organized interests at implementation stage, the chances of policy failure are likely to be even greater, for the advice and cooperation of 'street level bureaucrats' is usually essential, however frustrating it might be for national level policy makers to see their pet projects being modified as they pass through a series of 'decision points'. Compared with the outright policy failure which is likely to occur in the case of completely bypassing or ignoring street level bureaucrats, accepting policy modification as a consequence of 'decision points' is invariably the lesser of two evils from the perspective of a minister or government department. Furthermore, while multiple decision points do often yield implementation problems, they can also improve a policy, by enabling street level bureaucrats to take decisions in response to problems of practicability, or the specificity of local circumstances, which had not been foreseen by the progenitors of a policy. In this respect, though, street level bureaucrats need to be granted a degree of discretion which enables them to make decisions in response to particular or unique circumstances at individual or local level, or on a day-to-day basis.

Problems encountered or revealed by 'decision points' and street level bureaucrats will often 'loop back' to the original policy makers, who can learn from these problems, either in terms of developing new policies in the future, or in modifying the existing policy to render it more effective and practicable. Again, therefore, we emphasize the extent to which implementation represents, not the final stage in a linear policy sequence process, but part of an ongoing and interactive process, whereby policy formulation, ratification, implementation and modification are interlinked, and where implementation problems often serve to push an issue back onto the institutional agenda, thereby prompting reconsideration and revision (while also possibly perpetuating the 'issue attention cycle').

Implementation problems arising from a plethora of actors, agencies and concomitant decision points are particularly likely to occur – as Pressman and Wildavsky's case study clearly illustrated – in urban policies, such as those concerned with ameliorating urban deprivation and/or fostering urban regeneration, and tackling social problems such as poverty or crime. The laudable intentions of central or national level policy makers may well flounder when they encounter the myriad local level policy actors with a role to play in the administration of such policies, each of whom might well need to be consulted at some stage, and thus effectively granted an opportunity to modify or adapt the practical application of the policy 'on the ground'. Clearly, the more policy actors involved, the more 'decision points' which are likely to arise, thereby increasing the likelihood that the policy which is actually implemented is somewhat different to that originally devised by ministers and civil servants, and given legislative effect by Parliament. As John observes, those pursuing urban policies in particular have 'to negotiate the maze of central government departments, their regional organisations, the numerous government agencies, and private-sector and local-authority bodies' (1998: 28). Since the late 1980s, this 'maze' has become considerably more complex, as we note in the next chapter.

This aspect, perhaps more than any other, illustrates the crucial fact that the policy which emerges after formulation, followed by executive (and possibly parliamentary) endorsement, is by no means the ultimate version, for policies are often subject to modification and adaptation during their implementation 'stage'. This vital observation also serves, once again, as a salutary reminder that policy making is invariably an ongoing and organic process, so that 'stages' models should be viewed primarily as analytic or heuristic devices, rather than accurate depictions of what actually happens in political practice.

Resources are adequate

In this context, resources refer not only to finance and funding, vital though these invariably are, but also other criteria, most notably sufficient time, and adequate levels of staffing (including staff with requisite expertise, experience and competence). The absence, even partial, of any of these resources will invariably have a detrimental impact on the successful implementation of public policy.

Of course, finance and staffing are often inextricably linked, for the number – and calibre – of staff employed by any organization involved in policy implementation will be heavily dependent on its levels of funding. In this respect, a 'perfect' health service or education system is unattainable, because finance is finite, and so only a certain number of consultants, doctors and nurses can be employed, just as only a certain number of police officers can ever be employed at any given moment, so that attempts at eradicating crime will only be partially successful. Consequently, many public services and organizations either aim for targets which can never realistically be 100%, so that their success is always 'relative', or they have to prioritize, by focusing on particular aspects of their overall policy responsibilities. This might be in response to priorities determined by central or national level policy makers, or it might be priorities which 'street level bureaucrats' themselves deem to be the most urgent or feasible, given the unavoidable resource constraints within which they operate. In the latter instance, the street level bureaucrats will again be exercising discretion, and making their own judgements, in deciding how to pursue particular policies.

However, the staff shortages which might militate against perfect implementation are not always a direct consequence of limited financial resources, but sometimes the result of an insufficient number of suitably qualified personnel. No government's desire to improve the health service will be particularly successful if hospitals cannot recruit enough qualified nurses, doctors or consultants, nor is a drive to raise educational standards likely to be a resounding success if schools cannot attract enough qualified teachers.

One of the many problems encountered by the CSA, immediately following its launch in 1993, was inadequate staffing – inadequate both in relation to the volume of case loads it was attempting to deal with, and the administrative complexities involved in the assessments of those cases. The 5,000 staff initially employed – half of them from outside the civil service, and having received just 4–8 weeks training (Garnham and Knights, 1994: 54) – immediately found themselves struggling to process the cases submitted to them. The formulae devised to determine how much child support should be paid were so complex that 100 pieces of information were sometimes required to make the calculation for one case or application. This complexity was compounded by the inevitable delays involved in waiting for relevant documentation – such as, for example, salary slips, proof of rent or mortgage paid, etc. – to be submitted.

However, because the staff in the CSA were also subject to performance indicators and targets, the haste with which they were obliged to process cases meant that numerous mistakes and miscalculations were inevitably made. While these were subsequently being corrected, the backlog of new cases increased further. The problems of the CSA were such that within six months of its launch, the House of Commons social security Select Committee decided to conduct an inquiry into its operation – the first of several over the next few years.

With regard to finance itself, though, an interesting example of a policy initiative being undermined by lack of money was the second (1983–7) Thatcher government's professed desire to expand sciences and technology in universities *vis-à-vis* arts and social sciences. The then Education Secretary, Keith Joseph, was among those Conservatives at the time who viewed social science subjects especially as being less useful or necessary to the needs of the British economy, as well as being inherently Left-wing or enshrining a Marxist bias – indeed, Joseph is alleged to have insisted also that the Social Science Research Council be renamed the Economic and Social Research Council, on the grounds that 'social science' was an oxymoron. However, science and engineering faculties are capital intensive, requiring extensive and regularly updated technology and machinery, which are expensive to purchase and maintain, whereas arts and social sciences used relatively little hardware and mainly required just lecturers, thereby rendering them rather cheaper overall.

Consequently, a government committed to cutting public expenditure found that its ideological disposition in favour of 'proper' academic disciplines such as science and technology was undermined somewhat by the fact that they cost rather more than 'soft' subjects in the arts and social sciences. This was quite apart from the fact, of course, that more students – as customers or consumers in the Conservatives' free market perspective – chose to study arts or social science-based degrees anyway.

Policy is based on a valid theory of cause and effect

Virtually any policy will be based, directly or indirectly, on an assumption that '*a* causes *b*', so that if *b* is adjudged undesirable – is defined as a problem by agenda setters – then a policy will be devised to tackle *a*. Clearly, however, if policy makers' assumptions about the underlying cause of a particular problem are erroneous, then their subsequent policy is unlikely to be effective, thus resulting in failure at the implementation stage.

For example, throughout most of the 1960s and 1970s, successive governments resorted to incomes policies as a means of securing wage restraint (Dorey, 2001a: Chapters 3–6). This reflected the widely held assumption that inflation was caused by 'excessive' pay increases secured by 'greedy' trade unions and workers, which then resulted in employers raising their prices in order to fund the pay increase. The result was ever-increasing inflation, manifesting itself in increases in the cost of living, which would then prompt other trade unions to seek pay rises to offset these increases, resulting in a vicious circle of pay and price rises. Consequently, governments devised various types of incomes policy to restrain pay increases, in the expectation that price increases would similarly slow down, thereby reducing inflation, a process depicted in Figure 7.1.

However, from the late 1970s onwards, this theory concerning inflation and the appropriate policy response was increasingly rejected, as a growing number of New Right academics, journalists, think tanks and Conservative politicians advanced a monetarist account of inflation (although a few individuals, such as Enoch Powell, had been espousing this perspective throughout the 1950s and 1960s, but to no avail – Kingdon's three policy streams did not flow together during this period), whereby the cause was, ultimately,

Figure 7.1   Theory of cause and effect underpinning incomes policies in the 1960s and 1970s

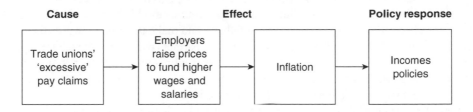

Figure 7.2   Theory of cause and effect leading to the Child Support Agency

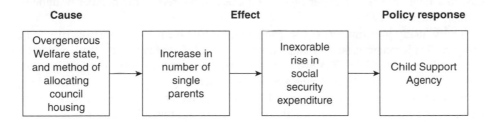

excessive increases in the money supply by governments, without any corresponding increase in productivity or industrial output. This effectively resulted in too much money in circulation chasing too few goods, whereupon the laws of supply and demand resulted in prices being increased (demand for goods exceeding supply).

This new theory of inflation meant that incomes policies were deemed irrelevant, for it was not wage increases *per se* which ultimately caused inflation. Instead, the way to curb inflation was assumed to be strict control of the money supply by government, and curbs in public expenditure, which was itself a major factor in pumping too much money into the economy, thereby fuelling inflation.

More recently, in the 1990s, a number of senior Conservative ministers, mainly on the Thatcherite wing of the party, professed deep concern about the increasing number of single parents in Britain, but particularly unmarried mothers. As Figure 7.2 shows, a major cause of this phenomenon was deemed to be an overgenerous welfare state, in which the ready availability of social security benefits, coupled with being granted priority on local councils' housing lists, was allegedly making it too easy, or even an attractive option, either for women to leave their husbands/boyfriends, taking their child(ren) with them, or for young women to become pregnant without any intention or desire to marry the father of their child, safe in the knowledge that the welfare state would then support them for the next 16 years. Similarly, it was assumed that this last consideration encouraged young men to behave in a sexually irresponsible or promiscuous manner, subsequently accepting no financial or paternal responsibility if their 'macho' pursuit of casual sex resulted in an unplanned pregnancy.

On the basis of this cause-and-effect account of lone parenthood, and the concomitant increase in social security expenditure, the Conservatives established, in 1993, the CSA, the avowed intention being to trace 'absent fathers' and make them pay towards the maintenance of their children, rather than leaving their ex-partners dependent on welfare support. This, in turn, was supposed to encourage greater sexual responsibility or restraint on the part of young men, while also yielding significant savings in terms of social security expenditure *vis-à-vis* single parents and unmarried mothers.

Yet basing such a policy initiative on this particular theory of cause and effect disregarded the possibility that many women who subsequently became 'lone parents' did *not* do so on the basis of a rational cost-benefit analysis about the amount of social security they could subsequently claim. Increases in divorce and separation can doubtless be attributed to a range of social and personal factors, as can the rise in the number of unmarried mothers since the 1970s.

Finally, many governments (but especially Conservative ones) in postwar Britain have assumed that a major cause of rising crime has been lax sentencing by 'soft' judges, and an insufficiently harsh regime inside prisons, so that criminals were not afraid of being convicted: they would either escape a custodial sentence, perhaps by virtue of their lawyer offering a 'sob story' about the wretched life the defendant had endured, or even if imprisoned, would experience a comfortable regime inside, followed by early release for good behaviour. This perspective has underpinned many initiatives to impose a tougher law and order regime over the years, involving longer prison sentences, coupled with granting the police greater powers of arrest. In 2003, meanwhile, the Blair government, concerned that too many defendants were escaping custodial sentences, attempted to place certain limits on trial by jury.

However, it is unlikely that longer sentences, and harsher regimes inside prison, will themselves serve to reduce crime, not least because most criminals probably assume that they will not get caught in the first place. Given the conviction rates for various types of crime, linked to the number of crimes which go undetected or unsolved, some criminals seem to make a 'rational' calculation that they will not get caught, so that the potential prison sentence associated with their particular crime does not act as a deterrent.

The objectives are clear, coherent and consistent

The greater the number of objectives attributed to a particular policy, the more likely it is that discrepancies or inconsistencies will become apparent at implementation stage. By way of illustration, Marsh and Rhodes cite the example of the Thatcher governments' privatization policies of the 1980s, which suffered from enshrining 'multiple and conflicting objectives' (1992b: 182). One of the key goals variously attributed to privatization was to increase competition and consumer choice, yet in many cases, nationalized industries were sold with only limited fragmentation into separate competitive companies. This was partly because some of the senior managers or potential managers successfully persuaded Conservative ministers against breaking up the industries, and partly because ministers themselves recognized that the potential value of shares in a national company would inevitably be higher than those of a regional company, thereby making the initial sale of shares more attractive to investors.

A further contradiction arising from this particular aspect of privatization concerns the issue of regulation. A major feature of the Thatcherites' critique of the pre-privatization British economy was the alleged degree of regulation to which industry was subjected, and as such, privatization was to herald a new era of freedom and autonomy for industries liberated from political meddling and bureaucratic interference. Yet because many of the privatized industries effectively retained their monopoly status, the Thatcher governments recognized that some mechanism was required to protect the interests of the consumer. Consequently, privatization merely exchanged one mode of regulation for another, as each of the privatized industries became subject to a regulatory body – OFWAT, OFGAS, OFTEL, etc. – which were intended to ensure certain standards of service were provided to consumers, and also to approve proposed price increases. Consequently, the privatization programme of the 1980s and 1990s did not so much result in a 'rolling back' of the state as a restructuring of it, and this process contributed towards the development of 'governance' in Britain, and the rise of the 'regulatory state' (both of which are discussed in the next chapter).

As we noted above, though, Britain's privatized railways were characterized by the opposite problem, namely a degree of fragmentation, both territorially and functionally, which rendered it virtually impossible to provide the improvement in services which rail users were promised. Indeed, Britain's privatized railways have become renowned for their delays, cancellations, overcrowding due to shortages of 'rolling stock (carriages), speed restrictions or diversions due to engineering works, and breakdowns *en route* have proved a common experience for millions of railway customers (see, for example, Batchelor, 1999; Bennett, 1998; Department of the Environment, Transport and the Regions, 1999: Table 5; Groom, 2000; Haubrich, 2001: 321–2; Jowit, 2000). Within five years of Britain's railways being privatized, opinion polls were indicating that even many Conservative voters were in favour of bringing the railways back into public ownership. Meanwhile, by 2003, the delays in journey times on some train services were such that proposals were put forward for some services to be cut, on the grounds that fewer trains would mean less congestion on the railways, and thus increased punctuality among those trains still running.

Privatization was also depicted as a major means of extending share ownership to ordinary people, thereby embedding support for 'popular capitalism'. Yet while the initial sales of shares in key industries such as British Gas and British Telecom were oversubscribed, as millions of ordinary people sought to buy shares over the counter of their high street bank, for example, many people soon sold their shares in order to yield an instant profit, particularly when the sale price of the shares had been set at below their market value in order further to attract 'small investors'. For example, although 2,051,373 million people purchased shares in British Telecom when it was privatized in 1984, this figure had declined to 1,236,870 by 1990. Similarly, while 4,407,079 million people originally purchased shares during the 1986 privatization of British Gas, the number of people owning shares in British Gas had fallen to 2,780,813 by 1990 (although Conservatives could still claim that this was precisely 2.78 million more shareholders than before the industry was privatized). Elsewhere, of the 2 million people who purchased shares in the 1986 privatization of Rolls Royce, less than half still retained them by 1990. Similarly, during the same period, the number of shareholders in British Airways declined from 1,100,000 to 347,897 (Abromeit, 1988). Meanwhile, although individual shareholders owned 58 per cent of all shares in Railtrack Group PLC when the company was floated on the stock market in April 1996, only 30 per cent still did so just two years later (Haubrich, 2001: 325).

Another problem encountered by the Thatcher governments as a result of pursuing objectives which proved inconsistent concerned the twin goals of curbing inflation and cutting public expenditure, particularly the welfare budget. The economic strategy deployed for reducing inflation entailed, among other things, recourse to high interest rates, in order to make borrowing more expensive, and thus less attractive, thereby reducing the amount of money in circulation. This policy was accompanied by a reduction in government subsidies to industry, partly to curb expenditure *per se*, but also to encourage greater efficiency among economic actors. However, these measures served to exacerbate the recession affecting the British economy, with a resultant increase in company bankruptcies and closures. By 1982, the official rate of unemployment had risen to approximately 3 million (virtually double what it had been when the Conservatives entered office in May 1979). This, in turn, sent social security expenditure soaring by billions in the form of unemployment benefit (now Jobseekers' Allowance), supplementary benefit (now Income Support) and housing benefit. In other words, the goal of reducing inflation invoked consequences which led to a massive increase in public expenditure, even though Conservative ministers were committed to reducing it.

Yet again, the CSA can be cited by way of example. As we noted in Chapter 2, a major impetus for the 1993 establishment of the CSA had been a 'moral panic' during the late 1980s and early 1990s about the increasing number of single parents, particularly unmarried mothers, an anxiety which was linked to ministerial concern about the impact on public expenditure, in the form of social security payments, at a time of economic recession. It was widely assumed, therefore, that the primary targets when seeking child support payment would be those men who had fathered illegitimate children, but paid little or nothing towards their upbringing (apparently happy to leave their ex-girlfriend/wife to fend for herself, or become reliant on the welfare state/taxpayer).

However, because of the performance indicators and targets which the CSA had been set, including figures for the amount of child support payments to be obtained, in order to yield savings on social security payments of £530 million during its first year, it was either men who were already paying 'maintenance' to their ex-partners (and who could thus readily be contacted to secure increased payments), or higher-earning middle-class men, who were initially targeted. Indeed, leaked internal memos sent to area managers within the CSA confirmed this strategy, with one such memo declaring: 'This is not the time for the cases we know should get early attention, but which will need a lot of effort to extract money. The name of the game is maximising the maintenance yield – don't waste a lot of time on non-profitable stuff!' (quoted in *The Guardian*, 13 September 1993).

This strategy was reiterated by a member of the CSA's management board, through another internal memo to divisional managers, which pointed out that: 'Higher savings can be achieved if we prioritise as follows', the subsequent list starting with 'absent parents in work with higher than average earnings', followed by 'absent fathers in regular contact with the parent with care' (quoted in *The Guardian*, 13 September 1993).

This strategy, pursued in order to meet with the target set for social security savings (which was not met, anyway), was in direct contrast to what had widely been deemed a key objective of the CSA, namely ensuring that most, and eventually all, 'absent fathers' made a financial contribution towards their children, but especially those deemed to be part of the irresponsible, 'feckless' underclass. Instead, those already paying maintenance were pursued for additional sums, rather than those (often lower-income) men who were not paying anything, and who might take a long time to 'track down'. A further consequence of this strategy was that many Conservative MPs found a significant proportion of their post bags and constituency surgeries occupied by irate middle-class 'absent fathers' angry that they, rather than genuinely 'feckless' fathers, were being pursued for more money (see, for example, David Ashby MP, House of Commons Debates, 20 March 1995, col. 26; Andrew Rowe MP, *ibid*, col. 62).

Occasionally, lack of clarity or consistency manifests itself by the pursuit of a particular policy which then has unintended or unforeseen consequences for another, separate policy; policy *a* is inadvertently undermined by the introduction of policy *b*. For example, having introduced various measures to combat homophobia, and grant equal rights to gays and lesbians, the Blair government then introduced EU-inspired statutory employment regulations to eradicate various forms of discrimination, in the workplace, particularly discrimination on grounds of religious belief or sexual orientation. However, the relevant legislation granted exemptions to employers or organizations 'with an ethos based on religion or belief', which, critics quickly pointed out, would provide bodies such as churches and 'faith schools' with a lawful justification to dismiss gay and lesbian staff (*The Independent on Sunday*, 11 May 2003).

The objectives are fully understood and/or accepted by 'street level bureaucrats'

If policy makers do not appear sure or agreed as to what the precise objectives of a particular policy are, then 'street level bureaucrats' themselves are almost inevitably going to be uncertain, thereby exacerbating problems at implementation stage. The case of the CSA, cited above, again provides a good illustration of this, with officials in the agency's six regional offices – as just noted – encouraged by their divisional managers to 'track down' fathers who were better-off, or already paying maintenance, rather than pursuing those who were not paying anything, even though it was the latter who most people agreed were the ones who ought to be pursued.

Elsewhere during the mid-1990s, growing concern over a burgeoning bureaucracy in the NHS – resulting largely from the introduction of internal markets and agencification via the establishment of NHS Trusts – prompted John Major's government to call for a 5 per cent reduction in NHS managers. However, as managers are unlikely to want to make themselves redundant, some NHS Trusts apparently classified senior nurses, such as ward sisters, as managers (on the grounds that they managed wards, staff and certain types of funding), and consequently made some of them redundant instead. This merely compounded the problem of insufficient numbers of nurses in Britain's hospitals, particularly those with considerable experience derived from length of service and seniority. To overcome the ensuing shortages of nurses, many NHS Trusts and hospitals then resorted to recruiting 'agency staff', who were often actually more expensive to employ (due to their hourly rates of pay, and the fee payable to the agency) than full-time nurses employed directly by the Trusts or hospitals themselves.

Meanwhile, the Blair governments have advocated a better 'work-life balance' to counter the 'long hours' work culture in Britain (where employees, on average, work several hours longer each week than their European counterparts). Ministers – especially the Trade and Industry Secretary, Patricia Hewitt – have thus exhorted men to spend more time with their children, and to play a more active (and more equal) role in child rearing. To this end, since April 2003, both men and women with young children have been granted the right to request (from their employers) reduced or flexible working hours, so as to enable them to enjoy more time with their families. However, the portents for this policy initiative were not particularly promising, for just months before its introduction, a joint study conducted by the Work Foundation think-tank, and the Equal Opportunities Commission, discovered that men's applications for unpaid parental leave were more likely to be rejected by their employers than applications by women. The survey also found many men feared that even asking for 'family time' might damage their careers, because employers might consider that they were not fully committed to their work or company.

Part of the problem was generational, the survey found, because many men in managerial positions were in their 50s, and had therefore pursued their careers in an era when more women were expected to remain at home as full-time mothers. These men, therefore, were generally less sympathetic to younger men's desire to share child-rearing responsibilities. In this respect, then, the attitudes or practices of many employers – 'street level bureaucrats', in this context – were likely to impede the government's policy initiative to promote 'family-friendly' employment (*The Observer*, 20 October; *The Guardian*, 21 October 2002).

The extent to which 'street level bureaucrats' implement a policy in the manner intended by national level policy makers will depend not only on whether they fully understand the objectives and purpose enshrined in the policy, but also, perhaps, on its compatibility with their own values or organizational goals. Just as government departments – as we noted in Chapter 4 – have often been characterized by a particular internal philosophy or operational paradigm, so too might the organizations acting as 'street level bureaucrats' have their own particular ethos or institutional ideology, and this may have practical consequences for their interpretation or acceptance of a policy emanating from above. Or as Barrett and Fudge observe, public policy 'is mediated by actors who may be operating with different assumptive worlds from those formulating the policy and, inevitably, it undergoes interpretation and modification and, in some cases, subversion' (1981b: 251).

That those to whom a policy is applied or targeted respond in the anticipated manner

This is an aspect of policy implementation which has tended to be overlooked somewhat, yet which often has a crucial bearing on whether or not policies are effective and successful.

When formulating and finalizing programmes and laws, policy makers will generally assume that the vast majority of people will accept the measure concerned and act accordingly. This clearly implies either a high level of compliance from those to whom a particular policy is targeted, or a positive response, in terms of potential recipients availing themselves of the provisions of a new policy (such as claiming a social security benefit to which they have become entitled). In this respect, the successful implementation of a particular policy may well be beyond the control of both formal policy makers and the street level bureaucrats, because the citizens who constitute the 'target audience' do not respond as expected.

The sphere of post-1960 industrial relations provides a number of useful examples of this 'implementation gap'. The various incomes policies pursued by policy makers throughout most of the 1960s and 1970s were predicated, in part, on the assumption that the trade unions would adhere to their side of agreements entered into (with ministers and employers' representatives) by union leaders. Yet these incomes policies were repeatedly undermined by the reluctance or refusal of rank-and-file trade unionists and employees to abide by the pay limits or 'norm' determined at national level. This meant that actual pay awards, particularly at local or regional level, were often somewhat higher than policy makers and trade union leaders envisaged, thereby giving rise to the phenomenon of 'wage drift', as actual earnings increased at a higher rate than allowed for by national level agreements.

The 1971 Industrial Relations Act, meanwhile, sought to place legislative curbs on trade union power and activities, and assumed that once on the statute book, trade unions and their members would abide by the new law. What Edward Heath and his Conservative colleagues had clearly not anticipated was the trade unions' orchestrated campaign of non-compliance with the legislation, which virtually rendered it ineffective and inoperable. With a number of court cases and legal challenges, related to the Act, also going against the government, Heath and his Cabinet all but abandoned it, and spent much of 1972 seeking a rapprochement with the trade unions (Dorey, 1995b: 100–2; Moran, 1977; Taylor, 1996: 176–80).

Although the 1979–90 Thatcher governments subsequently learnt from the experience of the Industrial Relations Act, so that their trade union reforms were generally much more successful, there was one notable exception, concerning the 1984 Trade Union Act. Among other things, this Act stipulated that trade unions had to ballot their members, at least once every 10 years, to obtain their approval to operate a political fund. As such political funds were financed via a proportion of each trade union member's annual subscription fee, and often provided part of various trade unions' donations to the Labour Party, Conservative ministers envisaged that many, if not most, members would vote against the operation of a political fund by their trade union, either on the assumption that many of them did not support the Labour Party – after all, in the 1983 general election, Labour had received just 27 per cent of votes cast – or because they objected to their subscription fees being spent on political campaigns, rather than directly providing services and benefits for trade union members themselves.

However, in each of the trade union ballots held during the remainder of the 1980s, in compliance with the 1984 Act, a majority of trade union members voted to retain their union's political fund. Furthermore, during the same period, a number of trade unions balloted their members to gauge the level of support for the introduction of political funds, when and where such funds had not previously been operated. Each of these ballots also yielded majorities in favour of launching a political fund. Such results were doubtless deeply disappointing to Conservative ministers, and not what they had envisaged. The most that they could claim was that at least these political funds had now been democratically approved by the trade union members who were effectively financing them, although there was some grumbling that in conducting the ballots, various unions had not made fully clear to their members the extent to which their political funds were actually being deployed to support the Labour Party.

Perhaps the most dramatic example of a policy whose implementation was seriously affected by the failure of citizens to respond as anticipated was the 1990 (1989 for Scottish readers) Community Charge, or Poll Tax, as it was more commonly known. Conservative ministers could not have anticipated that so many citizens would refuse to pay the Poll Tax, even to the extent of 'disappearing' from the electoral register in order to avoid liability to pay. In Scotland, for example, about 600,000 people (representing 15 per cent of the Scottish population) had 'failed' to pay their poll tax by the autumn of 1989, at least six months after its introduction, while in England, during the summer of 1990, it was becoming apparent that in Liverpool and some inner-London districts, about 50 per cent of eligible adults had not paid their poll tax (since the April introduction). In London as a whole, about 27 per cent of adults had still not paid their poll tax by August 1990 (Butler et al., 1994: 165, 167).

However, there was another way in which many citizens did not act as anticipated following the introduction of the Poll Tax. Conservative ministers assumed that once *every* adult began contributing towards local government finance (rather than just the main householder, as with the old domestic rates system), they would take more interest both in the amount they paid, and how it was then spent by their local council. The underlying premise was that following the introduction of the Poll Tax, local voters would either vote for parties and councils whose Poll Tax bills were lower, and/or who spent local citizens' monies wisely, providing value for money. In other words, it was assumed, voters would increasingly vote Conservative in local elections, rather than for high-spending or 'profligate' Labour councils.

However, ministers underestimated the extent to which many voters actually use local elections to register their general feelings about central government, or the national issues at the time, particularly if they are not happy with aspects of central government's performance. With the Poll Tax introduced against the backdrop of a second recession, particularly affecting white collar workers, and a slump in the housing market, many voters used the 1990 local elections, as well as by-elections, to register their dissatisfaction with the Thatcher government at that time. For example, in the May 1990 local elections, 'the Conservatives fared disastrously, being left with fewer councillors than at any time since the war' (Butler et al., 1994: 261).

The Conservatives also suffered some dramatic by-election defeats in 1990 in previously safe seats, losing Mid-Staffordshire to Labour in March 1990 (Labour benefiting from a 22 per cent swing), while the same month also saw the Liberal Democrats win a by-election in Ribble Valley – previously the Conservatives' thirteenth safest seat (Butler et al., 1994: 174). Later that year, in October, the Liberal Democrats overturned a 17,000 majority in Eastbourne, winning the by-election by a majority of 4,500. Margaret Thatcher's resignation came just a few weeks later.

Finally, to return to the case of the CSA, ministers and civil servants, primarily in the Department of Social Security, and the Treasury, undoubtedly anticipated that single parents would be grateful to the Agency for locating their ex-partners, and obliging them to provide financial support in respect of their child(ren). Yet such a premise proved erroneous in many instances, because a significant number of single parents either resented the 'intrusion' of the CSA into their family affairs (although ministers took the view that when people are claiming public funds in the form of social security, the taxpayer has a right to expect that these funds are not paid to people who do not need or deserve them), or feared reprisals – quite possibly in the form of violence – from their former partner if the latter was suddenly presented with a demand for regular maintenance in respect of their child. Ministers might also have underestimated just how many men would not be willing to make financial contributions to the raising of their child(ren), but were apparently quite happy to leave the woman struggling, or to let the taxpayer incur the costs of their irresponsibility.

To add to its various other travails, therefore, the CSA was immediately beset by the non-compliance of 'absent fathers' and single parents alike, each of whom had their own particular reasons for refusing to cooperate. Indeed, it became apparent that some single parents and their ex-partners were colluding together against the CSA. In such cases, when a single parent in receipt of social security refused to divulge details about her (the overwhelming majority of single parents are women) ex-partner, she would be penalized by having a proportion of her benefit withheld. However, some absent fathers proved willing to 'reimburse' the mother for the amount withheld from her social security payments, because this was considerably less than they would have to pay if their whereabouts and circumstances became known to the CSA.

Certainly, the CSA encountered many single parents who were adamant that they neither knew where their ex-partners were, nor what they were now doing. Other women insisted that they feared violent reprisals if they provided information which would then lead to their ex-partners being 'tracked down' and made to pay maintenance by the CSA. This was a particularly pertinent concern for women who were now 'single parents' because they had fled from violent boyfriends or husbands, sometimes quite literally in fear of their life; their recently-acquired 'single parent' status was a consequence of escaping from an abusive relationship and domestic violence, *not* the result of promiscuity, irresponsibility or casual, unprotected sex. For some such women, the CSA was no ally, but an institution whose intervention might inadvertently expose them – and their children – to renewed physical danger.

More recently, sections of the Countryside Alliance have warned the Blair government that if it perseveres with its attempt at outlawing fox hunting, there will be a campaign of civil disobedience and defiance by the fox hunting fraternity, involving such activities as blockades of roads, and possibly of some depots supplying food or milk, with the express aim of causing disruption to daily life in Britain (the hope presumably being that this will fuel public anger towards the ministers and Labour MPs who enacted the ban on blood sports; of course, it might actually create hostility towards fox hunters instead, if they are clearly seen to be defying the law and causing considerable inconvenience to ordinary people). Some fox hunters have also warned that they will refuse to pay any fines imposed for actively defying the ban, and are prepared to go to prison and become 'martyrs' to the cause of fox hunting and 'liberty' in the countryside.

So far, our examples here have focused on the behaviour of ordinary citizens, where they have failed or refused to respond in the manner expected or envisaged by national level policy makers. However, it can also be the case that those in formal positions of authority or power fail to act as intended, thereby contributing to policy failure, or, at least, only partial success of an initiative. We referred above, for example, to the problems engendered by the 1971 Industrial Relations Act, but a further factor which undermined it was the way in which various judges interpreted the law differently to how it was intended by Conservative ministers. By not interpreting the Act quite in the manner that had been expected, the judiciary effectively – but unwittingly – contributed to the Act's downfall.

Much more recently, the Blair Government's initiatives to tackle antisocial behaviour have been hindered by the apparent reticence of the courts fully to use the powers available to them. For example, in spite of enacting legislation in 1998 and 2001, empowering courts to impose Anti-social Behaviour Orders (ASBOs) and night-time curfews on troublesome youths, by November 2002, only 654 such ASBOs had actually been imposed in England and Wales, rather fewer than the 5,000 which the government had originally envisaged (Burney, 2002; Randall, 2004: 182). With regard to another aspect of antisocial behaviour or public order, autumn 2004 heralded the publication of a report to Tony Blair – by Hazel Blears, a Minister of State at the Home Office – noting that local authorities and the police were failing to make full use of the powers vested in them (by the government) to tackle binge drinking and public drunkenness and related disorderly behaviour. Part of the problem, the report noted, was a lack of coordination and communication between the police and local authorities. Blears also reported that in spite of the government's efforts to tackle under-age drinking, 35 per cent of off-licences which were tested, and 65 per cent of tested bars and clubs, were still selling alcohol to under-age drinkers (Cracknell, 2004: 13).

Such problems seemed to vindicate Tony Blair's repeated emphasis on the vital need for 'joined-up government', entailing much greater dialogue and cooperation between the departments, agencies and various other policy actors involved in devising and implementing particular policies.

Seeking to overcome the 'implementation gap'

Given that the above criteria or conditions are, by definition, unattainable in the real world, any government will enjoy only partial policy success. This perhaps provides one explanation for the British electorate's growing disillusion and disenchantment with governments and politicians, as indicated by declining turn out in elections (turn out in the 2001 election was down to 59 per cent) and successive opinion polls indicating diminishing trust in politicians, along with the saloon-bar wisdom that 'they're all as bad as each other'.

Although politicians will frequently cite statistics to 'prove' that policies are working, or at least beginning to take effect, the public will often remain unconvinced, as indicated by opinion polls, focus groups and attitude surveys, which invariably reveal that many people are convinced that crime is spiralling out of control and that courts are 'too lenient' with criminals, that Britain is a 'soft touch' for asylum seekers, that we are over-taxed, that educational standards have deteriorated, etc. These common assumptions partly derive from the problems which governments encounter in successfully implementing policies, whereupon public and media attention tends to dwell upon the apparent failures or inadequacies.

If they are cognizant of the implementation problems which await them, then governments are likely to tailor their policy objectives and policy style accordingly, in an attempt at enhancing their likely success rate. For example, the Thatcher governments of the 1980s had a clear set of policy objectives, such as curbing public expenditure, shrinking the welfare state, cutting trade union power, privatization (although this did not become a clear policy goal until after 1982), reforming local government, and introducing into the public sector elements of competition, coupled with responsiveness to customers and clients. In so doing, the Thatcher governments apparently sought to ensure that they enunciated a 'clear, coherent and consistent' set of objectives, although even this was problematic in some policy areas, such as privatization, where multiple objectives were often cited, but not all of which were compatible or consistent with each other.

However, the Thatcher governments also sought to weaken, remove or bypass many of those 'street level bureaucrats' who might otherwise impede successful policy implementation, thereby seeking to minimize dependency relationships, and *inter alia* reduce the number of 'decision points'. Hence the reduced consultation with trade unions and other professional bodies or producer groups, the reduction of the role and powers of local authorities, and the increasing use of ministerially-appointed or approved 'quangos' and executive agencies to implement policies.

In so doing, and largely in accordance with the model of perfect implementation previously delineated, the Thatcher governments were attempting to invoke a 'top-down' approach, whereby implementation is effectively viewed as the imposition of clear and explicit policy objectives on a small number of hierarchically-organized and compliant actors in each policy domain, at subnational level.

Yet the Thatcher governments still encountered a range of implementation problems (see Marsh and Rhodes, 1992b, for a good overview), not least of these deriving from the continued ability of organized interests and street level bureaucrats to impede the successful administration of key policies, such as education and health reform, while local authorities, in spite of their reduced powers, still retained sufficient strength, both in terms of structural or strategic position, and residual resources, to thwart various attempts at reducing local government expenditure (see, for example, Rhodes, 1992).

Although the Blair governments appear to have accepted many of the overall policies of the preceding Conservative governments – the primacy of the market, private sector involvement in financing capital projects in the public sector, refusal to raise income tax, close(r) links with employers rather than with the trade unions, public service reform, welfare reform, etc. – they seem nonetheless to have acknowledged various of the problems enshrined in the top-down approach to implementation, and tailored their policy style accordingly.

Consequently, rather than seeking to marginalize subnational policy actors, or impose policies on them by ministerial decree, the Blair governments have opted for a more inclusionary policy style, whereby the importance of non-governmental policy actors and street level bureaucrats is accepted, thus leading to greater consultation, dialogue and partnerships. Ministers still declare certain key policy objectives – although often depicted as 'aspirations' – and targets or performance indicators, but in conjunction with this, there has been a discernible trend towards co-option rather than coercion, and devolution rather than diktat.

Indeed, as we noted in Chapter 4, the core executive itself under Blair has been characterized by concerted efforts at pursuing 'joined-up government' through cross-departmental initiatives and coordination – such as the Social Exclusion Unit – and this approach has, in certain respects, been replicated at regional and local level. Whereas the 'top-down' model of perfect implementation presupposed a vertical chain of command within a specific policy domain or subsystem, the policy style of the Blair governments acknowledges – sometimes explicitly, but sometimes hesitantly – that implementation in contemporary Britain increasingly necessitates horizontal consultation and coordination between policy actors at subnational level, rendering vertical, top-down command even less appropriate or feasible.

Rather than seeing implementation as a choice between 'top-down' control by national level policy makers, *or* 'bottom up' policy administration and adaptation by 'street level bureaucrats', the Blair governments seem to have developed a 'third way' or 'mixed economy' of implementation, with ministers establishing broad objectives in certain policy areas, but leaving subnational actors to devise ways of achieving them – albeit with a judicious blend of incentives and sanctions for success and failure respectively – while also establishing devolved institutions at regional level, with varying degrees of autonomy to determine either their own policy objectives, or their particular means of attaining centrally determined goals.

Conclusion

While the model of 'perfect implementation' was never remotely attainable (and was not intended to be, of course), many of the conditions enshrined within it have become even less feasible since it was originally devised. In an increasingly global, interconnected world, policies are even more subject to external constraints and agencies than ever before. Similarly, within Britain itself, there are more organized interests, agencies and sundry other policy actors than ever before, partly reflecting the increasingly cross-cutting or interconnected nature of many policy issues or problems, particularly as policies are increasingly formulated at different levels within the polity.

As such, implementation has increasingly been recognized as a dynamic, ongoing, two-way process: 'a policy/action continuum in which an interactive and negotiative process is taking place over time between those seeking to put policy into effect and those upon whom action depends' (Barrett and Fudge, 1981a: 25). Consequently, 'there has been a growing trend towards multi-organisational forms of policy implementation' (Gray, 2000: 284). What this means, ultimately, is that much implementation in Britain reflects a transition from government towards governance, a trend which forms the basis of the next chapter. This will further illustrate the deficiencies of top-down models of implementation, and the notion that implementation constitutes the final 'stage' in a linear or sequential policy process.

Recommended Texts and Further Reading

1　David Marsh and R.A. Rhodes (1992b) 'The Implementation Gap: Explaining Policy Change and Continuity' in David Marsh and R.A.W. Rhodes (eds) *Implementing Thatcherite Policies: Audit of an Era*, Milton Keynes: Open University Press.

Although focusing on policies pursued during the 1980s, draws more general and useful lessons about the factors which determine the success or failure of policy implementation.

2　Jeffrey Pressman and Aaron Wildavsky (1973) *Implementation: How Great Expectations in Washington Are Dashed in Oakland*, Berkeley, CA: University of California Press.

Seminal text which effectively established 'implementation studies' as a vitally important aspect of the policy process in its own right, and identifies the kinds of problems which policies encounter when being put into practice 'on the ground'.

3　Susan Barrett and Colin Fudge (eds) (1981a and b) *Policy and Action*, Methuen.

Good (if rather dated) series of essays which provides a judicious blend of empirical case studies from specific policy areas and events, and discussion of the academic literature on implementation studies.

4　Michael Hill and Peter Hupe (2002) *Implementing Public Policy*, Sage.

Traces the development of 'implementation studies' to the present day, examining the key concepts and debates concerning both the theories and the practice of implementation. In many respects, a rich and in-depth literature review.

8 From Government to Governance

The concept of *governance* has become increasingly popular among political scientists and policy analysts since the 1980s, for it represents an intellectual innovation which aims to characterize key empirical changes in the structure of the British polity, and the impact that these changes have had on public policy in Britain. Previously, textbooks tended to refer to 'government', reflecting the notion of a unitary state, in which central government or the 'core executive' – Cabinet, ministers, departments and senior civil servants – administered public policy in a top-down manner, in spite of the important, but often overlooked or underestimated role of street level bureaucrats, as noted in the previous chapter. This notion of 'government', both as a noun, and a verb (as in 'to govern'), was both implicit and extensive in most political science and policy studies literature.

Since the late 1980s, however, the character, role and structure of government in Britain have changed considerably, to the extent that many writers no longer deem the term 'government' to be adequate or appropriate when delineating how public policy is formulated and implemented. This is because the British polity has undergone a process of fragmentation and decentralization since the late 1980s, which has affected administrative units, political institutions and the policy process itself. As Wright observed, there has been:

> a tendency … towards the increased Balkanisation and privatization of the public domain, as the result of devolving authority to a diversified network of agencies, regulatory bodies, sub-contractors, third sector bodies, private companies. This network is bound together by a 'nexus of contracts' which has replaced integrated hierarchies. Exchange or bartered relationships are slowly replacing authoritative command structures … [all leading to an] increasing process of policy obfuscation, or 'boundary-blurring', in which public and private interact in inextricable ways.
>
> (1994: 127)

It is these changes, and their consequences, which have resulted in the concept of governance acquiring wider currency among political scientists and policy analysts.

The meaning of governance

In this context, governance refers to the fact that 'the government' now has 'to operate in a diverse, fragmented, complex, and decentralised environment', in which there are: 'more actors involved, the boundaries between the public and the private sphere are less precise, and the Government's command over the policy process is seen to have receded ... the Government is only one actor (although a crucial one) among many others in the policy arena.'

Consequently, the contemporary study of public policy in Britain requires consideration of 'all the actors and locations beyond the "core executive" involved in the policy making process' (Richards and Smith, 2002: 15, 4, 2).

Similarly, Pierre and Stoker observe that with the apparent advent and advance of governance: 'Local, regional and national political elites alike seek to forge coalitions with private businesses, voluntary associations and other societal actors to mobilize resources across the public-private border in order to enhance their chances of guiding society towards politically defined goals' (2000: 29).

Goldsmith, meanwhile, emphasizes that governance 'places an emphasis on vertical co-operation between institutions and tiers or levels of government, and on horizontal co-operation between public, private and voluntary sectors at the local level' (1997: 7).

Certainly, with regard to local politics, Wilson notes that: 'Governance refers to the development and implementation of public policy through a broader range of public and private agencies than those traditionally associated with elected local government. Partnerships, networks and contracts have therefore become integral parts of the local political scene' (2000: 258).

Indeed, some writers deploy the term 'multilevel governance' to emphasize the different levels and layers at, and through, which policies and public services are increasingly devised and delivered.

Of course, various policies and services have always been administered by local boards and authorities, but the process of agencification pursued by the Thatcher-Major governments, coupled with the increased role which was simultaneously ascribed to the private and voluntary sectors in service provision, and then the first Blair government's measures to establish a Scottish Parliament, Welsh Assembly, and Regional Assemblies in England, have served to imbue the concept of multilevel governance with added resonance and relevance, both conceptually and empirically. This is because multilevel governance characterizes a political regime in which there are 'negotiated exchanges between systems of governance at different institutional levels', be they international (the EU, for example), national, regional or local. Consequently, the contemporary policy process is increasingly 'fragmented into a maze of institutions and organizations', entailing 'many centres and diverse links between many agencies of government at local, regional, national and supranational level' and each of these discrete levels, in turn, 'has a diverse range of horizontal relationships with other government agencies, privatized utilities, private companies, voluntary organizations and community groups' (Pierre and Stoker, 2000: 30–1).

For example, a policy to tackle drug abuse and associated problems will not be successful if it relies solely or primarily on parliamentary legislation or ministerial exhortation. Instead, it will require interaction, cooperation and coordination between a wide range of policy actors, not only at different vertical levels, ranging from the supranational or intergovernmental down to the local, but also horizontally, spanning a range of policy actors from a range of policy subsystems, such as charities, community groups, housing associations, health authorities and NHS Trusts, police forces, probation services, schools and social services. Similarly, initiatives to tackle drug trafficking will require the involvement and coordination of airline companies, civil aviation authorities, coastguards, customs and excise, and port authorities, as well as cooperation at international level by various national police forces and/or Interpol. Such an initiative would almost invariably involve the EU too.

Crucially, though, while this form of governance clearly entails the interaction of policy actors and service providers at different vertical levels, there is relative lack of hierarchical control. Whereas older, traditional models of government invariably depicted ministers, deriving their political authority and legitimacy from Parliament, announcing policies and piloting legislation through the House of Commons, which were then expected to be faithfully implemented at subnational level (irrespective of how unrealistic or inaccurate such a neat process was in reality), multilevel governance makes explicit the absence of a clear chain of command, and draws attention, instead, to the vital importance of cooperation and coordination in an increasingly complex policy process.

For example, following the Morecambe Bay disaster early in 2004, when 19 Chinese workers collecting cockles drowned after they were marooned on the treacherous sands by a rapid incoming tide, it was revealed that no less than 50 organizations had been attempting to regulate the employment of such workers, some of them illegal immigrants exploited by ruthless 'gang-masters' who had little regard for their health and safety, and knowing that given their status, they were hardly likely to complain to 'the authorities' about their treatment. Indeed, prior to the tragedy, the local MP had already arranged a 'multi-agency meeting' on the issue of cocklers in Morecambe. Among the 'agencies' involved in this policy issue were the Immigration Service, the Joint Council for the Welfare of Immigrants, the local council, Lancashire police, various trade unions, and the fisheries committee (*The Independent on Sunday*, 8 February 2004). Meanwhile, at national level, a number of government departments or agencies could also be deemed to have had a political responsibility for particular aspects of the issue: the Home Office with regard to illegal immigration; the Health and Safety Executive for enforcing the safety of employees at work; the Department of Environment, Food and Rural Affairs for matters pertaining to agricultural workers (a category which the cocklers arguably fitted into); and the Department of Work and Pensions for dealing with rogue employers, such as illegal or unlicensed 'gang-masters' (*The Guardian* (*Editorial*), 7 February 2004).

Indeed, like the individuals and institutions in the core executive, as well as in policy communities, the policy actors involved in multilevel governance are invariably involved in an often complex web of exchange relationships, derived, once again, from resource dependency. Hence the tendency towards voluntary or self-organized partnerships and forums at local and regional level, as policy actors seek to establish priorities, develop common strategies, share intelligence, exchange resources, and determine mutual roles and responsibilities. To the extent that central government, traditionally conceived, retains a role, it is increasingly to establish overall objectives or policy frameworks, and/or establish targets and performance indicators, but with the policy actors themselves developing the strategies and partnerships through which the goals can best be achieved. Or to put it another way, central government stipulates the desired outcomes, but increasingly leaves the relevant policy actors to devise the appropriate processes.

The political scientist who has probably done more than anyone else to popularize the concept of governance is Rod Rhodes (1996, 1997), and while he identifies a number of potential meanings and applications of the term, he ultimately opts for a definition (1997: 53) which emphasizes:

- Interdependence between organizations, which includes not only traditional state actors and political institutions, but also private sector and voluntary bodies. The boundaries between these actors have become 'shifting and opaque'.
- Interaction between the various actors, derived from resource dependencies and exchange relationships, and their mutual need to develop common objectives or agreed strategies. These interactions also entail the development of trust and acceptance of the 'rules of the game' between the various policy actors.
- Relative autonomy from the state, with the policy actors often establishing their own processes and practices to pursue objectives, strategies or targets, even though the latter might have been decreed by the state (or central government) itself.
- A 'coordinating', rather than 'commanding', role for the state, or central government. The plethora of policy actors now involved at all levels of British society mean that while the 'core executive' is still a vitally important institutional entity – as illustrated in Chapters 3 and 4 – its ability to play a directive role has been somewhat curtailed, and replaced by a more indirect 'steering' and 'supervisory' role, particularly with regard to policy implementation.

Rhodes emphasizes how governance 'blurs the distinction between state and civil society', because the state 'becomes a collection of interorganizational networks made up of governmental and societal actors with no sovereign actor able to steer or regulate' (Rhodes, 1997: 57). We would suggest, however, that Rhodes' definition perhaps exaggerates the state's apparent loss of steering or regulatory capacity, for as we shall see shortly, when we discuss the rise of the 'regulatory state', it is still actors within the core executive who tend to establish targets and objectives that societal actors are expected to attain, and to which funding is increasingly linked. It is undoubtedly much more difficult for the state to 'steer or regulate' in an increasingly fragmented, 'marketized', and pluralistic socio-political system, but in recognition of this, the state seems to have redoubled its efforts in this respect, albeit by developing new ways and means of encouraging subnational actors to pursue particular policy goals and meet specific performance indicators.

No one who works in a university, for example, could claim that they were today subject to *less* state direction and 'steerage' than in the past, for virtually every aspect of academic life is now subject to requirements and targets imposed on universities from outside, and to which funding is linked (as will be illustrated below). The proposed creation of an 'access regulator', to ensure that universities are admitting more students from poorer or 'disadvantaged' backgrounds (and, again, to which funding will be linked, as well as permission to charge 'top-up fees'), is just the latest institutional innovation whereby the state still seeks to 'steer' societal institutions, in order to ensure that they act in accordance with governmental aims and aspirations, with the threat of financial penalties if they are subsequently adjudged to have failed.

According to Kooiman and Van Vliet (1993: 66), the role of central government in a system of governance entails a number of discrete, but clearly interlinked, obligations and objectives, namely:

- *Coordination*, which involves identifying the key actors or 'stakeholders' with regard to a particular policy issue or objective, and then promoting linkages between them.
- *Collaboration and steering*, which logically follows on from the above, involves central governments seeking to ensure that these policy actors work effectively together in the pursuit of 'desired outcomes'.
- *Integration and regulation*, entailing the development of institutional mechanisms and procedures for ensuring that these 'desired outcomes' are actually achieved.

That Britain has experienced a transition from government to governance can be attributed to several developments and trends since the late 1980s. The most notable of these are: globalization; Europeanization; 'agencification'; the Blair governments' penchant for establishing 'task forces', 'working groups' and advisory groups; devolution to Scotland and Wales; English 'regionalization'; the increased involvement of voluntary bodies, alongside the public and private sectors, in service provision and delivery; the rise of the 'regulatory state'. Each of these phenomena will now be discussed.

Globalization

Globalization is a relatively new concept (although its antecedents, and the processes leading to it, are centuries old), referring to the extent to which countries, their economies and political institutions appear to be increasingly interconnected in the contemporary world, and therefore raising serious questions about the notion of the autonomous nation-state and national sovereignty. Although capital(ism) has never recognized or confined itself to national borders and geopolitical boundaries, many commentators believe that the world has now entered a qualitatively new phase of international economic interdependence, hastened – as well as symbolized – by the collapse of the former Soviet Empire during 1989–91, although some authors believe that the scope or apparent originality of globalization has been exaggerated (Hardt and Negri, 2000; Hirst and Thompson, 1996).

For writers such as Fukuyama, however, the collapse of the Soviet regime heralded 'the end of history', the end-point in mankind's ideological evolution, for the collapse of 'socialism' (assuming, for argument's sake, that this was what existed in the old East European regimes, although one seriously doubts whether a reincarnated Karl Marx would have approved of the awful tyranny and atrocities perpetrated in his name) signified the point at which all ideological alternatives to the market economy (capitalism) and liberal democracy were intellectually exhausted and politically vanquished; individualism and liberalism had triumphed, or would imminently do so in so-called Third World societies (Fukuyama, 1989: 3–18).

In this context, globalization refers to:

the multiplicity of linkages and interconnections that transcend the nation-states (and by implication the societies) which make up the modern world system … Nowadays, goods, capital, people, knowledge, images, communications, crime, culture, pollutants, drugs, fashions, beliefs all readily flow across territorial boundaries … the existence of global systems of trade, finance and production binds together, in very complicated ways, the prosperity and fate of households, communities and nations across the globe.

(McGrew, 1992: 65–6)

As such, globalization is deemed to involve both a widening and deepening of 'interconnect-edness' between countries and institutions of governance (Giddens, 1991: 187). It entails 'widening' by virtue of the increasing number of linkages between nation-states, which are themselves increasingly mediated between international institutions, such as the EU (discussed below), G7 (or G8, as it has become since the accession of Russia), the International Monetary Fund (IMF) and the North Atlantic Treaty Organization (NATO). Although these particular organizations predate the current (or latest) phase of globalization, they nonetheless symbolize the manner in which countries, their governments and other national policy actors are increasingly forming or joining transnational bodies to coordinate economic, military and political activities and policy making. For example, in 1909, there existed 37 international governmental organizations (IGOs) and 176 international non-governmental organizations (INGOs), but by 1996, there were 260 IGOs and 5,472 INGOs (Held et al., 1999: 4).

It also entails a 'deepening' of these interconnections, though, as they become more complex, and exert a correspondingly greater impact on the citizens and policy makers of particular countries. There is deemed to be a growing interdependence between countries and national governments, as they are increasingly obliged to confront common problems – AIDS, asylum seekers, drug trafficking, organized crime, global warming, pollution, terrorism, etc. – which cannot be effectively tackled independently by nation-states or national governments acting in isolation. For example, the USA has repeatedly called upon the 'international community' to help defeat terrorism.

Explaining the development of globalization

Different writers have prioritized different factors in seeking to identify the underlying impetus of globalization, with Immanuel Wallerstein, for example, emphasizing capitalism's relentless expansionist tendencies, deriving from its constant search for new markets, raw materials, cheap labour and, ultimately, new sources of profit. He believes that during the latter part of the 20th century, capitalism became truly global, to the extent that 'the entire globe is operating within the framework of ... the capitalist world economy', although just as capitalism is characterized by marked inequalities within any individual country, so the new 'capitalist world economy' entails structural inequalities between countries, with a 'core' of economically wealthy and politically powerful western nations exercising considerable dominance and influence over the less industrially-advanced societies in what Wallerstein terms the 'semi-periphery' or 'periphery' of this new international capitalist regime (Wallerstein, 1983, 1991). The countries who comprise the 'core' of this capitalist world order are therefore deemed to retain a greater degree of relative national autonomy and political sovereignty, although clearly, in economic affairs, their independence is still constrained and compromised.

Sklair, meanwhile, analyses the establishment of a 'global system' in terms of 'transnational practices', of which the transnational corporation is the primary economic manifestation, 'the major locus of transnational economic practices', while a parallel 'transnational capitalist class is the major locus of transnational political practices'. (1991: 5–6).

For other writers, though, the underlying impetus of globalization emanates primarily from technological advances, whereby:

> technology ... has so greatly diminished geographic and social distances through the jet-powered airliner, the computer, the orbiting satellite and many other innovations that now move people, ideas and goods more rapidly and surely across space and time than ever before. It is technology that has profoundly altered the scale on which human affairs take place ... technology, in short, that has fostered the interdependence of local, national and international communities that is far greater than any previously experienced.

> (Rosenau, 1990: 17)

Some writers, though, such as Gilpin, prefer to explain the impetus underpinning globalization with reference to political dynamics, whereby national political and policy actors develop organizational and institutional linkages with each other, in recognition of the need to secure stability and order in an otherwise increasingly unstable and unpredictable world. Consequently, a growing number of linkages have been established between political actors from various countries, as each tries to balance the desire to retain some degree of sovereignty and autonomy with recognition of the need to seek alliances with their foreign counterparts in order to pursue shared objectives and foster some semblance of order and stability. While recognizing the development of a global economy, Gilpin views its establishment as being at least partly contingent on the politico-institutional framework established by dominant or *hegemonic* states, without whom the international economic order would be characterized by considerable instability and disorder. According to Gilpin:

> a hegemon is necessary to the existence of a liberal international economy ... historical experience suggests that in the absence of a dominant liberal power, international economic co-operation has been extremely difficult to attain or sustain and conflict has been the norm ... The expansion and success of the market in integrating modern economic life could not have occurred without the favourable environment provided by the liberal hegemonic power.

> (1987: 88, 85)

However, while different authors 'privilege' a particular dynamic or underlying cause of globalization, it could readily be argued that all of the above factors are relevant to explaining 'global interconnectedness', and that these dynamics are themselves interlinked and interdependent. For example, technological advances have surely themselves contributed towards the development of a global economy, by facilitating instantaneous (as well as 24 hours per day) financial transactions across the globe, while 'the spectacular development of electronically transmitted information ... enables geographically distant units to be organisationally unified' (Urry, 1989: 97; Held, 1989: 193). Or as Castells notes:

> Capital is managed around the clock in globally integrated financial markets working in real time for the first time in history: billion dollars worth of transaction take place in

seconds in the electronic circuits through the globe. It is now the case that due to the expansion of capital and technological changes, savings, investments and currencies are now interconnected world-wide.

(1996: 93)

At the same time, social phenomena such as population shifts or environmental pollution, can at least partly be attributed to economic factors (in terms of the search for employment by 'economic migrants', or the relentless drive to maximize industrial output respectively). Certainly, Anthony Giddens prefers a 'multicausal' account of the dynamics of globalization, emphasizing that 'the world system should be seen as influenced by several sets of primary processes associated with the nation-state system, coordinated through global networks of information exchange, the world capitalist economy and the world military order' (1987: 288; see also Robertson, 1990: 22; Robertson and Lechner, 1985: 113).

Implications of globalization for British policy making

Globalization has impacted – and continues to impact – upon Britain, both in institutional terms, and with regard to various policies, particularly those of an economic character. However, there appears to have been less public and political concern about the impact of globalization on Britain compared with the anxiety about 'Europeanization', partly, perhaps, because the process and its ramifications are somehow more subtle and more difficult to discern, and partly because Britain has been one of the 'core' nations anyway, so that membership of various international institutions has not yielded the same fears about 'surrendering' sovereignty in quite the same manner as EU membership and integration have done. Indeed, one might suggest that the psychological and historical legacy of formerly presiding over an empire, and then, Commonwealth, which spanned the globe, has rendered Britain more at ease about involvement in global politics – particularly in view of the alleged 'special relationship' with the present-day hegemon, the USA – whereas considerable unease continues to underpin Britain's relationship with Europe.

For example, Britain is a member of several key economic and military bodies beyond the EU level, as illustrated by Figure 8.1.

However, it is with regard to economic and industrial policies that globalization seems to have imposed the greatest constraints on the autonomy of British policy makers. In an era of multinational corporations and international finance, coupled with the ability of large companies and financial institutions to shift billions of pounds from one location to another around the globe, it has been deemed axiomatic that Britain ensures that economic, employment and fiscal policies are conducive to attracting, and then retaining, overseas companies, thereby maintaining the flow of inward investment upon which so many jobs have come to depend. With multinational companies accounting for about 70 per cent of world trade (McGrew, 1997: 6), policy makers in Britain have increasingly had to accept certain limits with regard to aspects of economic and employment policies, such as tax rates, the level of the statutory minimum wage, the scope of employment protection legislation, etc., for fear that setting any of these 'too high' will prompt a 'flight of Capital'

Figure 8.1 Britain's membership of key international bodies (beyond the EU)

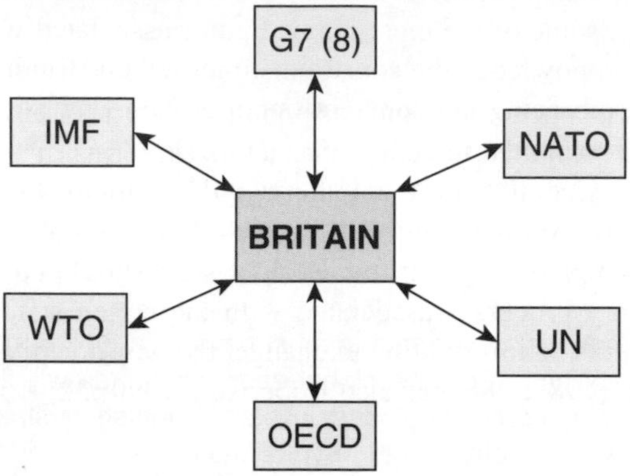

Abbreviations used: IMF = International Monetary Fund; NATO = North Atlantic Treaty Organization; WTO = World Trade Organization; OECD = Organization for Economic Cooperation and Development; UN = United Nations

or a decision by a foreign company *not* to open a factory or headquarters in Britain. Or as one political theorist has expressed it:

> the internationalisation of production, finance and other economic resources is unquestionably eroding the capacity of the state to control its own economic future. At the very least, there appears to be a diminution of state autonomy, and a disjuncture between the idea of a sovereign state determining its own future and the conditions of modern economies, marked as they are by the intersection of national and international economic processes.

(Held, 1989: 194)

Some writers go even further, and argue that an international capitalist class has developed, due to globalization 'unifying the world into a single mode of production and a single global system, and bringing about the organic integration of different countries and regions into a global economy' (Robinson, 2001: 158: see also Sklair, 1998).

The economic aspects of globalization also have ramifications for ostensibly non-economic policies and institutions, as evinced by political attempts at 'reforming' (invariably a euphemism for reducing) various aspects of social policy and the welfare state. Not only have most British policy makers accepted that funding the welfare state in its current form entails a level of taxation which acts a deterrent to investors from overseas, it is also assumed that 'generous' welfare provision undermines 'labour market discipline' or 'flexibility', thereby further deterring employment-generating inward investment.

Although, as we have noted above, some writers believe that the scale of globalization has been exaggerated, many policy makers act as if it were a self-evident fact which must be responded to, rather than refuted. Or as Higgott has remarked: 'The reconfiguration of UK politics, especially the management of the functions of the state, is ... increasingly determined by – or at least influenced by – the perceptions of the impact of globalisation' (1998: 20). Certainly, some of the most senior figures associated with New Labour insist on the need both to acknowledge the constraints imposed on Britain by globalization, and on the necessity of embracing the apparent opportunities which it offers, albeit through forging alliances with other countries.

With regard to the constraints imposed on Britain's economic policies by globalization, for example, the Chancellor, Gordon Brown, in a July 1998 speech to a News International Conference, explained that:

> The first objective national governments must have, in a global market place, is to max-imise economic stability ... For in a global economy, funds will flow to those countries whose policies inspire confidence, and investors punish mistakes more quickly and severely than in the past. Both the old Keynesian fine-tuning, and the rigid application of fixed monetary targets were policies designed for sheltered national economies, and based on apparently stable and predictable relations which have now broken down in modern, liberalised and global capital markets.

However, while globalization is clearly placing certain constraints on the autonomy of national policy actors, this does not mean that the nation-state and its political institutions are becoming obsolete (as some of the more extreme or utopian theorists of globalization sometimes assume). Instead, international policy responses to international problems are still mediated through national-level actors or representatives, both when policies are being developed via forums such as NATO or G7(8), and when agreed policies are subsequently being implemented at national level. Or as Robinson observes, nation-states increasingly function as 'transmission belts and filtering devices for the imposition' of policies and programmes agreed at the global level (2001: 188).

At the same time, it is an exaggeration or over-simplification to assume that the need to attract inward investment, or prevent a flight of capital, will automatically and inevitably lead policy makers to seek to dismantle the welfare state and constantly curb public expenditure (in order to minimize taxation and other economic costs). Such a highly reductionist or determinist account of the impact of globalization on domestic or national policy makers overlooks the extent to which companies will consider other factors when making decisions about investment and (re)location of production, such as education and training provision, and the skills of the indigenous labour force. In other words, some investment decisions will involve a trade-off between low taxes and low unit labour costs on the one hand, and the level of provision of collective or public goods, human capital and various supply-side measures on the other. In this respect:

> the conventional view about the impact of the multi-nationalization of production and financial integration on national economic policy regimes is overly simplistic. Managers of multi-national enterprises and mutual funds are not unsophisticated capitalists whose reaction to interventionist government is everywhere and always the same. Mobile capital may well choose to invest and produce in economies with interventionist governments.

> As a result, governments may retain considerably more autonomy in the era of global markets than is often presumed.
>
> (Garrett, 2000: 114)

Similarly, Holton has argued that, while globalization certainly places limits on what national governments and domestic policy makers can do, multinational companies 'remain dependent on nation-states for certain types of resources in a range of circumstances' (1998: 92). The implication of this is that 'there is still room for a good deal of effective domestic economic management' (Thompson, 1992: 214).

It also remains the case that even when a country's policy makers are signatories to international agreements or commitments, the national government and/or other domestic policy actors will ultimately be responsible for the enactment of the programme or policy, often with at least some discretion about how to implement it. In this respect, the increasing involvement of states (such as Britain) in international organizations and summits represents something of a paradox, but one which itself reflects the uneven, dialectical and contradictory character of globalization itself (for a discussion of which see Held and McGrew, 2002; Holton, 1998; McGrew, 1992; Smith, 1992). On the one hand, such involvement, and the obligation to abide by certain international agreements, reflects the acknowledged erosion of national autonomy caused by globalization, and the extent to which many problems cannot be adequately addressed on a purely national basis. On the other hand, though, international cooperation and mutual agreements provide a degree of order and predictability in an otherwise unstable and insecure world. This enables states to retain a degree of efficacy and competence, without which they would probably be completely destabilized and rendered impotent, whereupon their legitimacy in the eyes of their citizens would be grievously undermined. In this context, it has been suggested that: 'Reciprocal sovereignty still constitutes the basis of the international order, and nation-states ... have been empowered because of their status as constitutive parts of a recognized [international] order' (Axford, 1995: 139). Or as Tony Blair expressed it, in a speech in Chicago in April 1999: 'If sovereignty means control over one's destiny and strength, then strength and control, in today's world, means forging alliances or falling behind.'

As such, although globalization undoubtedly places certain limits and constraints on the autonomy of British policy makers, either in the sense that they need to secure international cooperation for the pursuit of certain policies, or in the sense that they are obliged to adopt particular policies which they might not otherwise have freely chosen, it can also be argued that globalization offers new opportunities to British policy makers: international cooperation and agreements can enable policy makers in Britain to tackle problems which they would otherwise have been unable to address in isolation. Much the same can be said with regard to Britain's membership of the EU.

Europeanization

The phenomenon of Europeanization can be discerned at two discrete levels, the substantive and the procedural. At the substantive level, Europeanization is apparent in the expansion and extension of policy competencies assumed by the EU, these usually extended via periodic treaties and intergovernmental conferences.

At the procedural level, Europeanization can be seen in the increasing authority imbued in key EU institutions, some of these increases similarly derive directly from particular treaties and intergovernmental summits, while other increases are a consequence of the steadily developing policy competencies of the EU.

Policies endorsed by the EU's decision-taking and policy-making institutions (outlined below) then effectively become law in Britain (and other member states), although their format varies, with the main ones being:

- *Regulations,* which are fully binding on member states in their entirety.
- *Directives*, which are binding with regard to the policy objective or outcome to be achieved, but which leave member states with the discretion to determine *how* to attain it.
- *Case law*, arising from the decisions of the European Court of Justice.
- *Decisions*, which are binding on those to whom they are specifically addressed, be they member states, particular companies or industries or private individuals.

Institutionally, the EU comprises a number of policy-making bodies, each playing different roles, and possessing different powers. The main bodies are, briefly, as follows.

Council of Ministers

The Council of Ministers – also known as Council of the European Union – comprises the relevant minister from each member state, concerned with the policy issue or subsystem under consideration. As such, the Council of Ministers meets in different guises – the Council of Agriculture Ministers, the Council of Economic and Finance Ministers, the Council of Education Ministers, etc. Altogether, there are about 90 such council meetings per annum, with the Council of Ministers concerned with agriculture, economic and financial affairs, and external relations, meeting the most frequently, while those concerned with social issues such as education, and health, meet more sporadically (Nugent, 2000: 210). There is also a General Affairs Council, consisting of the Foreign Secretary (or equivalent) from each member state, which meets on a monthly basis.

One of the most notable and important increases in authority concerns the Council of Ministers, in which a system of Qualified Majority Voting (QMV) was introduced by the 1986 Single European Act. Previously, decisions taken by the Council of Ministers – these decisions then effectively constituting EU law, and therefore taking precedence over domestic law – were on the basis of unanimity, meaning that *all* ministers had to endorse a proposal. This meant that any one minister was able to oppose a proposal which he/she considered to be detrimental to their country's interests, and in so doing, prevent the measure from being adopted, an ability which Britain, in particular, considered a major means of upholding national sovereignty. However, among the provisions of the Single European Act was the introduction of QMV, whereby a policy proposal could be endorsed on the basis of 62 votes out of 87 (71 per cent), with each member state being allocated a number of votes based approximately on the size of its population, although smaller nations were slightly 'overcompensated'. For example, Britain was allocated 10 votes, whereas Belgium

Table 8.1 Allocation of votes in Council of Ministers before and after November 2004

Country	Votes prior to November 2004	Votes from November 2004
Austria	4	10
Belgium	5	12
Cyprus	N/A	4
Czech Republic	N/A	12
Denmark	3	7
Estonia	N/A	4
Finland	3	7
France	10	29
Germany	10	29
Greece	5	12
Hungary	N/A	12
Ireland	3	7
Italy	10	29
Latvia	N/A	4
Lithuania	N/A	7
Luxembourg	2	4
Malta	N/A	3
Netherlands	5	13
Poland	N/A	27
Portugal	5	12
Slovakia	N/A	7
Slovenia	N/A	4
Spain	8	27
Sweden	4	10
United Kingdom	10	29
Total	**87**	**321**

was given 5 (see Table 8.1). The introduction of QMV effectively removed the national veto, for even if the British minister cast his/her 10 votes against a proposal, endorsement by 62 of the remaining 77 votes would be sufficient to ensure the proposal's formal adoption, whereupon it would become official EU policy.

The May 2004 enlargement of the EU, involving the accession of 10 new member states – most of them from Eastern Europe – has necessitated corresponding changes to the allocation of votes in the Council of Ministers, as illustrated in Table 8.1. It can be seen that Britain now has 29 (out of 321) votes, compared with 10 (out of 87) previously.

From November 2004, a minimum of 232 (72%) votes out of a new total of 321 is necessary for a 'qualified majority' to be attained. Furthermore, a majority (sometimes as many as two-thirds) of member states must approve a decision.

Much of the work of the Council of Ministers involves taking decisions – in tandem with the European Parliament, via the codecision-taking procedure (see below) – on proposals put forward by the European Commission (discussed below), and in this respect, the Council is largely a reactive body. However, in this context, being reactive does

Table 8.2 **Directorates-General of the European Commission**

EU policies	EU external relations
Agriculture	Development
Competition	Enlargement
Economic and Financial Affairs	EuropeAid – Cooperation Office
Education and Culture	External Relations
Employment and Social Affairs	Humanitarian Aid Office – ECHO
Energy and Transport	Trade
Enterprise	
Environment	
Fisheries	
Health and Consumer Protection	
Information Society	
Internal Market	
Joint Research Centre	
Justice and Home Affairs	
Regional Policy	
Research	
Taxation and Customs Union	

not imply weakness or subordination, for only the Council of Ministers can give the formal approval which the Commission's proposals require in order to be enacted. This 'makes it the EU's crucial decision-making forum from Whitehall's point of view' (James, 1999: 22).

European Commission

The Commission is widely viewed as the 'civil service' of the EU, for its primary role is to develop public policy, and then oversee its implementation by member states and their relevant policy actors, although any policies which the Commission proposes have to be formally approved by other institutions, most notably the Council of Ministers and the European Parliament. Mazey and Richardson have suggested that the Commission 'constitutes a kind of *bourse*, acting as a market for policy ideas and innovation within the EU policy process' (1996: 41).

As Table 8.2 illustrates, the European Commission comprises 23 Directorates-General, each concerned with a particular policy area or issue, 17 of which are concerned directly with policies pertaining to member states, and the other 6 dealing with the external relations of the EU.

If a member state – or policy actors within it – are adjudged to be failing or refusing to abide by relevant EU decisions or directives, then the European Commission can invoke sanctions and penalties, including the levying of fines. For example, in October 2004, the Commission 'named and shamed' a number of companies for being the worst industrial polluters in the EU. Some of these were leading British companies, including GlaxoSmithKline, and BP, while some were overseas firms with factories, plants or other subsidiaries based in Britain. An EU spokeswoman judiciously suggested that such companies 'might want to evaluate their potential for improving their environmental performance'. Failure to do so would almost certainly result in them being fined (*The Guardian*, 9 October 2004).

Prior to the 2004 enlargement of the EU, there were 20 Commissioners (two each from the five largest members, namely Britain[1], Germany, France, Italy and Spain, and one each from the 10 other member states). However, there is now just one commissioner from each member state. Britain's EU Commissioner, as of 2004, is Peter Mandelson, who has been allocated the high-profile trade portfolio. However, upon appointment, each EU Commissioner is required to work in accordance with, and in pursuit of, the goals and objectives of the EU: they are *not* national representatives (a point clearly overlooked by Peter Mandelson's critics when they questioned whether he was the right person to promote and defend Britain's interests in the EU).

It is worth noting, incidentally, that while its critics berate the European Commission for being a bloated bureaucracy, it actually: 'employs fewer people than the French Ministry of Culture and the British Lord Chancellor's office, neither of which is a major Department of State. It is smaller than the governments of cities like Amsterdam and Madrid' (Geddes, 1993: 43–4).

European Parliament

Also imbued with somewhat greater authority, by virtue of the 1992 (Maastricht) Treaty on the EU, and then the 1997 Treaty of Amsterdam, is the European Parliament. The Maastricht Treaty introduced, and the Amsterdam Treaty extended, a codecision procedure, whereby many policy proposals emanating from the European Commission require the approval of both the Council of Ministers *and* the European Parliament in order to be formally adopted, and thereby become EU law. The European Parliament also has the power to pass a 'motion of censure' against the European Commission, which, if supported by an overall majority of MEPs, and two-thirds of the votes cast, would compel the Commission to resign.

European Court of Justice

Also acquiring greater authority *pari passu* with the increasing policy jurisdiction of the EU is the European Court of Justice (not to be confused with the entirely separate, non-EU, European Court of Human Rights, which was established in 1949, eight years before the formation of the European Communities). Based in Strasbourg, the European Court of Justice is concerned with ensuring the effective enforcement of EU law, which takes precedence over domestic law. The European Court of Justice therefore adjudicates in cases where it is alleged that a member state, or one of its policy actors, has failed to implement EU law, or is pursuing a domestic policy which is deemed to be in contravention of that law. With the EU steadily extending its policy jurisdiction, the European Court of Justice

[1]Britain's two Commissioners, until 2004, were Chris Patten (former Conservative Cabinet Minister and Party chairman) and Neil Kinnock (leader of the Labour Party from 1983 to 1992).

has become an increasingly important and influential institution, and is increasingly called upon to adjudicate over an expanding range of policies.

The European Council

The European Council (not to be confused with the Council of Ministers/Europe) is the EU forum in which the heads of member governments, their foreign ministers and the President of the Commission meet. Meetings are held twice a year (though extra meetings may be called in exceptional circumstances), the main aim being to discuss major policy issues. It has been suggested that:

> The growing dominance of the European Council ... is one of the biggest EU changes since its inception. When it began in the early 1970s, the idea was that heads of government should meet informally for a fireside chat. Now each presidency works towards a climax of decisions at summits normally held in June and December. And the conclusions from each summit tend to map out the agenda for the whole EU.

> (*The Economist,* 8 March 1997)

It can be seen, therefore, that the European Council provides a framework and strategic direction for other EU policy-making bodies, while also enabling European political leaders to discuss problems which may subsequently arise, and thereby seek common solutions.

The uneven character and impact of Europeanization

It must be emphasized that while 'Europeanization' is widely perceived to be a top-down process affecting nation-states, and arguably challenging their very viability and efficacy as geopolitical institutions, it is also the case that the EU itself needs the cooperation and compliance of member nation-states in order to achieve its objectives. In other words, Europeanization should not be simply viewed as a linear, one-way, top-down policy process, in which Britain always fatalistically or grudgingly accepts policy initiatives invoked from above, from the EU. Instead, opportunities exist for member states to influence, to varying degrees, and according to circumstances, policies at European level, through a process of 'uploading' policy proposals or preferences.

In this context, one writer has discerned three broad responses by member states towards the EU with regard to public policy: pace-setting, fence-sitting and foot-dragging. This approach emphasizes the extent to which 'Europeanization is a two-way process. It entails a "bottom-up" and "top-down" dimension'. As such, member states wil sometimes take the initiative, or seek to set the EU's institutional agenda, by 'actively pushing policies at the European level, which reflect a Member State's policy preferences' (Börzel, 2002: 194). In such instances, individual member states can act as pace-setters in the EU, so that 'domestic policies are exported to the European level and subsequently adopted by other Member States' (2002: 197).

For example, it could be argued that the process of liberalization pursued by the EU since the 1980s, and enshrined in the 1986 Single European Act, was partly influenced by

Table 8.3   The uneven character of Europeanization

Policy competence mainly located at EU level	Policy competence shared between EU and Britain	Policy competence mainly located in Britain, or through intergovernmental agreement
Agriculture	Environmental	Defence
Competition	Regional	Education
Consumer Protection	Social	Foreign
Fisheries	Transport	Health
Trade		Law and order
		Macro economic
		Welfare

Source: Richards and Smith, 2002: 152

the neo-liberal economic policies and privatization programme pursued by the Thatcher governments in Britain during the 1980s. In this context, far from being the EU's foot-dragging member state, Britain acted as a pace-setter within the EU, promoting policies of economic liberalization and deregulation which have since been disseminated through other member states in the EU, and become primary objectives of the Commission. Certainly, a senior official in the Department of Trade and Industry has claimed that: 'We have … become one of the Departments that has been arguing for deregulation in Europe, or at least better regulation', while another departmental official not only claimed that 'the EU has enhanced the autonomy of the DTI', it had also 'allowed the DTI to make policy at the EU level rather than in Whitehall' (Marsh et al., 2001: 220).

Even when a member state such as Britain is unable to influence the formulation of an EU policy in a particular manner, the EU will still be heavily dependent on the member state(s) to implement the policy in the manner intended, so that national or subnational-level policy actors become, in effect, the street level bureaucrats. Seen from this perspective, 'the interplay between the EU system and the British polity appears to be characterized by complex feedback loops', and 'European [policy] inputs rarely, if ever, enter Britain without modification' (Rosamond, 2003: 59).

Crucially, it should be reiterated that some areas of public policy in Britain have been more 'Europeanized' than others – hence the uneven character and impact of Europeanization – meaning that various policy subsystems and departments retain considerable autonomy. We noted in Chapter 4 how some departments, most notably the Ministry of Agriculture/DEFRA, and the Department of Trade and Industry have been strongly influenced by the EU, whereas others, such as the Department of Education and Skills and the Department of Health, have been rather less so. The unevenness of 'Europeanization' is illustrated by Table 8.3, which shows the varying degrees to which specific policy subsystems in Britain have – so far – been 'Europeanized'.

Yet even for those departments which have been most affected by the process of Europeanization, the process is not necessarily a negative one whereby they lose their autonomy. On the contrary, in certain respects, closer involvement in the EU policy process has actually served to enhance the authority and autonomy of some departments in Whitehall, such as the DTI, MAFF/DEFRA and the Foreign and Commonwealth Office (Buller and Smith, 1998; Bulmer and Burch, 1998; Marsh, Richards and Smith, 2001: Chapter 9).

'Agencification'

Since the late 1980s, there has been a major reform of the core executive, with regard to the organization and operation of government departments and the civil service. In 1987, Sir Robin Ibbs, the then Head of the Efficiency Unit in the Cabinet Office, published its Report – *Improving Management in Government: The Next Steps* (but commonly referred to merely as *The Next Steps*) – into the future structure and operation of the civil service. The report reflected Margaret Thatcher's desire to reform – a euphemism for reducing the size and scope of – the civil service, as part of her wider desire to reduce costs, cut red tape and 'roll back the state'. Whether these objectives were really achieved is beyond the scope of this particular study; our concern is with the implications for the policy process which accrued from the implementation of *The Next Steps* report. The report proposed a much clearer demarcation in each government department between those responsible for policy advice and formulation on the one hand, and policy delivery and implementation on the other. To secure this division of responsibility, *The Next Steps* proposed that the sections and staff responsible for administering a department's services should be made semi-autonomous, in the form of 'executive agencies' which would have responsibility and considerable freedom *vis-à-vis* day-to-day operational matters, management of their budgets and staffing levels, albeit within a 'framework agreement' laid down by the 'parent department' (for a detailed account of the origins and introduction of the Next Steps programme, see Flynn et al., 1990: 159–78; Jordan, 1994: Chapter 5).

It was envisaged that a smaller, leaner, fitter core of policy advisers and policy makers would remain at the heart of the core executive, inside the central government departments, while most civil servants focused almost exclusively on policy implementation and service delivery at subnational level. Consequently, the traditional civil service hierarchy 'has been replaced by an almost federal system of core and periphery, with the periphery not being directly controlled by the centre' (Smith, 1999: 194).

By the time that the first Blair government was elected in May 1997, more than 110 agencies had been established, employing 400,000 civil servants. Examples of such agencies include the Defence Procurement Agency, Highways Agency, Rural Payments Agency and the UK Passport Service (not all agencies actually include the term in their title). Indeed, as Table 8.4 indicates, individual departments will often preside over several agencies, such as the Department of Work and Pensions, under whose auspices are the CSA, Jobcentre Plus and Pension Service, for example.

Having been elected in 1997, the Blair government made no attempt to abandon or reverse the Next Steps programme; on the contrary, further agencies have been established since 1997, as the Blair governments sought to maintain the envisaged distinction between policy making and policy implementation or service delivery.

This apparent distinction was clearly delineated in the original *The Next Steps* report, which suggested that ministers would remain constitutionally responsible for the

Table 8.4 Examples of Executive Agencies operating under the aegis of selected government departments

Environment, Food and Rural Affairs	Health	Home Office
Countryside Agency	Medical Supplies Agency	Criminal Records Bureau
Food Standards Agency	NHS Estates	Forensic Science Service
Rural Payments Agency	NHS Modernization Agency	HM Prisons Service
Veterinary Laboratories Agency		UK Passport Service
Trade and Industry	**Transport**	**Work and Pensions**
Companies House	Driver and Vehicle Licensing Agency	Benefits Agency
Employment Tribunals Service	Driving Standards Agency	Child Support Agency
Insolvency Service	Highways Agency	JobCentre Plus
Patent Office	Maritime and Coastguards Agency	Pension Service
Radiocommunications Agency	Vehicle Certification Agency	
	Vehicle and Operator Services Agency	

formulation of public policies, while the administration and implementation of those policies would henceforth be the responsibility of the agencies. However, this theoretical distinction between policy formulation and policy implementation (or service delivery) has been rather less clear-cut in practice, yielding some high-profile, and acrimonious, disputes in cases of policy problems or apparent failure. For example, the CSA has encountered numerous problems, and attracted considerable criticism, since it commenced its work in 1993. Responsible for locating 'absent fathers' and ensuring that they fulfil their financial responsibilities towards their children and ex-wife or girlfriend, particularly when the mother is in receipt of (or submits a claim for) social security, the CSA has encountered criticism from 'absent fathers' and single parents alike, and led to many MPs being approached by constituents aggrieved at the way the CSA was impacting upon their lives or circumstances. The CSA has consequently been subject to a number of inquiries – and ensuing critical reports – by the Social Security Select Committee, and various subsequent reforms and modifications by Social Security ministers.

Although many of the CSA's problems have derived from staffing problems, and non-compliance by its 'clients' ('absent fathers' and single parents, many of whom have resented its 'interference' in their affairs), a more general issue which it has highlighted is whether the original policy proposal and objectives were themselves ill-judged or ill-defined. Or to put the conundrum more starkly, is it the DSS, at the policy making level, which should be held responsible for devising a 'bad' policy, and perhaps imposing unrealistic targets or performance indicators, or is it the CSA which should shoulder responsibility, for failing to implement the policy effectively or competently, and reaching the targets set for it? Actually, one academic expert on the British civil service suggests that the answer is 'both', for he described the CSA as 'an administrative shambles', but notes that 'it was also handicapped by poorly designed policy and legislation' (Theakston, 1999b: 29). However, after the first tranche of criticisms, negative press coverage about errors (and the 'human heartbreaks' which apparently resulted) and condemnatory select committee reports, it was the CSA's first chief executive, Ros Hepplewhite, who resigned, not the Secretary of State for Social Security.

Even more controversial was the case involving the Home Office and the Prisons Agency in 1995. When three prisoners escaped from the Isle of Wight's high-security Parkhurst Prison in January 1995, the question was raised about whether the government's – or, more specifically, the Home Office's – prison policy was inadequate (possibly due to staff shortages and thus a lack of prison officers to maintain adequate security and supervision), or whether the escapes could be attributed entirely to incompetent management of the prisons and inadequate supervision of inmates by prison governors, and, in this case, the Director of the Prisons Agency, Derek Lewis. What ensued was a highly public and protracted bitter dispute between Lewis, and the then Home Secretary, Michael Howard.

Howard was emphatic that prison security (and in this instance, the apparent lack of it) was firmly the responsibility of those charged with day-to-day management of Britain's prisons. A breakout by any prisoner(s) was deemed the responsibility of lax security, and thus ineffective management at prison level, on a day-to-day basis; the Home Secretary could hardly be expected to be held responsible, and blamed, for a prison breakout. Howard insisted that: 'With regard to operational responsibility, there has always been a division between policy matters and operational matters', and that as Home Secretary, his responsibility was for the former (House of Commons Debates, 10 January 1995: col. 40). Yet Derek Lewis begged to differ, maintaining that it was indeed the Home Office's policy on prisons which was at fault, coupled with ministerial interference, and which thus impeded the ability of prison officers and managers to supervise inmates adequately and thereby ensure prison security (Lewis, 1997: Chapters 12–13).

The episode resulted in an inquiry into prison security, chaired by Sir John Learmont, whose report in October 1995 scathingly observed that the Parkhurst Prison escapes had 'revealed a chapter of errors at every level and a naivety that defies belief' (1995: para 2.257). Yet Howard maintained that the Learmont Report did not attribute blame for the breakout to any decision of his, adding that the Director General of the Prison Service, Derek Lewis, had 'ceased to hold his post with effect from today' (House of Commons Debates, 16 October 1995: cols. 31–33).

These examples indicate the manner in which agencification has raised important questions about responsibility for public policy in contemporary Britain (see Barker, 1998). True, even before the Next Steps programme of establishing executive agencies to implement policies and deliver services, there had been a long-standing constitutional debate about the degree to which ministers could seriously be expected to accept full responsibility for mistakes perpetrated by their civil servants during the implementation of policies which ministers themselves had agreed to. The doctrine of individual ministerial responsibility held that 'Advisers [civil servants] advise, Ministers decide', the clear implication being that policy decisions were the responsibility of ministers, who, ought therefore, to accept the blame if and when a major policy failed. However, it was always tacitly accepted that ministers could not be expected to resign every time a policy did not work as intended, quite apart from the fact that ministers could not supervise every aspect of the implementation of their policies. In this respect, the theoretical distinction between policy formulation and policy implementation has always been rather more opaque in empirical reality. Consequently, ministerial resignations in response to policy failures are rather rare, and since the 1980s, the occasional resignations which have been tendered, ostensibly in accordance with the constitutional doctrine of individual ministerial responsibility, have tended either to reflect a minister's loss of popularity, and therefore loss of support, among their own ministerial or backbench colleagues, or a desire to protect the government – or the Prime Minister in particular – from embarrassment, and the possibility that further awkward, probing questions might be asked by journalists (Pyper, 1991). Rare indeed is the minister who actually resigns in response to genuine repentance and remorse for the failure of one of their polices.

The trend to 'agencification' has been reinforced by the parallel expansion of a plethora of 'non-executive agencies', advisory bodies, authorities, boards, commissions and councils. While most of these are semi-autonomous, or even independent of government, they are clearly located within the various policy sectors or subsystems over which government departments and their Secretaries of State preside, as Table 8.5 illustrates.

The expansion of such bodies, formally independent or semi-independent of central government, but often financed via public funds, and with many of their senior appointments subject to ministerial approval, has led some writers to talk of a 'new magistracy' (Hall and Weir, 1994; Jenkins, 1995; Morris, 1994; Skelcher and Davis, 1996: Stewart, 1995; 1996). Certainly, the proliferation of such bodies prompted serious questions concerning (lack of) accountability and a growing 'democratic deficit'.

Task forces, working groups and *ad hoc* advisory groups

While 'task forces', 'working groups' and *ad hoc* advisory groups are not in themselves new or novel, the period since the election of the first Blair government, in May 1997, has witnessed a massive expansion of such bodies. During the first 18 months of the first Blair government's term of Office, for example, no less than 295 task forces, and *ad hoc* advisory groups were created (Barker et al., 1999: 12), while in 2001–2, there were 41 task forces and 133 *ad hoc* advisory groups, as well as 32 departmental policy reviews in progress (Cabinet Office, 2003b: xvi).

Task forces, working groups and *ad hoc* advisory groups are primarily concerned either 'to investigate and recommend new policies and practices or, in some cases, practical means of implementing policies on which Labour had already settled' (Barker et al., 1999: 11).

Table 8.5 Examples of 'non-executive agencies', advisory bodies, authorities, boards, commissions and councils

Culture, Media and Sport	Defence	Education and Skills
British Tourist Authority	Army Base Repair Organisation	Learning and Skills Council
Broadcasting Standards Commission	Defence Scientific Advisory Council	Higher Education Funding Council for England
English Heritage	Royal College of Defence Studies	Qualifications and Curriculum Authority
National Lottery Commission	Meteorological (Met) Office Strategic and Combat Studies Institute	
Environment, Food and Rural Affairs	**Health**	**Home Office**
Meat and Livestock Commission	Dental Practice Board	Advisory Council on the Misuse of Drugs
Radioactive Waste Management Advisory Committee	Expert Advisory Group on AIDS	Alcohol Education and Research Council
Sea Fish Industry Authority	Human Fertilization and Embryology Authority	Commission for Racial Equality
Sustainable Development Commission	Standing Nursing and Midwifery Advisory Commission	Criminal Cases Review Commission
		Criminal Injuries Compensation Authority
		National Criminal Intelligence Service
		Parole Board
Trade and Industry	**Transport**	**Work and Pensions**
Advisory, Conciliation and Arbitration Service	British Waterways	Employment Service
Competition Commission	Civil Aviation Authority	Employment Tribunals Service
Economic and Social Research Council	Commission for Integrated Transport	Industrial Injuries Advisory Council
	Disabled Persons' Transport Advisory Committee	Social Security Advisory Committee
	Strategic Rail Authority	
	Trinity House Lighthouse Service	

Examples of task forces and working groups established by the Blair governments since 1997, and operating under the auspices of the main government departments or ministries, are provided in Table 8.6, while Table 8.7 gives an indication of the eclectic range of *ad hoc* advisory groups functioning during the same period.

Table 8.6 Task forces (tf) and working parties (wp) established by the Blair governments

Culture, Media and Sport	Education and Skills	Environment, Food and Rural Affairs
Alternatives to Tobacco Sponsorship (tf)	Literacy (tf)	Coalfields (tf)
Creative Industries (tf)	Numeracy (tf)	Construction (tf)
Football (tf)	School Standards (tf)	Cowboy Builders (wp)
Regional Museums (tf)	Study Support (wp)	Hills (tf)
Tourism (wp)		Leylandii (wp)
		Livestock Farming (tf)
		Milk (tf)
		Mobile Homes (wp)

Health	Home Office	Trade and Industry
Cancer (tf)	Child Protection on the Internet (tf)	Competitiveness – Encouraging Innovation (wp)
Chronic Fatigue Syndrome (wp)	Community Fire Safety (tf)	Employment Tribunal System (tf)
Coronary Heart Disease (tf)	Human Rights (tf)	Manufacturing Industry (tf)
Inequalities and Public Health (tf)	National Crime Reduction (tf)	Oil and Gas Industry (tf)
Mental Health (tf)	Older Volunteers (wp)	Tackling Overindebtedness (tf)
Older People (tf)	Review of the Tote (wp)	Work and Parents (tf)
Prison Health (tf)	Youth Justice (tf)	

Transport	Treasury	Work and Pensions
Cleaner Vehicles (tf)	Financial Management (wp)	Disability Rights (tf)
Shipping (wp)	Financing of High Technology Business (wp)	New Deal (tf)
	Private Finance Initiative (tf)	Pensions Education (wp)
	Smaller Quoted Companies (wp)	Skills (tf)

Source: Barker, Byrne and Veall, 1999; Cabinet Office, 2004

Why should the number of task forces, *ad hoc* advisory groups and 'working parties' have expanded so significantly under the Blair governments? The cynical response might be that establishing a task force provides the appearance of addressing a problem, and satisfying media, or public, demands that the government 'must do something'. From this perspective, creating a task force on a particular policy issue might be a means of agenda management, in the sense that once such a body has been established, the 'issue attention cycle' (identified in Chapter 2) will result in the media or public losing interest.

There are, though, three rather more charitable or constructive interpretations of why the Blair governments have been so prolific in their recourse to task forces. First, task forces might be viewed as a means of achieving the 'more inclusive' approach to politics that Tony Blair has variously espoused. Involving a wide spectrum of individuals and organizations in the consideration of policy issues might be deemed a major means of

Table 8.7 Examples of *ad hoc* advisory groups by government department, 1997–2003

Culture, Media and Sport	Education and Skills	Environment, Food and Rural Affairs
Audio-visual Industries Training Group	Citizenship Education Working Party	Air Quality Forum
Hotel and Restaurants Monitoring Group	Education Funding Strategy Group	Corn Returns Working Group
Music Industry Forum	Gifted and Talented Advisory Group	Design Advisory Group
	Literacy and Numeracy Strategy Group	Food Chain Group
	Music and Dance Scheme	Hedgerows Regulations Review Group
	School Libraries Advisory Group	
Health	**Home Office**	**Trade and Industry**
Adoption Support Stakeholder Group	Mobile Phone Theft Group	Advisory Group Consumer Affairs
Defibrillator Advisory Committee	Advisory Group on Retail Crime	Advisory Group on Nanotechnology
Emergency Services Action Team	Property Crime Reduction Action Team	Age Advisory Group
Hepatitis C Strategy Steering Group	Vehicle Crime Reduction Action Team	Better Payment Practice Group
Integrated Sexual Health and HIV Strategy Steering Group		Clusters Policy Steering Group
		Information Age Partnership
Transport	**Treasury**	**Work and Pensions**
Advisory Group on Motorcycling	Business Advisory Group on Economic and Monetary Union	Benefits Agency Standards Commission
Aviation Health Working Group	Construction Industry Scheme User Panel	Jobcentre Plus Stakeholder's Forum
Disruptive Passengers Working Group	Royal Mint Shareholder Panel	Partnerships Against Poverty
Road Haulage Forum		Pension Sharing Consultative Panel
Road Safety Advisory Panel		

Source: Barker, Byrne and Veall, 1999; Cabinet Office, 2004

'depoliticizing' various problems, and of thus fostering a wider basis of support or legitimacy for ensuing policy initiatives.

Second, but closely linked to this last point, task forces might be viewed as an important way of enhancing the degree of expertise in developing public policy, in the hope that the involvement of experts will facilitate an improvement in the 'quality' – and thus

Table 8.8 Composition of four task forces during the second Blair government

Department of Health – NHS Quality Task Force	Home Office – Task Force on Child Protection on the internet
• 3 × ministers	• 1 × minister
• 16 × civil servants	• 5 × civil servants
• 8 × public/professional	• 2 × public/professional
• 3 × voluntary/charity sector	• 5 × voluntary/charity sector
• 3 × private sector	• 20 × private sector
Foreign and Commonwealth Office – Britain Abroad Task Force	**Ministry of Defence – Service Families' Task Force**
• 7 × ministers	• 6 × ministers
• 2 × civil servants	• 1 × civil servant
• 4 × public/professional	• 5 public/professional
• 1 × private sector	• 3 × voluntary/charity sector

Source: Cabinet Office, 2003b

success – of particular policies. Indeed, incorporation of such experts can also contribute towards the development of 'evidence-based policy making'. An indication of the breadth of membership which task forces can encompass is indicated by the four examples in Table 8.8.

Third, the Blair government's penchant for establishing task forces also reflects the professed desire to secure 'joined-up government' in order to tackle the so-called 'wicked issues'. In this respect, task forces offer a means of countering the phenomenon of 'departmentalism' (identified in Chapters 3 and 4), and of ensuring that particular policy problems or proposals are considered more holistically.

They are also a further consequence of the Next Steps' theoretical demarcation between policy making and policy implementation, for with many (but by no means all) senior civil servants supposedly responsible primarily for operational management and service delivery – via the various agencies previously referred to – ministers have increasingly turned to other individuals and institutions for advice and ideas in formulating policies, and the Blair governments' recourse to task forces is a clear manifestation of this phenomenon.

Devolution to Scotland and Wales

The transition from government to governance has been enormously enhanced by the Blair governments' policies concerning Scottish and Welsh devolution, coupled with the more tentative moves towards devolution to the English regions. These devolutionary and decentralizing trends have had profound implications for Britain's hitherto 'unitary state' tradition, in which political power was applied from the centre – via Whitehall and Westminster – in a top-down manner.

Ironically, it was the policies and policy style of the Thatcher-Major governments which enhanced the demands for devolution in Scotland and Wales during the 1980s and 1990s, for while these governments waxed lyrical about 'rolling back the state' and reducing government 'interference' in economic affairs and civil society, the state was to be strengthened in certain respects, and certain ideologically-motivated reforms imposed from above. This caused considerable resentment in Scotland and Wales, partly because electoral support for Thatcherite conservatism was lower here than in England, and also, following on from this, because of a perception that Thatcherism was a quintessentially provincial, suburban, English phenomenon, both in terms of its social bases and its political outlook.

Even when the Thatcher governments did purport to 'roll back the state' via such initiatives as the Next Steps agencies and 'reforming' local government, there was often a concern in Scotland and Wales that this process was being accompanied by a parallel process of increased, albeit indirect, control, via subnational bodies and appointments. This was particularly so in Wales, where concern increased in some quarters about the expansion of non-elected, ministerially-appointed or approved, bodies, often responsible for the allocation of significant sums of public monies. For example, by 1996, there were more than 1,400 'quangos' appointees in Wales, compared with 1,273 elected councillors. Furthermore, these 'quangos' presided over a combined annual budget of some £2 billion, which was almost as much as that spent by elected local authorities (Davies, 1999: 16, note 13).

The Thatcher-Major governments therefore prompted growing concern in Scotland and Wales about a 'democratic deficit', which, in turn, served to imbue the Labour Party's professed commitment to Scottish and Welsh devolution with greatly added relevance and resonance, even though there remained different views within the Labour Party about the precise form that devolution should take, and how much power should be devolved. For example, it has been variously suggested that in spite of presiding over the actual implementation of devolution, Tony Blair has never been particularly enthusiastic about it, but somehow felt obligated by a policy commitment inherited from his two predecessors, Neil Kinnock and John Smith. Certainly, it has sometimes appeared as if (New) Labour's devolution policies were not carefully thought through, either in terms of the constitutional implications, or the likely consequences for public policy (particularly in the context of the professed commitment to 'joined-up government'). However, lack of overall consistency and coherence appears to be a characteristic of the Blair governments' constitutional reform 'programme' in general!

Devolution to Scotland

Following the ill-fated attempt, by James Callaghan's 1976–9 Labour government, to introduce devolution for Scotland (and Wales), it was to be another 20 years before Scotland was finally granted its own Parliament. A referendum to gauge the degree of support in Scotland for a Parliament was held in September 1997 (resulting in a convincing 'yes' vote), with the legislation then passed in 1998, and the Scottish Parliament itself finally launched in 1999 (see Mitchell, 1999).

Comprising 129 Scottish Members of Parliament (SMPs), elections to the Scottish Parliament are based on the Additional Member System, with 73 SMPs directly elected on a first-past-the-post basis, using existing constituencies (although one additional constituency was created especially), with the remaining 56 MSPs selected from party lists, in accordance with their party's share of the vote. A major consequence of deploying a partly proportional electoral system for elections to the Scottish Parliament has been to ensure that the single largest party in the 1999 election, Labour, lacked an overall majority, and was therefore obliged to form a coalition, its chosen partners being the Liberal Democrats. This itself was to have significant implications for some of the policies subsequently pursued in Scotland, and served to provide a clear indication of how devolution itself contributed considerably to increasing policy diversity within Britain, and *inter alia* signalled some of the problems of securing policy coordination and 'joined-up' government in the 'differentiated polity' which the new governance entails.

Devolution imbued the Scottish Parliament with considerable legislative powers, and responsibility for a wide range of policy areas, as shown below.

- Agriculture
- Economic development
- Education and training
- Environment
- Fisheries and forestry
- Health
- Housing
- Law and order
- Local government
- Social work
- Sports and the arts
- Transport.

Central (Westminster) government and the core executive in London retained control of macro-economic strategy, monetary and fiscal policy, foreign affairs and relations with the EU, defence, national security, and social security. In this respect, Tony Blair was adamant that ultimate sovereignty remained with the UK Parliament.

The Scottish Parliament was also granted revenue-raising powers, enabling it to raise or reduce the basic rate of income tax 3%. However, by autumn 2004, it had not invoked this power, but if and when it does so in the future, conflict may well arise with the UK government based in London. This is because a decision by the Scottish Executive to raise income tax might have significant – potentially detrimental – implications for central government's determination of macro-economic strategy, along with monetary and fiscal policy, at UK level.

Scottish policy divergence

In spite of Westminster and Whitehall retaining jurisdiction over such important and extensive areas, the powers and policy competencies which were devolved were sufficient to provide the Scottish Parliament with the potential to pursue significantly different policies to those pursued in England, and in certain respects, this is precisely what it has done. However, it should be emphasized that, for various cultural, historical and judicial reasons, Scotland already enjoyed greater autonomy or policy distinctiveness *vis-à-vis* England than Wales (see, for example: Brown et al., 1998; Kellas, 1984). The main policy areas where Scottish devolution has presaged a divergence from corresponding policies in England are:

- *University tuition fees*: abolished.
- *Care for the elderly*: free personal/home care reintroduced for the elderly.
- *'Foundation Hospitals'*: to be opposed by the Labour-Liberal Democrat Executive.
- *Nursery education*: pre-school provision for all three- and four-year-olds.
- *Children's health*: free fruit distributed in schools.
- *Teacher's pay*: 23 per cent increase, to be phased in over three years.
- *Schools 'opting-out' of LEA control*: right to 'opt-out' abolished.
- *School league tables and national tests for 5–14-year-olds*: to be abolished.
- *Section 28*[2]: abolished.
- *Fox hunting*: outlawed.
- *Warrant sales*[3]: abolished.

It is clear that the Scottish Parliament and its Executive have placed considerable emphasis on educational initiatives, not least because this is seen as key to tackling social exclusion and inequalities (Stewart, 2004: 106–9). However, the emphasis on education, and the type of measures so far introduced – coupled with explicit commitments to the principle of comprehensive education – can also be partially viewed in ideological terms, with Scotland deemed to enshrine a relatively strong and resilient 'social democratic communitarianism', as opposed to the 'Blairite liberalism' south of the border (Paterson, 2002: 125). Certainly, with regard to education, Bromley and Curtice have discerned 'a distinctly Scottish policy' which reflects a 'distinctive strand of public opinion' north of the border (2003: 10–11).

Summer 2003, meanwhile, heralded proposals by the Scottish Executive to launch an offensive against juvenile crime, which could result in the imprisonment of parents who consistently failed to control their children's antisocial behaviour, while children as young as 10 could be electronically tagged if they persistently engaged in such behaviour.

One point worth noting is that legislation approved by the Scottish Parliament does not then have to be endorsed by a second chamber. This partly explains the successful abolition of fox hunting and Section 28 in Scotland, whereas at Westminster, similar policy initiatives have effectively been blocked by the House of Lords. On the other hand, some commentators believe that the absence of a second (revising or scrutiny) chamber in Scotland is likely to prove detrimental to the quality of some laws approved by the Scottish Parliament. However, it should also be noted that the Scottish Parliament makes regular use – far more so than Westminster – of prelegislative committees to scrutinize Bills *before* they are debated by Members of the Scottish Parliament (MSPs). As such, Scottish

[2]'Section 28' of the 1988 Local Government Act. This Section prohibited the 'promotion' of homosexuality by schools and teachers via sex education lessons.

[3]Warrant Sales are (were) the selling of a person's property in order to pay off local tax arrears.

devolution seems to have yielded not only a divergence (from Westminster) on a number of policy issues, but also a somewhat different mode of parliamentary policy making.

It has also yielded some variation in executive (ministerial) posts and structures, with the appointment of a Minister for Social Justice during the first (1999–2003) Scottish Parliament. Following the 2003 Scottish Parliament election, the holder of this post was retitled Minister for Communities. This post was given a strong coordinating role, the primary aim being to ensure that the policy initiatives of the Scottish Executive contributed to the tackling of social inequalities and exclusion. Indeed, since devolution, the Scottish Executive has placed a strong emphasis on rebuilding the welfare state in Scotland – as evinced by some of the policies listed above – following decades of Westminster-imposed retrenchment and curbs (Stewart, 2004: 105). However, the welfare-orientated approach of the Scottish Executive is still contingent upon the funding allocated to Scotland by the Treasury, coupled with the fact that the Scottish Parliament is not empowered to vary social security rates or pensions – these being among the 'reserved powers' retained by Westminster and Whitehall.

Devolution to Wales

The first Blair government granted devolution to Wales in tandem with that granted to Scotland, with a referendum in Wales in 1997, followed by the relevant legislation the following year, and the National Assembly for Wales launched in 1999. However, there remained several significant differences between the devolution granted to Wales, and that enacted in Scotland.

First, the referendum in Wales was held a week later than that in Scotland, apparently in the expectation that Scotland's (expected) 'yes' vote would create a 'bandwagon effect', ensuring that Wales also endorsed devolution. It did, but only by the narrowest of margins, 559,419 (50.3 per cent) votes to 552,698 (49.7 per cent), a majority of just 6,721, and on a turnout of 50.1 per cent, which effectively meant that only 1 in 4 of the Welsh electorate actually voted for devolution.

Second, unlike the Scottish Parliament, the National Assembly for Wales is not a legislative body, but is primarily an executive body. It is not, therefore, empowered to introduce legislation pertaining to Wales, but, instead, is primarily responsible for administering policies previously overseen by the Secretary of State for Wales and the Welsh Office. Policy areas for which the National Assembly for Wales has executive authority are:

- Agriculture
- Arts and heritage
- Education
- Environment
- Health
- Industry and training
- Planning
- Roads.

Many pro-devolutionists in Wales partly attribute the low turn out, and narrow 'yes' majority, in the September 1997 referendum, to the limited form of devolution being offered to the Welsh people, which, compared with that on offer to Scottish citizens, was hardly likely to generate real enthusiasm. Some Labour ministers in London, on the other hand, doubtless interpreted the relatively low turnout and narrow margin of victory as an indication that the Welsh people were less keen on devolution than their Scottish counterparts, thus vindicating the Blair government's decision to offer Wales an (executive) Assembly, rather than a (legislative) Parliament.

However, in the months preceding the second elections to the National Assembly for Wales, in May 2003, surveys revealed that an increasing number of Welsh people wanted the National Assembly to be granted greater powers, while Labour's First Minister (leader in the Welsh Assembly), Rhodri Morgan, called for 'clear red water' to be placed between Wales and Westminster, in order to facilitate greater autonomy and radicalism by the Welsh Assembly, and the Labour Party therein.

Third, the National Assembly for Wales does not possess any tax-raising powers. It is permitted, however, to determine how its block grant will be apportioned between the various services in Wales, thereby enabling the Welsh Assembly to give greater priority to some policy areas than others in any financial year.

Like the Scottish Parliament, the National Assembly for Wales is elected using the Additional Member System. Of the 60 Assembly Members for Wales (ASMs), 40 are elected on a first-past-the-post basis, from existing Westminster constituencies, while the other 20 are recruited from party lists, according to their party's share of the 'top-up' vote. As in Scotland, this method of election led to Labour being the single largest party, but lacking an overall majority. Initially, the Labour Party in Wales sought to form a minority administration governing alone, but when Rhodri Morgan replaced Alun Michael as Labour's First Minister in the Welsh Assembly, Labour formed a coalition with the Welsh Liberal Democrats.

Welsh policy divergence

In spite of its limited powers, the National Assembly for Wales has still pursued a number of policies and initiatives which constitute a divergence from corresponding policies in England, and which were also doubtless viewed with some displeasure by the Blair government in London. The main examples of such policy innovations following Welsh devolution are:

- *Prescription charges*: since 1 April 2001, prescriptions have been free for those either under 25, or over 60, years of age. It is intended that prescription charges will be phased out entirely by 2007.
- *Bus travel*: pensioners in Wales receive free travel on buses.
- *Education*: (a) Abolition of school league tables; (b) Abolition of tests for 7-year-olds; (c) free school milk for children under 7 years of age.
- '*Foundation Hospitals*': to be resisted by Labour–Liberal Democrat Coalition in National Assembly for Wales.

One particular source of conflict which emerged virtually from the outset between the National Assembly for Wales and Westminster/Whitehall concerned Objective One funding. When the Welsh (former) mining regions and rural West of Wales were ascribed 'Objective One' status by the EU (due to their extreme socio-economic deprivation), the Treasury initially declined to provide the requisite 'match-funding' – a refusal which ultimately prompted the 'no confidence' motion in Labour's then First Minister, Alun Michael, who was widely perceived to be 'too Blairite' to be able effectively to represent Welsh interests. Eventually, in the summer of 2000, and following Michael's enforced resignation, the Treasury relented, and Wales was awarded the match-funding upon which the EU monies depended. However, the episode provided a clear indication of the limited powers of the Welsh Assembly, and the extent to which Wales lacked the degree of autonomy enjoyed by Scotland *vis-à-vis* Westminster and Whitehall.

Nonetheless, some writers discern an increasingly distinct Welsh dimension emerging, both with regard to an inclusive policy making process, and the substance of the policies pursued, particularly in the twin spheres of social policy and welfare provision, reflecting (historically) 'a greater willingness to embrace socialist and communitarian values at the ballot box than has been the case in England', whereupon:

> the Welsh Executive has attempted to articulate such values in the development of a social policy agenda based upon the following notions: universalism; a rejection of marketisation; and co-operation rather than competition in the provision of collective goods ... devolution ... has created an enabling context in which these values can be applied to social policy.
>
> (Chaney and Drakeford, 2004: 136)

The continued application of such values is likely to ensure the concomitant continuation of Welsh policy divergence, particularly if the National Assembly's powers are increased, in accordance with the recommendations of the Richard Commission, which published its report in the spring of 2004.

English regionalization

Although the Blair governments have displayed considerable hesitancy about proceeding with the formal commitment to elected English Regional Assemblies – John Prescott has often appeared to be the only senior minister genuinely committed to devolution for England – there has, nonetheless, been a discernible process of 'regionalization' in England, particularly since the 1990s. Ironically, it was the staunchly antidevolution Conservative government, led by John Major, which provided the impetus for English regional governance, by establishing, in April 1994, Government Offices for the Regions, their professed purpose being to provide 'a single point of contact for local authorities, businesses and local communities' (Department of the Environment, 1993; see also Mawson and Spencer, 1997a, 1997b; Spencer and Mawson, 1998).

In establishing these Government Offices of the Regions, however, the Major government inadvertently provided a fillip to the Labour Party, which was itself seeking to develop a policy for the English regions that would parallel its proposals for Scottish and

Welsh devolution. Not only did the Major government's initiative imbue Labour's developing policy with greater relevance and legitimacy, it also ensured that at least part of the administrative and institutional framework would be in place once a Labour government was elected.

During the Blair government's first term of office, its main innovation with regard to English regional government was the inauguration of the eight Regional Development Agencies (RDAs) and concomitant Regional Assemblies. The RDAs were inaugurated in April 1999, their remit being to act as 'economic powerhouses' which would undertake or coordinate initiatives to regenerate their respective regions, particularly with regard to attracting investment and providing employment opportunities (Peele, 2003: 206; Greenwood et al., 2002: 204).

At the same time, the establishment of these RDAs was paralleled by the creation of Regional Chambers (one for each of the eight English regions outside London), comprising representatives from local authorities in the relevant region, as well representatives from the regions' businesses, education and voluntary sectors, and trade unions. These Regional Chambers were to monitor the work of 'their' RDA, with whom there would also be regular consultation (reflecting the Blair governments' emphasis on 'partnership politics').

However, critics claim that in spite of the establishment of RDAs and Regional Chambers, and ministerial rhetoric about decentralization and devolution to the English regions, the Blair government has still retained considerable control from the centre, both through the allocation of public expenditure and resources to the regions, and through the determination of strategic policy objectives (see, for example, Lee, 2000).

One of the reasons why the Blair governments' motives were suspected by some commentators was that the original proposals for 'English devolution' included directly-elected Regional Assemblies, which would be created on a rolling basis, once the RDAs and Chambers had become established, and when and where a referendum indicated that sufficient popular support existed in a region. Yet once the RDAs and Chambers had been launched, most ministers – with the exception of John Prescott – appeared to lose interest, as indicated by the subsequent period of prevarication and procrastination. Many Labour MPs were also deeply sceptical about the need or desirability of such Assemblies, while other Labour backbenchers were concerned that it might be unwise to proceed with referenda campaigns so close to the (expected) spring 2005 general election (Hetherington, 2004: 13). It was not until November 2004, therefore, that the first referendum was finally held, with people in the north-east of England permitted to vote on whether they wished to have a directly-elected Regional Assembly for the north-east, although it had still not been decided precisely what powers such a body would subsequently be granted, beyond oversight and coordination of stragic planning, economic development, housing and possibly transport. A 'yes' vote would be followed by legislation to establish a 25-member elected Assembly, with the first elections likely to be held in 2006, following the necessary reorganization of local government in the region to establish a unitary authority.

However, when the referendum was held in the north-east, at the beginning of November 2004, the result was an emphatic rejection – by 696,519 votes to 197,310 – of an elected Regional Assembly (in spite of the 'Vote Yes' campaign spending £10 million). Such a resounding defeat made it virtually inconceivable that planned referenda in north-west England, and Yorkshire, would be conducted in the foreseeable future (for an initial analysis of the north-east referendum result, see Chittenden and Fielding, 2004: 13).

The Greater London Authority

The only elected English Assembly which was actually established by the first Blair government was the Greater London Authority (GLA), which was launched in 2000. The primary role of the GLA is to promote the economic, environmental, and social development of London, while also exercising the function of scrutiny *vis-à-vis* the directly elected Mayor, through his presentation of a monthly report, and via an equally regular personal appearance for 'Mayor's Question Time' (for a useful overview, see Bax, 2002: 103–19; Peele, 2003: 208–10; Pimlott and Rao, 2002).

The role of the Mayor of London, meanwhile, was mainly strategic, the objective being to provide leadership and coordination of the designated policy areas just mentioned, but with particular regard also for transport in the capital. Given the vital importance – and problems – of transport in London, this particular remit has since proved particularly conflictual. The issue which dominated the first 15 months of Livingstone's mayorship was that of the future of London Underground, which, it was universally accepted, required major and urgent investment. However, whereas Livingstone strongly favoured raising the necessary revenues via the issuing of bonds, the Blair government was committed to partial privatization, via the Public-Private Partnership scheme which New Labour had become so enamoured with, whereby private consortiums would assume responsibility for track and tunnel maintenance, while the trains and stations remained publicly owned and managed.

Such was the depth of disagreement between Livingstone and the government over the issue that it was only finally resolved via a High Court judgement in favour of the government, although the judge was nonetheless critical of the government's handling of the affair, and in particular, its apparent failure to make sufficiently clear, when establishing the GLA and the mayorship, that whoever became mayor would only acquire overall responsibility for London Underground after the Public-Private Partnership scheme had been implemented (*The Guardian,* 31 July 2001). The week prior to this court case had also seen Tony Blair sack Bob Kiley as chairperson of London Underground, due to his refusal to implement the Public-Private Partnership, although Kiley remained as Ken Livingstone's appointed Transport Commissioner.

Transport continued to constitute a source of tension between Livingstone and the Blair government due to the former's determination to impose 'congestion charges' on private motorists in London, in an attempt at reducing the volume of traffic in the capital. On this issue, Livingstone prevailed, to the extent that a policy which many – including several New Labour ministers – had envisaged would prove to be a disaster, subsequently proved so successful that several other cities in Britain began drafting similar proposals (thereby providing an excellent example of policy transfer).

Interaction between voluntary, public and private sector bodies

The establishment of the English Regional Assemblies, coupled with the prior fragmentation of service delivery into a 'mixed economy' of public, private and voluntary sectors and agencies, has itself contributed to a major feature of the new governance, namely the establishment of partnerships and regional networks to coordinate policies and service delivery. The West Midlands Regional Assembly, for example, has established four 'strategic partnerships', covering transport, regional housing, social inclusion, and a 'European and International Partnership', but is also served or supported by a host of 'associate' and advisory bodies, such as a Regional Rural Affairs Forum, a Faith Task Group, a Public Health Issues Group and a Business Policy Group.

These sundry strategic partnerships and associated bodies will bring together representatives from a wide range of public, private and voluntary bodies which are service providers and/or can offer expertise in a particular policy subsystem. This is clearly illustrated by the membership of the Transport Partnership established by the West Midlands Regional Assembly, as listed below, whose remit is primarily to 'broker consensus around solutions to key regional transport issues and facilitate their implementation' (www.wmra. gov.uk/transport_partnership).

- 5 Regional Assembly Members
- 1 Bus/Metro operator
- 1 Rail industry
- 1 Airport
- 1 West Midlands Passenger Transport Authority
- 1 Highways Agency
- 1 Strategic Rail Authority
- 1 Government Office of the Regions (West Midlands)
- 1 Advantage West Midlands
- 1 Sustainability West Midlands
- 1 West Midlands Local Government Association
- 1 Business Sector
- 1 Commercial Road Transport
- 1 Public Transport Users Group.

Meanwhile the composition of the Housing Partnership of the West Midlands Regional Assembly is illustrated below:

- National Housing Federation
- Housing Corporation
- Chartered Institute for Housing
- West Midlands Voluntary and Community Sector Housing Network
- Government Office of the Regions (West Midlands)
- West Midlands Local Government Association
- Countryside Agency

- House Builders Federation
- Local Authorities in the West Midlands Region, of which there are 38.

Housing also provides another example of the extent to which governance increasingly entails consultation and coordination between public, private and voluntary bodies, this time in connection with the Mayor of London's 2001 initiative to develop a GLA strategy to tackle homelessness and 'rough sleeping' in the capital. The initial stage in devising such a strategy was to elicit responses to a consultation paper entitled *Evening the Odds*. There was an eclectic range of 57 respondents:

- Alone in London Service
- Ashiana Project
- Big Issue Foundation
- Bina Gardens
- Bondway Outreach
- Borderline
- Bridge Housing Association
- Broadway
- Centrepoint
- CRASH
- Crisis
- De Paul Trust
- Eaves Housing for Women
- Empty Homes Agency
- English Churches Housing Group
- Equinox
- Foyer Federation
- Great Chapel Street Medical Centre
- Groundswell
- HAS
- Homeless Network
- Horseferry Road
- Huge Move
- In Kind Direct
- Kipper Project
- London Borough of Camden
- London Borough of Croydon
- London Borough of Haringey
- London Borough of Southwark
- London Connection
- London Housing Federation
- London NHS Region
- Look Ahead Housing and Care Ltd
- Metropolitan Police Authority
- NACRO
- National Homelessness Alliance
- National Housing Federation
- New to London
- Off the Streets and Into Work
- Passage Day Centre
- Providence Row
- Recycle IT
- Resource Information Centre
- Rough Sleepers Unit
- Safe in the City
- Salvation Army Homeless Service
- Sheffield Institute for Studies on Ageing
- Shelter
- Single Homeless Project
- St Botolph's
- St Martin in the Fields Social Care Unit
- St Mungo's
- Thames Reach
- UNLEASH
- Westminster Advice and Assessment Centre
- Westminster City Council
- YMCA.

Source: Yvernault, 2003: Appendix A

including homelessness charities, local authorities, pressure groups and voluntary bodies, as well as the Metropolitan Police Authority (Yvernault, 2003)

A final example here of the manner in which governance entails establishing partnerships between, and coordinating, a range of policy actors is provided by management of London Underground, commonly known as 'the tube'. The range of public and private actors involved is illustrated in Figure 8.2.

Figure 8.2   Managing London Underground

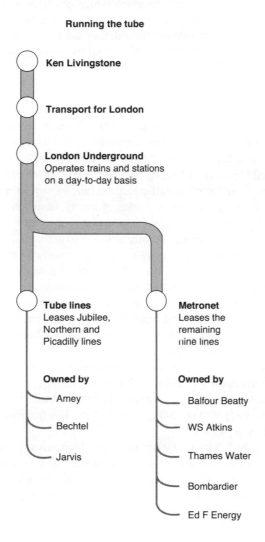

Running the tube

Ken Livingstone

Transport for London

London Underground
Operates trains and stations
on a day-to-day basis

Tube lines
Leases Jubilee,
Northern and
Picadilly lines

Metronet
Leases the
remaining
nine lines

Owned by
— Amey
— Bechtel
— Jarvis

Owned by
— Balfour Beatty
— WS Atkins
— Thames Water
— Bombardier
— Ed F Energy

Clearly, with the delivery of various services now shared between a range of public, private and voluntary bodies, partnerships, coordination and strategic oversight all become vitally important, and this aspect of the contemporary policy process will become even more important as, or when, English Regional Assemblies are established.

Furthermore, as in other policy arenas, the emphasis is on shared resources and exchange relationships, with the Assemblies, their partnerships' groupings, regional and local service providers and delivery agencies, obliged to work together and forge alliances in order to achieve policy objectives and performance indicators. Consequently, the various consultative and exchange relationships which characterize both the core executive, and policy networks, at national level, are increasingly a key feature of regional and local policy making and implementation. Indeed, they are both vertical (between national, regional *and* local level policy actors), and horizontal (between policy actors at specific – national, regional *or* local – levels).

The 'regulatory state'

The privatization programme pursued by the 1979–97 Thatcher-Major governments was imbued with several objectives – extending competition, increasing efficiency, empowering the consumer, fostering an enterprise culture, etc. (Dorey, 2001b) – but it was also frequently linked to the professed objective of 'rolling back the state'. Thatcherism frequently depicted the state and its allegedly self-serving anti-enterprise bureaucracy as a major impediment to the operation of private enterprise and the market economy, based on the immutable laws of supply and demand. By removing the 'dead hand' of state intervention and control, privatization was heralded as a major means of unleashing entrepreneurial talent and innovation, and allowing the consumer-responsive private sector to provide the goods and services that the British public wanted, rather that what the 'gentlemen in Whitehall' assumed they wanted, needed, or ought to have. Even in areas of the public sector where privatization was not considered feasible or appropriate, certain 'market' principles and private sector practices were introduced. Privatization and 'marketization' would therefore usher in a new era of limited government, less political interference and freedom from bureaucratic meddling. Or so neo-liberal Thatcherite ideologues purported to believe.

In fact, since the 1980s, the state has not so much been 'rolled back' as restructured and reorientated, and intervention has taken new forms. Consequently, a number of writers have identified the emergence of a new 'regulatory state' (Hood et al., 1999; Loughlin and Scott, 1997; Majone, 1994; Moran, 2001). This, in turn, has fostered the establishment of the 'audit society' (Power, 1997).

The most obvious manifestation of the manner in which privatization has yielded a new mode of regulation is through the plethora of regulatory bodies which have been established since the 1980s. Calculating the precise number of such bodies is problematic, due to the different definitions deployed as to what actually constitutes a 'regulatory body' in an era of agencification and sundry other semiautonomous commissions and councils. In 1997, for example, Rhodes believed that there were at least 32 regulatory bodies in post-privatization Britain (Rhodes, 1997: 91–2), while Hood et al. have identified no less than 135 in 1995. Whatever the precise figure, the list below identifies the main regulatory bodies in Britain today, whereupon it immediately becomes apparent that most of the privatized industries are subject to their own regulatory body:

- Advertising Standards Authority
- Consumers' Association
- Financial Services Authority
- General Consumer Council for Northern Ireland
- Funding Agency for Schools

- Higher Education Funding Council for England
- Higher Education Funding Council for Wales
- National Consumer Council
- Office for Standards in Education (OFSTED)
- Office for the Regulation of Electricity and Gas
- Office of Communications
- Office of Gas and Electricity Markets
- Office of Telecommunications (OFTEL)
- Office of the Rail Regulator
- Office of Water Services (OFWAT)
- Police Complaints Authority
- Postal Services Commission
- Postwatch
- Press Complaints Commission
- Quality Assurance Agency (Higher Education)
- Scottish Consumer Council
- Social Services Inspectorate
- Strategic Rail Authority
- Teacher Training Agency
- Trading Standards Institute
- Welsh Consumer Council.

Many of these are commonly known by their acronyms, which have entered the lexicon of ordinary conversation and news reportage, such as the Office of Telecommunications, which is invariably referred to as OFTEL, and the Office for Standards in Education, commonly known (especially by tremulous school teachers) as OFSTED.

With regard to the privatized industries in particular, these regulatory bodies are concerned to ensure some degree of protection for consumers, either by restricting price increases, in the case of OFTEL and OFWAT, for example, or imposing financial penalties for poor service, as the (former) Strategic Rail Authority did *vis-à-vis* railway companies. As Feigenbaum et al. (1998: 80) have noted, these regulatory bodies 'possess considerable power over the operation, service standards and pricing structure of the privatized utilities'.

As such, they reflect the fact that in spite of the Thatcherite discourse of competition and consumer choice, many of the privatized industries and services remained near-monopolies, albeit no longer in the public sector. Consequently, it was recognized that the consumer still required some form of 'protection' against excessive price increases, unfair practices or poor service. Thus it was that privatization heralded the development of a new tranche of bodies to regulate the practices and activities of the privatized industries, so that government effectively 'substituted regulation for ownership' (Rhodes, 1997: 91).

However, it is certainly not just privatized utilities which are subject to such regulation. Virtually all public services and bodies are today subject to forms of regulation by various governmental, semiautonomous or funding agencies and councils, who impose targets, establish performance indicators, conduct regular 'audits' (see below) to measure the extent to which these targets and indicators have been met, and often allocate (or withhold) funding accordingly. Figure 8.3 illustrates the various regulatory

Figure 8.3   The governance of British universities

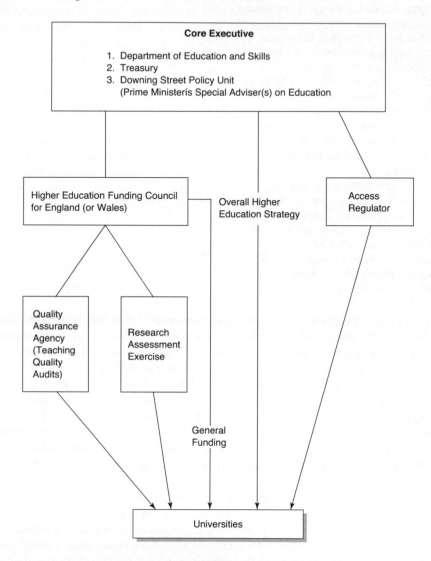

bodies which universities are 'policed' by today, for example, and their linkages to the core executive.

It is therefore a major paradox yielded by the regulatory state and its relentless attempt at improving public sector or public service performance that new modes of intervention and surveillance from, or at the behest of, the core executive, are established. This particular paradox has been well noted by Moran, who observes that while the new governance is characterized by central government's relinquishing of direct control, and a fragmentation of administrative processes and institutions at subnational level, it has nonetheless been accompanied by new attempts at exercising forms of control and direction from the centre. According to Moran: 'The regulatory State has replaced nationalisation with regulation' so that while 'privatisation removed a large area of command from the British economy ... it did so at the cost of creating huge new areas of intervention and institution building.' In this respect, Moran suggests that 'the supposed rise of governance has been accompanied by something that looks like its very antithesis', namely new forms of command, control, regulation and surveillance, either from, or on behalf of, and at the behest of, the centre. The ultimate irony, therefore, is that the rhetoric of deregulation which pervaded the 1980s and 1990s has belied a parallel trend towards increased regulation: 'the social world of 2000 is infinitely more tightly controlled than the world of 1950' (Moran, 2000: 6–8; see also Moran, 2001). In similar vein, Gamble observes that: 'One of the consequences of the rise of the regulatory state may therefore be an increase rather than a decrease in government' (1997: 370), while Majone notes how privatization and 'deregulation' have actually 'created the conditions for the rise of the regulatory state to replace the *dirigiste* state of the past'(1994). Certainly, as Muller and Wright suggested (writing in 1994), 'it would be perfectly plausible to contend that the last 15 years have seen more 'state reshaping' than 'state retreat', with the state remaining a central policy actor, retaining 'a nodal decision-making position' even though 'their action is more indirect, more discreet and more bartered' (1994: 7–8).

Similarly, in his book on *Economic Policy in Britain*, Wyn Grant notes how, after an apparent 'rolling back' initially, 'the state starts to expand again, but in a more chameleon-like form', so that 'the emergence of a regulatory state does not mean that state power necessarily diminishes, but that its form changes ... becomes more diffuse ... becomes less direct, but also more penetrating. A regulatory state is in many ways a more fragmented state with responsibility divided amongst a host of different regulators or auditors' (2003: 226–7). This last point draws attention to the fact that 'regulation' requires evaluation, measurement and quantification, in order to gauge the extent to which performance indicators and targets are being met by service providers and 'street level bureaucrats' responsible for policy implementation. Consequently, the regulatory state begets the 'audit society'.

The 'audit society'

The emergence of the regulatory state has proceed *pari passu* with the development of the 'audit society' (Power, 1997), whereby public services have increasingly become subject to detailed monitoring and evaluation, in order to ensure that performance targets are being achieved, and that cost-effectiveness, 'value for money' or 'quality' are being attained. Indeed, Power highlights three specific characteristics of this new 'audit society':

1 The imposition of 'increasingly detailed accounting requirements' on public institutions, such as hospitals, schools and universities.
2 The imposition of 'increasingly detailed and explicit performance standards and indicators'.
3 The emergence of an audit regime, entailing 'a system of surveillance designed to ensure that these standards [and indicators] are met'.

With regard to the second above characteristics, public services have become subject to an ever-increasing range of 'targets', which are deemed to indicate either increased productivity, 'value-added', or improved responsiveness to the needs of consumers. Hospitals, schools and universities are doubtless the most notable examples of public service providers or institutions which have become subject to an increasing array of 'performance targets' since the late 1980s, but they are by no means the only ones. For example, in the spring of 2003, it was reported that Thames Valley police were setting a plethora of monthly quotas to traffic police in their region, obliging them to: make three arrests for traffic offences per month; issue 10 'fixed-penalty' notices for speeding; fine 10 motorists or their passengers for not wearing seat belts. They were also instructed to 'book' three motorists each month for number plate offences, and fine at least 10 motorists or motorcyclists for sundry other offences, such as failing to stop at a red light (*The Sunday Times,* 11 May 2003).

To provide incentives – 'incentivization' in modern management-speak – levels of funding are often partly linked to the attainment of performance indicators and the 'hitting' of specified targets. Just as funding might well be increased when targets and performance indicators are verifiably met, so failure to meet specified goals might be punished by reductions in funding. In this respect, the 'audit society' entails the replication of commercial criteria in the private sector or public services (even when the latter have been formally transferred to the private sector, such as the railways), so that just as successful private companies will make a profit, and unsuccessful ones will incur a loss, so public services meeting their targets will (in principle) be rewarded with increased funding, with a corresponding loss of funding for those adjudged to have failed. This, therefore, is a key means by which the contemporary state seeks to 'steer' various public, private or voluntary sector bodies and policy actors towards the delivery of 'quality services' or attainment of particular standards of performance , in the absence of formal or direct control by the state.

It is largely to gauge the extent to which public services and those employed in the residual public sector are meeting the performance indicators and targets imposed on them that the audit society has emerged, for public services are now subject to a constant process of auditing, not simply in a traditional or narrow financial sense, but to measure and evaluate their performance in both quantitative and qualitative terms.

Of course, the process of auditing is also a form of managerial or political control over those who have previously enjoyed considerable professional discretion and autonomy. Indeed, many public service professionals are now subject simultaneously to pressure from below, in terms of their clients' demands and rights (often stipulated in the guise of 'charters'), and pressure from above, in terms of ever closer and stringent managerial monitoring.

The most obvious manifestation of this 'audit society' is the plethora of 'league tables' which purport to rank the success of public services, according to a range of criteria. Schools, for example, can now be ranked in 'league tables' according to such variables as the percentage of pupils obtaining GCSEs and/or A levels (and even the grades obtained therein), and the proportion of students subsequently going on to university. Universities, meanwhile, are now placed in league tables according to such criteria as 'teaching quality', 'value-added' and research (via the Research Assessment Exercise, or RAE as it is known among academics). Early in 2003, the Blair government announced that future funding of universities would be partly linked to a new criterion, namely their recruitment of more students from working-class or other socially disadvantaged backgrounds. To audit their success in meeting this new target, an 'Access Regulator' was to be created, thereby adding to the sundry other bodies auditing the 'performance' of Britain's universities.

Again, part of the rationale for ranking performance in published league tables is to instil a major feature of the private sector or 'the market', into the public sector or public services, namely competition, and a constant determination to improve one's position against rivals. This, in turn, it is assumed, will result in a constant improvement in the quality of service provided to, and received by, public sector consumers.

However, as part of the new 'governance' in contemporary Britain, the audit society engenders a number of problems and paradoxes. First, there can be a tension between quantitative and qualitative targets or criteria, such as whether a hospital should be judged on the total number of patients treated, and perhaps, therefore, how short its waiting lists are, or the quality of patient care, which might result in individual patients staying in hospital a day or two longer, perhaps, but which would then result in longer waiting lists for the other (would-be) patients, and a shortage of beds.

Second (but following on from the above), some targets can create 'role conflicts' in institutions, because the pursuit of a particular target might be detrimental to other aspects of an organization's functions. For example, although the number of university students has increased significantly since the 1990s (and is scheduled to increase further by 2010), coupled with the fact that students are now paying directly for higher education, university lecturers are under intense pressure to focus on research and publications, due to the need to improve their institution's ranking in the next RAE. Clearly, lecturers' extensive focus on research may not be in the interests of students and their education, yet academics are increasingly caught between the legitimate expectations of undergraduates to be taught properly, and the demands of university management to improve 'research output', in order to secure additional funds.

One other example of the perverse consequences which can accrue from the pursuit of incompatible performance indicators and targets in the new audit society concerns Britain's privatized railways. By the winter of 2002–3, following constant criticism about late-running trains and poor punctuality, it was announced that various train services were to be reduced. The argument was that many trains were late because of congestion on the tracks, whereby one late-running train caused delays to the trains behind it. The more train services there were in operation, therefore, the more scope there was for such delays and hold-ups, and hence the greater the likelihood of a poor ranking in the 'punctuality league table'. Consequently, with wonderfully perverse logic, it was proposed that by cutting some services, so that there were fewer trains on the tracks at any given time, there would be fewer delays, and so punctuality would improve. Of course, even if this proves to be the case, then unless trains are provided with more carriages, they are likely to be (even more) overcrowded, as passengers who previously travelled on two trains, henceforth all seek to travel on the one train still running.

A further problem engendered by the imposition of innumerable targets – particularly when there are implications for subsequent financial resources – is that the temptation sometime arises for public service managers to engage in a certain 'creativity' in order to 'prove' that they have met their targets. For example, in May 2003, it was alleged that various NHS Trust hospitals, knowing they were being audited on their Accident and Emergency (A&E) waiting-time targets during one particular week at the end of March, cancelled dozens of routine operations, in order to free-up beds, and redirect medical staff to their A&E departments, while also recruiting hundreds of temporary (agency) nurses (*The Observer*, 11 May 2003).

One other perverse consequence of 'the audit society' is the extent to which the auditing procedures can be rendered more important than the actual activities which are supposedly being measured. Or as Power notes, audits do not merely measure activities, they play a significant role in determining which activities are worth quantifying (1994: 33). If we return briefly to the example of the RAEs in higher education, we note that the RAE does not merely measure the number and 'value' of academic publications, but itself decrees which type of publications are worthy of evaluation. Academic research is thus increasingly preoccupied by considerations of what will be acceptable to the RAE itself, rather than any intellectual or educational criteria. For example, because the RAE prioritizes scholarly research and 'cutting-edge' originality, a specialist monograph which only sells 300 copies is ascribed much more 'weight' than a textbook which might be read or purchased by 10,000 undergraduates nationally. Indeed, some academics are now strongly discouraged from writing textbooks, because such publications are not deemed 'RAE-submissible'.

Certainly, many audits require that tasks are performed, or services delivered, in a manner which renders them more 'quantifiable', even if this means actually altering the tasks themselves, or the manner in which services are delivered – 'a preoccupation with the auditable process rather than the substance of activities' (Power, 1994: 48). Or to put it more simply, audits often entail the tail wagging the dog, something to which almost anyone employed in the public sector today will testify!

A final, stark, indication of the negative consequences of the 'audit society' for those employed in the public sector – and, ultimately, their 'customers' or 'clients' – is provided by the case of a Drugs Action Team in Bristol, whose overwhelmed and demoralized leader quit in May 2003. He pointed out that while trying to tackle drug abuse and addiction in the Bristol area, he was required, among other things, to:

- deal with 44 different 'funding streams', each of which imposed its own targets and detailed 'business plans', and demanded a quarterly report;
- sign 'endless' service agreements with other service providers, who also stipulated targets, and required quarterly reports on progress towards attaining them;
- cope with repeated changes in the allocation and level of funding and targets, which made it virtually impossible to plan or maintain staffing levels and prioritize objectives;
- prepare an annual 'treatment plan' of about 70 pages, outlining 82 objectives and containing 'nine planning grids';
- arrange cover for the staff who had to take sick leave due to the stress-related illnesses they incurred trying to cope with the job.

These, and various other, bureaucratic or target-driven requirements meant that he and his staff spent 60 per cent of their time on paperwork, form-filling, box-ticking and report-writing, and only 40 per cent on actually providing advice and services for drug users, ostensibly, the *raison d'être* of the Drugs Action Team.

Consequently, in his resignation letter, the leader of the Bristol Drugs Action Team complained of a culture of control in Whitehall which amounted to a 'monitoring fetish', and pointed out the irony that: 'The demand [by Whitehall] for quick hits … is driven by a central desire analogous to the instant gratification demands by drug users themselves.' Ultimately, he observed, while ministers lack a serious understanding of drug-related issues, 'they do know about management and monitoring and data collection, so that's what they do' (quoted in Davies, 2003: 1).

Conclusion

The fragmentation and increased number of policy actors engendered by the transition from government to governance has placed a premium on the need for coordination. Not only are there more actors involved in the contemporary British policy process, there are also an increasing number of social issues and problems which require the involvement and cooperation of a range of bodies: some governmental and some non-governmental; some public sector, some private or voluntary; some central or national level, and some regional or local (or EU) level. Consequently, the number of linkages between various policy actors has increased, both vertically, between national-level bodies and those at subnational level, but also horizontally, both between bodies at national level, and also between regional or local level bodies. Governance thus entails not only the weakening of old notions of hierarchy and clear chains of command, but also erodes the relative autonomy of many traditional policy 'sectors'. These trends further increase the importance of coordination and 'steerage', particularly, but not solely, from the core executive. At the same time, though, 'fragmentation erodes accountability because sheer institutional complexity obscures who is accountable to whom and for what' (Rhodes, 1997: 101).

Recommended texts and further reading

1. Robert Holton (1998) *Globalization and the Nation-state*, Basingstoke: Macmillan.

    Clear and concise overview of globalization, with particular attention paid to the economic manifestations and implications, and the impact on the contemporary nation-state (and domestic policy makers).

2. Loughlin, Martin and Scott, Colin (1997) 'The Regulatory State' in Patrick Dunleavy, Andrew Gamble, Ian Holliday and Gillian Peele (eds) *Developments in British Politics 5*, Basingstoke: Macmillan.

    Essay detailing how privatization and the ostensible 'rolling back' of the state have actually yielded new modes of regulation, behind which there remains considerable ministerial control.

3. Pierre, Jon and Stoker, Gerry (2000) 'Towards Multi-level Governance' in Patrick Dunleavy, Andrew Gamble, Ian Holliday and Gillian Peele (eds) *Developments in British Politics 6*, Basingstoke: Macmillan.

Useful essay discussing both the concept of (multilevel) governance, and the extent to which the concept provides a good characterization of the changes in the structure and functioning of Britain's political and policy-making institutions.

4. Power, Michael (1997) *The Audit Society: Rituals of Verification*, Oxford: Oxford University Press.

   Excellent account of the way in which public services in Britain are subject to increasing regulation, evaluation and performance indicators, in order to measure 'outcomes' and quantify service delivery.

5. Rhodes, R. A. W. (1997) *Understanding Governance: Policy Networks, Governance, Reflexivity and Accountability*, Buckingham: Open University Press.

   Very good discussion of the ways in which government has been replaced by governance, as policy making increasingly takes place at different levels, and between a range of actors, in the context of a 'hollowing out of the state'.

6. Ben Rosamond (2003) 'The Europeanization of British Politics' in Patrick Dunleavy, Andrew Gamble, Richard Heffernan and Gillian Peele (eds) *Developments in British Politics 7*, Basingstoke: Palgrave.

   Essay detailing the ways in which European integration is impacting upon Britain's political and policy making institutions, and both reflects and reinforces trends towards governance.

Policy Making in Britain: Trends and Trajectories

Writing in 1982, Jordan and Richardson identified a particular 'policy style' in Britain, one which, to a significant extent, operated irrespective of the ideological inclination of the governing political party. A major implication of Jordan and Richardson's 'British policy style' was that significant changes of policy are relatively rare. Instead, there was a strong trend either on broad policy continuity, or on only incremental changes to most areas of public policy.

Jordan and Richardson's 'British policy style'

Jordan and Richardson (1982) identified five particular features of a distinct 'British policy style', namely:

1. Sectorization.
2. Clientelism.
3. Consultation.
4. Institutionalization of compromise.
5. Development of exchange relationships.

Sectorization

This refers to the tendency for policy making in Britain to be concentrated in particular departments and subsystems, on a vertical basis, with only limited interaction between them, such as agriculture, education, transport, etc. This reflects policy making at the meso level, below the Cabinet, and away from Parliament, although both of these institutions will almost invariably be involved subsequently in providing (usually) formal approval and legitimation of sectoral policy decisions. According to Jordan and Richardson, Britain has long been characterized by 'a functionally differentiated and fragmented bureaucracy' based largely on discrete policy subsystems (1982: 86).

Sectorization also contributes considerably to the 'departmentalism' noted in Chapters 3 and 4, whereby a department enshrines a particular philosophy, while also jealously guarding its policy domain, and ministers and senior civil servants in the department are often inculcated into judging policies primarily in terms of how they will affect their department. It also means that, as noted in Chapter 4, 'Cabinet does not act as an impartial jury coolly assessing options put to it by departments. Politically, it is too difficult to proceed on a "critical assessment" basis' (Jordan and Richardson, 1982: 83). This tendency to sectorization has therefore enhanced the importance of cross-cutting or coordinating bodies in the core executive, such as cabinet committees and the various secretariats within the Cabinet Office, as well the Prime Minister's Office (particularly the Policy Unit/ Directorate within it).

Clientelism

We noted in Chapter 6 the manner in which certain departments tended to develop very close links with key organized interests in their policy sector or subsystem (policy communities), and this led Jordan and Richardson to posit clientelism as a key feature of a discrete 'British policy style'. This entails a symbiotic relationship, whereby the organized interests look to 'their' department to promote or defend their interests in the policy process, thereby rendering those groups the *de facto* 'clientele' of that department. These organized interests are, in turn, highly valued by the department's senior civil servants, due to the advice and assistance they can provide with regard to various policy issues, particularly those of a specialized, technical or administratively complex character, as well as their vital role in aiding implementation. Thus, in Jordan and Richardson's words: 'Group-Department relations tend to produce treaties of mutual advantage', thereby both reflecting and reinforcing a tendency for 'relations between department and sectoral interests ... to become closer' (1982: 85, 86).

Consultation

This characteristic refers to a long-standing tendency by government departments and their officials to elicit the views of organized interests and other 'affected parties' in the development of public policy. In this context, consultation reflects two broad motivations, namely 'cultural bias', and 'functional logic'.

'Cultural bias' is deemed by Jordan and Richardson to reflect a normative assumption that consultation is innately desirable, not least because it imbues decisions and policies with greater legitimacy. In its broadest sense, consultation seeks to secure the 'consent of the governed', and reflects a desire to ensure that as many policies as possible derive from consensus and compromise. This, in turn, ought to render those policies more successful, certainly more so than those policies which are implemented without effective prior consultation, and which are thus imposed, perhaps, by 'despotic power', or where concerns expressed during consultations have subsequently been disregarded.

The second motivation for the importance ascribed to consultation in the 'British policy process' is that of 'functional logic', which refers to the specialist knowledge and expertise which certain key organized interests possess, and which policy makers need access to. This, in turn, 'contributes to system maintenance, not only because it imparts a sense of involvement, but also because it should produce more acceptable policies' (Jordan and Richardson, 1982: 86).

As we have noted elsewhere in this book, some of the most dramatic policy failures in Britain since 1970, such as the 1971 Industrial Relations Act, and the 1989–90 Community Charge/Poll Tax, have at least partly derived from a failure properly to consult the 'affected parties'. Certainly, as we note below, the Thatcher governments' attempts at imposing radical reforms in areas such as education and health without adequately consulting the relevant trade unions or representative professional bodies, merely yielded a host of implementation problems which necessitated consultation with those organizations at a later stage. Had they been consulted at the outset, then many, if not most, of the ensuing problems would probably have been foreseen and thus avoided. Of course, though, from a Thatcherite perspective, bodies such as the teachers' unions and the BMA were themselves part of the problem, intrinsically opposed to the governments' objectives from the outset, so Conservative ministers decided that there was little to consult them about.

Institutionalization of compromise

The emphasis on consultation noted above was often regularized and rendered routine via an elaborate system of committees and sundry advisory bodies. Jordan and Richardson cite a 1980 Report on Non-departmental Public Bodies which listed more than 1,500 advisory bodies in British government (Cmnd 7797, 1980: 1). It is not simply the number of such advisory bodies which is significant in this context, but also the representation on them of key organized interests. For example, one commentator noted that by 1949, trade unions were represented on no less than 60 advisory bodies (Allen, 1960: 34; see also, Taylor, 1993: 39), and this figure doubtless increased steadily as the number of such bodies themselves multiplied in subsequent decades.

In spite of their official 'non-departmental' status, many of them clearly corresponded to, or operated under the auspices of, particular government departments, such as the Advisory Committee on Animal Experiments, linked to the Home Office, or the Committee on Medical Aspects of Food Policy, which corresponded to – and doubtless with – the (then) Department of Health and Social Security (Jordan and Richardson, 1982: 92). In seeking to ensure that the relevant organized interests or interested parties have been involved in discussions preceding a policy initiative or reform, formal policy makers sought to ensure that useful advice and expert views could be elicited, while also enabling the participants to appreciate the rationale or necessity of what was being proposed. This, in turn, was intended to ensure that policies were generally deemed acceptable and legitimate to those affected by them, thereby minimizing the risk of opposition or conflict at a later stage, such as during implementation: 'making sure that, at every stage of the policy process, the right chairs have been warmed at the right committee tables by the right appropriate institutions' (Henderson, 1977: 189).

Development of exchange relationships

The development of policy communities in key policy subsystems clearly symbolizes this fifth aspect of the 'British policy style', for they reflect the manner in which clientelistic relations within particular 'sectors' entail exchanges of resources. As we noted in Chapter 5, the participants who constitute a policy community possess resources, such as professional knowledge and expertise, structural or administrative importance, political authority, etc., which effectively binds them together – while generally excluding actors who do not possess such attributes – in a mutually beneficial and reciprocal relationship.

In support of their claim that these characteristics collectively constituted a distinct British policy style, Jordan and Richardson refer to an observation by Jack Hayward, who, writing in the mid-1970s, had declared that:

Firstly, there are no explicit, over-riding medium or long-term objectives. Secondly, unplanned decision-making is incremental. Thirdly, hum-drum or unplanned decisions are arrived at by a continuous process of mutual adjustment between a plurality of autonomous policy-makers operating in the context of a highly fragmented multiple flow influence. Not only is plenty of scope offered to interest group spokesmen to shape the outcome by participation in the advisory process. The aim is to secure through bargaining at least passive acceptance of the decision by the interests affected.

(1974: 398–9)

The reference to 'incremental' decision taking is crucial here, for incrementalism eschews explicit consideration of policy makers' goals and objectives, either because these are treated as self-evident, and/or because the primary concern is to take decisions and adopt policies which are 'realistic' and practicable. In the context of such defining features as clientelism, negotiation, the institutionalization of compromise, what counted as 'realistic' and 'practicable' were usually policies which were – or would be – acceptable to the professional or organized interests affected. For policy makers to reflect explicitly on their longer-term goals and objectives was deemed futile if the consequent policies proved unacceptable to the 'client' groups, hence the prioritization of what was adjudged 'realistic' and 'practicable'. Consequently, there was 'a preparedness to settle individual policies without complete agreement about ends' (Jordan and Richardson, 1982: 93). The strong emphasis on incrementalism was further underpinned by 'sectorization', for this provided 'a means of avoiding the intellectual overload of attempting to weigh up all the options' (1982: 82). At the same time, they noted: 'The need to consult and negotiate with a specific set of groups concerned with each policy problem, of course, has a direct bearing on the nature of policy outcomes. Essentially, it normally leads to incremental policy change, irrespective of the party forming the government at any one time' (1982: 92).

However, Jordan and Richardson were advancing their notion of a distinct British policy style at a time when Margaret Thatcher had only been Prime Minister for three years, and had yet to develop most of her more radical policy initiatives. She and her government had also barely begun to confront, or bypass, various organized interests when formulating policy. As such, the veracity of Jordan and Richardson's characterization of a distinct 'British policy style' ostensibly appeared less and less tenable as the 1980s progressed. Yet in spite of the combative character of Thatcher's 'conviction conservatism', her rebarbative rhetoric, and the ideological inclinations of many of her governments' policies, Richardson subsequently maintained that the impact of Thatcherism had probably been exaggerated. This was partly because some of the economic and industrial changes which became prominent during the 1980s were already discernible in the 1970s, to the extent that between 1976 and 1979, it was James Callaghan's Labour government which formally abandoned the hitherto commitment to full employment, insisted that spending its way out of an economic crisis was no longer a viable option, and instigated – partly due to external (IMF) pressure – cuts in public expenditure. Certainly, Thatcher embraced these trends with considerable enthusiasm (rather than sorrowful reluctance, as Labour had done), but the important point here, according to writers such as Richardson, is that while May 1979 did herald the election of an ideologically-motivated and avowedly anticonsensus government, which actively sought to confront certain 'vested interests', and acquired a reputation for eschewing consultations with various organized interests, and introducing policies with which those interests disagreed or disapproved, thereby resulting in 'a much more conflictual relationship within the policy process' (Richardson, 1993: 96), there were also subsequent attempts at re-establishing consultative relationships with previously excluded groups or professional bodies at implementation stage:

> The destabilization of policy communities ... was almost invariably followed, however, by a return to the accepted values and norms of the policy process. Thus, once a sector had been 'shaken and stirred', the affected interests were then soothed by being invited back into the inner circle of negotiations with government.
>
> (Richardson, 1993: 97)

While insisting that the reforms themselves – or at least the principles underpinning them – were non-negotiable, Conservative ministers would subsequently seek 'to negotiate the implementation phase with the affected interests and to make significant concessions in that process' (Richardson, 1993: 97–8).

This trend back towards consultation with organized interests was most apparent after John Major had replaced Margaret Thatcher as Conservative Party leader and Prime Minister in November 1990. Not only was Major's own personality and leadership style more amenable to consultation and dialogue – even if, for various reasons, the thrust of many of his policies remained Thatcherite (Dorey, 1999a: 226–35) – it was also during the first half of the 1990s, during the course of Major's premiership, that various problems associated with the Thatcherite reforms of the late 1980s became (more) apparent. In a number of policy areas, such as education, for example, there was an explicit attempt at re-establishing – to varying degrees – relationships with organized interests which had been largely eschewed and excluded from policy formulation during the 1980s (Dorey, 1999b: 159),with the notable exception of the trade unions in general, who continued to be excluded from the bulk of economic, industrial and training policy making.

The main implications of Jordan and Richardson's concept of a British 'policy style' were effectively endorsed by another eminent political scientist, Richard Rose, in two of his books: *Do Parties Make a Difference?*, first published in 1979, but with a second edition in 1984, to take account of the first Thatcher government, and *Inheritance in Public Policy*, published (with Philip Davies) in 1994. Rose also rehearsed some of the key arguments in a 1990 article, 'Inheritance before Choice in Public Policy' (Rose, 1990). In *Do Parties Make a Difference?*, Rose argued that the formal ideological differences between the Conservative and Labour Parties had generally been belied by the broad similarities of many of their policies and measures when each was actually in government. Those commentators – often advocates of electoral reform, many of whom seemed to hanker after some form of coalition government in order to secure centrist and consensus politics in Britain – who lamented Britain's 'adversarial political system', in which two ideologically-motivated parties confronted each other, and whose alternation in Office was deemed to entail repeated swings from Left to Right and vice versa, and thus sharp, short-term changes in policy every few years based on partisanship, apparently failed to distinguish between what the parties and their spokespersons said, and what they actually did in practice; rhetoric was mistaken for reality.

The reality was that, in spite of the ostensibly gladiatorial confrontations and partisan jousting the House of Commons at Question Time, and the bitter allegations and counter-accusations which the parties levelled against each other in election campaigns, when either was in governmental office, in the period until 1979, the Conservative Party and the Labour Party each pursued broadly similar policies much of the time – to the chagrin of their more partisan backbenchers and activists who bemoaned their leadership's 'betrayal' of their party's principles or the alleged 'reneging' on manifesto commitments. After all, the 1945–79 period was (arguably) one of 'consensus politics – although some commentators dispute the extent, or even existence, of 'consensus politics' during this period (this debate is beyond out remit here, though) – in which the Labour and Conservative Parties, when in Office, generally upheld a commitment to a mixed economy (in which some key industries or utilities were publicly owned, i.e. nationalized), a welfare state, full employment, and partnership with the trade unions (see, for example, Dorey, 1995a: Chapters 1–4; Kavanagh and Morris, 1989). The reversal or repeal of the previous government's legislation or other measures following a general election victory was actually rather rare: the exception rather than the norm (and thus in sharp contrast to the image painted by the 'adversarialists'). For example, those who dispute the existence of a postwar consensus (for example, Pimlott, 1988) often cite the 1951–55 Churchill government's denationalization of the iron and steel industries, along with road haulage, which had been nationalized just a few years earlier by Clement Attlee's 1945–50 Labour government. Yet what is more notable is that these were the only industries which the Conservatives denationalized during their 13 years in office from 1951 until 1964; the other industries and utilities nationalized by the 1945–50 Labour government remained under public ownership throughout. Furthermore, even when the Conservatives denationalized iron and steel, they subjected it to close supervision via an Iron and Steel Board. The only other major reversal of policy following a change of government was the February-October 1974[1] Labour government's repeal of the Industrial Relations Act, which had been introduced in 1971 by Edward Heath's Conservative government. Yet the Conservatives themselves had virtually permitted the Act to fall into abeyance within months of enacting it, not least because of the strength of trade union opposition it engendered, coupled with the fact that a series of prominent court cases in early 1972 revealed flaws and inconsistencies in the Act. As such, the subsequent Labour government was to repeal an Act which had tacitly been laid to rest by the Conservative government which had enacted it in the first place.

One other notable feature of various policy initiatives or innovations which were enacted during the 1945–79 period was the extent to which the (governing) party which implemented them was not the party which would have been ideologically or instinctively

---

[1]There were two general elections in 1974, one in February, when Labour formed a minority government 34 seats short of an overall majority, and then an election in October 1974, when Labour was re-elected with an overall majority of 3 (which soon dissipated through defections and by-election defeats.).

expected to have adopted them. For example, it was the Conservatives who presided over the building of a total of over 470,000 local authority (council) houses in 1953 and 1954, a tally which, along with the simultaneous building of just over 150,000 private dwellings during the same two-year period, more than fulfilled Harold Macmillan's pledge in the 1951 election that a Conservative government would build 300,000 houses per year. It was also a Conservative government – led by Harold Macmillan – which, in 1962, steered Britain firmly in a neo-corporatist direction by establishing the National Economic Development Council (NEDC), which involved trade union leaders and employers' representatives meeting regularly with various Cabinet Ministers and senior civil servants to seek agreement on a range of economic and industrial policies. The same 1959–64 Conservative government also explicitly claimed that wages should no longer be based on free collective bargaining and 'market forces', but ought to be determined via incomes policies (thereby constituting a significant rejection of the party's *laissez-faire* philosophy).

This Conservative government also submitted Britain's first application to join the (then) European Economic Community (EEC). Meanwhile, it was a Conservative government which nationalized Rolls Royce in February 1971, to save the company from bankruptcy, and to avoid the concomitant loss of jobs. The same (1970–4) Conservative government also passed the 1972 Industry Act, which 'provided the government with sweeping powers, enabling it to channel state support into companies that it believed needed financial assistance' (Taylor, 1993: 200). This was just two years after Heath's Conservative Party had been elected to office pledging a massive reduction in state aid or taxpayers' subsidies to 'lame duck' industries, as part of a wider commitment to encouraging private enterprise, greater self-reliance (from the state) and a more competitive economy.

In another sphere of policy, the first postwar attempt at placing statutory curbs on the trade unions, due to growing concern about their increasing militancy and the detrimental impact on the economy of strike activity, was made in 1969 – albeit unsuccessfully – by Harold Wilson's 1966–70 Labour government (see Dorey, forthcoming, for an account of this episode), a full two years before the Conservatives made a similar attempt. It was also a Labour government, during the latter half of the 1970s (and as mentioned above) which actually abandoned the commitment to full employment, and imposed – or, rather, had imposed upon it by the IMF – cuts in public expenditure and welfare provision, and which began – on a very modest scale – selling shares in British Petroleum (BP).

In short, the 1945–79 period was characterized by a considerable degree of continuity and similarity in many of the policies and programmes pursued by Conservative and Labour governments, to the extent that the reversal or repeal of a predecessor's policies or legislation were the exception rather than the norm. Although this (relative) similarity and continuity of public policy can be explicated by reference to Jordan and Richardson's notion of a 'British policy style' – which both reflected and reinforced the postwar consensus to a large degree – other factors also doubtless further underpinned it, not least of these being the relatively non-ideological character of the party leaderships during much of the postwar period until the late 1970s. The Labour Party was generally led from its centre-Right: Clement Attlee was certainly no Left-wing ideologue, while Hugh Gaitskell and James Callaghan were both widely identified with the party's social democratic or revisionist 'wing'. Harold Wilson, meanwhile, although he had acquired something of a Left-wing image in the early 1950s, soon became an arch-pragmatist, more concerned, it seems with managing the various economic and political difficulties which beset his 1964–70 and 1974–6 premierships, while also desperately seeking to hold an increasingly fractious Labour Party together.

Many other senior or influential Labour Cabinet or Shadow Cabinet Ministers during the 1950s, 1960s and 1970s were also located on, or strongly identified, with the Party's social democratic or revisionist wing, most notably Anthony Crosland, Denis Healey, Douglas Jay, Roy Jenkins, David Owen and Shirley Williams. Indeed, the latter three left the Labour Party in March 1981, to form the Social Democratic Party[2], due to disillusion with Labour's lurch to the Left following the 1979 election defeat.

The Conservative Party, meanwhile, was largely led from its centre-Left or 'one nation' wing for most of the postwar period until 1979, with leaders such as Harold Macmillan (Conservative leader and Prime Minister from 1957 to 1963) personifying the paternalist strand of 'caring capitalism'. This strand was also represented or articulated by many other senior Conservatives during the latter half of the 1940s through to the 1970s, such as Rab Butler, Selwyn Lloyd, Ian Macleod, Reginald Maudling and Peter Walker. The influence of this strand of Conservatism was particularly evident in the party's stance towards industrial relations and trade unionism during the 1950s and early 1960s, with ministers consistently rejecting calls from sundry backbenchers and conference delegates for legislation to deal with strikes and/or the trade union closed shop (Dorey, 2002b). Meanwhile, the Conservative 1947 policy document, *The Industrial Charter*, explicitly accepted a regulated economy (thereby rejecting *laissez-faire* and unrestrained market forces) and the goal of full employment (Conservative and Unionist Central Office, 1947). Meanwhile, Edward Heath's apparent move to the Right, during the late 1960s and early 1970s, proved to be a short-lived guise, for by 1972 – and thereafter – he was an enthusiastic advocate of economic and industrial partnership, and defender of full employment (he consistently warned of the danger to social stability of tolerating high unemployment). Heath was also willing to condemn business behaviour or practices which he deemed to be 'the unacceptable face of capitalism' (something which one could not imagine his successor, Margaret Thatcher, ever doing).

The overall degree of policy continuity or similarity evinced by governments from 1945 to 1979, in the context of the other factors outlined above, led Rose to argue that in the short term, political parties did not normally make much difference. If parties were to make a significant difference, then they generally needed at least two terms in office, thereby giving them 8–10 consecutive years of governmental power. After all, Rose emphasised: 'A newly installed government does not take command of the ship of state when it is at anchor: instead, a new government lands on a ship that is moving with the prevailing currents' (1990: 267). This perspective was borne out by the 1979–90 Thatcher governments, for it was only during the second and third terms (1983–7 and 1987–1990 respectively) that she and her governments pursued the radical policies – such as privatization of British Gas and

---

[2]The Social Democratic Party merged with the Liberal Party in 1998 to become the Liberal Democrats.

British Telecom, the poll tax, the introduction of a National Curriculum in secondary education, reorganization of the NHS, outlawing of the trade union closed shop, etc. – which underpinned the concept of Thatcherism. Had Thatcher *not* been re-elected in June 1983, she would almost certainly have been deposed as Conservative Party leader, and been rendered a mere footnote in history, famous only for having being Britain's first female Prime Minister.

Subsequently, in *Inheritance in Public Policy*, Rose and Davies elaborated on some of the themes delineated in *Do Parties Make a Difference?* They explained that many policies and programmes became embedded, often over several decades, and thereby proved extremely difficult to repeal or reverse. Indeed, many policies, they explain, attract the support of client groups or their beneficiaries, which means that any subsequent attempt at reversing or repealing the programme(s) is likely to arouse electoral or institutional opposition, particularly if a policy community or other important/influential section of British society is likely to be affected. For example, Rose and Davies note that of the legislation still on the statute book in 1979, 36 per cent had been enacted before 1901, and almost 63 per cent had been enacted before 1951. In other words, more than a third of laws operational in 1979 had been introduced during the 19th century (1994: 28). Rose and Davies also observe that between 1946 and 1989, the 95 'inherited' (pre-1946) programmes were responsible for an additional £69 billion of public expenditure overall, whereas the 143 new programmes and policies introduced during this period (and still operational by 1989) increased public expenditure by 'only' £37 billion (1994: 150).

In this context it is perhaps not surprising that the 1979–90 Thatcher governments' clearly proclaimed commitment to cutting public expenditure – underpinned as it was by a clear ideological rationale – proved impossible to achieve. For example, between the financial years of 1979–80 and 1990–91, expenditure on social security increased by £18 billion, on health by £8 billion, on law and order by £5 billion and on defence by £4 billion.

Thus did Conservative ministers judiciously alter the meaning of 'cutting' public expenditure: rather than reducing it in absolute terms, they sought to slow down its rate of increase, so that it increased at a (s)lower rate than the rate of economic growth. This was also intended *pari passu* to secure a reduction in public expenditure as a proportion of GDP. Although the Thatcher governments did enjoy some limited success in this respect, public expenditure subsequently increased as a proportion of GDP under the Major and Blair governments, invariably oscillating in the 38–42 per cent range.

Of course, Rose was not claiming that policies and programmes never change, or that governments and parties make no difference whatsoever over time. Instead, he was drawing attention to the myriad constraints and pressures which impinge on governmental autonomy and limit the realistic choices and options available to policy makers.

The implications for public policy and the policy process in Britain

The clear implication of Jordan and Richardson's 'British policy style', and Rose's notion of 'inheritance in public policy', was that policy making in Britain was highly reactive and incremental, with politicians enjoying only limited success in changing public policy, certainly with regard to introducing significant reforms. At the macro or general level, Rose's critique depicted policy makers as being heavily constrained by the programmes and policy commitments bequeathed to them by their predecessors, so that governments generally required at least two consecutive terms in office in order to start effecting notable, and potentially long-lasting, changes. In the short term, though, governing parties made relatively little difference to public policy, with their first term of office largely taken up with tackling problems left behind by, or arising from the policies of, the out-going government. At the same time, the newly-appointed Cabinet would usually need a period of acclimatization, with ministers seeking both to familiarize themselves with the various issues affecting their department, and establishing a rapport with their senior civil servants, along with the leaders of the relevant organized interests in their particular policy subsystem.

Yet even if a senior minister settled in very quickly, and/or had a clear policy objective, he/she would often encounter a 'departmental philosophy' which was generally sceptical or suspicious of new policy ideas and objectives. Such 'philosophies' would often be deeply entrenched among senior civil servants in particular departments, and further reinforced if the ministry formed part of a policy community, whereupon departmental officials and one or two key organized interests would probably be strongly committed to existing policies or programmes. In such circumstances, new ministers, however ambitious or visionary, often found it virtually impossible, in their relatively brief – usually two years at most between Cabinet reshuffles – tenure at a department, successfully to challenge existing orthodoxies and long-cherished departmental perspectives.

All too often, the minister succumbed to the philosophy of the department, and was readily persuaded by their senior officials either that a proposed new policy was simply not practicable, or that 'the time is not yet right', or that the proposal was 'certainly worth exploring', whereupon the mandarins would pass it to an official committee and/or conduct desultory consultations with relevant outside organizations, but with the real objective being to let the issue fall off the policy agenda: the minister would soon be reshuffled, or become preoccupied with other, more urgent, issues, and his/her proposal cast back into the primeval policy soup.

What should be emphasized, though, is that until the 1970s, there was, arguably, a broad consensus in British politics – although, as noted above, some political scientists and political historians dispute this, providing for a debate which is beyond our remit here – based on a shared commitment to full employment, Keynesian economic management, a mixed economy (with some key industries or utilities publicly owned), partnership with the trade unions and a welfare state. This welfare state reflected a common commitment to eradicating poverty and not permitting socio-economic inequalities to become excessive (even if what was deemed 'excessive' could not be clearly defined), providing services such as health and education free at the point of access – funded out of general taxation, of which the rich paid more – and promoting such principles as 'equality of opportunity'.

This consensus over broad policy goals and governmental objectives meant that irrespective of the formal ideological differences between the Conservative and Labour parties, and their verbal attacks on each other in Parliament, and during election campaigns, when either was in government, it generally pursued the policies and policy goals identified above. When Edward Heath's Conservative government did try to depart from the consensus in 1970–71, and encountered industrial unrest and criticism, it hurriedly switched back to policies of the consensus, desperately seeking to win back the trust of the trade unions, reverse the rise in unemployment, and intervening extensively in the economy, to the extent that it nationalized Rolls Royce in order to prevent bankruptcy and the ensuing loss of tens of thousands of jobs.

However, along with a broad commitment by the Labour and Conservative parties to certain policy goals, what also characterized the postwar consensus (criticisms of the concept notwithstanding!) was a concomitant belief in the apparent virtue of securing agreement from the relevant policy actors, particularly organized interests. As Richardson noted, the emphasis on consultation was both normative and practical. It was normative because there was a common assumption by many politicians and senior civil servants that those affected by particular policies *ought*, almost as a matter of courtesy, to be consulted, particularly if particular changes were being considered. There was also a tacit belief that many policies would enjoy greater legitimacy if they followed consultations with relevant or affected bodies.

At the same time, it was also widely accepted that there was a good *practical* reason for consulting with relevant organized interests or individuals, namely that public policies were much more likely to prove successful if they followed such dialogue. Consultation could highlight problems with the existing policy or flag potential problems with a proposed new policy. In either case, appropriate modifications could be carried out. Furthermore, it was widely recognized that those organized interests which could offer valuable advice and expertise when a policy was being formulated, were also likely to be able to affect the implementation of the ensuing policy. Failure either to consult, or to heed the advice of the relevant bodies, might well alienate the bodies concerned, possibly to the extent that they obstructed the implementation of the policy.

Changes and developments in British policy making since the 1980s

As the chapters in this book have shown, there have been a number of significant changes to policy making in Britain since the1980s, reflected and reinforced by both the increased number and range of policy actors – be they individuals or institutions – and their changing roles. This, in turn, has yielded corresponding changes in the relationships between the various policy actors, and the modes of interaction between them. The key changes which have occurred since the mid-1970s (the last decade of the 'old' British policy style) are listed in Table 9.1, and discussed more fully below.

Challenging sectorization within the core executive

The notion of sectorization which Jordan and Richardson referred to as a key feature of the 'British policy style' was inextricably linked to two other features of policy making in postwar Britain, namely the *relatively* self-contained or autonomous policy subsystems or 'funnels' based around, and flowing largely top-down from, government departments. Second, there was the prevalence of policy communities, deriving from the close and

Table 9.1   Main changes in the British policy process and policy style, 1975–2005

1975	2005
Sectorization and departmentalism	Interdepartmental coordination
Extensive vertical segmentation via policy subsystems	Greater horizontal linkages and coordination across policy subsystems
Policy communities strong and autonomous	Policy communities less closed or stable, and thus somewhat weaker
Many ministers departmental managers first and foremost	Many ministers agenda setters, 'innovators' and policy activists
Civil service advice sought prior to policy formulation	Special advisers and experts play greater role in proffering advice as well as policy development. Civil service role increasingly that of policy management and service 'delivery'
Policy making predominantly reactive (respond to problems when they arise)	Policy making increasingly proactive (anticipate problems in advance)
'Muddling through'	More evidence-based policy making
Policies from within core executive	Policies from abroad (policy transfer)
Unitary state applied policies nationally	Local level experiments and pilot schemes
Make existing policies work	Develop new policies
Government	Governance
Domestic/national policy	Devolution, Europeanization and globalization
Indivisible sovereignty	Pooled sovereignty

closed relationship between particular departments and their 'client' organized interests. In a relatively stable situation, the emphasis was on policy continuity, and where change was deemed necessary, a premium was placed on reactive, incremental policy initiatives whose departure from the status quo was minimized as far as practicably possible. Certainly, 'outsiders' generally remained excluded, but if they were occasionally incorporated, the effect – intentional or otherwise – was often to neutralize and assimilate them, thereby inculcating them with the norms and values of the existing members of the policy community.

Now, at the beginning of the 21st century, although much policy making can still be viewed in terms of particular departments and policy subsystems – sectorization – there has also developed a somewhat greater degree of fluidity and flexibility. Departmental independence and vertical policy segmentation are less prevalent and pervasive, both reflecting and reinforcing greater instability and uncertainty. The emergence of new problems and issues onto the policy agenda has heralded greater horizontal or interdepartmental policy making which cuts across traditional policy sectors, as well as the involvement of a greater number of policy actors beyond the core executive and traditional policy communities. Of course, there have always been cross-cutting policy issues and interdepartmental policies, even in the heyday of Jordan and Richardson's 'British policy style', but from the late 1980s onwards, these have undergone both a quantitative and qualitative change.

Quantitatively, there are now many more cross-cutting, interdepartmental policy issues, deriving from the need to develop 'joined-up' solutions to such problems as agricultural crises and aspects of food production, environmental pollution, increasing levels of obesity (and other health risks deriving from changing lifestyles), juvenile delinquency, social exclusion and transport. Qualitatively, these interdepartmental or 'multisector' policy issues are often more complex, with more variegated linkages between the myriad policy actors increasingly involved in consultation, coordination and the implementation of public policies.

At the level of the core executive, as we explained in Chapters 3 and 4, there has been a significant expansion in the number of Special Advisers appointed, not only by the Prime Minister, but also by Cabinet Ministers, most of whom now appoint two such advisers, but with larger departments, such as the Treasury, appointing four or five. The increased use of Special Advisers reflects the desire or perceived need of Prime Ministers and their Cabinet colleagues for a greater range of advice, and more original ideas, so that they are less reliant on senior civil servants. This is certainly not to say that civil servants no longer proffer advice and engage in 'fact-finding' for ministers, and thus have no role in policy formulation, but that this role is less prevalent than it was 30 years ago, and that senior civil servants are now required to focus more (than they used to) on policy management, and supervise the 'delivery' of policies. This crucial development is confirmed by Richards and Smith when they observe that:

> today, there is a splitting of roles, with Ministers concerning themselves with policy-making, and officials focusing on the 'management' of the policy process. What we are seeing is a significant change in the role of officials as their traditional monopoly of advice is being eroded, and Ministers are turning to a myriad of organisations and advisers for policy inputs.

(2004: 120)

Consequently, even when some senior civil servants do retain a role in offering policy advice to ministers, they no longer enjoy the exclusivity which they once enjoyed; their access to a minister is not as privileged as it used to be. Their advice is but one source which more proactive ministers now tap in to when developing policies.

Alongside the increasing deployment of Special Advisers, there are other institutional innovations at core executive level which reflect and reinforce the increasing range and complexity of linkages between departments and across traditional policy sectors. For example, we discussed in Chapter 4 the enhanced roles of both the 10 Downing Street

Policy Directorate (Unit before 2001), and the Cabinet Office, both of which play a vital role in the pursuit of 'joined-up government', and thus in preventing a reassertion of departmentalism and sectorization. As we explained, both of these bodies play a coordinating role, seeking to ensure that policies are compatible with the government's overall objectives and strategies, while also supervising their development and implementation via the relevant ministers and departments.

Furthermore, as we observed in the previous chapter, there has been a proliferation of task forces and 'working groups', usually comprising ministers and/or civil servants, representatives from public, private and voluntary sector bodies, and individual experts. These themselves reflect and reinforce Tony Blair's professed desire for a much greater degree of joined-up government, but they are also emblematic of the shift towards governance, whereby policy making and implementation occur at various levels and via a greater number of policy arenas and actors, both vertically and horizontally.

The partial transcendence of departmentalism and sectorization also reflects and reinforces two other trends with regard to the policy process within the core executive in contemporary Britain. First, as discussed in Chapters 3 and 4, senior ministers themselves have generally become more 'activist' in terms of their approach to policy making. With regard to Norton's typology of ministerial styles delineated in Chapter 3, more ministers today can be classified as 'commanders', or to use the typology advanced by Marsh, Smith and Richards, ministers are increasingly acting as 'agenda setters' and 'policy initiators'. This trend is doubtless reflected and reinforced by the increased role of Special Advisers, the Downing Street Policy Directorate and the Cabinet Secretariat in monitoring and 'chasing-up' the work of senior ministers and their departments. An increasing number of Cabinet Ministers are therefore adopting a more proactive role in developing policies and generating new ideas.

The second trend emanating from the above developments is the accelerated downgrading of the Cabinet as a detailed decision-taking forum. Although it has long been widely recognized by political scientists that weekly – until the 1960s, often twice weekly – three-hour meetings of the Cabinet are not conducive to detailed discussions of public policy, particularly if they were highly technical or specialized, and/or only concerned one minister and their department, the Cabinet's role has diminished further since the 1980s, with Cabinet meetings under Tony Blair often lasting not longer than 1½ hours. Although some writers attribute this to the style or 'presidentialization' of recent Prime Ministers, it can also be viewed as an entirely rational response to trends in contemporary policy making, whereby ministers, whose departments are involved in a particular policy, meet via bilaterals or trilaterals (when the public expenditure implications of a policy initiative warrant an input by the Chancellor), Cabinet committees, or other interdepartmental forums, such as 'working groups'. Of course, an increasing range of polices will also entail senior ministers in discussions with their counterparts in the EU, particularly via the Council of Ministers. These alternative arenas for the development of public policy further reduce the role of the Cabinet as a policy-making body in the core executive, although it still plays a role in formally approving policy proposals, and providing strategic oversight (although as we have already noted, this last role is increasingly fulfilled by the Policy Directorate and Cabinet Secretariat).

Destabilized policy communities

The increasing range of interdepartmental issues and cross-sector forums for developing policies, has, in turn, served to weaken some of the policy communities which prevailed prior to the 1990s. As we noted in Chapter 5, policy communities entailed a very close and mutually beneficial relationship between a government department and one or two 'insider' organized interests. However, the emergence of new or more complex problems has served to undermine the previously privileged position of certain organized interests, as groups – and increasingly, individuals (Special Advisers, experts, etc.) – find themselves being co-opted or incorporated into the policy process. Admittedly, their inclusion is often alongside, not instead of, established groups who previously formed the basis of a policy community, but nonetheless, this has serious implications for the traditional notion that many policies in Britain were the product of a closed relationship between individual departments and their 'key' client pressure group(s).

As we noted in Chapter 5, for example, the 1990s saw the formerly close and closed relationship between the NFU and MAFF weakened rather by the increased input and involvement of other organized interests, as well as medical or environmental experts who provided scientific evidence about the risks of certain methods of modern, intensive, agricultural production. In so doing, the NFU was undermined somewhat and viewed, by critics, as part of the problem of agricultural policy making in Britain. The abolition of MAFF following the 2001 general election – which had itself been delayed slightly by the foot-and-mouth epidemic – both reflected and reinforced the less privileged position of the NFU in the agricultural policy process – although this is certainly not to suggest it has been reduced to insignificance (see the chapter by Wyn Grant (2005) in the companion text, *Developments in British Public Policy*, for a fuller discussion of agricultural policy making).

Similarly, we noted how the 1990s witnessed a partial destabilizing of the transport policy community, as the dominant paradigm of private (car) transport and road building was challenged on a range of environmental grounds, as well as the manner in which certain pressure groups opposed to further road building made increasing use of alternative arenas, most notably public inquiries, to challenge proposals for the building of new roads, particularly in rural areas (see the chapter by Nick Robinson (2005) in the companion text, *Developments in British Public Policy*, for a fuller discussion of transport policy making).

Certainly, environmental challenges to the transport policy community's dominant paradigm of private (car) transport and road building have been buttressed by medical knowledge, as evidence has been discovered linking traffic fumes and exhaust emissions with various respiratory problems, such as asthma, as well as higher risks of lung cancer later in life, with young children identified as particularly vulnerable (their push-chairs or buggies, are effectively at the same physical level as car exhaust pipes, and they are therefore more likely to be breathing in 'pure' fumes) (*The Independent on Sunday*, 19 September 2004). Traffic exhaust emissions and fumes have also been identified as one of several toxic pollutants – along with others, such as pesticides, industrial effluents and some chemicals used in processed food – underpinning a significant increase in diseases of the brain, such as Alzheimer's and senile dementia (*The Observer*, 15 August 2004).

We have therefore seen extant policy communities being increasingly destabilized by the emergence of new, often scientific, evidence, which serves to challenge some of the principles and practices of the actors involved. In such instances, a 'paradigm shift' may occur, leading to a restructuring of the policy community, either entailing the incorporation of a somewhat wider range of organized interests and/or the adoption of rather different values and objectives to those which were previously hegemonic in that policy subsystem. Hence we have seen scientific evidence raise concerns about the impact on the environment or public health of certain farming methods, cigarette smoking (and 'passive smoking') and increased car usage and road-building, which, in turn, has contributed towards the destabilizing of the former agricultural, tobacco and transport policy communities respectively.

Policy transfer

We noted in Chapter 2 the concept and increasing importance of 'policy transfer', which reflects a greater willingness on the part of British policy makers to look elsewhere, often to other countries, for ideas and inspiration to tackle issues which have reached the institutional agenda. The two most obvious examples, we observed, were the adoption of US-style 'work-fare' (or welfare-into-work) schemes for tackling unemployment, particularly among the young, and the 1993 launch of the CSA, following a visit by Peter Lilley, the then Secretary of State for Social Security, to the US State of Wisconsin. By this time, though, the Conservatives had already been eliciting the views of the US sociologist, Charles Murray, who warned ministers (based on experience in the USA) of the damaging and destabilizing social consequences of permitting continued increases in the number of unmarried mothers on welfare.

Since the 1990s, policy transfer, and policy learning, have become more prevalent in Britain, both reflecting and reinforcing the trend towards more proactive Cabinet Ministers, and their quest for alternative or additional (to that traditionally provided by senior civil servants) sources of policy advice and inspiration. In the autumn of 2003, for example, the Health Secretary, John Reid, visited Washington, USA, to seek advice and ideas on how to make the NHS more efficient. Recognizing that the involvement of the private sector in US health care might make his visit controversial in Britain, Reid insisted that: 'Just because we in Britain reject the insurance-based health system run by private providers doesn't mean that we cannot learn lessons from how such systems operate elsewhere.' Reid's visit to Washington also provided a further illustration of the increasing use of experts, for the Health Secretary was accompanied by Professor Chris Ham, an academic expert on the NHS and health care policy, and head of the Department of Health's strategy unit (*The Independent on Sunday*, 19 October 2003).

Another example of British policy makers looking overseas for inspiration concerned the April 2004 launch of a new scheme to re-educate and rehabilitate men convicted of violence against women. Such men would be obliged to attend classes which would challenge their negative stereotypes and sexist attitudes about women and women's role in society. It was envisaged that this, in turn, would encourage such men to learn less aggressive or abusive ways of expressing themselves, thereby reducing levels of domestic violence in Britain. This scheme, involving weekly attendance for up to 10 months, was based on a similar programme operated in Duluth, Minnesota (*The Observer*, 8 February 2004).

Individual cities are also beginning to look abroad for ideas and inspiration on occasion to see if a new policy has proved successful, and thus worthy of adoption. For example, in the autumn of 2004, health officials and councillors from Manchester embarked on a fact-finding visit to Dublin, to examine the impact of a ban on smoking in public places and workplaces in the Irish capital. The visiting delegation was considering a ban on workplace smoking in Manchester, and wanted to see whether such a ban had proved successful in Dublin. The visit also included a meeting with the Irish Health Minister, Micheál Martin, who explained that prior to imposing the smoking ban in Dublin, officials had visited New York to evaluate how successful a similar ban had been across the Atlantic: Manchester was considering adopting a policy on the basis of its success in Dublin, and Dublin had adopted the policy on the basis of its success in New York (Carter, 2004: 12–13).

Meanwhile, during autumn 2004, senior officers from London's Metropolitan Police visited Johannesburg, South Africa, to look at a new form of policing, involving rapid response units monitoring crime and suspicious behaviour via CCTV. This often enabled the police to arrive at the scene of a crime within 60 seconds, and thereby apprehend the criminals in the act, which also made it easier to secure convictions. It was said that this new mode of policing had cut street crime by about 80 per cent since the late 1990s (*The Sunday Times*, 7 November 2004).

Evidence-based policy making

The recourse to policy transfer is itself aligned to a more general trend towards evidence-based policy making in contemporary Britain. Rather than merely 'muddling through' by making gradual, reactive adjustments to existing policies, British policy makers are increasingly commissioning or conducting research into problems, in order to gain a better understanding of the underlying causes, and thereby develop policies which are more likely successfully to tackle the problem. For example, the Blair governments' approach to law-and-order issues is significantly different to that associated with Old Labour (in spite of the recognition that socio-economic environment and background play a notable part in shaping behaviour and potential criminality). Certainly, a 'desire for "evidence– based" policy making has seen a fresh appetite for assimilating criminological research into policy' (Randall, 2004: 183).

This relatively recent recourse to evidence-based policy making has been reflected and reinforced by other trends noted above, such as: the partial destabilizing or restructuring of various policy communities (whose former dominance has itself sometimes been undermined by new evidence which challenges or undermines their previous normative paradigms and shared values); the emergence of more policy-innovating or proactive Cabinet Ministers; the downgrading of the civil service's policy formulation role (towards a greater emphasis on policy management and delivery); the appointment of Special Advisers; the greater use of 'working groups' and 'task forces', whose membership often includes academic or professional experts from the relevant policy subsystem(s); the restructuring of the Prime Minister's Policy Directorate (formerly Unit), as well as the reorganization of the Cabinet Office; the enhanced role of departmental select committees, coupled with the gradually increasing adoption of prelegislative inquiries by these committees.

This recent trend towards evidence-based policy making also signifies something of a shift away from the older, incremental approach, whereby policy makers seemed to pride themselves on 'muddling through', and generally contented themselves with marginal and minor adjustments to a deficient policy. In this context, the reliance on 'bureaucratic accommodation', entailing an emphasis on achieving maximum consensus between a subsystem's key policy actors, effectively precluded a more fundamental evidence-based approach: 'What is acceptable to the affected parties?' was generally deemed more important than a more rational or root-and-branch responses to a problem, which would have entailed consideration of a range of options prior to making a decision. Or to put it another way, rather than pursue evidence-based policy making to discover 'what works?', the *a priori* assumption seemed to be that without the agreement of the 'affected parties' achieved through 'bureaucratic accommodation', nothing was likely to work. Thus were evidence-based policies effectively ruled out by default.

Pilot schemes for new policies

A further manifestation of the increasing recourse to evidence-based policy making is the use of pilot schemes prior to the nationwide introduction of new policies. By testing new initiatives at local or regional level, ministers can gauge their efficacy in terms of the intended results and objectives, as well as ensuring that the actual administration of the scheme is effective and practicable. Only if both of these aspects yield a positive response is the policy initiative likely to be adopted officially, and subsequently implemented nationwide.

For example, the above-mentioned programme for re-educating men who physically abuse women is not only based on a similar scheme in the USA (and thus an example of policy transfer), it was also tested in London and West Yorkshire prior to being implemented throughout Britain in April 2004 (*The Observer*, 8 February 2004). Meanwhile, David Blunkett's 2004 announcement that the Home Office planned to introduce a national identity card – albeit phased in over several years – followed a pilot scheme, whereby the residents of a small (un-named) town used a prototype ID card for six months. This was intended to enable departmental officials to gauge citizens' responses and calculate the costs involved, whereupon the findings could then be incorporated into the national ID card scheme (*The Guardian*, 27 August 2003).

The Home Office has also been making extensive use of pilot schemes with regard to measures to tackle antisocial behaviour. Policy innovations such as Anti-social Behaviour Orders (ASBOs), and various on-the-spot-fines for minor offences or disorderly behaviour, have invariably been tested through pilot schemes initially, to gauge their effectiveness at local level, prior to implementing them on a national basis. Meanwhile, a White Paper on police reform, published in November 2004, included proposals for a new form of community-based 'reassurance policing', entailing local-based teams comprising a sergeant, two constables and three comminity support officers, who would seek to establish close links with the community which they patrolled. This initiative was not only intended to tackle crime more effectively, but to reassure local people who lived in fear of crime, and/or who felt that the police had become too remote. This initiative followed a successful pilot scheme by police in Merseyside, wherepon the Home Office sought to extend it throughout the country (*The Observer*, 7 November 2004).

The increasing use of such pilot schemes also reduces the likelihood of policies encountering one of the problems which Dunleavy identified as a key characteristic of British 'policy disasters', namely 'scale aggregation' (1995: 59–60). He suggests that one reason (among several others) why controversial policies, such as the Poll Tax, and the CSA, proved so 'disastrous', was that they were each introduced throughout England and Wales (the Poll Tax was introduced in Scotland in 1989, a year earlier than in England and Wales, but ministers apparently ignored the problems which arose) on a national basis, rather than being 'piloted' on a local or regional basis first. Had the Poll Tax, for example, been subject to a pilot scheme in a few English and Welsh towns or cities, the problems of implementation, enforceability and non-compliance which it subsequently encountered would almost certainly have been identified much earlier, and thereby led to the modification – if not the abandonment – of the Poll Tax prior to its country-wide introduction in April 1990.

The subsequent use of pilot schemes suggests that many policy makers have learnt from such experiences, and increasingly recognize that if future policy disasters are to be avoided or minimized, then politically controversial or administratively complex policy initiatives should initially be tested at local level. The evidence obtained from such pilot schemes and studies can then be evaluated and incorporated into the policy if and when it is subsequently adopted and implemented nationally. In this respect, pilot schemes also buttress the increasing recourse to evidence-based policy making referred to previously.

Furthermore, *de facto* pilot schemes are likely to be provided as a consequence of the trend towards governance, whereby policy initiatives successfully pursued in particular regions are monitored and subsequently adopted by other cities or regions, and possibly by central government itself. In this respect, devolution, and the trend towards regional government and governance, offers new scope for governing bodies in one part of the country to look around and see 'what works' in other parts of Britain. Where a new policy appears to have proved successful in one part of the country, it is likely to be introduced in other districts or regions too. For example, the unexpected success of 'congestion-charging' in London, having been introduced amidst considerable controversy in February 2003, has led other cities – including Cardiff and Edinburgh – to announce definite plans for similar schemes, while in other cities, such as Bristol, 'congestion-charging' was 'under discussion' or on the city council's institutional agenda (Jowit, 2004: 5).

Devolution

The former 'British policy style' was also predicated on the existence of a unitary state, in which Scotland and Wales were largely subject to laws and policies emanating from Westminster and Whitehall (although Scotland always retained a degree of relative autonomy by virtue of its own educational and legal systems, which both reflected and reinforced a distinctive Scottish culture and sense of distinctiveness north of the border). This relative autonomy has been significantly enhanced by the establishment of a Scottish Parliament in 1999, which has been granted legislative powers over a relatively wide range of policy areas, as well as limited – and, as yet, unused – tax-raising powers. Wales, meanwhile, was granted a directly-elected Assembly, albeit without primary legislative or revenue-raising powers.

Consequently, devolution to Scotland and Wales has occasioned increasing policy divergence between Scotland, Wales and England. As we noted in Chapter 8, Scotland abolished 'section 28' and outlawed fox hunting some time before similar legislation was passed by the House of Commons for England. Scotland also used devolution to forge a somewhat different path from England/Westminster with regard to a wide range of education policies, including abolition of tuition fees. In Wales, meanwhile, in spite of its rather more limited powers, the National Assembly has also exhibited policy divergence (from England/ Westminster) in matters pertaining to education, health and transport in Wales.

It is doubtful whether some of these policy initiatives have been warmly welcomed in 10 Downing Street, but then the whole point of devolution – in decentralizing power and policy making closer to the people directly affected – is to facilitate diversity and difference between the regions within a nation. This is particularly vexatious for a Westminster-based administration which consistently emphasizes its desire for 'joined-up government', for devolution and its concomitant divergence and diversity of public policy have revealed 'the potential for a dis-United Kingdom', and this is obviously 'proving a hard pill to swallow':

> Devolved governments do their own thing. They elect first ministers the UK government does not want to deal with. They adopt policies the UK government does not approve of, which embroil the centre in disputes not of its own making ... policy networks implement and vary policies in ways the centre dislikes.
>
> (Rhodes et al., 2003: 165)

Of course, devolution itself is a prime example of the trend towards governance, and the manner in which policy making in Britain is now conducted at more levels, and involves a greater number of actors, drawn from both the public and private spheres, as well as from the voluntary sector with regard to social policy especially.

Europeanization

While devolution represents one major form of governance, and a (partial) transfer of power downwards from London, Europeanization (and globalization) represent the other major manifestations of governance, and the erosion of national autonomy from above. As European integration continues apace, so an increasing number of policy subsystems in Britain will be affected, and departmental autonomy sometimes impinged upon as a result. However, as we noted in Chapters 4 and 8, Europeanization is something of a dialectical process, for while Euro-scepticism in Britain depicts it as a relentless, top-down, imposition of EU policies on Whitehall and Westminster, it can also assist departments in pursuing policy goals which they – or Britain in general – would be unable to achieve if acting in splendid isolation. As we noted in Chapters 4 and 8, some departments have actually embraced Europeanization, viewing it as a means of enhancing their ability to achieve particular policy goals. Indeed, occasionally, departments might be able influence the EU itself, and 'up-load' particular policies, or act as 'pace-setters' *vis-à-vis* other member states.

Furthermore, while its critics portray European integration as representing a corresponding diminution of Britain's national autonomy and parliamentary sovereignty, it can also be viewed more favourably as a manifestation of 'pooled sovereignty', whereby nation-states achieve far more for their citizens, by sharing policy making competencies and capacities, than they could achieve by acting in isolation.

Globalization

Similarly, globalization is also a dialectical phenomenon. Clearly, by virtue of being locked into a global economy, British policy makers enjoy less autonomy than 30 years ago with regard to various economic, industrial and labour market policies, for adoption of the 'wrong' policy in these spheres may well prompt a 'flight of capital', as multinationals shift investments and production abroad, to regimes with lower taxes or unit labour costs for example.

However, this perspective of the impact of globalization needs to be qualified in two ways. First, as we noted in the previous chapter, it is not always or automatically the case that companies will relocate to countries with the lowest rates of tax or expenditure, because minimal taxes and expenditure might also mean minimal infrastructure, or a low-skill workforce due to under-investment in education and training. This might not be what a company wants; it might actually seek a country in which there is relatively high expenditure on infrastructure, such as good transport links, or fairly high levels of investment in education and training, to ensure an educated or skilled workforce.

Second, as with the EU, the limitations imposed on the autonomy of British policy makers by globalization are often compensated for by the opportunities afforded to tackle problems which cannot be adequately addressed at the national level alone. In a world increasingly characterized by problems and events which are not confined – or whose impact is not confined – to one country alone, Britain's involvement in a range of international bodies can facilitate fruitful cooperation and partnership with policy makers from other countries, which, in turn, can yield more effective policies to tackle such problems as drug trafficking and global warming, for example.

Of course, the phenomenon of policy transfer discussed above can itself be viewed as a manifestation of the internationalization of public policy, as countries and national governments (or other domestic policy actors) – and even individual cities – increasingly look abroad for policy ideas and inspiration.

Conclusion

In the context of the above changes, the role of government and the state has itself undergone a somewhat paradoxical change. The rhetoric of the 1980s, particularly from Thatcherite Conservatives, proudly proclaimed that the state was being 'rolled back' and government intervention (interference) greatly reduced. Since then, under the Major and Blair governments, the rhetoric has continued to imply a reduced role for the state, due to the type of developments noted in Chapter 8, namely 'agencification', an enhanced role for the private sector and voluntary bodies in service delivery (a mixed economy of policy implementation), devolution, Europeanization and globalization. With the state apparently having been 'hollowed out', it might be expected that British government would now be weaker, and play a lesser role in the policy process.

In fact, it would be more accurate to claim that instead of having been 'rolled back', the state has been restructured, and that in many policy areas, government intervention has not so much diminished as manifested itself in different guises. Indeed, Richardson is among those who believe that since 1979, 'government intervention has increased quite considerably' (1994: 179), and that even 'by the mid-1980s, the balance of power has shifted decisively in favour of government in terms of setting the agenda and initiating policy change' (2000: 1010). After all, he points out: 'From the perspective of those groups now affected by increased governmental intervention at the sectoral level – for example, teachers, doctors, lawyers, university lecturers, water companies – the 'state' is now considerably more intrusive' (1994: 179).

Yet government remained heavily dependent on the cooperation of various other policy actors to ensure the successful implementation of many policies, and this dependency has clearly increased in the context of agencification, devolution and the general expansion of the private and voluntary sectors.

Hence the shift from government as traditionally defined (a single body imposing political decisions in a top-down manner) to governance, where 'the government' is but one of many actors in the policy process, albeit the key one overall, However, by virtue of being but one of many policy actors, British governments now have to deploy new methods to achieve policy success, hence the emphasis today on: 'joined-up government', in order to achieve greater coordination and overcome sectorization; the incorporation of a wider range of individuals and organizations (Special Advisers, task forces, sector working groups, etc.) to proffer advice when a new policy is being formulated or drafted; regulation, to ensure that those actors responsible for the implementation of public policy actually administer policies and programmes in a manner which ensures their effectiveness and success.

Hence the increasing extent to which funding is linked to compliance and success by 'street level bureaucrats' in terms of achieving the policy objectives decreed by senior ministers. Of course, to evaluate the extent to which such compliance or success has been attained, there has been a vast expansion in the number regulatory bodies and 'audits' to measure and monitor service delivery in the privatized industries and public sector. Hence, as we noted in Chapter 8, Moran's observations about the rise of the 'regulatory state' (Moran 2000; 2001; see also Richardson, 1994), and Power's notion about the growth of the 'Audit Society' (1994; 1997). The transition from government to governance does not mean that the state is less active and more *laissez-faire*, but that its activities and mode of intervention are of a qualitatively different character than previously, and that different means are now deployed in order to ensure that the increased range of policy actors and service providers act in accordance with the overall objectives of central government.

Glossary

All-party Committee   Parliamentary committee comprising MPs from any of the political parties, with a shared interest in a particular policy area. Much more broad-ranging in their topics and areas of interest, and hence much more numerous, than the backbench subject committees.

Backbench subject committee   Parliamentary committee in each of the main political parties, comprising MPs from the party who have a shared interest in a particular policy area. Often corresponding closely to the policy areas covered by the main government departments, hence they are far fewer in number than the All-party committees. Can provide a useful channel of communication between the governing party's MPs and the relevant minister(s), and may occasionally or indirectly influence particular policies.

Bilaterals   Meetings between two ministers, such as Prime Minister and a Cabinet Minister, Prime Minister and Chancellor, Chief Secretary to the Treasury and a 'spending' minister, or two senior ministers whose respective departments have a common concern over a policy initiative or problem, on which they need to work together.

Cabinet Office   Comprising six secretariats and four 'units', the Cabinet Office facilitates the work of the Cabinet and its various committees, while also coordinating the work of ministers and their departments. Also plays a vital role in helping the Prime Minister to oversee the development and progress of the government's policies and overall strategy.

Core executive   The key individuals and institutions concerned with policy making and coordination, at the heart of the British political system. In particular, the core executive comprises the Prime Minister, Cabinet and its ministers (particularly the senior ones), Cabinet committees, the Cabinet Office, government departments, senior civil servants, along with their 'official' committees, and Special Advisers.

Departmentalism   (i) The operational philosophy and outlook which has become embedded in a department over a long period of time, and which shapes its approach to particular policy issues; (ii) the tendency of some Cabinet Ministers to 'go native', and promote or defend their department's interests first and foremost, in Cabinet or Cabinet committee, possibly to the neglect of the Cabinet's overall objectives or strategy.

Differentiated polity   Term used to characterize the contemporary British political system, whereby the 'hollowing-out' or 'rolling back' of the state has apparently resulted in a more fragmented system, with both more levels and more policy actors. Inextricably linked to the notion of *governance* (see below), it has clear implications for the policy process, namely that the involvement of more actors at various levels – national, subnational, regional and local – as well as from the public, private and voluntary sectors, renders much policy making and implementation more complex and messy, with a premium placed on coordination, and with central government 'steering' rather than simply directing or controlling.

Europeanization   The increasing influence and impact of the European Union on public policies in Britain, and the manner in which Britain's policy-making institutions are responding and adapting to this trend.

Evidence-based policy making   Developing policies on the basis of 'what works', with policy makers examining the impact and evaluating the success of 'pilot schemes' before implementing a policy more generally or widely. Can also involve policy transfer, whereby the success of a policy implemented elsewhere (in another city, region or country) is evaluated before being adopted by other policy makers. Represents an attempt at instilling greater rationality into policy making.

Globalization   The increasing interconnectedness and interdependence of countries and their economic, political and social systems, and the increasingly international nature of various problems (AIDS, drug trafficking, pollution, terrorism, etc.). Usually viewed in terms of the constraints which globalization increasingly places on national policy makers and domestic public policies (particularly economic policies), and the growing need for international cooperation or coordination *vis-à-vis* public policy.

Governance   The trend, since the 1980s, towards increasing fragmentation and multiplication of policy making arenas, and a growing number of policy actors at national, regional and local levels. Leads to a growing need for bargaining, exchange of resources and contracts between a plethora of policy actors at different levels vertically, and across a range of policy sectors horizontally, with central government often confined to the nonetheless vitally important roles of coordination, steering, supervision, strategic oversight and target setting.

Incrementalism   Concept popularized by Charles Lindblom, referring to the step-by-step approach to developing public policy. Claims to be a 'realist' approach, in that it recognizes the various practical constraints – time, expertise, limited information, resources, potential opposition from other actors – facing policy makers, and the contexts within which they operate, and which therefore militate against radical changes and new initiatives. Instead, emphasizes the evolutionary character of most public policies, and the manner in which effective changes are usually gradual – what Lindblom referred to as 'muddling through'.

Institutional agenda   The policy issues, objectives or problems with which government departments and ministers are primarily concerned at any particular juncture. Comprises the issues which the elite level of formal policy makers consider to be most important at any given juncture.

Issue attention cycle   Concept developed by Downs, this refers to the manner in which public or political interest in an issue goes through a series of phases, whereby recognition of a problem leads to widespread or vocal demands for political action, and the issue reaches the institutional agenda. However, when the costs or other implications of solving the problem become apparent – or the problem is actually solved – interest in it evaporates, and the issue slips back down or off the agenda, but may well rise back up it at a later stage if the problem re-emerges.

Issue network   A relatively loose and open range of organized (some more organized than others) interests in a sphere of policy. However, the policy may well be interdepartmental, and this, along with the diversity of organized interests involved, means that involvement in policy making and implementation is less stable or consistent. Issue networks are therefore deemed to be at the opposite end of a policy networks continuum to policy communities (see below)

Junior minister   Ministers below Secretary of State or Cabinet rank, namely Minister of State, and (Parliamentary) Under-Secretary, who are allocated specific policy responsibilities within a government department. Their number has increased significantly during the last 100 years, reflecting the increasing range of policy responsibilities of governments, the increasing complexity of particular areas of public policy, and thus the increasing workloads of, and specialization needed within, government departments.

Special (Policy) Advisers   Appointed by ministers, including the Prime Minister, to provide an alternative (to the civil service) source of policy advice and ideas. In the case of the Prime Minister, such advisers can also provide counter-proposals to those advanced by Cabinet ministers. Their number and apparent influence have increased significantly since the 1980s, as ministers have sought wider or alternative sources of advice than that traditionally proffered by senior civil servants.

Policy community   A close and relatively closed relationship between a group of policy actors in a particular policy subsystem, usually based around a government department and its 'client' organized interest(s), who work closely together in developing and implementing public policy. Policy communities tend to foster relative policy continuity, with significant policy change occurring only rarely, usually prompted by a crisis, a substantial ideological shift, or the discovery of new evidence or knowledge which challenges the norms and assumptions which have hitherto sustained and legitimized the policy community.

Policy inheritance   Concept popularized by Richard Rose, to explain how and why new governments are invariably obliged to accept and continue with many, if not most, of the policies and programmes already operational upon entering office. Many of these are long standing (possibly decades old), deeply embedded, and possibly have millions of beneficiaries, including the departments who administer them. Consequently, new governments and ministers invariably find their room for manoeuvre limited, soon recognizing the difficulties in repealing or abandoning many existing programmes and policies. Hence a tendency towards incrementalism in many policy areas.

Policy learning   The process whereby policy makers examine previous policies, or similar policies pursued elsewhere, in order to ascertain what lessons can be learned, and/or how to avoid making mistakes.

Policy network   Overarching concept of which issue networks and policy communities are the most notable variants. It emphasizes the role and prevalence of organized interests in the policy process, and their relationship or interaction with formal policy makers and governmental institutions, particularly departments and ministries.

Policy stream   The second of the 'streams' identified by John Kingdon, whereby policy or policies favoured by some actors are recommended to tackle a particular problem. Crucially, however, because the polices may be based on particular values or ideological beliefs, they may be developed first, and only afterwards is a problem sought to which the policy can be applied, and the apparent necessity or attractiveness of the policy illustrated. Even then, however, the policy might not be adopted by formal policy makers if the circumstances are not appropriate (see *political stream* and *policy window* below).

Policy style   The dominant mode or process of policy making, usually at national level in a particular country, although can also refer to the prevailing mode of policy making in a policy subsystem. Until recently, for example, Britain was deemed to have a reactive and incremental policy style with a strong emphasis on 'bureaucratic accommodation'. Most policies were subject to only relatively minor or piecemeal changes, and there was a strong emphasis on short-term problem-solving, and reacting to issues as and when they arose, rather than seeking to anticipate them.

Policy sector/subsystem   The particular actors and processes in a specific sphere of policy, such as agriculture, education, health, transport, etc. Reflects the extent to which the political system is often characterized by 'sectorization', whereby departments and their 'client' groups have enjoyed relative autonomy in their sphere of policy.

Policy transfer   Concept popularized during the 1990s, in reference to the way that some policies are deliberately 'copied' from other countries or regimes, and applied in British context. Policy makers look to other countries to see how they have tackled certain problems and then develop similar policies to be implemented in Britain. A number of policies in Britain since the 1990s have been 'transferred' from the USA, although Australia has also been a source of ideas for some policy initiatives (see also *policy learning* and *evidence-based policy making*).

Policy window   A short-lived or temporary opportunity for pursuing significant policy change. Occurs when the three 'policy streams' (identified by John Kingdon) flow together, so that appropriate political circumstances exist to apply a particular policy solution to a particular policy problem or issue. If there is any delay – for example, a suitable policy is not readily available – then the policy window is likely to close, and circumstances change, so that the chance to introduce the policy may be lost indefinitely.

Political stream   The third of John Kingdon's policy streams, whereby the 'correct;' political situation or circumstances arises in which particular solutions to a particular problem can be implemented. This may entail a change of government, the rise to prominence of a particular ideological faction in the governing party, or a crisis which enables policy makers to jettison the existing policy in favour of a new one. When the political stream merges with the problem and policy streams, a *policy window* is said to open, but does not usually remain open for long.

Problem stream   One of the three streams which, according to John Kingdon, need to flow together to effect a change in public policy. This first stream entails the identification of a problem by a set of policy actors or advocates, although formal policy makers may not yet accept that the problems are serious enough to warrant attention. Alternatively, there may be a lack of feasible policies available to tackle the problem(s), and/or political circumstances may not be appropriate.

Policy Directorate   Crucial part of the Prime Minister's Office (known as the Policy Unit until 2001) which both provides policy advice for the Prime Minister, and provides a vital conduit between 10 Downing Street and the various government departments. Enables the Prime Minister to keep abreast of policy developments and progress in his/her ministers' departments, and can, on occasions, 'chase up' ministers whose progress in pursuing an agreed policy appears to be too slow.

Prelegislative scrutiny (or prelegislative committee)   Consideration of a draft or proposed Bill, usually by a departmental select committee, before it is formally presented to Parliament for its First Reading. This enables 'interested parties' or experts to offer advice or criticism about proposed legislation, in the hope that the draft Bill will be modified accordingly before being formally introduced. Prelegislative scrutiny/committees can be said to provide Parliament with a slightly more active policy role than it has enjoyed hitherto, and might also be viewed as part of the recent trend towards 'evidence-based policy'.

Private Members' Bill   A Bill introduced by a backbench MP, normally on a topic of his/her choosing (provided that it does not presage increased public expenditure), although they may be persuaded to a introduce a Bill on behalf of the government, or, more commonly, on behalf of an organized interest. Many Private Members' Bills fail to reach the statute book due to lack of parliamentary time, although they may serve to push an issue onto the policy agenda, and maybe prompt government legislation in the not too distant future.

Rational policy making   Associated with Herbert Simon, who devised a model of the policy process in which policy makers identify their goals, identify the options available to achieve them, evaluate the advantages, disadvantages and likely consequences of each one, and then select the option which is most advantageous. Simon recognized that this was not how decisions were actually taken, and he recognized that 'real life' policy makers would face a range of practical difficulties in adhering closely to this model, but he did suggest that the model could help introduce a greater degree of rationality into the policy-making process than had existed hitherto.

Report Stage Occurring immediately after a Bill's (standing) committee stage, this is the debate, open to all MPs, on the revised Bill, in the light of amendments made in committee. Further amendments can be tabled at this stage.

Second Reading A debate on the principles and purpose of a Bill, with the government (via the 'sponsoring' minister) explaining why the Bill is desirable and should therefore be supported, and the Opposition usually arguing that the Bill is inappropriate or irrelevant *vis-à-vis* the problem it purports to remedy, and ought thus to be opposed.

Select Committee Parliamentary body which examines the implementation and operation of government policies, as well as associated expenditure. Each of the main government departments is 'shadowed' by a particular Select Committee, which chooses its topic of inquiry, and then examines relevant documents, invites written submissions from individuals and organizations affected by the policy under investigation, and verbally questions invited individuals, representatives, senior civil servants and ministers themselves. Critical select committee reports sometimes prompt changes to existing policy.

Standing Committee Parliamentary stage of a Bill which follows a successful Second Reading. Usually comprising 16–25 MPs, a Standing Committee scrutinizes a Bill in detail, which usually entails a number of amendments being 'tabled' to improve it, and eradicate inconsistencies or ambiguities which have been identified.

Street level bureaucrats Those who actually implement policies 'on the ground', such as local government officers, nurses, police officers, social workers, teachers, traffic wardens, etc. The manner in which they interpret and implement policies can have a significant impact on whether the policies are a success or a failure.

Systemic agenda The range of issues and problems which formal policy makers are being urged to address, at any given juncture, by individuals and organizations in society be they academics, journalists, organized interests, political parties or think tanks, for example. These 'actors' will often advocate particular policies which they believe ought to be adopted, in order successfully to tackle the issue or problem they have identified. Ultimately, those who constitute part of the 'systemic agenda' are invariably seeking to influence the institutional agenda.

Third Reading Final Debate on a Bill in the House of Commons prior to it being sent to the House of Lords (or to the House of Commons if it was first introduced in the House of Lords) following Report Stage. No further amendments are tabled during Third Reading.

Trilaterals Meeting between three ministers, often comprising the Prime Minister, Chancellor and a departmental minister. Such meetings have become more popular during the premiership of Tony Blair.

References

Published in London unless stated otherwise

Abbott, Stephen (1966) *Industrial Relations*, Conservative Political Centre.

Abel-Smith, Brian (1975) *A History of Nursing*, Heinemann.

Abel-Smith, Brian and Townsend, Peter (1965) *The Poor and the Poorest*, G. Bell & Sons.

Abromeit, Heidrun (1988) 'British privatisation policy', *Parliamentary Affairs* 41:1.

Ahmed, Kamal (2002) 'Inside Labour's young boy (and girl) network', *The Observer* 2 June.

Ahmed, Kamal (2003) 'It's currency crunch time', *The Observer* 18 May.

Ahmed, Kamal, Hinsliff, Gaby and Bright, Martin (2002) 'How Estelle learnt the toughest lesson of all', *The Observer* 27 October.

Allen, V.L. (1960) *Trade Unions and the Government*, Allen and Unwin.

Alport, Cuthbert (1946) *About Conservative Principles*, publisher unknown.

Anderson, James E. (1975) *Public Policy-Making*, Nelson.

Annesley, Claire (2003) 'Americanised and Europeanised: UK social policy since 1997', *British Journal of Politics and International Relations*, 5:2.

Ashley, Jackie (2002) 'Brains at the heart of Brownland: Interview with Ed Balls', *The Guardian* 4 November.

Axford, Barrie (1995) *The Global System: Economics, Politics and Culture*, Cambridge: Polity.

Bachrach, Peter and Baratz, Morton (1970) *Power and Poverty: Theory and Practice*, New York: Oxford University Press.

Baggott, Rob and McGregor-Riley, Victoria (1999) 'Renewed Consultation or Continued Exclusion?: Organised Interests and the Major Government' in Peter Dorey (ed.) *The Major Premiership: Politics and Policies Under John Major, 1990–7*, Basingstoke: Macmillan.

Baker, Kenneth (1993) *The Turbulent Years: My Life in Politics*, Faber and Faber.

Bale, Tim (1996) 'Demos: Populism, Eclecticism and Equidistance in the Post-modern World', *Contemporary British History* 10:2.

Ball, Alan R. and Millward, Frances (1986) *Pressure Politics in Industrial Societies*, Basingstoke: Macmillan.

Balogh, Thomas (1963) *Planning for Progress: A Strategy for Labour*, Fabian Society, Fabian Tract 346.

Barber, James (1991) *The Prime Minister Since 1945*, Oxford: Blackwell.

Barberis, P. (2000) 'Prime Minister and Cabinet' in Robert Pyper and Lynton Robins (eds) *United Kingdom Governance*, Basingstoke: Macmillan.

Barker, Anthony (1998) 'Political Responsibility for UK Prison Security – Ministers Escape Again', *Public Administration*, 76:1.

Barker, Tony, with Byrne, Iain and Veall, Anjuli (1999) *Ruling by Task Force*, Politico's in association with Democratic Audit.

Barnard, C. (1995) 'A European Litigation Strategy: The Case of the Equal Opportunities Commission' in Jo Shaw and Gillian More (eds) *New Legal Dynamics of European Integration*, Oxford: Oxford University Press.

Barrett, Susan and Fudge, Colin (1981a) 'Examining the policy-action relationship' in Susan Barrett and Colin Fudge (eds) *Policy and Action: Essays on the Implementation of Public Policy*, Methuen.

Barrett, Susan and Fudge, Colin (1981b) 'Reconstructing the Field of Analysis' in Susan Barrett and Colin Fudge (eds) *Policy and Action: Essays on the Implementation of Public Policy*, Methuen.

Barnett, Joel (1982) *Inside the Treasury*, Andre Deutsch.

Baston, Lewis (1996) 'The Social Market Foundation', *Contemporary British History* 10:1.

Batchelor, C. (1999) 'Railtrack denies cutting back on basic renewal', *Financial Times* 9 June.

Bax, Alex (2002) 'The Greater London Authority' in Stanley Henig (ed.) *Modernising Britain: Central, Devolved, Federal?*, The Federal Trust.

Beckett, Andy (2003) 'The changing face of Melanie Phillips', *The Guardian* (*G2*), 7 March.

Benn, Tony (1981) 'The Case for a Constitutional Premiership', *Parliamentary Affairs* 33:1.

Benn, Tony (1989) 'Obstacles to Reform in Britain' in Ralph Miliband, Leo Panitch, and John Saville (eds) *Socialist Register 1989*, Merlin.

Bennett, N. (1998) 'The right way to run a railway', *The Sunday Telegraph* 4 October.

Beveridge, William (1942) *Report on Social Insurance and Allied Services*, Cmd 6404, HMSO.

Blackburn, Robert and Kennon, Andrew, with Wheeler-Booth, Sir Michael (2003) *Parliament: Functions, Practice and Procedures*, 2nd edition (1st edition written by John Griffith and Michael Ryle and published in 1989), Sweet and Maxwell.

Blick, Andrew (2004) *People Who Live in the Dark: The History of the Special Adviser in British Politics*, Politico's.

Bochel, Catherine and Bochel, Hugh M. (2004) *The UK Social Policy Process*, Basingstoke: Palgrave.

Borthwick, Robert (1995) 'Prime Minister and Parliament' in Donald Shell and Richard Hodder-Williams (eds) *Churchill to Major: The British Prime Ministership Since 1945*, Hurst.

Börzel, Tanja (2002) 'Member State Responses to Europeanization', *Journal of Common Market Studies*, 40:2.

Bown, Francis (1990) 'The Shops Bill' in Michael Rush (ed.) *Parliament and Pressure Politics*, Oxford: Clarendon Press.

Brand, Jack (1992) *British Parliamentary Parties: Policy and Power*, Oxford: Clarendon Press.

Bromley, Catherine and Curtice, John (2003) 'Devolution: Scorecard and Prospects' in Catherine Bromley et al. (eds) *Devolution – Scottish Answers to Scottish Questions?*, Edinburgh: Edinburgh University Press.

Brown, Alice, McCrone, David and Paterson, Lindsay (1998) *Politics and Society in Scotland*, Basingstoke: Palgrave.

Brown, Colin (1990) 'Thatcher rewards the defenders of her political faith', *The Independent* 21 December.

Buller, Jim and Smith, Martin J. (1998) 'Civil Service Attitudes Towards the European Union' in David Baker and David Seawright (eds) *Britain For and Against Europe: British Politics and the Question of European Integration*, Oxford: Oxford University Press.

Bulmer, Simon and Burch, Martin (1998) 'Organizing for Europe: Whitehall, the British State and the European Union', *Public Administration*, 76.

Bulpitt, Jim (1996) 'The European Question' in David Marquand and Anthony Seldon (eds) *The Ideas that Shaped Post-war Britain*, Fontana.

Burch, Martin (1988a) 'The British Cabinet: A Residual Executive', *Parliamentary Affairs*, 41:1.

Burch, Martin (1988b) 'The United Kingdom' in Jean Blondel and Ferdinand Muller-Rommel (eds) *Cabinets in Western Europe*, Basingstoke: Macmillan.

Burch, Martin (1995) 'Prime Minister and Whitehall' in Donald Shell and Richard Hodder-Williams (eds) *Churchill to Major: The British Prime Ministership since 1945*, Hurst.

Burch, Martin and Holliday, Ian (1996) *The British Cabinet System*, Hemel Hempstead: Prentice Hall/Harvester Wheatsheaf.

Burch, Martin and Holliday, Ian (1999) 'The Prime Minister's and Cabinet Offices: An Executive Office in All But Name', *Parliamentary Affairs*, 52:1.

Burney, E. (2002) 'Talking Tough, Acting Coy: What Happened to the Anti-social Behaviour Order?', *Howard Journal of Criminal Justice* 41:5.

Butler, David, Adonis, Andrew and Travers, Tony (1994) *Failure in British Government: The Politics of the Poll Tax*, Oxford: Oxford University Press.

Butler, Lord (Rab) (1971) *The Art of the Possible*, Hamish Hamilton.

Cabinet Office (1997) *Ministerial Code: A Code of Conduct and Guidance on Procedures for Ministers*, Cabinet Office.

Cabinet Office (2003a) *The Prime Minister's Strategy Unit*, Briefing February 2003.

Cabinet Office (2003b) *Public Bodies 2002*, The Stationery Office.

Cabinet Office (2004) *Public Bodies 2003*, The Stationery Office.

Callaghan, John (1996) 'The Fabian Society since 1945', *Contemporary British History* 10:2.

Campbell, Colin and Wilson, Graham (1995) *The End of Whitehall: Death of a Paradigm*, Oxford: Blackwell.

Carter, Helen (2004) 'Now the fug of smoke has lifted, all eyes are on Dublin', *The Guardian* 25 September.

Castells, Manuel (1996) *The Information Age: Economy, Society and Culture: The Rise of the Network Society*, Oxford: Blackwell.

Castle, Barbara (1993) *Fighting All the Way*, Pan Books.

Castle, Stephen (1997) 'How to tell Smithies from Wonks', *The Independent on Sunday* 8 June.

Catterall, Peter and Brady, Christopher (1998) 'Cabinet Committees in British Governance', *Public Policy and Administration*, 13·4.

Centre for Agricultural Strategy (1979) *National Food Policy in the UK*, Reading: CAS.

Channel 4 (1999) *'Can't Pay, Won't Pay': The Child Support Agency*, Part One (of a three part documentary), broadcast 12 September.

Chaney, Paul and Drakeford, Mark (2004) 'The primacy of ideology: social policy and the first term of the National Assembly for Wales' in Nick Ellison, Linda Bauld and Martin Powell (eds) *Social Policy Review 16*, Bristol: Policy Press (with the Social Policy Association).

Chittenden, Maurice and Fielding, Nick (2004) 'Prescott takes a Geordie kicking', *The Sunday Times* 7 November.

Chitty, Clyde and Simon, Brian (1993) *Education Answers Back*, Lawrence and Wishart.

Cmnd 7797 (1980) *Report on Non-departmental Bodies*, HMSO.

Cobb, Roger W. and Elder, Charles D. (1972) *Participation in American Politics: The Dynamics of Agenda-building*, Boston: Allyn and Bacon.

Cockett, Richard (1994) *Thinking the Unthinkable: Think Tanks and the Economic Counter-revolution 1931–83*, HarperCollins.

Conservative and Unionist Central Office (1947) *The Industrial Charter: A Statement of Conservative Industrial Policy*.

Cook, Robin (2003) *The Point of Departure*, Simon and Schuster.

Cortell, Andrew (1997) 'From Intervention to Disengagement: Domestic Structure, the State and the British Information Technology Industry, 1979–90', *Polity*, 30:1.

Cortell, Andrew and Peterson, Susan (1998) 'Altered States: Explaining Domestic Institutional Change', *British Journal of Political Science* 29:1.

Cracknell, David (2004) 'Police fail to use powers to tackle binge drinking', *The Sunday Times* 17 October.

Crenson, Maurice (1971) *The Un-Politics of Air Pollution: A Study of Non-Decision Making in the Cities*, Baltimore: Johns Hopkins Press.

Crossman, R.H.S. (1963) 'Introduction' in Walter Bagehot, *The English Constitution* (originally published in 1867), Fontana.

Crossman, Richard (1975) *The Diaries of a Cabinet Minister, Volume One: Minister of Housing, 1964–66*, Hamish Hamilton and Jonathan Cape.

Crossman, Richard (1976) *The Diaries of a Cabinet Minister, Volume Two: Lord President of the Council and Leader of the House of Commons*, Hamish Hamilton and Jonathan Cape.

Crossman, Richard (1977) *The Diaries of a Cabinet Minister, Volume Three: Secretary of State for Social Services*, Hamish Hamilton and Jonathan Cape.

Currie, Edwina (1989) *Lifelines*, Sidgwick and Jackson.

Daugbjerg, Carsten (1998) *Policy Networks Under Pressure: Pollution Control, Policy Reform and the Power of Farmers*, Aldershot: Ashgate.

David, M. (2002) 'Introduction: Themed Section on Evidence-based Policy as a concept for modernising governance and social research', *Social Policy and Society* 1:3.

Davies, Nick (2003) 'Special investigation: How Britain is losing the drug wars', *The Guardian* 22 May.

Davies, Ron (1999) *Devolution: A Process not an Event*, Cardiff: Institute of Welsh Affairs.

Day, Patricia and Klein, Rudolf (1992) Constitutional and Distributional Conflict in British Medical Politics: The Case of General Practice, 1911–1991', *Political Studies* 40:3.

Deacon, Alan (2000) 'Learning from the US? The Influence of American Ideas Upon "New Labour" Thinking on Welfare Reform', *Policy and Politics*, 28:1.

deLeon, Peter (1999) 'The Stages Approach to the Policy Process: What Has It Done? Where Is It Going?' in Paul Sabatier (ed.) *Theories of the Policy Process*, Boulder, CO: Westview Press.

Dell, Edmund (1980) 'Some Reflections on Cabinet Government', *Public Administration Bulletin* 32.

Denham, Andrew and Garnett, Mark (1996) 'The Nature and Impact of Think Tanks in Contemporary Britain', *Contemporary British History*, 10:1.

Denham, Andrew and Garnett, Mark (1998) *British Think Tanks and the Climate of Opinion*, UCL Press.

Denham, Andrew and Garnett, Mark (1999) 'Influence without responsibility?: Think tanks in Britain', *Parliamentary Affairs*, 52:1.

Denham, Andrew and Garnett, Mark (2004) 'A "Hollowed Out" Tradition?: British Think Tanks in the Twenty-First Century' in Diane Stone and Andrew Denham (eds) *Think Tank Traditions: Policy Research and the Politics of Ideas*, Manchester: Manchester University Press.

Department of the Environment (1993) *News Release* (731) 4 November.

Department of the Environment, Transport and the Regions (1999) *Bulletin of Rail Statistics – Quarter 4, 1998/9*, The Stationery Office.

Department of Social Security (1998) *A New Contract for Welfare*, Cmnd 3805, The Stationery Office.

Desai, Radhika (1994) 'Second Hand Dealers in Ideas: Think Tanks and Thatcherite Hegemony', *New Left Review 203*.

Dillon, Jo (2001) 'They may not run the country, but they run the people who do', *The Independent on Sunday* 21 October.

Dolowitz, David (2000a) 'Introduction: A New Face to British Public Policy' in David Dolowitz with Rob Hulme, Mike Nellis and Fiona O'Neill, *Policy Transfer and British Social Policy*, Buckingham: Open University Press.

Dolowitz, David (2000b) 'Welfare: The Child Support Agency' in David Dolowitz with Rob Hulme, Mike Nellis and Fiona O'Neill, *Policy Transfer and British Social Policy*, Buckingham: Open University Press.

Dolowitz, David and Marsh, David (1996) 'Who Learns What from Whom: A Review of the Policy Transfer Literature', *Political Studies, 44*.

Dolowitz, David and Marsh, David (2000) 'Learning from Abroad: The Role of Policy Transfer in Contemporary Policy-Making', *Governance*, 13:1.

Dolowitz, David, Greenwold, Stephen and Marsh David (1999) 'Policy Transfer: Something Old, Something New, Something Borrowed, Why Buy Red, White and Blue?', *Parliamentary Affairs*, 52:1.

Donoughue, Bernard (1987) *Prime Minister: The Conduct of Policy under Harold Wilson and James Callaghan,* Jonathan Cape.

Dorey, Peter (1991) 'The Cabinet committee system in British government', *Talking Politics*, Autumn.

Dorey, Peter (1992) 'Much maligned, much misunderstood: The role of the Party whips', *Talking Politics*, Autumn 1992.

Dorey, Peter (1993a) 'Corporatism in the United Kingdom', *Politics Review*, 3:2.

Dorey, Peter (1993b) 'One Step at a Time: The Conservatives' Approach to the Reform of Industrial Relations', *The Political Quarterly*, 64:1.

Dorey, Peter (1995a) *British Politics Since 1945*, Oxford: Blackwell.

Dorey, Peter (1995b) *The Conservative Party and the Trade Unions*, Routledge.

Dorey, Peter (1996) 'Exhaustion of a Tradition: The Death of "One Nation Toryism"', *Contemporary Politics* 2:4.

Dorey, Peter (1998) 'The New "Enemies Within": The Conservative Attack on Single Parents, 1989–97', *Revue Française de Civilisation Britannique*, 7:3.

Dorey, Peter (1999a) 'Despair and Disillusion Abound: The Major Premiership in Perspective' in Peter Dorey (ed.) *The Major Premiership: Politics and Policies Under John Major, 1990–1997*, Basingstoke: Macmillan.

Dorey, Peter (1999b) 'The 3 Rs – Reform, Reproach and Rancour: Education Policies under John Major' in Peter Dorey (ed.) *The Major Premiership: Politics and Policies under John Major, 1990–1997*, Basingstoke: Macmillan.

Dorey, Peter (2000) 'Public Policy: The Child Support Act and Agency' in Steve Lancaster (ed.) *Developments in Politics 11: An Annual Review*, Ormskirk: Causeway Press.

Dorey, Peter (2001a) *Wage Politics in Britain: The Rise and Fall of Incomes Policies in Britain Since 1945*, Brighton: Sussex Academic Press.

Dorey, Peter (2001b) 'Privatization' in Barry Clarke and Joe Foweraker (eds) *Dictionary of Democratic Thought*, Routledge.

Dorey, Peter (2002a) 'Britain in the 1990s: The Absence of Policy Concertation' in Stefan Berger and Hugh Compston (eds) *Social Partnership in the 1990s*, Oxford: Berghahn.

Dorey, Peter (2002b) 'Industrial Relations as "Human Relations": Conservatism and Trade Unionism, 1945–1964' in Stuart Ball and Ian Holliday (eds) *Mass Conservatism: The Conservatives and the Public Since the 1880s*, Frank Cass.

Dorey, Peter (2003a) 'Between Ambivalence and Antipathy: The Labour Party and Electoral Reform', *Representation* 40:1.

Dorey, Peter (2003b) 'Margaret Thatcher's Taming of the Trade Unions' in Stanislao Pugliese (ed.) *The Legacy of Margaret Thatcher: Liberty Regained?*, Politico's.

Dorey, Peter (forthcoming) 'Industrial Relations Imbroglio' in Peter Dorey (ed.) *The 1964–1970 Labour Governments*, Routledge.

Downs, Anthony (1972) 'Up and Down with Ecology – The Issue Attention Cycle', *The Public Interest 28*.

Drewry, Gavin (ed.) (1989) *The New Select Committees*, Oxford: Oxford University Press.

Driver, Stephen and Martell, Luke (1997) 'New Labour's Communitarianism', *Critical Social Policy* 17:3.

Dudley, G. and Richardson, J.J. (1996) 'Why Does Policy Change Over Time?: Adversarial Policy Communities, Alternative Policy Arenas and British Trunk Road Policy 1945–1995', *Journal of European Public Policy*, 3.

Dunleavy, Patrick (1995) 'Policy Disasters: Explaining the UK's Record' *Public Policy and Administration*, 10.

Dunleavy, Patrick and Rhodes, R.A.W. (1990) 'Core Executive Studies in Britain', *Public Administration*, 68:1.

Easton, David (1965) *A Systems Analysis of Political Life*, Chicago: University of Chicago Press.

Eckstein, Harry (1960) *Pressure Group Politics*, Allen and Unwin.

Edholm, Felicity (1991) 'The Unnatural Family' in Martin Loney et al. (eds) *The State or the Market: Politics and Welfare in Contemporary Britain*, Sage/Open University.

Elgie, Robert (1995) *Political Leadership in Liberal Democracies*, Macmillan.

Elliot, Larry, Wintour, Patrick and Maguire, Kevin (2002) 'Tensions at the top', *The Guardian* 16 April 2002.

Elms, Tim and Terry, Tracy (1990) *Scrutiny of Ministerial Correspondence*, Cabinet Office Efficiency Unit.

Englefield, Dermot (ed.) (1984) *Commons Select Committees: Catalysts For Progress?*, Harlow: Longman.

Etzioni, Amitai (1993) *The Spirit of Community*, New York: Touchstone Books.

Feigenbaum, Harvey, Henig, Jeffrey and Hamnett, Chris (1998) *Shrinking the State*, Cambridge: Cambridge University Press.

Fielding, Steven (2003) *The Labour Party: Continuity and Change in the Making of 'New' Labour*, Basingstoke: Macmillan.

Flynn, Andrew, Gray, Andrew and Jenkins, William (1990) 'Taking the Next Steps: The Changing Management of Government', *Parliamentary Affairs* 43:2.

Foley, Michael (1992) *The Rise of the British Presidency*, Manchester: Manchester University Press.

Foley, Michael (2000) *The Blair Presidency*, Manchester: Manchester University Press.

Foster, Christopher (2001) 'Transport Policy' in Anthony Seldon (ed.) *The Blair Effect: The Blair Government 1997–2001*, Little, Brown & Co.

Foster, Christopher and Plowden, Francis (1996) *The State Under Stress*, Buckingham: Open University Press.

Friedman, Milton (1962) *Capitalism and Freedom*, Chicago: University of Chicago Press.

Friedman, Milton and Friedman, Rose (1980) *Free to Choose*, Harmondsworth: Penguin.

Fukuyama, Francis (1989) 'The end of history?', *The National Interest*, 16.

Gamble, Andrew (1997) 'Conclusion: Politics 2000' in Patrick Dunleavy, Andrew Gamble, Ian Holliday and Gillian Peele (eds) *Developments in British Politics 5*, Basingstoke, Macmillan.

Garnham, Alison and Knights, Emma (1994) *Putting the Treasury First*, Child Poverty Action Group.

Garrett, Geoffrey (2000) 'Globalization and National Autonomy' in Ngaire Woods (ed.) *The Political Economy of Globalization*, Basingstoke: Palgrave.

Geddes, Andrew (1993) *Britain in the European Community*, Manchester: Baseline.

Giddens, Anthony (1987) *War, Violence and the Nation-state*, Cambridge: Polity.

Giddens, Anthony (1991) *Modernity and Self-identity*, Cambridge: Polity.

Giddings, Philip (1993) 'Questions and Departments' in Mark Franklin and Philip Norton (eds) *Parliamentary Questions*, Oxford: Clarendon Press.

Giddings, Philip (1995) 'Prime Minister and Cabinet' in Donald Shell and Richard Hodder-Williams (eds) *Churchill to Major: The British Prime Ministership Since 1945*, Hurst.

Gilpin, Robert (1987) *The Political Economy of International Relations*, Princeton, NJ: Princeton University Press.

Goldsmith, Michael (1997) 'Changing Patterns of Local Government', *ECPR News* 9:1.

Gould, Philip (1999) *The Unfinished Revolution: How the Modernisers Saved the Labour Party*, revised edition, Little, Brown.

Graham, Alistair (1995) 'The Accountability of Training and Enterprise Councils', *Parliamentary Affairs* 48:2.

Grant, Wyn (1983) 'The National Farmers Union: The Classic Case of Incorporation' in David Marsh (ed.) *Pressure Politics: Interest Groups in Britain*, Junction Books.

Grant, Wyn (1989) *Pressure Groups, Politics and Democracy in Britain*, Hemel Hempstead: Philip Allan.

Grant, Wyn (1997) 'BSE and the Politics of Food' in Patrick Dunleavy, Andrew Gamble, Ian Holliday and Gillian Peele (eds) *Developments in British Politics 5*, Basingstoke: Macmillan.

Grant, Wyn (2000) *Pressure Groups and British Politics*, Macmillan.

Grant, Wyn (2003) *Economic Policy in Britain*, Basingstoke: Palgrave.

Grant, Wyn (2005) 'Agricultural Policy' in Peter Dorey (ed.) *Developments in British Public Policy*, Sage.

Gray, Clive (2000) 'A "Hollow State"'? in Robert Pyper and Lynton Robins (eds) *United Kingdom Governance*, Basingstoke: Macmillan.

Greenwood, Justin (2003) *Interest Representation in the European Union*, Basingstoke: Palgrave.

Greenwood, John, Pyper, Robert and Wilson, David (2002) *New Public Administration in Britain*, 3rd edition, Routledge.

Greer, Alan (1999) 'Policy Co-ordination and the British Administrative System: Evidence from the BSE Inquiry', *Parliamentary Affairs* 52:4.

Grice, Andrew (2004) 'Brown shuffles advisers to prepare for Balls' departure', *The Independent* 10 January.

Griffith, John and Ryle, Michael (1989) *Parliament. Functions, Practice and Procedures*, Sweet and Maxwell.

Groom, Brian (2000) 'Rail industry structure set to remain', *The Financial Times* 21 October.

Gunn, Lewis (1978) 'Why is Implementation so Difficult?', *Management Services in Government* 33.

Halcrow, Maurice (1989) *Keith Joseph: A Single Mind*, Macmillan.

Hall, Robert (1961) 'Britain's economic problems', *The Economist* 16 September.

Hall, W. and Weir, S. (1994) *Ego-trip: Extra Governmental Organisations in the UK and their Accountability*, Democratic Audit and Charter 88.

Hall, W. and Weir, S. (1996) *The Untouchables: Power and Accountability in the Quango State*, Scarman Trust.

Ham, Christopher (1999) *Health Policy in Britain*, 4th edition, Basingstoke: Macmillan.

Hardt, Michael and Negri, Antonio (2000) *Empire*, Cambridge, MA: Harvard University Press.

Harris, Michael (1996) 'The Centre for Policy Studies: The Paradoxes of Power', *Contemporary British History* 10:2.

Haubrich, Dirk (2001) 'UK Rail Privatisation Five Years Down the Line: An Evaluation of Nine Policy Objectives', *Policy and Politics* 29:3.

Hayek, Friedrich (1944) *The Road to Serfdom*, Routledge and Kegan Paul.

Hayek, Friedrich (1960) *The Constitution of Liberty*, Routledge and Kegan Paul.

Hayward, Jack (1974) 'National Aptitudes for Planning in Britain, France and Italy', *Government and Opposition* 9:4.

Headey, Bruce (1974) *British Cabinet Ministers*, Allen and Unwin.

Healey, Dennis (1990) *The Time of My Life*, Harmondsworth: Penguin.

Heffernan, Richard (1996) '"Blueprint for a Revolution"? The Politics of the Adam Smith Institute', *Contemporary British History* 10:1.

Heffernan, Richard (2000) *New Labour and Thatcherism: Political Change in Britain*, Palgrave.

Held, David (1989) 'The Decline of the Nation State' in Stuart Hall and Martin Jacques (eds) *New Times: The Changing Face of Politics in the 1990s*, Lawrence and Wishart/Marxism Today.

Held, David, Goldblatt, David, McGrew, Anthony and Perraton, Jonathan, (1999) *Global Transformations: Politics, Economics and Culture*, Cambridge: Polity.

Held, David and McGrew, Anthony (2002) *Globalization and Anti-globalization*, Cambridge: Polity.

Hencke, David (1999) 'House of straw that Jack built', *The Guardian* 21 June.

Henderson, P. (1977) 'Two British Errors: Their Probable Size and Some Possible Causes', *Oxford Economic Papers* 29:2.

Hennessy, Peter (1986) *Cabinet*, Oxford: Blackwell.

Hennessy, Peter (2000) 'Why Mr Blair's premiership will end in tears', *The Independent* (*Weekend Review*) 20 May.

Hennessy, Peter (2001a) *The Prime Minister: The Office and its Holders Since 1945*, Penguin.

Hennessy, Peter (2001b) *Whitehall*, Pimlico.

Hetherington, Peter (2004) 'Knife-edge in north-east referendum', *The Guardian* 15 October.

Higgott, Richard (1998) 'Review of "Globalisation"', paper presented for the Economic and Social Research Council, 20 November.

Hill, Michael (1998) *Understanding Social Policy*, 3rd edition, Oxford: Blackwell.

Hill, Michael and Hupe, Peter (2002) *Implementing Public Policy*, Sage.

Hinchingbrooke, Lord (1944) *Full Speed Ahead: Essays in Tory Reform*, Simpkin.

Hinsliff, Gaby (2004) 'Tories seek the magic Right stuff', *The Observer* 10 October.

Hirst, Paul and Thompson, Grahame (1996) *Globalisation in Question*, Cambridge: Polity.

Hodder-Williams, Richard (1995) 'The Prime Ministership, 1945–1995' in Donald Shell and Richard Hodder-Williams (eds) *Churchill to Major: The British Prime Ministership Since 1945*, Hurst.

Hogg, Sarah and Hill, Jonathan (1995) *Too Close to Call: Power and Politics – John Major in No. 10*, Warner Books.

Hogwood, Brian (1987) *From Crisis to Complacency?: Shaping Public Policy in Britain*, Oxford: Oxford University Press.

Hogwood, Brian and Gunn, Lewis (1984) *Policy Analysis for the Real World*, Oxford: Oxford University Press.

Hogwood, Brian and Mackie, Thomas (1985) 'The United Kingdom: Decision Sifting in a Secret Garden' in Thomas Mackie and Brian Hogwood (eds) *Unlocking the Cabinet: Cabinet Structures in Comparative Perspective*, Sage.

Holliday, Ian (2000) 'Executives and Administrations' in Patrick Dunleavy, Andrew Gamble, Ian Holliday and Gillian Peele (eds) *Developments in British Politics 6*, Basingstoke: Macmillan.

Hollis, Patricia (1997) *Jennie Lee: A Life*, Oxford: Oxford University Press.

Holton, Robert (1998) *Globalization and the Nation-state*, Basingstoke: Macmillan.

Hood, Christopher (1976) *The Limits of Administration*, Wiley.

Hood, Christopher, Scott, Colin, James, Oliver, Jones, George and Travers, Tony (1999) *Regulation Inside Government: Waste-watchers, Quality Police and Sleaze-busters*, Oxford: Oxford University Press.

Hoskyns, John (2000) *Just in Time: Inside the Thatcher Revolution*, Aurum.

House of Commons Information Service (2003) *The Success of Private Members' Bills*, Legislation Series; Factsheet L3, December 2003.

House of Commons (2003) *Sessional Information Digest: 2001–02*, The Stationery Office.

House of Commons (2004) *Sessional Information Digest: 2002–03*, The Stationery Office.

Howe, Geoffrey (1995) *Conflict of Loyalty*, Pan Books.

Howlett, Michael and Ramesh, M. (1995) *Studying Public Policy*, Toronto: Oxford University Press.

Hulley, Tom and Clarke, John (1991) Social Problems: Social Construction and Social Causation' in Martin Loney et al. (eds) *The State or the Market: Politics and Welfare in Contemporary Britain*, Sage/Open University.

Ingham, Graham (2000) *Managing Change: A Guide to British Economic Policy*, Manchester; Manchester University Press.

Irvine, John, Miles, Ian and Evans, Jeff (eds) (1979) *Demystifying Social Statistics*, Pluto Press.

James, Oliver and Lodge, Martin (2003) 'The Limitations of "Policy Transfer" and "Lesson Drawing" for Public Policy Research', *Political Studies Review*, 1:2.

James, Simon (1993) 'The Idea Brokers: The Impact of Think Tanks on British Government', *Public Administration*, 71.

James, Simon (1999) *British Cabinet Government*, 2nd edition, Routledge.

Jenkins, Roy (1971) 'On Being a Minister' in Valentine Herman and James Alt (eds) *Cabinet Studies*, Macmillan.

Jenkins, Simon (1995) *Accountable to None: The Tory Nationalization of Britain*, Hamish Hamilton.

Jenkins-Smith, Hank and Sabatier, Paul (1993) 'The Study of the Public Policy Process' in Paul Sabatier and Hank Jenkins-Smith (eds) *Policy Change and Learning: An Advocacy Coalition Approach*, Boulder CO: Westview Press.

John, Peter (1998) *Analysing Public Policy*, Pinter.

Johnson, Nevil (1988) 'Departmental Select Committees' in Michael Ryle and Peter G. Richards (eds) *The Commons Under Scrutiny*, Routledge.

Jones, G.W. (1985) 'The Prime Minister's Power' in Anthony King (ed.) *The British Prime Minister*, 2nd edition, Macmillan.

Jones, Helen (2005) 'Health Policy' in Peter Dorey (ed.) *Developments in British Public Policy*, Sage.

Jones, J. Barry (1990) 'Party Committees and All-party Groups' in Michael Rush (ed.) *Parliament and Pressure Politics*, Oxford: Clarendon Press.

Jordan, A.G. (1981) 'Iron Triangles, Woolly Corporatism and Elastic Nets: Images of the Policy Process', *Journal of Public Policy*, 1:1.

Jordan, A.G. (1990) 'Sub-governments, Policy Communities and Networks: Refilling the Old Bottles', *Journal of Theoretical Politics*, 2.

Jordan, Grant (1994) *The British Administrative System: Principles Versus Practice*, Routledge.

Jordan, A.G. and Richardson, J.J. (1982) 'The British Policy Style or the Logic of Negotiation?' in J.J. Richardson (ed.) *Policy Styles in Western Europe*, George Allen and Unwin.

Jordan, A.G. and Richardson, J.J. (1987) *British Politics and the Policy Process*, Unwin Hyman.

Joseph, Keith (1987) 'Escaping the Chrysalis of Statism', *Contemporary Record*, 1:1.

Jowit, Juliette (2000) 'Britain's overstressed railways', *The Financial Times* 21 October.

Jowit, Juliette (2004) 'Congestion charging sweeps the world', *The Observer* 15 February 2004.

Judge, David (1990) 'Parliament and Interest Representation' in Michael Rush (ed.) *Parliament and Pressure Politics*, Oxford: Clarendon Press.

Judge, David (1993) *The Parliamentary State*, Sage.

Kassim, Hussein (2000) 'The United Kingdom's Co-ordination of European Union Policy' in Hussein Kassim, Guy Peters and Vincent Wright (eds) *The National Co-ordination of EU Policy: The Domestic Level*, Oxford: Oxford University Press.

Kaufman, Gerald (1997) *How to be a Minister*, Faber.

Kavanagh, Dennis and Morris, Peter (1989) *Consensus Politics: From Attlee to Thatcher*, Oxford: Blackwell.

Kavanagh, Dennis and Seldon, Anthony (1999) *The Powers Behind the Prime Minister: The Hidden Influence of Number Ten*, Harper Collins.

Kavanagh, Dennis and Seldon, Anthony (2000) 'Support for the Prime Minister: The Hidden Influence of No. 10' in R.A.W. Rhodes (ed.) *Transforming British Government, Volume 2: Changing Roles and Relationships*, Basingstoke: Macmillan.

Keegan, William (1984) *Mrs Thatcher's Economic Experiment*, Harmondsworth: Penguin.

Kellas, James (1984) *The Scottish Political System*, Cambridge: Cambridge University Press.

Kellner, Peter and Lord Crowther-Hunt (1980) *The Civil Servants: An Inquiry into Britain's Ruling Class*, Macdonald.

Kelly, Paul (2003) 'Ideas and Policy Agendas in Contemporary Politics' in Patrick Dunleavy, Andrew Gamble, Richard Heffernan and Gillian Peele (eds) *Developments in British Politics 7*, Basingstoke: Palgrave.

Keynes, John Maynard (1936) *The General Theory of Employment, Interest and Money*, Macmillan.

King, Anthony (1975) 'Overload: Problems of Governing in the 1970s', *Political Studies* 23:2.

King, Anthony (1991) 'The British Prime Ministership in the Age of the Career Politician' in G.W Jones (ed.) *West European Prime Ministers*, Frank Cass.

King, Desmond and Wickham-Jones, Mark (1999) 'From Clinton to Blair – the Democratic Party Origins of Welfare to Work', *Political Quarterly* 70:1.

Kingdon, John (1995) *Agendas, Alternatives and Public Policies*, 2nd edition, New York: HarperCollins.

Kooiman, Jan and Van Vliet, Martijn (1993) 'Governance and Public Management' in Kjell Eliassen and Jan Kooiman (eds) *Managing Public Organisations*, 2nd edition, Sage.

Lawson, Nigel (1992) *The View from No. 11: Memoirs of a Tory Radical*, Bantam.

Learmont, Sir John (1995) *The Learmont Report: Review of Prison Service Security in England and Wales and the Escape from Parkhurst Prison on Tuesday 3 January 1995*, Stationery Office, Cm 3020.

Lee, B.H. (1974) *Divorce Law Reform in England*, Peter Owen.

Lee, J.M., Jones, G.W. and Burnham, June (1998) *At the Centre of Whitehall: Advising the Prime Minister and Cabinet*, Basingstoke; Palgrave.

Lee, Simon (2000) 'New Labour, New Centralism: The Centralisation of Policy and the Devolution of Administration in England and its Regions', *Public Policy and Administration* 15:2.

Lewis, Derek (1997) *Hidden Agendas: Politics, Law and Disorder*, Hamish Hamilton.

Lewis, Jane (2001) 'Women, Men and the Family' in Anthony Seldon (ed.) *The Blair Effect: The Blair Government 1997–2001*, Little, Brown & Company.

Lindblom, Charles (1959) 'The science of "muddling through"', *Public Administration Review* 19.

Lindblom, Charles (1979) 'Still muddling, not yet through', *Public Administration Review* 39.

Loughlin, Martin and Scott, Colin (1997) 'The Regulatory State' in Patrick Dunleavy, Andrew Gamble, Ian Holliday and Gillian Peele (eds) *Developments in British Politics 5*, Basingstoke: Macmillan.

Lukes, Steven (1974) *Power: A Radical View*, Basingstoke: Macmillan.

Mackintosh, John (1977) *The British Cabinet*, 3rd edition, Stevens.

Maclean, Mavis and Eekelaar, John (1993) 'Child Support: The British Solution', *International Journal of Law and the Family*, 7.

Macmillan, Harold (1927) *Industry and the State*, Macmillan.

Macmillan, Harold (1937) *The Middle Way*, Macmillan.

Madgwick, Peter (1991) *British Government: The Central Executive Territory*, Hemel Hempstead: Philip Allan.

Majone, Giandomenico (1994) 'The Rise of the Regulatory State', *West European Politics*, 17:3.

Mandelson, Peter and Liddle, Roger (1996) *The Blair Revolution: Can New Labour Deliver?*, Faber.

March, James and Olsen, John (1976) *Ambiguity and Choice in Organisations*, Oslo: Universitetforlaget.

March, James, Olsen, John and Cohen, Michael (1972) 'A Garbage Can Model of Organisational Choice', *Administrative Science Quarterly* 17.

Marquand, David (1996) 'Moralists and Hedonists' in David Marquand and Anthony Seldon (eds) *The Ideas that Shaped Post-war Britain*, Fontana.

Marsh, David and Read, Melvyn (1988) *Private Members' Bills*, Cambridge: Cambridge University Press.

Marsh, David and Rhodes, R.A.W. (1992a) 'Policy Communities and Issue Networks: Beyond Typology' in David Marsh and R.A.W. Rhodes (eds) *Policy Networks in British Government*, Oxford: Oxford University Press.

Marsh, David and Rhodes, R.A.W. (1992b) 'The Implementation Gap: Explaining Policy Change and Continuity' in David Marsh and R.A.W. Rhodes (eds) *Implementing Thatcherite Policies: Audit of an Era*, Milton Keynes: Open University Press.

Marsh, David, Richards, David and Smith, Martin J. (2001) *Changing Patterns of Governance in the United Kingdom: Reinventing Whitehall?*, Basingstoke: Palgrave.

Marsh, David and Smith, Martin J. (2000) 'Understanding Policy Networks: Towards a Dialectic Approach', *Political Studies*, 48:1.

Marsh, Richard (1978) *Off the Rails*, Weidenfeld and Nicolson.

Mawson, John and Spencer, K. (1997a) 'The Government Offices for the English Regions: Towards Regional Governance?', *Policy and Politics* 25:1.

Mawson, John and Spencer, K. (1997b) 'The Origins and Operation of the Government Offices for the English Regions' in Jonathan Bradbury and John Mawson (eds) *British Regionalism and Devolution*, Jessica Kingsley.

Mays, Nick (2001) *The Dangerous Dogs Act*, http://www.staffordmall.com/bsi-thedangerousdogsact.htm.

Mazey, Sonia and Richardson, Jeremy (1996) 'EU Policy making: A Garbage can model on an Anticipatory and Consensual Policy Style?' in Yves Mény, Pierre Muller and John-Louis Quermonne (eds) *Adjusting to Europe: The Impact of the European Union on National Institutions and Policies*, Routledge.

McAllister, Laura (1998) 'The Welsh Devolution Referendum: Definitely, Maybe?', *Parliamentary Affairs* 51:2.

McAllister, Laura (1999) 'The Road to Cardiff Bay: The Process of Establishing the National Assembly for Wales', *Parliamentary Affairs*, 52:4.

McCarthy, Michael (1983) 'Child Poverty Action Group: Poor and Powerless?' in David Marsh (ed.) *Pressure Politics: Interest Groups in Britain*, Junction Books.

McConnell, Allan and Stark, Alastair (2002) 'Foot-and-Mouth 2001: The Politics of Crisis Management', *Parliamentary Affairs* 55:4.

McGregor-Riley, Victoria (1997) *The Politics of Medical Representation: The Case of the British Medical Association. 1979 to 1995*, unpublished PhD thesis, Leicester: De Montfort University.

McGrew, Anthony (1992) 'A Global Society?' in Stuart Hall, David Held and Anthony McGrew (eds) *Modernity and its Futures*, Cambridge: Polity/Open University Press.

McGrew, Anthony (1997) *The Transformation of Democracy*, Buckingham: Open University Press.

McIlroy, John (1995) *Trade Unions in Britain Today*, 2nd edition, Manchester: Manchester University Press.

McSmith, Andy (2002) 'Student fees row was "last straw" for Morris', *The Independent on Sunday* 27 October.

McSmith, Andy (2004) 'The Mandy revolt and the reshuffle that never was', *The Independent on Sunday* 25 July.

Middlemas, Keith (1979) *Politics in Industrial Society*, Andre Deutsch.

Middlemas, Keith (1983) *Industry, Unions and Government*, Macmillan.

Mills, Michael (1992) 'Networks and Policy on Diet and Heart Disease' in David Marsh and R.A.W. Rhodes (eds) *Policy Networks in British Government*, Oxford: Oxford University Press.

Mitchell, Austin (1986) 'A House Buyer's Bill: How Not to Pass a Private Member's Bill', *Parliamentary Affairs*, 39:1.

Mitchell, James (1999) 'The Creation of the Scottish Parliament: Journey Without End', *Parliamentary Affairs* 52:4.

Moran, Michael (1977) *The Politics of Industrial Relations*, Macmillan.

Moran, Michael (2000) 'From Command State to Regulatory State', *Public Policy and Administration* 15:4.

Moran, Michael (2001) 'The Rise of the Regulatory State in Britain', *Parliamentary Affairs* 54:1.

Morgan, Kenneth O. (1997) *Callaghan: A Life*, Oxford: Oxford University Press.

Morris, Robert (1994) 'New Magistracies and Commissariats', *Local Government Studies*, 20:2.

Muller, Christopher (1996) 'The Institute of Economic Affairs: Undermining the Post-war Consensus', *Contemporary British History*, 10:1.

Muller, Wolfgang and Wright, Vincent (1994) 'Reshaping the State in Western Europe: The Limits of Retreat', *West European Politics* 17:3.

Murray, Charles (1989) 'Underclass', *The Sunday Times* (*Magazine*) 26 November.

Murray, Charles (1994a) 'Underclass: the crisis deepens', *The Sunday Times* 22 May.

Murray, Charles (1994b) 'The new Victorians and the new rabble', *The Sunday Times* 29 May.

Nakamura, Robert (1987) 'The Textbook Process and Implementation Research', *Policy Studies Review* 1.

Naughtie, James (2001) *The Rivals: The Intimate Story of a Political Marriage*, Fourth Estate.

Norton, Philip (1975) *Dissension in the House of Commons 1945–74*, Macmillan.

Norton, Philip (1978) *Conservative Dissidents*, Temple Smith.

Norton, Philip (1979) 'The Organization of Parliamentary Parties' in S.A. Walkland (ed.) *The House of Commons in the Twentieth Century*, Oxford: Clarendon Press.

Norton, Philip (1980) *Dissension in the House of Commons 1974–1979*, Oxford: Oxford University Press.

Norton, Philip (1981) *The Commons in Perspective*, Oxford: Martin Robertson.

Norton, Philip (1985) 'The House of Commons: Behavioural Change' in Philip Norton (ed.) *Parliament in the 1980s*, Oxford: Basil Blackwell.

Norton, Philip (1987) 'Prime Ministerial Power: A Framework for Analysis', *Teaching Politics* 16:3.

Norton, Philip (1990a) 'The Lady's not for turning, but what about the rest? Margaret Thatcher and the Conservative Party 1979–89', *Parliamentary Affairs* 43:1.

Norton, Philip (1990b) 'Public Legislation' in Michael Rush (ed.) *Parliament and Pressure Politics*, Oxford: Clarendon Press.

Norton, Philip (1993a) *Does Parliament Matter?*, Hemel Hempstead: Harvester Wheatsheaf.

Norton, Philip (1993b) 'Questions and the Role of Parliament' in Mark Franklin and Philip Norton (eds) *Parliamentary Questions*, Oxford: Clarendon Press.

Norton, Philip (2000) 'Barons in a Shrinking Kingdom: Senior Ministers in British Government' in R.A.W. Rhodes (ed.) *Transforming British Government, ii: Changing Roles and Relationships*, Basingstoke: Macmillan.

Nugent, Neill (2000) 'The European Union and UK Governance' in Robert Pyper and Lynton Robins (eds) *United Kingdom Governance*, Basingstoke: Macmillan.

Pahl, Ray and Winkler, Jack (1974) 'The Coming Corporatism', *New Society*, 10 October.

Parry, Rhona (2003) *The Impact of Foot-and-Mouth Disease on the Agricultural Policy Community: A Policy Case Study*, Undergraduate dissertation, LLB Law and Politics, Cardiff University.

Paterson, Lindsay (2002) 'Scottish Social Democracy and Blairism: Difference, Diversity and Community' in Gerry Hassan and Chris Warhurst (eds) *Tomorrow's Scotland*, Lawrence and Wishart.

Patten, John (1995) *Things to Come*, Sinclair-Stevenson.

Paxman, Jeremy (2003) *The Political Animal*, Penguin.

Peele, Gillian (2003) 'Politics in England and Wales' in Patrick Dunleavy, Andrew Gamble, Richard Heffernan and Gillian Peele (eds) *Developments in British Politics 7*, Basingstoke: Palgrave.

Perkin, Harold (1990) *The Rise of Professional Society: England Since 1880*, Routledge.

Peters, B. Guy (1984) *The Politics of Bureaucracy*, 2nd edition, New York: Longman.

Pierre, Jon and Stoker, Gerry (2000) 'Towards Multi-level Governance' in Patrick Dunleavy, Andrew Gamble, Ian Holliday and Gillian Peele (eds) *Developments in British Politics 6*, Basingstoke: Macmillan.

Pimlott, Ben (1988) 'The Myth of Consensus' in Lesley Smith (ed.) *The Making of Britain: Echoes of Greatness*, Basingstoke: Macmillan.

Pimlott, Ben (1993) *Harold Wilson*, HarperCollins.

Pimlott, Ben and Rao, Nirmala (2002) *Governing London*, Oxford: Oxford University Press.

Ponting, Clive (1986) *Whitehall: Tragedy and Farce*, Sphere.

Ponting, Clive (1990) *Breach of Promise: Labour in Power, 1964–1970*, Penguin.

Power, Michael (1994) *The Audit Explosion*, Demos.

Power, Michael (1997) *The Audit Society: Rituals of Verification*, Oxford: Oxford University Press.

Pressman, Jeffrey and Wildavsky, Aaron (1973) *Implementation: How Great Expectations in Washington Are Dashed in Oakland*, Berkeley, CA: University of California Press.

Prior, James (1986) *A Balance of Power*, Hamish Hamilton.

Pryce, Sue (1997) *Presidentializing the Premiership*, Macmillan.

Public Administration Committee (2002) *Public Administration – Minutes of Evidence*, Inquiry into 'The New Centre', HC262-ii, published 18 January 2002.

Pym, Francis (1984) *The Politics of Consent*, Hamish Hamilton.

Pyper, Robert (1991) 'Ministerial Departures from British Governments, 1964–90: A Survey', *Contemporary Record*, 5:2.

Radice, Lisanne, Vallance, Elizabeth and Willis, Virginia (1990) *Member of Parliament: The Job of a Backbencher*, Basingstoke: Macmillan.

Raison, Timothy (1979) *Power and Parliament*, Oxford: Basil Blackwell.

Randall, Nick (2004) 'Three Faces of New Labour: Principle, Pragmatism and Populism in New Labour's Home Office' in Steve Ludlam and Martin J. Smith (eds) *Governing as New Labour: Policy and Politics Under Blair*, Basingstoke: Palgrave.

Rawnsley, Andrew (2001) *Servants of the People: The Inside Story of New Labour*, Penguin.

Rawnsley, Andrew (2002) 'It's never been worse', *The Observer* 24 November.

Read, Melvyn (1992) 'Policy Networks and Issue Networks: The Politics of Smoking' in David Marsh and R.A.W. Rhodes (eds) *Policy Networks in British Government*, Oxford: Clarendon Press.

Regan, Paul (1988) 'The 1986 Shops Bill', *Parliamentary Affairs* 41:2.

Rhodes, R.A.W. (1990) 'Policy Networks: A British Perspective', *Journal of Theoretical Politics*, 2.

Rhodes, R.A.W. (1992) 'Local Government Finance' in David Marsh and R.A.W. Rhodes (eds) *Implementing Thatcherite Policies: Audit of an Era*, Buckingham: Open University Press.

Rhodes, R.A.W. (1995a) 'Introducing the Core Executive' in R.A.W. Rhodes and Patrick Dunleavy (eds) *Prime Minister, Cabinet and Core Executive*, Basingstoke: Macmillan.

Rhodes, R.A.W. (1995b) 'From Prime Ministerial Power to Core Executive' in R.A.W. Rhodes and Patrick Dunleavy (eds) *Prime Minister, Cabinet and Core Executive*, Basingstoke: Macmillan.

Rhodes, R.A.W. (1996) 'The New Governance: Governing Without Government', *Political Studies* 44:

Rhodes, R.A.W. (1997) *Understanding Governance: Policy Networks, Governance, Reflexivity and Accountability*, Buckingham: Open University Press.

Rhodes, R.A.W., Carmichael, Paul, McMillan, Janice and Massey, Andrew (2003) *Decentralizing the Civil Service: From Unitary State to Differentiated Policy in the United Kingdom*, Buckingham: Open University Press.

Rhodes, R.A.W. and Marsh, David (1992) 'Policy Networks in British Politics' in David Marsh and R.A.W. Rhodes (eds) *Policy Networks in British Government*, Oxford: Clarendon Press.

Richard, Lord (2004) *Report of the Richard Commission on the Powers and Electoral Arrangements of the National Assembly for Wales*, Cardiff.

Richards, David (1997) *The Civil Service Under the Conservatives 1979–97: Whitehall's Political Poodles?*, Brighton: Sussex Academic Press.

Richards, David and Smith, Martin J. (1997) 'How Departments Change: Windows of Opportunity and Critical Junctures in Three Departments', *Public Policy and Administration* 12:2.

Richards, David and Smith, Martin J. (2002) *Governance and Public Policy in the UK*, Oxford: Oxford University Press.

Richards, David and Smith, Martin J. (2004) 'The "Hybrid State": Labour's Response to the Challenge of Governance' in Steve Ludlam and Martin J. Smith (eds) *Governing as New Labour: Politics and Policy Under Blair*, Basingstoke: Palgrave.

Richards, Peter G. (1970) *Parliament and Conscience*, George, Allen and Unwin.

Richards, Peter G. (1979) 'Private Members' Legislation' in S.A. Walkland (ed.) *The House of Commons in the Twentieth Century*, Oxford: Clarendon Press.

Richards, Steve (2000) 'Yes, minister, it's safer to leave it to us …', *The Independent on Sunday* 29 October.

Richards, Steve (2003) 'Tony and Gordon: a troubled double act that needs to change its script', *The Independent on Sunday* 11 May.

Richardson, Jeremy J. (1993) 'Interest Group Behaviour in Britain: Continuity and Change' in Jeremy J. Richardson (ed.) *Pressure Groups*, Oxford: Oxford University Press.

Richardson, Jeremy (1994) 'Doing Less by Doing More: British Government 1979–1993', *West European Politics* 17:3.

Richardson, Jeremy (2000) 'Government, Interest Groups and Policy Change', *Political Studies*, 48.

Richardson, J.J. and Jordan, A.G. (1979) *Governing Under Pressure: The Policy Process in a Post-parliamentary Democracy*, Oxford: Martin Robertson.

Richardson, J.J. and Stringer, J.K. (1980) 'Managing the Political Agenda: Problem Definition and Policy-making in Britain' *Parliamentary Affairs* 33:1.

Riddell, Peter (1989) *The Thatcher Decade: How Britain Has Changed During the 1980s*, Oxford: Basil Blackwell.

Riddell, Peter (2001) 'Blair as Prime Minister' in Anthony Seldon (ed.) *The Blair Effect: The Blair Government 1997–2001*, Little, Brown & Co.

Robertson, Roland (1990) 'Mapping the Global Condition' in Mike Featherstone (ed.) *Global Culture: Nationalism, Globalization and Modernity*, Sage.

Robertson, Roland and Lechner, Frank (1985) Modernization, Globalization and the Problem of Culture in World Systems Theory', *Theory, Culture and Society* 2:3.

Robinson, W. (2001) 'Social Theory and the Globalization: The Rise of a Transnational State' in *Theory and Society* 30.

Robinson, Nick (2000) *The Politics of Agenda Setting*, Aldershot: Ashgate.

Robinson, Nick (2005) 'Transport Policy' in Peter Dorey (ed.) *Developments in British Public Policy*, Sage.

Rosamond, Ben (2003) 'The Europeanization of British Politics' in Patrick Dunleavy, Andrew Gamble, Richard Hefferman and Gillian Peele (eds) *Developments in British Politics 7*, Basingstoke: Palgrave.

Rose, Paul (1981) *Backbencher's Dilemma*, Frederick Muller.

Rose, Richard (1984) *Do Parties Make a Difference?*, 2nd edition, Macmillan.

Rose, Richard (1990) 'Inheritance before choice in public policy', *Journal of Theoretical Politics*, 2:3.

Rose, Richard (2001) *The Prime Minister in a Shrinking World*, Oxford: Polity.

Rose, Richard and Davies, Philip (1994) *Inheritance in Public Policy: Change Without Choice in Britain*, New Haven CT: Yale University Press.

Rosenau, James (1990) *Turbulence in World Politics*, Brighton: Harvester Wheatsheaf.

Rowan, David (2003) 'Profile: Matthew Taylor – Ideas man', *The Observer* 7 September.

Ruben, Peter (1996) 'The Institute for Public Policy Research: Policy and Politics', *Contemporary British History* 10: 2.

Rush, Michael (1990) 'Select Committees' in Michael Rush (ed.) *Parliament and Pressure Politics*, Oxford: Clarendon Press.

Rush, Michael (2000) 'Parliamentary Scrutiny' in Robert Pyper and Lynton Robins (eds) *United Kingdom Governance*, Basingstoke: Macmillan.

Sabatier, Paul (1986) 'Top-down and Bottom-up Approaches to Implementation Research: A Critical Analysis and Suggested Synthesis', *Journal of Public Policy* 6:1.

Sabatier, Paul (1999) 'The Need for Better Theories' in Paul Sabatier (ed.) *Theories of the Policy Process*, Boulder CO: Westview Press.

Schattschneider, E.E. (1960) *The Semi-sovereign People*, New York: Holt, Rinehart and Winston.

Searing, Donald (1994) *Westminster's World: Understanding Political Roles*, Cambridge, MA: Harvard University Press.

Sedgemore, Brian (1980) *The Secret Constitution*, Hodder & Stoughton.

Seldon, Anthony (1990) 'The Cabinet Office and Co-ordination 1979–87', *Public Administration*, 68:1.

Seldon, Anthony (1996) 'Ideas are not Enough' in David Marquand and Anthony Seldon (eds) *The Ideas that Shaped Post-war Britain*, Fontana.

Seldon, Anthony (1997) *Major: A Political Life*, Weidenfeld and Nicolson.

Seldon, Anthony (2004) *Blair*, Free Press.

Sewill, Brendon (1975) 'A View from the Inside: In Place of Strikes' in Ralph Harris and Brendon Sewill, *British Economic Policy 1970–74: Two Views*, Institute of Economic Affairs.

Shell, Dennis (1995) 'Prime Ministers and their Parties' in Donald Shell and Richard Hodder-Williams (eds) *Churchill to Major: The British Prime Ministership Since 1945*, Hurst.

Shell, Donald (1992) *The House of Lords*, 2nd edition, Hemel Hempstead: Harvester Wheatsheaf.

Silk, Paul and Walters, Rhodri (1998) *How Parliament Works*, 4th Edition, Longman.

Simon, Herbert (1957) *Administrative Behaviour*, 2nd edition, New York: Macmillan.

Sklair, Leslie (1991) *Sociology of the Global System*, Brighton: Harvester Wheatsheaf.

Sklair, Leslie (1998) 'Transnational Practices and the Analysis of the Global System', paper presented to London School of Economics Transnational Communities Programme Seminar Series, May.

Skelcher, Chris and Davis, Howard (1996) Understanding the New Magistracy: A Study of Characteristics and Attitudes', *Local Government Studies*, 22:2.

Smith, Martin J. (1990) *The Politics of Agricultural Support in Britain: The Development of the Agricultural Policy Community*, Aldershot: Dartmouth.

Smith, Martin J. (1991) 'From Policy Community to Issue Network: Salmonella in Eggs and the New Politics of Food', *Public Administration* 69:2.

Smith, Martin J. (1993) *Pressure, Power and Policy: State Autonomy and Policy Networks in Britain and the United States*, Hemel Hempstead: Harvester.

Smith, Martin J. (1995) 'Interpreting the Rise and Fall of Margaret Thatcher: Power Dependence and the Core Executive' in R.A.W. Rhodes and Patrick Dunleavy (eds) *Prime Minister, Cabinet and Core Executive*, Basingstoke: Macmillan.

Smith, Martin J. (1999) *The Core Executive in Britain*, Basingstoke: Macmillan.

Smith, Martin J. (2000) 'Prime Ministers, Ministers and Civil Servants in the Core Executive' in R.A.W. Rhodes (ed.) *Transforming British Government, Volume 1: Changing Institutions*, Basingstoke: Palgrave.

Smith, Martin J. (2003) 'The Core Executive and the Modernization of Central Government' in Patrick Dunleavy, Andrew Gamble, Richard Heffernan and Gillian Peele (eds) *Developments in British Politics 7*, Basingstoke: Palgrave.

Smith, Martin J., Marsh, David and Richards, David (1993) 'Central Government Departments and the Policy Process', *Public Administration*, 71:4.

Smith, Martin J., Marsh, David and Richards, David (1995) 'Central Government Departments and the Policy Process' in R.A.W. Rhodes and Patrick Dunleavy (eds) *Prime Minister, Cabinet and Core Executive*, Basingstoke: Macmillan.

Smith, Martin J., Richards, David and Marsh, David (2000) 'The Changing Role of Central Government Departments' in R.A.W. Rhodes (ed.) *Transforming British Government, Volume 2: Changing Roles and Relationships*, Basingstoke: Palgrave.

Smith, Michael (1992) 'Modernization, Globalization and the Nation-state' in Anthony McGrew and Paul Lewis (eds) *Global Politics*, Cambridge: Polity.

Solesbury, William (1976) 'The environmental agenda', *Public Administration* 54.

Spence, David (1993) 'The Role of Civil Servants in European Lobbying: The British Case' in Sonia Mazey and Jeremy Richardson (eds) *Lobbying in the European Community*, Oxford: Oxford University Press.

Spencer, K. and Mawson, John (1998) 'Government Offices and Co-ordination in the English Regions', *Local Governance* 24:2.

Stanley, Martin (2000) *How to be a Civil Servant*, Politico's.

Stewart, John (1995) 'Appointed Boards and Local Government', *Parliamentary Affairs* 48:2.

Stewart, John (1996) 'Reforming the new magistracy' in Lawrence Pratchett and David Wilson (eds) *Local Government and Local Democracy*, Macmillan.

Stewart, John (2004) '"Scottish solutions to Scottish problems"? Social welfare in Scotland since devolution' in Nick Ellison, Linda Bauld and Martin Powell (eds) *Social Policy Review 16*, Bristol: Policy Press (with the Social Policy Association).

Stone, Diane (1996) 'From the margins of politics: The influence of think tanks in Britain', *West European Politics*, 19:4.

Stone, Diane (1999) 'Lesson Drawing and Policy Transfer', *Politics*, 19:1.

Strong, Philip and Robinson, Jane (1990) *The NHS Under New Management*, Milton Keynes: Open University Press.

Taylor, Robert (1993) *The Trade Union Question in British Politics*, Oxford: Blackwell.

Taylor, Robert (1996) 'The Heath Government and Industrial Relations: Myth and Reality' in Stuart Ball and Anthony Seldon (eds) *The Heath Government 1970–74*, Harlow: Longman.

Tebbit, Norman (1988) *Upwardly Mobile*, Weidenfeld and Nicolson.

Thatcher, Margaret (1993) *The Downing Street Years*, HarperCollins.

Thatcher, Margaret (1995) *The Path to Power*, HarperCollins.

Theakston, Kevin (1987) *Junior Ministers in British Government*, Oxford: Blackwell.

Theakston, Kevin (1999a) 'A Permanent Revolution in Whitehall: The Major Governments and the Civil Service' in Peter Dorey (ed.) *The Major Premiership: Politics and Policies Under John Major, 1990–1997*, Basingstoke: Macmillan.

Theakston, Kevin (1999b) 'Junior Ministers in the 1990s', *Parliamentary Affairs*, 52:2.

Theakston, Kevin (2000) 'Permanent Secretaries: Comparative Biography and Leadership in Whitehall' in R.A.W. Rhodes (ed.) *Transforming British Government, Volume 2: Changing Roles and Relationships*, Basingstoke: Palgrave.

Thompson, Grahame (1992) Economic Autonomy and the Advanced Industrial State' in Anthony McGrew and Pail Lewis (eds) *Global Politics*, Cambridge: Polity Press.

Thompson, Helen (1995) 'Joining the ERM: Analysing a Core Executive Policy Disaster' in R.A.W. Rhodes and Patrick Dunleavy (eds) *Prime Minister, Cabinet and Core Executive*, Basingstoke: Macmillan.

Thompson, Helen (1996) *The British Conservative Government and the European Exchange Rate Mechanism, 1979–1994*, Pinter.

Titmuss, Richard (1962) *Income Distribution and Social Change*, Unwin.

Urry, John (1989) 'The End of Organised Capitalism' in Stuart Hall and Martin Jacques (eds) *New Times: The Changing Face of Politics in the 1990s*, Lawrence and Wishart/Marxism Today.

Vance, Carol (1989) 'Social Construction Theory: Problems in the History of Sexuality' in Anja van Kooten Niekerk and Theo van der Meer (eds) *Homosexuality, Which Homosexuality?*, Routledge.

Walker, Robert (1998) 'The Americanisation of British Welfare: A Case Study of Policy Transfer', *Focus* 19:3.

Wallerstein, Immanuel (1983) *Historical Capitalism*, Verso.

Wallerstein, Immanuel (1991) 'The Lessons of the 1980s' in Immanuel Wallerstein (ed.) *Geopolitics and Geoculture*, Cambridge: Cambridge University Press.

Wass, Douglas (1983) *Government and the Governed*, Routledge and Kegan Paul.

Weeks, Jeffrey (1992) 'The Body and Sexuality' in Robert Bocock and Kenneth Thompson (eds) *Social and Cultural Forms of Modernity*, Cambridge: Polity/Open University.

Whitelaw, William (1989) *The Whitelaw Memoirs*, Aurum.

Whiteley, Paul and Winyard, Stephen (1987) *Pressure for the Poor*, Methuen.

Williams, Marcia (1972) *Inside Number 10*, Coward, McCann and Geoghegan.

Wilson, David (2000) 'New Labour, New Local Governance?' in Robert Pyper and Lynton Robins (eds) *United Kingdom Governance*, Basingstoke: Macmillan.

Wilson, Graham K. (1990) *Interest Groups*, Oxford: Blackwell.

Wintour, Patrick (2002) 'Blair's enforcer … whose agenda does he serve?', *The Guardian* 1 November.

Wistow, Gerald (1992) 'The Health Service Policy Community: Professional Pre-eminent or Under Challenge' in David Marsh and R.A.W. Rhodes (eds) *Policy Networks in British Government*, Oxford: Oxford University Press.

Wright, Vincent (1994) 'Reshaping the State: Implications for Public Administration', *West European Politics 17*.

Yvernault, Audrey (2003) *A Study of the Homelessness Policy Network in London*, Undergraduate dissertation, BSc (Econ) Politics, Cardiff University.

Index

Compiled by INDEXING SPECIALISTS (UK) Ltd, Regent House, Hove Street, Hove, East Sussex BN3 2DW. Tel: 01273 738299.
email: richardr@indexing.co.uk Website: www.indexing.co.uk